UNSETTLING COLONIALISM

SUNY series in Latin American and Iberian Thought and Culture
———————
Jorge J. E. Gracia and Rosemary G. Feal, editors

UNSETTLING COLONIALISM

Gender and Race in the
Nineteenth-Century Global Hispanic World

Edited by

N. Michelle Murray and Akiko Tsuchiya

Cover art: José Tapiró Y Baró, *A Tangerian Beauty*. Dahesh Museum of Art, New York. 1995.117

Published by State University of New York Press, Albany

© 2019 State University of New York

All rights reserved

No part of this book may be used or reproduced in any manner whatsoever without written permission. No part of this book may be stored in a retrieval system or transmitted in any form or by any means including electronic, electrostatic, magnetic tape, mechanical, photocopying, recording, or otherwise without the prior permission in writing of the publisher.

For information, contact State University of New York Press, Albany, NY
www.sunypress.edu

Library of Congress Cataloging-in-Publication Data

Names: Murray, N. Michelle, editor. | Tsuchiya, Akiko, editor.
Title: Unsettling colonialism : gender and race in the nineteenth-century global Hispanic world / edited by N. Michelle Murray and Akiko Tsuchiya.
Description: Albany : State University of New York, [2019] | Series: SUNY series in Latin American and Iberian thought and culture | Includes bibliographical references and index.
Identifiers: LCCN 2018056830 | ISBN 9781438476452 (hardcover) | ISBN 9781438476469 (pbk.) | ISBN 9781438476476 (ebook) Subjects: LCSH: Spanish literature—19th century—History and criticism. | Imperialism in literature. | Race in literature. | Gender identity in literature. | Sex in literature.
Classification: LCC PQ6072 .U64 2019 | DDC 860.9/005—dc23
LC record available at https://lccn.loc.gov/2018056830

10 9 8 7 6 5 4 3 2 1

Contents

List of Illustrations   vii

Acknowledgments   ix

Introduction   1

I. Colonialism and Women's Migrations

1. The Colonial Politics of Meteorology: The West African Expedition of the Urquiola Sisters   19
   Benita Sampedro Vizcaya

2. Eva Canel and the Gender of Hispanism   55
   Lisa Surwillo

3. Gender, Race, and Spain's Colonial Legacy in the Americas: Representations of White Slavery in Eugenio Flores's *Trata de blancas* and Eduardo López Bago's *Carne importada*   81
   Akiko Tsuchiya

II. Race, Performance, and Colonial Ideologies

4. A Black Woman Called *Blanca la extranjera* in Faustina Sáez de Melgar's *Los miserables* (1862–63)   107
   Ana Mateos

5. Colonial Imaginings on the Stage: Blackface, Gender, and the Economics of Empire in Spanish and Catalan Popular Theater   135
   Mar Soria

III. Gender and Colonialism in Literary and Political Debates

6. Becoming Useless: Masculinity, Able-Bodiedness, and Empire in Nineteenth-Century Spain   173
   Julia Chang

7. From Imperial Boots to Naked Feet: Clarín's Views on Cuban Freedom and Female Independence in *La Regenta*   203
   Nuria Godón

8. *Dalagas* and *Ilustrados*: Gender, Language, and Indigeneity in the Philippine Colonies   231
   Joyce Tolliver

9. The Spanish Carceral Archipelago: Concepción Arenal against Penitentiary Colonization   255
   Aurélie Vialette

Contributors   279

Index   283

Illustrations

Figure 1.1	Sebastiana Estala at the center, surrounded by her four children; from left to right, Manuela, Esteban, Juliana, and Isabel Urquiola Estala, in Vitoria, Spain.	22
Figure 1.2	Postcard sent from the colonial city of Santa Isabel in Fernando Poo to Seville in 1955.	26
Figure 1.3	Postal stamps commemorating the centenary of the birth of Manuel Iradier, on the first day of circulation.	26
Figure 1.4	Manuel Iradier Bulfy, photograph taken upon his return from the second expedition to Africa.	27
Figure 1.5	Petition to the governor by Manuel Iradier Bulfy, Fernando Poo, January 1, 1877. "Instancia de Manuel Iradier y Bulfy. Fernando Poo, 1 de enero, 1877."	32–33
Figure 1.6	Petition to the governor by Isabel Urquiola de Iradier, Fernando Poo, October 16, 1876. "Instancia de Isabel Urquiola de Iradier. Fernando Poo, 16 de octubre de 1876."	36–38
Figures 1.7 and 1.8	Unpublished diary of Manuel Iradier Urquiola. This five-page-long diary has been reproduced in the DVD that accompanies Gutiérrez Garitano's *Apuntes de la Guinea*.	43
Figure 6.1	O'Donnell junto a las tropas de la Campaña de África pasando por la Puerta del Sol en 1860 (O'Donnell with troops from the African campaign passing through Puerta del Sol in 1860).	190

Acknowledgments

This project is the fruit of collaboration among a group of specialists on nineteenth-century Iberian studies, who have been meeting over the past few years to exchange ideas and share works in progress on the intersections of gender and empire in the nineteenth-century Iberian world. We would like to acknowledge each and every member of our research group for their contributions to this project, for their collegiality and support.

Michelle would like to thank her colleagues in the Department of Spanish and Portuguese at Vanderbilt University who encouraged her while she worked on the project, especially Andrés Zamora, who generously shared his expertise in nineteenth-century Spanish studies. She is also thankful for Jeffrey Coleman, Ana Corbalán, Elena Delgado, Kathy Everly, Jessica Folkart, Jo Labanyi, Jill Robbins, Rosi Song, Akiko Tsuchiya, and the members of her writing group for giving her ideas and feedback as she edited the volume. She is most grateful for Joshua Murray's daily insights, inspiration, and support.

Akiko would like to thank the many colleagues in the field, who have inspired her through intellectual dialogue, assisted her in locating research materials, and made invaluable suggestions along the way, as this project took life. She is especially grateful to Billy Acree, Pura Fernández, Michelle Murray, Íñigo Sánchez-Llama, the late Chris Schmidt-Nowara, Elzbieta Sklodowska, Lisa Surwillo, Joyce Tolliver, and Aurélie Vialette for the conversations and for their advice during various stages of the project.

We thank Rebecca Colesworthy, Acquisitions Editor at SUNY Press, for having faith in the project and for her unflagging support throughout the editorial process. Finally, we are very grateful to the two anonymous reviewers of the press, whose suggestions helped to improve the final manuscript.

Introduction

N. MICHELLE MURRAY AND AKIKO TSUCHIYA

Colonialism, its aftermath, and its discontents have long posed a challenge to scholars across the disciplines, given the androcentric and northern European focus through which these problems have often been approached. In contrast, *Unsettling Colonialism: Gender and Race in the Nineteenth-Century Global Hispanic World*, examines the entanglements of gender and race in the cultural productions of the long nineteenth century,[1] as they relate to Spanish imperialism. Our approach is feminist, insofar as our aim is to critically shed light on the multifaceted role of gender in discourses on Spain's colonies. By drawing our attention to women's central place as agents, symbols, or even objects of representation in colonial discourse, we scrutinize the ways in which women both upheld and destabilized colonial designs in the fin-de-siècle Hispanic world. The studies in this anthology unsettle monolithic narratives on the relationship between gender and colonialism, exposing the complex and oftentimes unpredictable tensions of identities and positionalities in cultural representations of nineteenth-century Spain.

The Iberian world has occupied a marginal place in feminist postcolonial studies, despite the geographical reach and global impact of the Spanish empire. Since the origins of its colonial enterprise in the fifteenth century, Spain has maintained most of its imperial holdings for nearly four hundred years. Spain embarked upon the first colonial voyage in 1492,[2] when Queen Isabella of Castile sponsored Christopher Columbus's journey to the Americas. The colonial era instituted social hierarchies around gender, nationalism, race, and sexuality in alignment with Eurocentric principles. Indeed, overseas expansion and local religious expulsions—coextensive, violent colonization that united the Spanish nation to overseas territories—worked together to consolidate the nation.

The nineteenth century marks a crucial turning point in Spain's imperial narrative, as the entry of Napoleonic forces into the Iberian Peninsula in 1808 triggered a series of independence movements in the Americas that led to the fracturing of an empire that had existed for more than three hundred years.[3] The loss of some of Spain's largest colonies in Spanish America, following the formation of independent *juntas* in 1810 in Mexico, Argentina, and Chile, would culminate later in the century in the Spanish-American War, with the loss of Cuba and Puerto Rico—Spain's last colonies in the Americas—and of the Philippines in the Pacific. As a response to these losses—and after unsuccessful attempts to reconquer parts of its old empire between 1840 and 1860 (Balfour 2)—Spain launched a pursuit of a "new imperial future" in Africa as a compensatory gesture, leading to repeated attempts to recolonize northern Africa (Martin-Márquez 17–18). In Sebastian Balfour's view, even as Spain found itself in imperial decline while its European counterparts were expanding their empires, "Spanish nationalism took pride in asserting old-fashioned imperial values as opposed to those of the new colonial expansionism of other European powers" (2).[4] For Balfour, Spanish nation building and national identities in the nineteenth century and beyond were inextricably tied to its colonial past.[5] Yet, as Alda Blanco has noted, the "modern empire . . . paradoxically originates around the moment when Spain loses the majority of its overseas colonies" ("Spain at the Crossroads" 2). That is to say, Spain's decision to embark on imperial expansion in Africa during the late nineteenth century was motivated, in part, by the belief on the part of liberal thinkers that to be an empire was to be modern.[6] Colonialism, then, represented not a throwback to "old-fashioned" values but was, rather, understood to be a precondition for modernity.

While colonialism's global impact is undeniable, colonialism itself remains unsettled as a topic of critical inquiry. The field of Iberian studies has recently begun to contribute to analyses that sustain the academic project of unsettling colonialism. While there are numerous geographical distinctions, theoretical approaches, and vantage points from which to examine the problem of colonialism, postcolonial studies has examined the legacies of colonialism largely within European contexts. Leading scholars in postcolonial studies, such as Homi Bhabha and Gayatri Spivak, drew upon the work of Edward Said to theorize the legacies of British imperialism in the Middle East and South Asia (Bhambra 115). This line of inquiry is relevant to Iberian studies, as it purports to break with systems of knowledge rooted in colonial ideologies. By reconceptualizing knowledge about colonialism and its legacies in Spain, *Unsettling Colonialism* enters into dialogue with postcolonial scholarly inquiry. In assessing the lasting impact of Spanish colonialism in the political and cultural discourses—including literature—of the long nineteenth century, *Unsettling Colonialism* reflects a growing interest in postcolonial Europe. Postcolonial Europe, of which Spain forms a part, is a critical geographical distinction that resituates Europe in relation to its past imperial dynamics, thus accentuating the often-understudied significance of northern Europe's vision of Spain as part of the Orient.

Iberian studies scholars have noted the theoretical limitations even of groundbreaking works such as Edward Said's *Orientalism*, which fails to grapple with Spain's role in Orientalizing populations in Africa and Asia,[7] while simultaneously internalizing northern Europe's vision of Spain as part of the Orient. Moreover, while postcolonial scholarship is typically limited to Africa, Asia, and the Middle East, this volume expands those horizons to include insights into Spain's linkages with formerly colonized nations commonly overlooked in postcolonial debates, such as the Philippines and Equatorial Guinea. Indeed, the contributors to this volume examine the Spanish empire from within the new framework of Global Hispanophone studies, which has expanded the geographical and methodological scope of our discipline to consider the impact of Spanish colonialism beyond the Americas.[8] In this fashion, we hope to generate new disciplinary spaces for the analysis of the intersections of colonialism, race, and gender in the global nineteenth-century Hispanic world.

Despite Iberian studies' unique position from which to intervene in postcolonial critique, studies of empire and colonialism have been slow to emerge in the discipline of nineteenth-century Iberian literary and cultural studies. As Tsuchiya notes in her chapter, it is only since the turn of the twenty-first century that scholars in this field have begun to address the colonialist subtext of the literary works of nineteenth-century Spain, bringing to light the ways in which the Spanish nation was shaped by empire in the economic, political, and cultural arena.[9] In 2003, Alda Blanco was one of the first critics of nineteenth-century Iberian studies to acknowledge the erasure of empire from Spanish literary and cultural history, providing a corrective to this erasure by calling our attention to a group of *fin-de-siglo* literary works that inscribed the history of empire and colonialism within their pages ("El fin" 4). A few years later, Blanco reiterates the need to analyze the inscriptions of empire in the cultural production of Spain as a nation that continued to remain the metropolis of an empire, even after the loss of a majority of its colonies (Blanco, "Spain" 5–6, cited in Tsuchiya, *Empire's End* 4). In fact, as Lisa Surwillo affirms, literary and cultural representations, in particular, are crucial to the project of analyzing modernity's roots in empire and colonialism, as they provide "a space of fantasy . . . for imagining what was generally known but officially unacknowledged" (6). It is this "space of fantasy"—as represented in a wide range of cultural forms—that the contributions to this volume explore.

Iberian colonialism—like colonialism in many other parts of the world—remains unsettled, from both a temporal and geographical perspective. Historically speaking, a large majority of formerly colonized nations, including previous colonies of the Iberian empire, achieved independence throughout the nineteenth and twentieth centuries; nevertheless, the traces of colonial laws, logics, and procedures continue to bear upon nations that comprise the "Global South," once subjected to European domination.[10] Cameroonian philosopher Achille Mbembe has pointed out the incongruities of the post-colony, noting that "the post-colony . . . is really a combination of several temporalities. . . . [T]o postulate the existence of a 'before' and an 'after' of colonization could not exhaust the problem of the relationship between temporality and subjectivity" (15). Anne McClintock, likewise, points to the irony that although "a good deal of postcolonial studies has set itself against the imperial idea of linear time," the very term *postcolonial* "is haunted by the very figure of linear development that it sets out to dismantle" (10). While colonialism appeared to be dismantled in official law, its legacy in postcolonial societies continues to haunt both nations and citizens in much of the Global South, not only in the economic and political realms, but also in the cultural one. In the case of the Iberian empire, as Ángel Loureiro has argued, nineteenth-century Spanish nationalism itself is linked to the "ghost of empire," its inability to extricate itself from the "specter of its former colonies" (65).[11] The legacies of colonialism continue to emerge, both in cultural relations that sustain its injustices and in cultural representations—and critique—that produce new knowledge about the colonial past, in the metropolis as well as in the colonies.

From a geographical standpoint, colonialism, which unfolded in divergent ways in the global Hispanic world, also remains unsettled. Within the Iberian empire, the Río de la Plata region under Spanish rule logically differed enormously from that of the Philippines or the African colonies in Morocco, Western Sahara, or Equatorial Guinea. The global Hispanic empire of the nineteenth century extended far beyond the borders of

Spanish America through its entangled histories, and colonialism led to the reconfiguration of gender, class, and racial relations that were unique to the geopolitical context in which they unfolded.[12] The task of postcolonial critique, in which most of the contributors in this volume are engaged, is to explore the geopolitical impact of colonization for those who exploited the Global South and created an accompanying body of knowledge about colonized regions and peoples to justify this exploitation. The resonances of colonialism for metropolitan subjects are vast, in that these global outposts did not only alter the course of history in the colonies, but also "at home," where European societies reconfigured themselves in alignment with new epistemologies and relationships forged through violent domination abroad.

While specialists in Iberian literatures and cultures in the last decade have begun to scrutinize the ways in which the legacies of imperialism, colonialism, and slavery shape Iberian history and historiography, most of these studies do not foreground the role of gender in generating narratives about the colonial condition. In contrast, *Unsettling Colonialism* proceeds from the premise that gender is an essential category of social analysis that enables us to deepen our study of race, nationalism, colonialism, and social relations in nineteenth-century Spain. Charles Mills, a renowned philosopher working in critical race theory, has signaled the parallels among women, people of color, and the colonized, in that the difficult recognition of their "personhood" results from nineteenth-century ideologies of colonialism, domesticity, and slavery ("The Political Economy of Personhood"). Indeed, both women and the colonized were seen as partial members of European nation-states, as the political debates surrounding Spain's first liberal Constitution of 1812 illustrate.[13] This Constitution set forth the idea of Spain as a democratic nation and continues to be considered a fundamental part of the country's centuries-long democratization process. Yet, it excluded women, domestic servants, and Afro-descendants from citizenship. Questions over citizenship and which colonized people could take part in the democratic, liberal proceedings of 1812 emphasize the entanglement of gender, colonialism, and nationalism, even as the nation lost its imperial footing. The aforementioned concerns over the question of national belonging show the ways in which both gender and colonialism are linked to geopolitics—especially for women in domestic service, enslaved women, and Spanish women living in Africa, the Americas, and Asia.

By exploring the different positions of women—as both subjects and objects of representation—in relation to colonialism, we illustrate the entanglements of race, gender, and colonialism in the cultural discourses of the Hispanic world. Indeed, as the essays in the volume demonstrate, many women, who were marginalized because of their gender, participated directly in the colonizing mission or were complicit in upholding imperialist ideology, consciously or otherwise. By the same token, other contributions show male authors in Spain and its colonies who inscribe African, Asian, Latin American, and European women into literary and political writings, reflecting—and reifying—the power relationships that colonialism forged. The need to acknowledge the multiple positions of women as colonial subjects and agents compels us to reconsider colonialism as representing a complex and, oftentimes, contradictory relationship between gender, embodiment, and positionality. Our approach to the representation of colonialism resonates with Chandra Mohanty's assertion that "questions of subjectivity are always multiply mediated through the axes of race, class/caste, sexuality, and gender . . . [and] while questions of identity are crucially important, they can never be reduced to automatic self-referential, individualist ideas of the political (or feminist) subject" ("Cartographies" 33). Following this line of reasoning, it is not surprising that women took part in colonialism, or that male writers imagined women from all regions of the (former) Spanish empire as essential symbols of the nation's overseas expansion. To "unsettle colonialism" is, therefore, the practice by which we interrogate monolithic or totalizing narratives, representational paradigms, and ideologies underlying approaches to colonialism and imperialism. These essays seek to tease out the intricacies and contradictions of women's relationship to colonialism in the nineteenth-century Spanish context.

Gender is a fundamental component of colonialism and a privileged trope of colonial discourse, apparent in sexualized representations of territories to be conquered, discourses of domestication as a way of portraying the relationship between colonizers and colonized, and women's symbolic function as repositories of national values and ideologies. In recent years, postcolonial feminist theorists such as Jacqui Alexander, Anne McClintock, Chandra Mohanty, and Ann Laura Stoler have explored the ways in which colonialism engendered social relations—based on hierarchies of gender and sexuality, as well as race and class—in a parallel, if not identical, fashion in both European and formerly colonized nations.[14] Many of these postcolonial feminist studies have provided evidence that "women and men did not experience imperialism in the same way" and, more specifically, that the outcome of the reordering of the sexual and economic labor for colonized women was very different from the consequences for men (McClintock 6). As Anne McClintock argues, race, gender, and class "come into existence *in and through* relation to each other—if in contradictory and conflicted ways" and that "gender dynamics were, from the outset, fundamental to securing the maintenance of the imperial enterprise" (5, 7). Likewise, in *Carnal Knowledge and Imperial Power*, Ann Laura Stoler bases her study of colonialism on the premise that "imperial authority and racial distinctions were fundamentally structured in gendered terms"; that is, gender was foundational to the power relations that prescribed racial boundaries in colonial life (42).

Unsettling Colonialism seeks to make a unique contribution to the dialogue on the intersections of gender and colonialism by highlighting the gendered dynamics that were fundamental to the imperial enterprise and its representations in literary fiction, travel narratives, political treatises, periodical literature, medical discourse, the visual arts, and other cultural forms in fin-de-siècle Spain. In this way, the book reflects Jacqui Alexander and Chandra Mohanty's position that "[t]o talk about feminist praxis in global contexts would involve shifting the unit of analysis from local, regional, and national culture to *relations across cultures*" (xix; our emphasis). The volume will, therefore, carve out a much-needed space for studies of the Iberian empire within feminist postcolonial studies, from which Iberian literatures and cultures have been excluded or marginalized.

Given that Spain's imperial legacy extends far beyond the loss of its final American colonies and the Philippines at the end of the nineteenth century, particularly, as this legacy is reflected in metropolitan cultural representations, it is impossible to maintain an artificial separation between the "before" and "after" of the official end of Spanish colonialism in these regions. In fact, two of the chapters include a consideration of texts written in the early twentieth century by those whose lives and travels unfolded across the temporal threshold of the turn of the century, across colony and post-colony, as well as across the Atlantic or the Pacific. A crossing-over into the twentieth century, in these cases, is crucial to demonstrating the ways in which female subjects engaged and negotiated imperial discourses across geopolitical borders, even if they did not always contest these discourses.

If colonialism remains unsettled, both as a temporal marker and as a topic of scholarly inquiry, this volume intends to unsettle it further, offering new perspectives on the connections linking gender, race, and colonialism and their implications for knowledge production and cultural relations. To that end, the contributors to this volume present critical rereadings of canonical works, as well as recover previously marginalized gendered and racialized voices, to show the resonances of colonialism within Spain. The contributions also shed light upon the generative tensions arising from the use of feminist and postcolonial theories that originated in other contexts to serve cultural and historical analysis within the framework of Iberian studies. Finally, a number of essays address—implicitly if not explicitly—the role of archival research as a means to feminist knowledge production: that is, the ways in which the archive both facilitates and limits knowledge production on women who were relegated to the margins of official history. While the recovery of female and subaltern perspectives could potentially lead to the revision of literary and cultural history within the field of Iberian studies, the dearth of such materials in the Spanish archives poses unique methodological challenges for feminist knowledge production in this context. These are some of the recurrent issues explored in the contributions forming part of this volume.

Unsettling Colonialism is divided into three thematic sections that intersect and are mutually related. Part I, "Colonialism and Women's Migrations," examines women's mobility through migrations, trafficking, and colonial resettlement. In chapter 1, "The Colonial Politics of Meteorology: The West African Expedition of the Urquiola Sisters," Benita Sampedro Vizcaya traces the journeys of Basque sisters/scientists to the farthest reaches of Spain's African domains. Through their travels, these sisters made scientific advancements, accomplishments frequently reserved for men of the period. Sampedro contends that the astonishing and still-underappreciated scientific work of the Urquiola sisters served, in the end, to consolidate awareness in Spain of the economic value of Equatorial Guinea. This nation has been marginalized in the scant scholarship on European colonialism in Africa, a pivotal node in Atlantic imperial networks, and a vital source of Spanish nationalism after the colonial losses of 1898. Rather than undermining colonialism, these women ultimately served to consolidate empire, even as they challenged the boundaries of gender convention and advanced the frontiers of science in the nineteenth century.

Lisa Surwillo's essay in chapter 2, "Eva Canel and the Gender of Hispanism," contributes to understanding the role of gender in the political ideology of Hispanism and its cultural neoimperialism. For Surwillo, the writer Eva Canel (1857–1932), who traveled to Spanish America and lived on both sides of the Atlantic, exemplifies how Spain addressed its recently concluded slave policies. Through analysis of Canel's work *Lo que vi en Cuba* (1916), Surwillo interrogates the author's self-fashioning as an itinerant Hispanic writer attempting to negotiate the threshold between America and Spain in the contested space of Cuba.

Akiko Tsuchiya's contribution in chapter 3, for its part, focuses on the relationship between nineteenth-century sex trafficking and chattel slavery in literary fictions authored by Spanish men who were apologists of empire. Until 1888, the Atlantic World suffered two interrelated systems of human bondage. Since the fifteenth century, the Atlantic slave trade brought Africans to the Americas to support the institution of colonial slavery. The Atlantic slave trade and a parallel and often interconnected sex trafficking system across international borders transported, confined, and exploited women in Europe, Africa, and the Americas, by subjecting them to forced sex work. Tsuchiya's essay, "Gender, Race, and Spain's Colonial Legacy in the Americas: Representations of White Slavery in Eugenio Flores's *Trata de blancas* and Eduardo López Bago's *Carne importada*," brings to light the imperial/colonial subtexts of these two representative Spanish novels on transatlantic sex trafficking through a close attention to gendered and racialized tropes that establish an explicit connection between prostitution and the colonial project, particularly slavery. She examines the ways in which the intersecting discourses of literature and medicine transformed the prostitute figure into a privileged trope of racial and sexual otherness, highlighting the paradox implicit in the masculine metropolitan gaze: while it seeks to control and contain prostitution as a "social disease," it also fetishizes the prostitute's body as an erotic spectacle. Tsuchiya's argument is that, in the end, the representation of the European prostitute as the degenerate racial other is about asserting what Anne McClintock has called the "male imperial body politic" (47) in the neocolonial setting.

The essays in Part I thus capture the ways in which mobile women embodied imperial designs, either as exploited laborers forcibly brought to the colonies to sustain the imperial economy or as creators of knowledge that ultimately served to sustain colonization. The analysis of the literary, medical, and ethnographic gaze in these works calls attention precisely to the problem of representing women's role and agency—or the lack thereof—in a colonial or postcolonial context.

The chapters that comprise Part II, "Race, Performance, and Colonial Ideologies," examine the construction and performance of race in literary works. Ana Mateos's essay in chapter 4, "A Black Woman Called *Blanca la extranjera* in Faustina Sáez de Melgar's *Los miserables* (1862–63)," explores the intersections of gender and race through the figure of Alejandrina, the protagonist of Faustina Sáez de Melgar's *Los miserables*. Alejandrina is a mixed-race woman able to pass as white, who adopts an artificially black appearance. Mateos takes this act to invoke the slave analogy, specifically to represent the ways that marriage deprived white women of ownership of their own bodies. This essay contributes to the study of the intersection of abolitionist and proto-feminist discourses in post-Romantic Spain by presenting a case contrary to the general tendency at the time of avoiding comparisons of white women to bondage slaves, on the grounds that Christianity had already liberated the former from bondage. In doing so, it explores the intersectionality of race and gender in the context of Spain's participation in slavery, both in denouncing the situation of Spanish women and in proposing a transatlantic emancipatory model of womanhood across racial lines.

As in Mateos's work, the performances of race—as reflected in the practice of blackface—figure prominently in chapter 5, Mar Soria's "Colonial Imaginings on the Stage: Blackface, Gender, and the Economics of Empire in Spanish and Catalan Popular Theater." Focusing on theatrical production in fin-de-siècle Spain, Soria examines how the comical staging of blackface in the *género chico*—mass-produced one- and two-act plays—served to reinstate the metropolis' superiority over Cuba in the Spanish and Catalan national imaginaries, thus forging a sense of national identity. Through her analysis of *Las Carolinas* (1886) and *La perla cubana* (1890), two plays prominently featuring blackface, Soria shows that *género chico* blackface relies on the (re-)creation of racial hierarchies, based on the dominant Eurocentric episteme, thus buttressing the Spanish imperial economy, founded on the slavery system. Soria further contends that these plays aim to recover Spain's bygone imperial power through appeals to a distinctively traditional and colonial masculinity. The two essays in Part II, therefore, tease out the ideological implications of the relationship between empire and the performances of race (and gender) in the literary works of fin-de-siècle Spain.

The third and final part of *Unsettling Colonialism*, "Gender and Colonialism in Literary and Political Debates," consists of four essays that scrutinize the ways in which gender intersects with discourses of empire and colonialism in *fin-de-siglo* literary and political debates. In chapter 6, "Becoming Useless: Masculinity, Able-Bodiedness, and Empire in Nineteenth-Century Spain," Julia Chang focuses on the discourse of Spanish racial decline in relation to gender and disability in Benito Pérez Galdós's historical novel, *Aita Tettauen*. To this end, she studies the production of Spanish soldiers, as well as their counterpart—*los inútiles*—amid growing concerns around virility and racial decline in the context of anti-imperial struggle and colonial loss. Examining the medical requirements for military conscription alongside Galdós's novel, the chapter probes the biopolitical and aesthetic contours of military masculinity. This gender ideal, which enfolds normative notions of race and ability, Chang argues, is ultimately rendered unstable by the very colonial wars that necessitate its production. Nuria Godón, the author of chapter 7, examines the place of Leopoldo Alas's *La Regenta* in the context of fin-de-siècle discourses of colonialism and domination. Her essay, "From Imperial Boots to Naked Feet: Clarín's Views on Cuban Freedom and Female Independence in *La Regenta*," combines a reading of the nineteenth-century realist novelist's literary masterpiece with correspondence from the social movements for colonial independence and women's emancipation. Centering her analysis on the power relationship between the novel's male protagonist—a greedy clergyman who dreams of territorial control—and his daughters of confession, Godón argues that this relationship reflects the identification between patriarchal domination in the face of incipient feminism, on the one hand, and an apology of imperialism, in light of the independence of the colonies, on the other.

Analyzing works in which two key figures of Philippine nationalism address themselves explicitly to indigenous *dalagas* [girls], Joyce Tolliver's contribution in chapter 8, "*Dalagas* and *Ilustrados*: Gender, Language, and Indigeneity in the Philippine Colonies," offers new insight into the nexus of indigeneity, gender, and language in discourses on Spanish and U.S. imperialism in the Philippines. José Rizal's essay, "To the Young Women of Malolos," originally written in Tagalog in 1889, praises a group of Filipina women who petitioned the Spanish government to establish a Spanish language school, but suggests that only a return to their essential indigenous identity will make them pure enough to serve the emerging nation. By the same token, Pedro Paterno's tale, "La dalaga virtuosa [The Virtuous Girl]" (1910), echoes Rizal's affirmation of the Filipinas' indigenous identity as a key to their essential spiritual goodness, while linguistically undercutting the cultural authority of the U.S. occupation by writing in Spanish.

In chapter 9, "The Spanish Carceral Archipelago: Concepción Arenal against Penitentiary Colonization," Aurélie Vialette shows how Spain's recourse to penal colonies was the ultimate option to save the empire, transforming some of the Spanish islands—the Philippines and Fernando Poo—into spaces of exception. Vialette argues that this plan implied a paradox: the act of sending the convicts to remote islands created the illusion of their rehabilitation and conversion into citizens; yet, the criminals become citizens in the colony only, thus creating a mechanism for transforming them into neocolonizers of these islands. Vialette's point of entry in exploring the problem of penitentiary colonization is the work of Galician feminist social reformer and anthropologist Concepción Arenal, who provided crucial insight into how a woman, in a field dominated by male intellectuals, could participate in legal debates surrounding the relationship between prison reform and empire.

Unsettling Colonialism closes by charting Spain's imperial decline through the intertwining of gender, race, and colonialism in literary, historical, and cultural narratives that aim symbolically to recover the nation's geopolitical gains and losses. We thus highlight the rich and complex set of relations that complicate narratives about colonial rule grounded in the histories of other European nations. While we cannot presume that representations of women and colonized subjects will necessarily challenge dominant discourses of gender and race, these representations have the potential to reorient our analysis of colonialism in ways that take into account the process of negotiation of these subjects' identities and locations. Whether or not women and subaltern subjects can ultimately be viewed as agents of decolonization in a given discursive context, it is incumbent on the literary and cultural critic to take on the task of unsettling colonialism by analyzing these representations critically—and, in some instances, by identifying potential spaces of resistance within the dominant discourses of colonialism. The chapters of *Unsettling Colonialism* show how colonialism reconfigured social dynamics in Europe and how women travelers, writers, and scholars contributed to nationalist and colonial theorizing and agency. By focusing on the particularity of Spanish colonialism, the volume offers new approaches to race and gender studies from the singular context of a colonizing nation facing staggering imperial loss. Our hope is that this anthology will not only place Iberia on the map of colonial and postcolonial studies, from which it has largely been absent, but will also foster a greater awareness of the legacies of empire within the global nineteenth-century Hispanic world.

Notes

1. While the term *the long nineteenth century*—referring to the period between the French revolution and the outbreak of World War I—was coined by the historian Eric Hobsbawm in the British context, the end of the eighteenth century through the early twentieth century also marks a watershed moment in Spanish imperial history. At the same time, the exact temporal parameters of this "long century" have been subject to debate among scholars of Iberian and Latin American studies. For example, in *A New History of Iberian Feminisms*, the editors define the "long nineteenth century" as the period between 1808 and 1920. As Tsuchiya notes in her introduction to *Empire's End*, while the tendency among Iberian studies specialists

has been to conceptualize the Spanish-American War (1898) as the endpoint of the Spanish empire, not only did Spain's imperial domination continue in Morocco and Equatorial Guinea well into the twentieth century, but the Spanish colonial legacy extended beyond the end of the nineteenth century, both within the metropolis and in the postcolony (Spanish America and the Philippines).

2. It should be acknowledged, however, that Spain and Portugal did already have colonial holdings in North Africa prior to 1492, which turned out to be instrumental in the launching of the Atlantic expansion. See the special issues of the *Journal of Spanish Cultural Studies*: *A Forgotten Empire: the Spanish North African Borderlands*, ed. Barbara Fuchs and Yuen-Gen Liang; and "Entering the Global Hispanophone: An Introduction," ed. Benita Sampedro Vizcaya and Adolfo Campoy-Cubillo. We thank Benita Sampedro for these references.

3. While the Napoleonic Wars are often considered to be the critical event that led to the declaration of autonomous governments (juntas) by a number of Spain's largest colonies in Spanish America beginning in 1810, launching a period of more than ten years of wars of independence, the struggle for liberation had already begun in the late eighteenth century with the indigenous uprising in Peru in 1780. See Tsuchiya, Introduction (3).

4. According to Balfour: "The components of national culture in late nineteenth-century Spain, therefore, were made up of traditional icons of Spanish identity: the Reconquest of Spain in the Middle Ages, the Discovery of America, the Second of May uprising against the French, victories against rebellious Moroccans in the nineteenth century" (2).

5. For a discussion of the relationship between Spanish nationalism and imperial expansion in the nineteenth century, see Álvarez Junco (499–531). Javier Krauel, for his part, proceeds from the foundation laid by the work of historians Josep Fradera and Christopher Schmidt-Nowara to argue for "the centrality of the colonial empire for the nation-building process during the nineteenth century" (14).

6. In Blanco's words: "El que se argumentara que España debía expandir su territorio y asumir la *misión civilizadora* haciendo de Marruecos una colonia española era querer integrar a España en el proyecto moderno colonial y ubicar al país, que todavía estaba en los albores del desarrollo capitalista, dentro del concierto de naciones imperiales, a la vez que en el discurso colonial moderno. Es decir, ser un imperio que colonizaba era estar en la modernidad" (*Cultura y conciencia imperial* 46). We thank the anonymous reader of the manuscript for the reference to Blanco's work.

7. See, for example, Hooper, Jubran, Tofiño-Quesada, and Ugarte ("The Spanish Empire").

8. We are aware of the debates surrounding the choice of terminology in the context of recent (re)formulations of "Iberian studies"; however, we believe that this debate, too, remains unsettled. In our view, of greater importance is the fact that we have begun to interrogate and to debate vigorously the terminology—"Spanish," "Peninsular," "Hispanic," etc.—that we have previously taken for granted to define our field of study, based on unquestioned assumptions about both nation and empire.

9. Book-length studies, published since 2000, that foreground the problem of Spanish imperialism in nineteenth- and early-twentieth-century literature and culture include Alda Blanco's *Cultura y conciencia imperial en la España del siglo XIX* (2012), Michael Iarocci's *Properties of Modernity: Romantic Spain, Modern Europe, and the Legacies of Empire* (2006), Javier Krauel's *Imperial Emotions: Cultural Responses to Myths of Empire in fin-de-siècle Spain* (2013), Susan Martin-Márquez's *Disorientations: Spanish Colonialism in Africa and the Performance of Identity* (2008), Lisa Surwillo's *Monsters by Trade: Slave Traffickers in Modern Spanish Literature and Culture* (2014), Michael Ugarte's *Africans in Europe: The Culture of Exile and Emigration from Equatorial Guinea to Spain* (2010), and Akiko Tsuchiya and William Acree's *Empire's End: Transnational Connections in the Hispanic World* (2016).

10. Postcolonial critics have questioned dichotomies such as North/South, "first" and "third" worlds, as of late. As Chandra Mohanty has noted, these terms, which were "meant to loosely distinguish the northern and southern hemispheres, affluent and marginal nations and communities, obviously do not line up neatly within this geographical frame." At the same time, she maintains that these terms do have a certain value as political designations "that attempt to distinguish between the 'haves' and 'have-nots'" (*Feminism* 226). We are using the term *Global South* in this latter sense.

11. For Krauel, this specter takes the form of the nation's emotional investment in empire, reflected in the essays of early-twentieth-century canonical male writers; imperial myths, based on collective memory, engendered national narratives that endured long beyond the crisis of 1898 (6–12).

12. On these entangled histories, see *Empire's End* (Tsuchiya, Introduction 3–4).

13. See Herzog and Schmidt-Nowara for a discussion of the historical context in which the Cádiz delegates determined Spanish citizenship (Herzog 152–62; Schmidt-Nowara, *Slavery* 110–11). See Kirkpatrick on how gender figured into the debates on who should be included or excluded as a citizen (237).

14. For Chandra Mohanty, relations of power are not reducible to the binary opposition of colonizer/colonized. She notes the importance of taking into account the intersections of "multiple, fluid structure of domination" that shape women's social and political lives (13).

Works Cited

Alexander, M. Jacqui, and Chandra Talpade Mohanty, eds. *Feminist Genealogies, Colonial Legacies, Democratic Futures*. Routledge, 1999.
Álvarez Junco, José. *Mater dolorosa: La idea de España en el siglo XIX*. Taurus, 2001.
Balfour, Sebastian. *The End of the Spanish Empire 1898–1923*. Clarendon P, 1997.
Bermúdez, Silvia, and Roberta Johnson, eds. *A New History of Iberian Feminisms*. U of Toronto P, 2018.

Bhabha, Homi. *The Location of Culture*. Routledge, 1994.
Bhambra, Gurminder K. "Postcolonial and Decolonial Dialogues." *Postcolonial Studies*, vol. 17, no. 2, 2014, pp. 115–21.
Blanco, Alda. *Cultura y conciencia imperial en la España del siglo XIX*. Publicacions de la U de València, 2012.
———. "El fin del imperio español y la generación del 98: nuevas aproximaciones." *Hispanic Research Journal*, vol. 4, no. 1, February 2003, pp. 3–18.
———. "Spain at the Crossroads: Imperial Nostalgia or Modern Colonialism?" *A Contracorriente: Una Revista de Historia Social y Literatura de América Latina* vol. 5, no. 1, 2007, pp. 1–11.
Fuchs, Barbara, and Yuen-Gen Liang, eds. *A Forgotten Empire: The Spanish North African Borderlands*, special issue of the *Journal of Spanish Cultural Studies*, vol. 12, no. 3, 2011.
Herzog, Tamar. *Defining Nations: Immigrants and Citizens in Early Modern Spain and Spanish America*. Yale UP, 2003.
Hobsbawm, Eric. *The Age of Empire 1875–1914*. Abacus, 1987.
Hooper, Kirsty. "Reading Spain's 'African Vocation': The Figure of the Moorish Priest in Three *fin de siglo* Novels (1890–1907)." *Revista de Estudios Hispánicos*, vol. 40, no. 1, 2006, pp. 171–95.
Iarocci, Michael. *Properties of Modernity: Romantic Spain, Modern Europe, and the Legacies of Empire*. Vanderbilt UP, 2006.
Jubran, Carl. "Spanish Internal-Orientalism, Cultural Hybridity, and the Production of National Identity: 1887–1940." Diss. U of California, San Diego, 2002.
Kirkpatrick, Susan. "Constituting the Subject: Race, Gender, and Nation in the Early Nineteenth Century." *Culture and the State in Spain: 1550–1850*, edited by Tom Lewis and Francisco J. Sánchez, Garland, 1999, pp. 225–51.
Krauel, Javier. *Imperial Emotions: Cultural Responses to Myths of Empire in fin-de-siècle Spain*. Liverpool UP, 2013.
Loureiro, Ángel. "Spanish Nationalism and the Ghost of Empire." *Journal of Spanish Cultural Studies* vol. 4, no. 1, 2003, pp. 65–76.
Martin-Márquez, Susan. *Disorientations: Spanish Colonialism in Africa and the Performance of Identity*. Yale UP, 2008.
Mbembe, Achille. *On the Postcolony*. U of California P, 2001.
McClintock, Anne. *Imperial Leather: Race, Gender, and Sexuality in the Colonial Contest*. Routledge, 1995.
Mills, Charles. "The Political Economy of Personhood." On the Human: A Project of the National Humanities Center. October 18, 2017; https://nationalhumanitiescenter.org/on-the-human/2011/04political-economy-of-personhood/.
Mohanty, Chandra. *Feminism without Borders: Decolonizing Theory, Practicing Solidarity*. Duke UP, 2003.
———. "Cartographies of Struggle: Third World Women and the Politics of Feminism." *Third World Women and the Politics of Feminism*, edited by Chandra Mohanty, Ann Russo, and Lourdes Torres, Indiana UP, 1991, pp. 1–47.

Sampedro Vizcaya, Benita, and Adolfo Campoy-Cubillo, eds. *Entering the Global Hispanophone: An Introduction*, special issue of the *Journal of Spanish Cultural Studies* vol. 20, nos. 1–2, 2019.

Schmidt-Nowara, Christopher. *Slavery, Freedom, and Abolition in Latin America and the Atlantic World*. U of New Mexico P, 2011.

Stoler, Ann Laura. *Carnal Knowledge and Imperial Power: Race and the Intimate in Colonial Rule*. U of California P, 2002.

Surwillo, Lisa. *Monsters by Trade: Slave Traffickers in Modern Spanish Literature and Culture*. Stanford UP, 2014.

Tofiño-Quesada, Ignacio. "Spanish Orientalism: Uses of the Past in Spain's Colonization in Africa." *Comparative Studies of South Asia, Africa and the Middle East*, vol. 23, no. 1–2, 2003, pp. 141–48.

Tsuchiya, Akiko. Introduction. *Empire's End: Transnational Connections in the Hispanic World*, edited by Akiko Tsuchiya and William G. Acree Jr., Vanderbilt UP, 2016, pp. 1–13.

———, and William G. Acree Jr., eds. *Empire's End: Transnational Connections in the Hispanic World*. Vanderbilt UP, 2016.

Ugarte, Michael. *Africans in Europe: The Culture of Exile and Emigration from Equatorial Guinea to Spain*. U of Illinois P, 2010.

———. "The Spanish Empire on the Wane: Africa, Galdós, and the Moroccan Wars." *Empire's End: Transnational Connections in the Hispanic World*, edited by Akiko Tsuchiya and William G. Acree Jr., Vanderbilt UP, 2016, pp. 177–90.

PART I

COLONIALISM AND WOMEN'S MIGRATIONS

1

The Colonial Politics of Meteorology

The West African Expedition of the Urquiola Sisters

BENITA SAMPEDRO VIZCAYA

En 1853 se erigió una escuela-internado para niñas bènga en Evangesimba. Se le dio el nombre de *Itândĕ ja Iluku* ("amor de hermana"), mas pronto fue conocida como *Maluku* ("hermanas"). Dieciocho chicas cursaron inicialmente, de las cuales doce eran internas. *Maluku* fue dirigida por la señora Isabella Sweeney Mackey y por sus dos asistentes afroamericanas, Julia Smith y Margaret Webb. La señorita Smith había residido en Monrovia durante once años antes de llegar a la isla en 1853. Miss Webb fue una de las pioneras en Mànji, donde arribó en 1850 junto a los reverendos presbiterianos y sus esposas. Mackey escribió al Consejo de Nueva York que una chica bènga de la escuela realizó la asombrosa hazaña académica de memorizar por entero los cuatro Evangelios.

(In 1853, a boarding school for Bènga girls was built in Evangesimba. It was given the name of *Itândĕ ja Iluku* ["sisterly love"], but was soon known as *Maluku* ["sisters"]. Eighteen girls attended initially; of them, twelve were boarders. *Maluku* was run by Mrs. Isabella Sweeney Mackey and her two African-American assistants, Julia Smith and Margaret Webb. Miss Smith had resided in Monrovia for eleven years before arriving on the island in 1853. Miss Webb was one of the pioneers in Mànji, where she arrived in 1850 together with the Presbyterian

Reverends and their wives. Mackey wrote to the New York Council that a Bènga girl from the school achieved the amazing academic feat of memorizing the four Gospels in full.)

—Enénge A'Bodjedi, "Las Iglesias Presbiterianas Ndowé"

Señor: Doña Isabel Urquiola de Iradier, española peninsular, residente en esta Colonia con su legítimo esposo a los Reales Pies de V. M. devidamente espone [sic], que hallándose cerrada la Academia de Instrucción Primaria de Niñas de la misma, creyéndose con aptitud suficiente para dar la instrucción, solicitó la Plaza al Gobierno General bajo calidad de interina y sobresueldo asignado a la propietaria, a la sazón ausente por causa de enfermedad. Fecha 1º de Agosto obtuvo el respectivo nombramiento y desde ese día tomó posesión del cargo y abrió la instrucción con tan favorables auspicios que no cree la esponente [sic] haberse visto muy rivalizada respecto al número de niñas que vienen asistiendo a la clase. El día 24 del mismo mes fue instruida por el Habilitado de Clases Civiles a cerca de que el haber que se le asignaba no era el de dos mil quinientas pesetas consignadas en el Presupuesto, sino una gratificación mensual de ciento veinte y cinco pesetas. . . . Siendo insuficientes para su alimentación las ciento veinte y cinco pesetas mensuales que se le han otorgado en definitiva, y bajo cuya cuota nunca se hubiera brindado a desempeñar el cargo, acude rendidamente a los pies del trono y: Suplica a S. M. se digne otorgar a la que tiene el honor de dirigirse a su Soberano la concesión del sobresueldo correspondiente a la Maestra de Niñas de esta Colonia, contándose desde la fecha en que tomó posesión de dicho cargo.

(Sir: Mrs. Isabel Urquiola de Iradier, peninsular Spaniard, residing in this colony with her legitimate husband, duly submits at the Royal Feet of Your Majesty that, the Academy of Elementary Instruction of Girls having been closed and believing herself sufficiently well trained to teach, she applied to the General Government for the post, with interim status and with the same compensation assigned to the principal teacher, who was at that time absent due to illness. On the 1st of August, she obtained the appointment in question, and from that day she assumed possession of the position, beginning instruction with such favorable results that she was in her view without rival in respect to the number of girls who began attending classes. On the 24th of the same month, she was instructed by the Officer for Civil Education that the amount assigned to her was not the two thousand five hundred pesetas stipulated in the budget, but a monthly payment of one hundred and twenty-five pesetas instead. . . . Since the one hundred and twenty-five pesetas a month that she was offered were insufficient for her living expenses, and since with this stipend she would have never accepted the position, she humbly approaches the feet of the throne and requests His Majesty to grant her, who has the honor of addressing His Sovereign Highness, the sum which had been granted to the girls' elementary teacher in this colony, counting from the date on which she assumed possession of this position.)

—Isabel Urquiola de Iradier, "Instancia elevada al Rey. Fernando Poo, 8 de septiembre de 1876"

The story I am about to unfold is not intended to memorialize, but rather to resituate, the participatory role of women in colonial sciences as well as the political and pragmatic role of local guides in the nineteenth-century Spanish mapping of African territories. It is also intended as a supplement—stressing the centrality of the colonial politics of meteorology—to the founding narratives of surveying and settlement, and as a challenge to the unmitigated single voice of gendered history, a voice which served as a basis for the European construction of scientific knowledge about Africa. Addressing the frontiers of empire as delineated by Manuel Iradier y Bulfy (1854–1911) in his chronicling of the expeditions to the Gulf of Guinea, I will scrutinize the ways in which Iradier's prose both undermined and underwrote the hierarchical framework that governed the territory's colonial exploration.

In late 1874, twenty-year-old Isabel Urquiola[1] began a journey with her younger sister Manuela (aged eighteen)[2] to the southernmost edge of Spain's territorial possessions: to the Muni Estuary, on the border between today's Gabon and Equatorial Guinea. Initially accompanying Isabel's new husband, Manuel Iradier—also aged twenty and, like Isabel and Manuela, hailing from Vitoria in the Basque Country—the two young women were stationed on the small Atlantic island of Elobey Chico for an eight-month period. Iradier and the Urquiola sisters had embarked on a mail steamboat on December 16, 1874, in the north of Spain. After spending a few months in the Canary Islands to acclimate themselves and prepare the expedition, they boarded another steamboat in April, heading toward the Spanish territories in the Gulf of Guinea.[3] They reached their first destination, the island of Fernando Poo, on May 16, 1875. While in Santa Isabel, the capital of Fernando Poo, they were received by the Spanish governor, Diego Santiesteban,[4] who tried (and failed) to dissuade them from continuing their journey further south to Elobey Chico, in the Muni Estuary, citing the fact that the island lacked fresh water, protection from the Spanish crown, and proper infrastructure. Nothing deterred them. They reached Elobey two days later.

The only other non-African women who undertook such journeys to the region during this decade were the wives of a handful of missionaries and government officials. Yet, in the coming months, Isabel and Manuela Urquiola resided alone for extended periods of time, while Iradier explored the coastal region and ventured into the inland territories of the Muni. Despite the limitations of their equipment, the restrictions of the budget at their disposal, their inexperience, and their general unpreparedness for the tasks ahead, the Urquiola sisters soon initiated what may be considered a groundbreaking program of scientific data collection: one of pivotal significance not only for the history of science, but also for the history of Spanish colonial exploration and occupation of the territory.[5]

In the year 1893, almost a generation after the Urquiola sisters' expedition, a thirty-year-old London-born woman, Mary Henrietta Kingsley, would also board a cargo vessel to West Africa. She would stop—on

Figure 1.1. Sebastiana Estala at the center, surrounded by her four children; from left to right, Manuela, Esteban, Juliana, and Isabel Urquiola Estala, in Vitoria, Spain. (Gutiérrez Garitano, *Apuntes de la Guinea [Notes on Guinea]*)

occasion for a considerable amount of time—in some of the same islands (Fernando Poo, Corisco, Elobey), and on the same estuary in which the Urquiola sisters had their base of operations, living with the same Benga or Bubi communities. One year after her first West African trip, she traveled through the Muni Estuary from Corisco to Gabon, up the Ogooué River and into the interior, first by steamboat and then by canoe. Mary Kingsley has been acknowledged as one of the first European women to have visited inland parts of Gabon and the French Congo, and to have had contact with the Fang peoples in the interior, as well as with the Mpongwe communities on the estuary. According to her own testimony, during this second trip she traded British cloth for ivory, ebony, and rubber, using the profits of this trade to offset the costs of her travels.

Kingsley—unlike the Spanish sisters—received full credit for the extensive graphic, written, and material archive which she compiled as part of the commercial and scientific enterprises with which she was engaged. She published her acclaimed *Travels in West Africa* in London in 1897, and chronicled her experiences at numerous invited lectures upon her return.[6] While exploring the lower Congo River, she collected many scientific specimens for the British Museum, including insects and freshwater fishes, and (in the years before her death in 1900) her trips to West Africa afforded her a rewarding career as a writer, lecturer, and consultant in London. Her narrative of the expeditions, although at times seeming to anticipate more modern attitudes toward gender and race, falls in many ways squarely within the patriarchal and imperialist prejudices of the Victorian establishment. Certainly, Kingsley was also quite critical of many of the European colonial practices in Africa, including the role of the missionaries, and she often expressed sympathy toward the local populations. She contributed to the advancement of anthropological fieldwork, arguing that it was essential to live within these communities in order to understand them, and she enhanced European knowledge of Africa.[7] However, her narrative hardly passes the test of resisting the colonial archetype of self-discovery.[8] Even if her gender, motivations, and general sensibility do not exactly match the profile of the traditional colonial hero, her career recalls the claim made by Priyasha Mukhopadhyay in reviewing Berny Sèbe's recent book, *Heroic Imperialists in Africa*: "[T]he popular construction of the colonial explorer subduing native populations and, more often than not, saving them from themselves, was universally deployed in Britain and France as a 'justifying principle, whilst conveying an exotic vision of an expanding and successful empire'" (771).

To a considerable degree, it would seem that these pioneering female expeditionaries—while challenging the boundaries of gender convention and advancing the frontiers of the natural sciences, geography and ethnography—served ultimately as facilitators to the consolidation of European territorial expansion in Africa. Mary Kingsley's contribution to European views on the continent, her later role as colonial advisor, and the connections she made between theories of sexual, environmental, and racial determinism, all reveal a woman firmly rooted in the geopolitical interests of her own time and, specifically, those of colonial Great Britain at the turn of the century. Equally, the remarkable—and still largely unknown and unacknowledged—scientific work carried out by Isabel and Manuela Urquiola on the island of Elobey served indirectly, through the publications and public engagements of Isabel de Urquiola's husband, Manuel Iradier, to chart out Spanish possessions in the Gulf of Guinea, and to increase Spanish political and economic expectations regarding their potential for colonial purposes.

In order to appraise the full impact of the Urquiola sisters' role, however, it is necessary to revisit the historical moment in which their expedition took place and, in particular, the ongoing debates about the viability of these Spanish territories in Africa in the 1870s. Ignacio García Tudela—who had been appointed governor of Fernando Poo shortly before their arrival, in 1872—officially proposed the abandonment of the colony in a lengthy report that advised the central administration in Madrid to withdraw completely from their possessions in the Gulf of Guinea.[9] His argument rested on what he saw as the present and future incapability of Spain to infiltrate local networks, and the concomitant commercial and religious dominance of the British in this region. Britain, he claimed, was the only nation that was making real profit from the territories.[10] Yet, his successor as governor, Diego Santiesteban—a fifty-five-year-old navy captain well acquainted with colonial affairs, and with experience serving in the Philippines prior to his assignment to Fernando Poo—had begun to advocate for a very different position. Santiesteban enthusiastically defended maintaining the colony, stressing the benefits that he believed Spain might gain from these hitherto neglected territories. To that effect, on July 1, 1875, he dispatched to Madrid a counter-report illustrated with fourteen photographs by Francis W. Joaque, a well-regarded Sierra Leonean photographer with a studio in Fernando Poo.[11] He sent the fourteen views of the colony to the Ministerio de Ultramar in Madrid, hoping to harness economic backing for a fully functioning colonial administration in the Spanish Territories of the Gulf of Guinea.

The report and the photographs evidently worked miracles: Madrid's reaction was positive and expeditious. It is in this context that we should frame the warm welcome that Santiesteban offered to Manuel Iradier and Isabel and Manuela Urquiola, when they reached Fernando Poo in May 1875 and, consequently, their seminal role in helping pave the way for colonial mapping, possession, and settlement. Historian Gustau Nerín aptly summarizes the circumstances of their arrival:

> La de Iradier fue una expedición atípica: tres protagonistas jovencísimos e inexpertos, con escasísimo presupuesto y sin apoyo oficial, trataban de emular a los grandes exploradores ingleses. Poco les pudo ofrecer el Gobierno General, siempre falto de recursos. Iradier solo gozó del dudoso privilegio de alojarse en la casa del Subgobierno de Elobey, que estaba por aquel entonces abandonada. (Iradier's was an atypical expedition: three very young and inexperienced players, with an extremely limited budget and without official support, were trying to emulate the great English explorers. The General Government, always lacking in resources, could offer little to them. Iradier enjoyed only the dubious privilege of staying in the house of the Sub-government of Elobey, which was abandoned by then.) (126)

While they had not been funded by any government agency or geographical society for this first expedition—traveling instead on a practically self-subsidized mission with a budget of less than eight thousand pesetas—their interests converged with those of the governor.[12] Scholarship connecting this region with larger cross-Atlantic circuits during this period is still scant, but it is fair to claim that the territories would come to serve as a pivotal node in Spanish colonial networks, and as an anchor point both prior to and after the Spanish imperial defeat in Cuba, Puerto Rico, and the Philippines in 1898.[13]

During the Franco regime, the figure of Manuel Iradier as the epitome of the African explorer would be enshrined and exploited in the national public imaginary. To celebrate the centenary of his birth in 1954, the Spanish administration placed into circulation a series of postal stamps and postcards with his image, taken from his various photographs and portraits, and embellished with classically colonial iconography of Africa in circulation during mid-twentieth-century Europe.[14]

Figure 1.2. Postcard sent from the colonial city of Santa Isabel in Fernando Poo to Seville in 1955.

Simultaneously, the researchers at the Instituto de Estudios Africanos of the Consejo Superior de Investigaciones Científicas in Madrid organized a series of academic events in the late 1940s and throughout the 1950s, and issued various biographical works, aiming to recover Manuel Iradier as an iconic historical figure in the exploration of the African continent. Among these works are José María Cordero Torres's *Iradier* (1944), Ricardo Majó Framis's *Las generosas y primitivas empresas de Manuel Iradier Bulfy en la Guinea Española: el hombre y sus hechos* (*The Generous and Primitive Enterprises of Manuel Iradier Bulfy in Spanish Guinea: The Man and his Deeds*) (1954),

Figure 1.3. Postal stamps commemorating the centenary of the birth of Manuel Iradier, on the first day of circulation.

The Colonial Politics of Meteorology 27

and the collective volume *Iradier: Conmemoración de su primer centenario* (*Iradier: Commemoration of his First Centenary*) (1956). This scholarly production marked the culmination of a cumulative process; as Nerín suggests, "El invento de Iradier como gran explorador se iniciaría durante la dictadura de Primo de Rivera y lo consolidaría el franquismo, deseoso de construir una mitología colonialista africana a la altura de la de las grandes potencias coloniales" (The invention of Iradier as a great explorer would begin during the dictatorship of Primo de Rivera and would be consolidated by the Franco regime, eager to build an African colonialist mythology on a par with that of the great colonial powers) (126–27).

The organic intellectuals of the Franco regime were less keen, however, to reveal the full collaborative extent of the expedition headed by Manuel

Figure 1.4. Manuel Iradier Bulfy, photograph taken upon his return from the second expedition to Africa. (Gutiérrez Garitano, *Apuntes de la Guinea*)

Iradier and Isabel and Manuela Urquiola in 1875–77.[15] Specifically, the silencing of the participation of the Urquiola sisters in the first expedition effectively erased the women's participation in a formative period of Spanish expansion in Africa.[16] The journeys would set in motion a multifaceted circuit of diplomats, geographers, missionaries, military, and medical personnel that transferred valuable information, instrumental in the consolidation of ambitious political, religious, and economic projects for the region; the role of Spanish women in these processes has yet to be critically assessed.[17] While Manuel Iradier has been mythologized, Isabel and Manuela Urquiola were in fact responsible for pivotal scientific contributions through the meteorological observations they carried out from the small island of Elobey Chico (little more than one square kilometer in surface), located on the Muni Estuary not far from the coast of Gabon and the islands of Corisco and Elobey Grande. It was on this island that a number of European commercial houses had their base of operations: due to its strategic location, these companies enjoyed prime maritime connections to the West African coast. Among the firms with local representation were Woermann, John Holt, Hatton & Cookson, Cooper Scott, Morris, Friedrich, Glasgow Company, and, later, the Compañía Transatlántica.

The tasks carried out by the Urquiola sisters in the field of meteorology, through their daily data collection, are noteworthy from a scientific point of view. The records of the American Meteorological Society reveal that many network-based meteorological stations were established in the late nineteenth century, partly in response to the deliberations of the Vienna Meteorological Conference held in 1873.[18] However, large parts of Africa, Asia, South America, and Australia were represented poorly, if at all. This was particularly the case for Africa, since the Vienna convention predated the Berlin Conference of 1884–85 and, hence, the full-scale European redistribution and occupation of the continent, in the so-called scramble for Africa. Systematic contacts of Europeans with many parts of the continent, both coastal and inland, were still at a relatively embryonic travel/exploration phase. The Urquiola sisters, during their 1874–77 expedition, were responsible for one of the oldest meteorological datasets that had been preserved in the sub-Saharan region, and certainly the earliest in Central Africa.[19] Their work at the observatory in the island of Elobey is likely to have been one of many daily tasks they performed, but also one of their highest priorities. Its construction and setup was among their first projects upon arrival.

Mapping a region's weather conditions was understood not only as an important feature of scientific research but also as a critical first step to exploration and settlement. Weather—meteorologists rightly claim—is one of the natural phenomena most intimately linked to people's everyday lives: "Weather affects everything; there is no single social act that could be excluded from the influence of its conditions" (Koczanowicz 775). This clearly encompasses livelihoods and social actions that unfold within the frame of imperial expansion. Research on climate, geography, and natural and environmental sciences, is inextricably linked to the early stages of imperial state projects. Charting the territory, and the conditions that shape the territory, is a materialist and a fundamentally economic practice: a form of appropriation of the natural world that precedes its seizure and occupation. Apprehending the natural helps to structure the social and the political. Iradier's writings account for this fact with earnest sincerity; in stating the principal aims of his expedition, he writes, "esta tenía por objeto, más bien que el levantamiento de planos, la adquisición de noticias sobre el clima, las producciones y tribus del interior" (this had as its objective, more than the drafting of plans, the acquisition of information about the climate, the productions, and the tribes of the interior) (*Fragmentos de un diario* 54).

According to the meteorological charts preserved, data collection began in earnest shortly after the Urquiola sisters' arrival in Elobey in June 1875, and covered a span of seven full months, until December that year. From a scientific standpoint, their observatory contained a number of advanced technological instruments: several thermometers (to compare the accuracy of temperature measurement), including a maximum and a minimum shade thermometer, a Saussure hygrometer, an evaporation glass, a pluviometer, an anemometer, a photometer, a dew collector, a spectroscope, a compass, and a pendulum, among others.[20] In his book *África: Fragmentos de un diario de viajes de exploración en la zona de Corisco* (*Africa, Fragments of a Travel Diary of Explorations in the Zone of Corisco*) (1878)—which is an abbreviated version of his opera magna in two volumes, *África: Viajes y trabajos de la asociación euskara la exploradora* (*Africa: Travels and Activities of the Basque Association "The Explorer"*) (1887)—Iradier repeatedly regrets his failure to register all of the weather measurements, since his barometer and chronometer were damaged before the expedition began. From a rhetorical perspective, it is curious to note how the self-assertive "I," which permeates his prose throughout ("estoy en África" [I am in Africa]), "el objeto de mi expedición es" [the object of my expedition is]), switches to a more ambiguous, passive voice sentence structure when he enters into meteorological descriptions: "Las observaciones meteorológicas han sido hechas en el islote Elobey a la latitud de 1º Norte y longitud 27º–42' próximamente" (The meteorological observations have been made on the Elobey islet at latitude 1º North and longitude 27º–42' approximately) (*Fragmentos de un diario*

54); "Las mediciones se han verificado a las mismas horas que se anotaba la temperatura" (The measurements were verified at the same time that the temperature was recorded) (*Fragmentos de un diario* 57). The all-consuming dedication to daily weather measurements—taken up to eight times per day, and never fewer than four times—must have been as exhausting as it was exhaustive: "Las observaciones se efectuaban periódicamente a las 6 y a las 10 horas de la mañana, y a las 2 y 6 horas de la tarde" (The observations were made periodically at 6 and 10 o'clock in the morning, and at 2 and 6 o'clock in the afternoon) (*Fragmentos de un diario* 54). With a combination of almost all possible variables, they quantified humidity levels, temperature, cubic rain amounts and duration, wind speed and direction, types of clouds and cloud formation, storms and a variety of other atmospheric phenomena. What follows is a sample of the meteorological annotations:

> Temperatura: Las observaciones se han verificado diariamente a las seis y a las doce de la mañana y a las tres y seis de la tarde, dejando incompleta la serie de estos valores termométricos por no aventurar una interpolación en extremos demasiado distantes como son las doce horas de noche, durante las que no se han verificado observaciones . . . Humedad relativa: El higrómetro Saussure ha sido observado a las mismas horas que los termómetros, dejando también incompleta la serie de observaciones para evitar la interpolación. . . .
>
> Vientos: El anemómetro se ha consultado a las 6, 8, 10 y 12 horas de la mañana; a las 2, 4 y 6 de la tarde, y a las 8 de la noche.
>
> (Temperature: The observations have been verified daily at six and twelve in the morning and at three and six in the afternoon, leaving incomplete the series of these thermometric values, not venturing an interpolation for distant extremes such as the twelve hours overnight, during which no observations have been verified. . . . Relative humidity: The Saussure hygrometer has been observed at the same times as the thermometers, also leaving the series of observations incomplete to avoid interpolation. . . . Winds: The anemometer was consulted at 6, 8, 10 and 12 o'clock in the morning; at 2, 4 and 6 in the afternoon, and at 8 at night.) (Iradier, *Fragmentos de un diario* 190ff.)

Such detailed meteorological data was never again collected for the region. The nearest station has been operating since the 1950s in Cocobeach, Gabon. The charts comprising these earlier observations are far more precise than any others recorded in western Africa during that period, not only because of the consistency of the data collected, but also because of their temporal resolution: other stations during this period were recording at most three observations per day. Spanish naval and administrative personnel were typically responsible for measurements on the island of Fernando Poo. Their scientific measurements were conducted from various improvised stations, from the governor's house to ships docked at the harbor. The charts preserved illustrate a lack of consistency, reveal the omission of more complex criteria, and exhibit gaps in dates recorded, as well as other obvious imprecisions.

The challenges of daily life for Isabel and Manuela Urquiola at Elobey Chico were surely greater than what Manuel Iradier's publications reveal: on the island, they did not have fresh water, which needed to be transported from the nearby island of Elobey Grande. They were living among people whose languages—Benga and English among them—they had to learn. Unlike Manuel Iradier, who had a university degree from the Facultad de Filosofía y Letras prior to their expedition, they had not been afforded the opportunity of higher education, and, like him, they lacked any prior travel experience beyond the Basque province of Álava. The sisters spent long periods of time awaiting Iradier's return while he explored the territory, often without receiving news from him. While Isabel was pregnant with their firstborn child, there was a period of almost three months in which he was absent; he had fallen ill while exploring the northern bank of the Muni River. Over time, all three of them succumbed to tropical fevers on numerous occasions during their expedition. The couple's daughter, also named Isabel, born in Elobey on January 1876, would die from malarial fever that same year, on November 28, in the island of Fernando Poo, a life-changing episode that Iradier records in volume II of his *África: Viajes y trabajos de la asociación euskara la exploradora*:

> El 28 de Noviembre de 1876 mi adorada Isabela, elobeyana de nacimiento, cayó herida por la última fiebre. Todo fue inútil: se declaró el acceso pernicioso: aquellos hermosos ojos se cerraron para no abrirse más. La muerte se cernió en el seno de la familia, y, a objeto de evitar más desgracias, mandé a los seres queridos, que con tanta abnegación me habían acompañado a aquellos climas, a

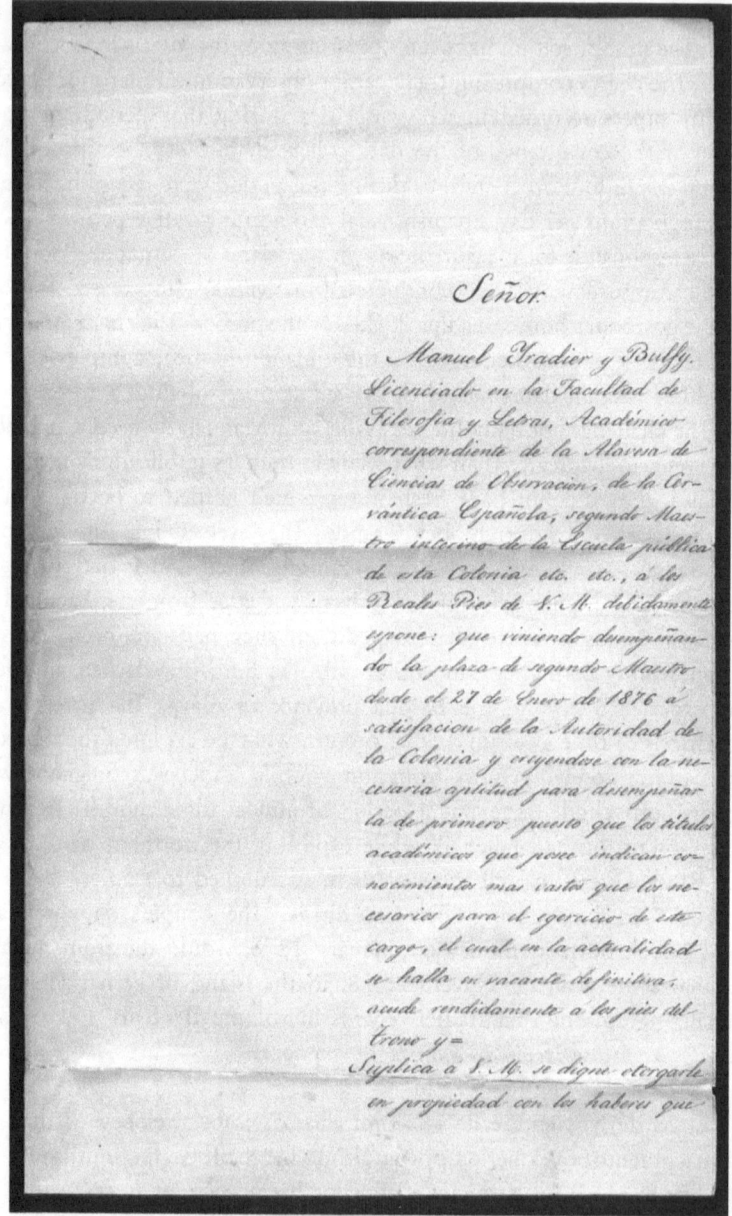

Figure 1.5. Petition to the governor by Manuel Iradier Bulfy, Fernando Poo, January 1, 1877. "Instancia de Manuel Iradier y Bulfy. Fernando Poo, 1 de enero, 1877." Source: Archivo General de la Administración, Alcalá de Henares. Fondo África, Sección 15 (4). Caja 81/06956.

le corresponde la plaza de Primer Maestro de esta Colonia, á el que tiene el honor de dirigirse á su Soberano.

Dios guarde la importante vida de V. M. muchos años para bien y felicidad de los españoles. Fernando Póo 1º de Enero de 1877.

Señor

A. L. R. P. D. V. M.

Manuel Yradier

reponer su quebrantada salud en las hermosas playas canarias. No quedé solo. El recuerdo de mi hija me perseguía por todas partes. (On November 28, 1876 my beloved Isabela, born on Elobey, fell victim to the last fever. Everything was in vain: the fever was declared pernicious: those beautiful eyes closed, never more to open. Her death filtered into the very bosom of the family, and, in order to avoid further misfortunes, I sent my loved ones, who with such self-denial had accompanied me to those climates, to restore their broken health on the beautiful beaches of the Canary Islands. I was not alone. The memory of my daughter followed me everywhere.) (15–16)

After eight full months in Elobey Chico, the family moved back to Fernando Poo's capital, Santa Isabel, with their newborn baby. There, both Manuel Iradier and Isabel Urquiola were granted teaching positions at the request of Governor Diego Santiesteban. Manuel worked as an interim teacher at the public school for boys, for a period of slightly less than two years: starting in January 1876 and ending with a resignation letter submitted in August 1877, "por padecer algunas fiebres después de año y medio que lleva de residencia en este punto [for suffering from fevers after the year and a half for which he has been residing in this place]."[21]

Isabel obtained an equivalent position as interim teacher in the public school for girls, with an appointment date of 1 August 1876, and a resignation date of 14 March 1877, but with only a fraction of the salary that had been granted to her husband. His appointment entailed an annual salary of 5,000 pesetas; hers, a theoretical 2,500 per year.

The disparity became further exacerbated when, due to an administrative glitch, she failed to receive the full 2,500 pesetas stipulated in the appointment letter and assigned in the school budget, but rather a mere 125 per month. Deeply disenchanted and dissatisfied with her remuneration, she formally petitioned the governor, and subsequently elevated her petition to the King of Spain in the highly formal letter that serves as epigraph to this essay, originally written on 2 September 1876 and subsequently rewritten and expanded six days later. The governor fully supported her claim, stating in his correspondence to the Ministerio de Ultramar in Madrid:

Esta señora española peninsular [tiene] dotes apreciables . . . la experiencia ha venido a demostrar la competencia de la reclamante. Alumnos y padres se encuentran satisfechos y la instrucción ha recobrado mucha parte de lo perdido en interinidades anteriores por lo que estimo que Doña Isabel Urquiola es acreedora de la munificencia.

(This peninsular Spanish lady has demonstrable gifts. . . . Experience has shown the competence of the petitioner. Students and parents are fully satisfied and instruction has recovered much of what had been lost with prior interim appointments; I therefore consider that Doña Isabel Urquiola is fully deserving of the compensation.)[22]

Her claims, however, were denied and, in March 1877, after completing almost eight months on the job, she returned to Spain with her sister Manuela. Iradier followed them shortly thereafter, in December of the same year. Once in Spain, he started to share some of the results of their West African expedition in a series of lectures and in reports issued by the Boletín de la Real Sociedad Geográfica de Madrid (1879). These would be elaborated at much greater length in his two volumes, *África: Viajes y trabajos de la asociación euskara la exploradora*, published in Vitoria in 1887. They are loosely organized as chronological travel diaries of the Iradier/Urquiola expedition of 1874–77, and of the second expedition he would embark on in 1884 in the company of Spanish doctor Amado Osorio. Susan Martin-Márquez has suggested that the second volume seems more organically structured "into chapters representing major scientific fields of the day, and [it] includes Iradier's observations of, for instance, the Guinean climate, physical anthropology, and language" (71). It is in these two volumes that he includes the extensive daily weather observations, with numerous pages devoted to meteorological tables, instruments used, measurements, nature and descriptions of political geography.

Although nowhere in either of his volumes is this fact acknowledged, the meteorological observations in particular appear to have been taken exclusively by Isabel and Manuela Urquiola. Most of the time, during the observational period, Iradier himself had been absent from the observatory itself, exploring the continent's interior on foot or on boat, or doing trade. There is only one personal admission to this fact on record: he confessed in an aside, at the end of a lecture he delivered at the Royal Geographical Society of Madrid in May 1886, that it would have been impossible for only one man with limited resources to measure and keep record of all the astronomical, geological, zoological, botanical, mineralogical, ethnological,

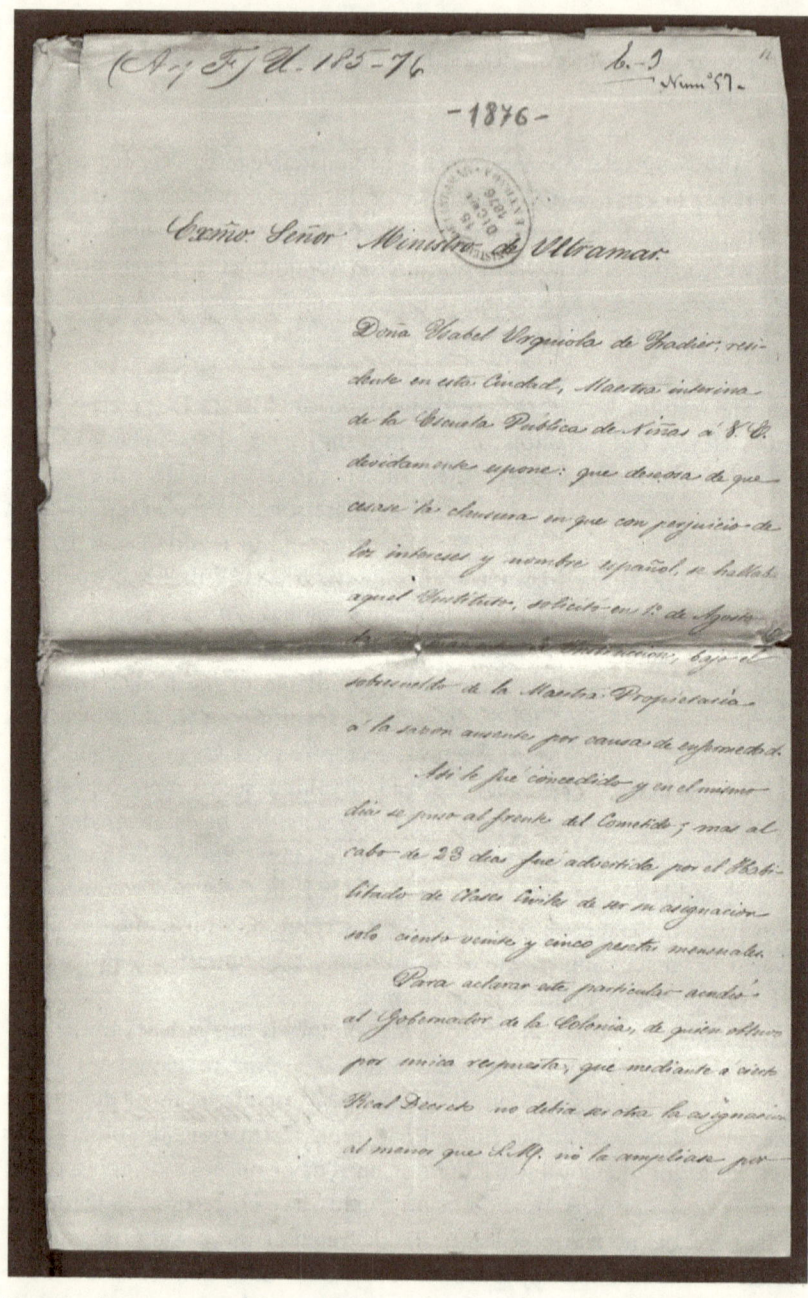

Figure 1.6. Petition to the governor by Isabel Urquiola de Iradier, Fernando Poo, October 16, 1876. "Instancia de Isabel Urquiola de Iradier. Fernando Poo, 16 de octubre de 1876." Source: Archivo General de la Administración, Alcalá de Henares. Fondo África, Sección 15 (4). Caja 81/06956.

instancia de la exponente, que seria apoyada
por razones de justicia. Lo hizo así
acompañando los documentos é instancia
misma que tiene hoy el honor de elevar por
conducto de V. E., mas no logró se le diese el
curso ordinario al menos de que aquella no
se reformara suprimiendo los documentos que
contenia. Fiel á su deseo, de pres. acu-
dió á lo propuesto; y como hasta el presente ningun resultado se le haya hecho noto-
rio, se ve la exponente en el imprescindible
caso de acudir á S. M. El Rey (Q. D. G.) por
conducto de S. E. con la primera de las expo-
siciones tal y como fué redactada en un
principio y =

Suplica á S. E. que teniendo en consideración
lo espuesto como causa bastante, para molestar
su alta atención, se sirva dar á aquel docu-
mento el curso que corresponda. Así lo
espera de la notoria justificación de S. E.

Dios guarde á S. E. muchos años

Fernando Pío

Figure 1.6. Continued.

and meteorological observations. Having addressed the subject of his meteorological observations, he concluded as follows:

> Antes de terminar, debo hacer una confesión que yo estaba decidido a ocultar. . . . Si yo en mis primeros viajes estaba ocupado explorando los bosques, los ríos, escalando montañas y visitando tribus. . . . ¿cómo podía observar la columna termométrica, la escala del udómetro, la aguja del higrómetro, la evaporación del agua, las oscilaciones plomadas, la dirección de los vientos y de las nubes y las tormentas? No fui yo quien tomó esas observaciones. El mérito es de mi compañera, que ni con las razones más poderosas ni los consejos más prudentes, ni los ruegos más afectuosos pudo renunciar a su determinación de permanecer siempre conmigo. Esta compañera es mi esposa.
>
> (Before I finish, I must make a confession that I was determined to hide. . . . If on my first trips I was busy exploring the forests, the rivers, climbing mountains and visiting tribes . . . how could I observe the column of the thermometer, the scale of the udometer, the needle of the hygrometer, the evaporation of the water, the oscillations of the lead, the direction of the winds and the clouds and the storms? It was not I who took those observations. The merit is that of my companion, who would not surrender her determination to remain with me, either with the most powerful reasoning, with the most prudent advice, or with the most affectionate pleas. This companion is my wife.) (Cited in Gallegos et al., 319)

Even this heartfelt admission, however, fails to include any mention of the scientific contributions of his sister-in-law, Manuela Urquiola. On the rare occasions on which he makes reference in his writings to the presence of Isabel and Manuela during their stay in Africa, he invokes leisure activities and conveys the impression that they had enjoyed an idyllic pastoral life on Elobey. He states they entertained themselves with fishing, taking care of the garden, walking, collecting beautiful butterflies, and observing the sunrise and sunset. He neglects entirely to mention the methodical and precision-based daily meteorological observations for which they would have been responsible—four to eight times per day—during this period. He sets the scene of their encampment in Elobey as a *locus amoenus,* introducing for the first time the two women in his company at the beginning of his first volume of *África: Viajes y trabajos de la asociación euskara la exploradora*:

> Cuando cambió la faz de aquella casita de madera; cuando quedó habitable y hasta confortable; arreglado el jardín y repleta de víveres la despensa, quedé tranquilo respecto al porvenir de mis compañeras, que sonreían de gozo y de contento, encantadas de la nueva vida Robinsón que tendrían que hacer, y que para ellas estaba llena de atractivos. Verían salir el sol por el continente, y verían su puesta en el horizonte del mar; contemplarían, desde la hermosa galería de la casa, el cuadro encantador de la bahía de Corisco, surcada de piraguas y de aves marinas; cogerían preciosas flores de abundante aroma, sembradas por sus manos, en el jardín, formarían colecciones de preciosas mariposas africanas; pasearían, gozando de la fresca sombra de la selva; pescarían pececillos en las orillas del mar, y, servidas por criadas negras, a quienes enseñarían lo bueno de los conocimientos de la mujer europea, no podrían notar la falta de las comodidades de su patria, ni sentir los terribles efectos del hastío y del aburrimiento.

> (When the face of that little wooden house changed, when it became habitable and even comfortable, when the garden had been arranged and the pantry well stocked, I became more assured about the future of my companions, who would smile with joy and contentment, delighted with the new "Swiss Family Robinson" life that they would need to lead, full of attractions for them. They would see the sun rise on the continent, would see it on the horizon of the sea; they would contemplate, from the beautiful gallery of the house, the charming picture of the bay of Corisco, crisscrossed by canoes and sea birds; they would collect precious flowers with rich aromas, sown by their hands in the garden, they would form collections of precious African butterflies; they would go for walks, enjoying the cool shade of the jungle; they would catch little fish on the seashore, and— served by black maids to whom they would teach all the good things of European women's knowledge—they would not miss the comforts of their homeland or feel the terrible effects of weariness and boredom.) (24–25)

Miguel Gutiérrez Garitano, who conducted extensive research at the Iradier family's archives in Vitoria and published a biography of the explorer to coincide with the hundredth anniversary of his death in 2011, has pointed to the existence of an additional family written source—besides Iradier's writings—which serves as further testimony to the Urquiola sisters' scientific enterprise in meteorology, biology, and travel writing: an unpublished, five-page, diary by Manuel Iradier Urquiola, the couple's son. The diary reads:

> Han pasado de esto 50 años y aún resulta el caso incomprendido. Iradier, antes de que el feminismo se sospechase, ya hacía partícipe a la mujer de las más altas misiones. Isabel Urquiola, aquella primera viajera africana, se instaló en el islote de Elobey siendo la colaboradora del explorador que mejor podía encontrar. Con paciencia religiosa rejistra [sic] cada tres horas los aparatos del observatorio, renueva los secantes a las plantas, guarda el insecto, pone en limpio las notas de viaje, y con fe inmensa domina el dolor de ver partir a su esposo a lo desconocido muchas veces.
>
> (50 years have passed and the case is still misunderstood. Iradier, before feminism was even suspected, already involved women in the highest missions. Isabel Urquiola, that first European woman to have traveled in Africa, settled on the islet of Elobey, becoming the best collaborator the explorer could have found. With religious patience, the observatory devices are replenished every three hours, the plant blotters are renewed, the insect is put away, the travel notes are transcribed, and with immense faith, she overcomes the pain of seeing her husband depart into the unknown many times.) (Cited from DVD included with Gutiérrez Garitano's *Apuntes de la Guinea*)

As Gallego et al. have remarked:

> Sociohistorically, those of the sisters are the only [meteorological observations] made by women, and they were made in a far more hidden-away location and under more precarious circumstances than those made by the men in Santa Isabel, because this was a "civilized" city, as the capital was described by Iradier on arrival there after his stay at Elobey. (322)

Yet, throughout their lives, Manuela and Isabel Urquiola's accomplishments were silenced, reappropriated by others, in much the same fashion as was the case for other women who also traveled in the region during those decades, some of whom Isabel and Manuela may have encountered, and who actively participated in shaping early interactions with the peoples of the Muni Estuary. Among these women were Anna DeHeer (wife, and then widow, of Reverend Cornelius DeHeer) and Mary Louise Reutlinger (also wife, and later widow, of Reverend Solomon Reutlinger), who were part of the personnel of the Presbyterian Mission between approximately 1868 and 1908.[23] Reutlinger in particular was responsible for having taught literacy to children at the Presbyterian Mission School.

The husbands of some of these missionary women, meanwhile, made claims for their exclusive authorship of translations of the Gospel into Benga, and of other publications, including a Benga grammar.[24] Robert Hamill Nassau, a prolific writer during his more than forty-year appointment in Africa, authored *Crowned in Palm-Land: A Story of African Mission Life [being a Life of M. C. Nassau]*, a memoir—composed of diary entries and personal correspondence—that had in fact been written by his wife Mary Cloyd Latta Nassau. She died at the Benito Mission (today Bolondo, in coastal Río Muni) in 1870. Nassau's sister, Isabel Nassau, had also been one of the pioneering women to live in the Ogooué region, roughly the same territories that Mary Kingsley would visit a few years later, and not far from Elobey Chico, where Isabel and Manuela Urquiola had been stationed. According to Ndowé scholar Enénge A'Bodjedi:

> Las mujeres presbiterianas americanas se dedicaban primordialmente a la enseñanza de las chicas Benga y otras Ndowé en Maluku, la escuela presbiteriana para niñas Ndowé en el poblado de Evangesimba. The Maluku Presbyterian Girls' Boarding Mission School, estuvo en funcionamiento desde 1853 hasta 1868. Además de enseñar a las chicas Benga y otras Ndowé a leer y escribir, les enseñaban otras herramientas útiles según los cánones de las mujeres protestantes americanas: lavar y planchar la ropa, la costura, cómo cocinar comida occidental/americana. Los hombres presbiterianos americanos se dedicaban a la enseñanza de los varones Benga y otros Ndowé en los poblados de Manji llamados Evangesimba, Elongo y Ugobe. La única mujer presbiteriana americana que enseñaba a los hombres Ndowé era Miss Isabel Nassau (1829–1906) en Bolondo.

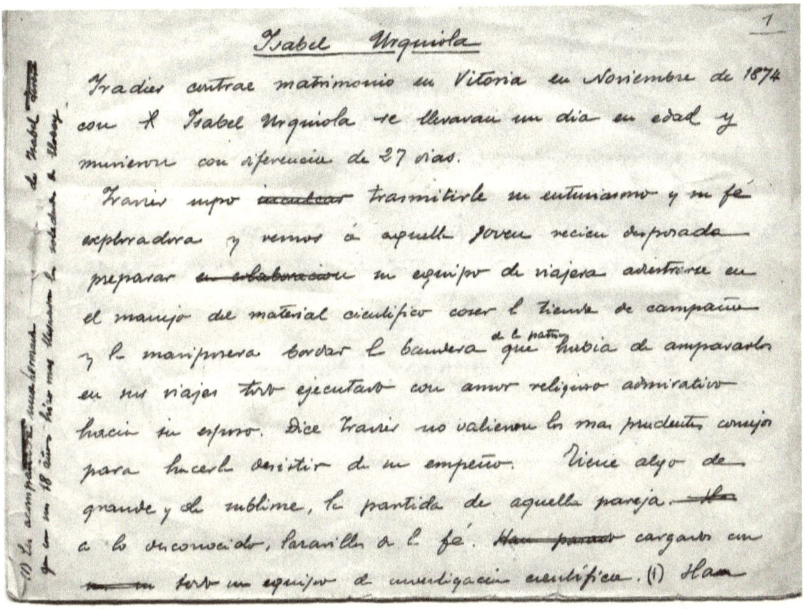
Isabel Urquiola

1

Iradier contrae matrimonio en Vitoria en Noviembre de 1874
con D. Isabel Urquiola se llevaban un dia en edad y
murieron con diferencia de 27 dias.
Iradier supo ~~inculcar~~ trasmitirle su entusiasmo y su fe
exploradora y vemos á aquella joven recien desposada
preparar ~~en colaboracion~~ su equipo de viajera adentrarse en
el manejo del material cientifico coser la tienda de campaña
y la mariposera bordar la bandera de la patria que habia de ampararlos
en sus viajes todo ejecutado con amor religioso admirativo
hacia su esposo. Dice Iradier no valieron los mas prudentes consejos
para hacerla desistir de su empeño. Tiene algo de
grande y de sublime, la partida de aquella pareja. ~~Ha~~
a lo desconocido, Lazarillo de la fé. ~~Han pasado~~ cargados con
~~......~~ todo un equipo de investigacion cientifica. (1) Han

(1) La ~~acompañante~~ ... una hermana de Isabel ... que con sus 18 años hizo mas llevadera la soledad de Elobey.

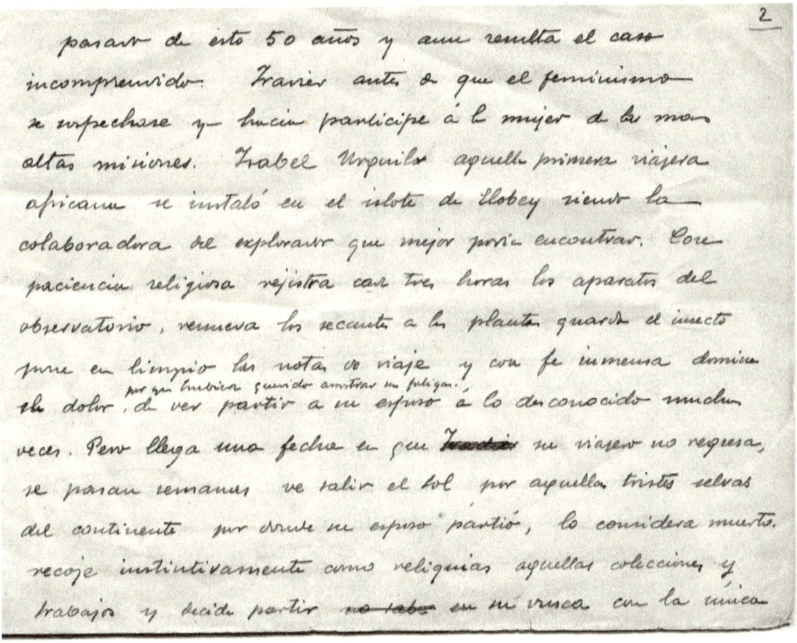
2

pasado de esto 50 años y aun resulta el caso
incomprendido. Iradier antes de que el feminismo
se sospechase ya hacia participe á la mujer de las mas
altas misiones. Isabel Urquiola aquella primera viajera
africana se instaló en el islote de Elobey siendo la
colaboradora del explorador que mejor podia encontrar. Con
paciencia religiosa registra cada tres horas los aparatos del
observatorio, renueva los recuentos a las plantas guarda el insecto
pone en limpio las notas de viaje y con fe inmensa domina
el dolor, por que hubiera querido arrostrar sus peligros. de ver partir a su esposo á lo desconocido muchas
veces. Pero llega una fecha en que ~~Iradier~~ su viajero no regresa,
se pasan semanas ve salir el sol por aquellas tristes selvas
del continente por donde su esposo partió, lo considera muerto.
recoje instintivamente como reliquias aquellas colecciones y
trabajos y decide partir ~~no sabe~~ en su busca con la única

Figures 1.7 and 1.8. Unpublished diary of Manuel Iradier Urquiola. This five-page-long diary has been reproduced in the DVD that accompanies Gutiérrez Garitano's *Apuntes de la Guinea.*

(American Presbyterian women were primarily engaged in the teaching of the Benga girls, and other Ndowé girls, in Maluku, the Presbyterian school for Ndowé girls in the village of Evangesimba. The Maluku Presbyterian Girls' Boarding Mission School was in operation from 1853 to 1868. In addition to teaching the Benga girls and other Ndowé to read and write, they taught them other useful tools according to the canons of American Protestant women: washing and ironing the clothes, sewing, how to cook western/American food. The American Presbyterian men dedicated themselves to the teaching of Benga boys and other Ndowé boys in the villages of Manji called Evangesimba, Elongo and Ugobe. The only American Presbyterian woman who taught the Ndowé men was Miss Isabel Nassau [1829–1906] in Bolondo.)[25]

Colonial and postcolonial histories are replete with examples of the topoi of education of Africans. Missionaries arrived to provide not only religious instruction, but also to run primary schools, clinics, and model farms, sometimes with surprising revelations vis-à-vis the limits and loci of their pedagogical transformations. Isabella Sweeney Mackey, who took charge of the Presbyterian Girls' School at Corisco in 1853, wrote to the New York Council that "una chica bènga de la escuela realizó la asombrosa hazaña académica de memorizar por entero los cuatro Evangelios" (a Bènga girl from the school achieved the amazing academic feat of memorizing the four Gospels in full) (A'Bodjedi 56).[26]

The story of the West African expedition of the Urquiola sisters to the Gulf of Guinea in 1874–77 squarely intersects in more than one direction with the history of imperialism and the Spanish expansion in Africa. As David Bunn puts it, "violence enters the fabric of daily life, including the order of representation" (75). Their case also serves to elucidate questions of colonial writing and authorship. According to Luis Fernández Cifuentes, Manuel Iradier, "a much more pathetic example of national deficiencies and confusions in the matter of scientific expeditions, would author two five-hundred-page volumes" (194). Yet, digging into the archives of the colonial administration grants us a more nuanced understanding of the white metropolitan male and female pantheons, including the agency exercised by women in colonial enterprises, gender dynamics, and writing and sciences in the nineteenth century.

The archives have many layers; engaging with oral history sources—through the memory of the elderly Benga and Combe inhabitants of the Muni Estuary—might further corroborate how the exploratory routes, treaties, diplomatic mediations, and cartographic delimitations attributed to Manuel Iradier y Bulfy are a mirage, disguising the real extent of collaboration, consent, and negotiation by others: the local guides, interpreters, porters, personal assistants, and communities that aided him, as well as the Urquiola sisters, during the expedition. Chief among these people was Elombuangani,[27] the local guide from the island of Corisco, a member of the Bodikito clan of the Benga, and the indisputable central historical figure of the expedition. Both at the phase of the exploration and annexation, colonial geographies and colonial economies have inescapably been dependent on local knowledge, labor, interrelations, and abilities. According to Benga oral sources, "Elombuangani y otros hombres Benga aprendieron a leer y escribir español con los misioneros católicos en Manji [Corisco] hacia 1864. Elombuangani y otros Benga hablaban español desde los tiempos del negrero Pedro Blanco y Miguel Pons, hacia 1820–1840" (Elombuangani and other Benga men learned how to read and write in Spanish with the Catholic missionaries in Mandji (Corisco) circa 1864. Elombuangani and other Benga spoke Spanish since the times of the slave-traders Pedro Blanco and Miguel Pons, around 1820–1840).[28]

Colonial travel accounts are always signifiers of past violence; nonetheless, rather than focusing on the impossible task of removing oneself from this memory of violence, I chose to recreate the traditional narrative within a contemporary reading. By virtue of this, I consider the story of the Iradier/Urquiola expedition as a corrective to conventional historical and national renditions. This revisionist exercise—reliant on the material and epistemological possibilities of the archive—is loaded with gendered, rhetorical, and social implications. While the archival and oral sources allow us a fuller narrative line, they do not automatically preclude us from a deliberate, political refusal to participate in the discourse of the exceptional individual. Set against the masculine storyline of the colonial explorer, and the spatially reduced and ideologically secured foundational articulation of Africa in nineteenth-century Europe, we cannot easily escape the expansion of the white settler narrative through gender inclusion alone. Thus, this is not simply an appeal for the individual female subject expeditionary, but a question of attribution, representation, and inclusiveness. It is also, and perhaps primarily, about the way in which colonial historical subjectivity is embedded in the whirlwind of time and narrative, as it simultaneously evokes the emerging, collective subject of colonization and settlement.

Notes

I thank Lisa Surwillo, who invited me to a panel at the Berkshire Conference of Women Historians, for which this project was originally conceived. A revised version was later shared at a seminar organized by Mayka de Castro and Rosa María Medina Doménech, at the Universidad de Granada (Spain), entitled "Márgenes académicos: poética, literatura y escritura de la historia," and I also thank them for the debates it helped foster. Another version of the project was subsequently shared at a conference organized by María Hernández-Ojeda at Hunter College, entitled "Los límites del Atlántico: tránsitos y migraciones," where I benefited from the panel response by Aurélie Vialette and others. I thank my colleagues at the Centro de Estudios Afro-Hispánicos of the UNED in Madrid, and the multiyear research grant from the Spanish government we enjoy for the project entitled "Towards a comparative study of Spanish colonialism in Africa and its effects on the colonized peoples of Equatorial Guinea and the Rif" [Code #HAR2016-79164-P]. Special acknowledgment is due to Enénge A'Bodjedi, for his insights and contributions to this research on Benga oral history and ethnography, and to Miguel Gutiérrez Garitano and the Asociación Africanista Manuel Iradier, for granting me permission to reproduce some of the images in this essay, gratitude extended as well to the Archivo General de la Administración in Alcalá de Henares. Last but not least, I am deeply grateful to Akiko Tsuchiya and Michelle Murray for their invitation to put this project into dialogue with other research on the intersection of gender and colonization in the nineteenth-century Hispanic world.

1. Born in Vitoria on July 5, 1854, she died in Madrid the same year as her husband, on September 16, 1911, according to the biographical notes of their son Manuel Iradier Urquiola (Garitano, *Apuntes de la Guinea* 206).

2. Several of the bibliographical sources refer to Iradier's sister-in-law as Juliana. Yet the sister that accompanied Isabel on the West African expedition of 1874–77 seems to have been—according to Gutiérrez Garitano—not Juliana, but Manuela. The error might have emanated from a family photograph of the mother with her four children in Vitoria, of which only a fragment—displaying Isabel and her younger sister Juliana standing next to her—circulated widely.

3. "El 16 de Diciembre de 1874 salgo de Vitoria con objeto de ver si la costa occidental de África, frente á nuestras posesiones del golfo de Guinea, presenta un punto accesible para el interior. . . . El 13 de Enero llego a la isla de Gran Canaria donde permanezco tres meses esperando la buena estación del Ecuador, y dando tiempo para no sufrir un rápido cambio de temperatura. . . . El 25 de Abril de 1875 parto hácia las costas de África, y en Mayo llego al islote Elobey, centro de

mis exploraciones" (On December 16, 1874, I leave Vitoria in order to see if the western coast of Africa, facing our possessions of the Gulf of Guinea, presents an accessible point for the interior. . . . On January 13 I arrive at the island of Gran Canaria where I remain three months waiting for better weather in the Equatorial zone, and allowing time to avoid suffering a rapid change of temperature. . . . On April 25, 1875, I depart towards the coasts of Africa, and in May I arrive at the islet of Elobey, center of my explorations) (Iradier y Bulfy, *Fragmentos de un diario* 3–4).

4. Diego Santiesteban Chamorro was appointed General Governor to Fernando Poo on October 1, 1874, arriving at Santa Isabel on January 23, 1875; he remained in the position until February 13, 1877 (Álvarez Chillida 159).

5. A collectively authored article by M. Cruz Gallego, Domínguez-Castro, Vaquero, and García-Herrera, published in 2011 by the American Meteorological Society, and entitled "The Hidden Role of Women in Monitoring Nineteenth-Century African Weather. Instrumental Observations in Equatorial Guinea," was the first piece of scholarship in the sciences to acknowledge the role of the Urquiola sisters during their 1874–77 expedition to the Gulf of Guinea.

6. In addition to *Travels in West Africa* (1897), Mary Kingsley also published, upon her return to London, *West African Studies* (1899) and *The Story of West Africa* (1900).

7. The late nineteenth century witnessed the rapid expansion of a new, primarily urban, literate class, which became the principal channel through which imperial expansion in Africa most effectively reached the European households. Mary Kingsley's writings undoubtedly benefited from this factor. For a nuanced analysis of the construction of the British colonial traveler as a social hero, from the period between the 1870s and World War II, see Sèbe.

8. For a critical assessment of Mary Kingsley's writings on Africa, and the intersection of travel narratives and colonialism, see the work of Alison Blunt and Karen Bennett.

9. "Informe del Gobernador de Fernando Poo, D. Ignacio García Tudela, demostrando y enardeciendo la necesidad y la conveniencia de abandonar dicha colonia y sus dependencias. Santa Isabel, 14 de diciembre de1873" (Report from the Governor of Fernando Poo, Mr. Ignacio García Tudela, demonstrating and ardently recommending the need and convenience of abandoning the said colony and its dependencies). (Archivo General de la Administración, Alcalá de Henares. Fondo África, Sección 15 (4). Caja 81/06939). Ignacio García Tudela was appointed as governor of Fernando Poo on August 9, 1872, arriving at Santa Isabel on December 5, 1872; he stayed in the position until November 22, 1874 (Álvarez Chillida 159).

10. For a detailed historical analysis of the report, and the political climate in which it was generated, see García Cantús.

11. "Oficio del Gobernador Diego Santiesteban al Ministro de Marina. Fernando Poo, 1 de julio de 1875." Archivo General de la Marina 'Álvaro de Bazán,' Ciudad Real (Spain), Sección Expediciones, Legajo número 356. For an innovative

analysis of the photographs, and the role of photography within the wider framework of European colonial expansion in West and Central Africa between 1840 and 1890, see Schneider and Vilaró i Güell.

12. The Iradier/Urquiola expedition of 1874–77 was modestly financed by the Asociación Euskara para la exploración y civilización del África Central La Exploradora, established in Vitoria (Spain) shortly before their departure. The Sociedad Geográfica in Madrid would not start business until 1876. Álvaro Llosa Sanz correctly points out that the Geographical Societies were "entidades privadas cercanas al poder y conformadas por variados profesionales . . . que a partir de 1870, momento de su multiplicación en todo el orbe, colaborarán con los intereses de los estados y sus fines militares-colonialistas. . . . En España . . . sólo en 1876 queda instituida la Sociedad Geográfica de Madrid liderada por Francisco Coello, que se unirá a la que fue definitiva institucionalización del africanismo español: la Sociedad Española de Africanistas y Colonialistas (1884)" (private entities close to political power and formed by a wide range of professionals . . . which from 1870, the moment of their multiplication across the globe, would collaborate with the interests of the states and their military-colonialist ends. . . . In Spain . . . only in 1876 is the Geographical Society of Madrid founded, led by Francisco Coello, which would join the definitive institutional organization of Spanish Africanism: the Sociedad Española de Africanistas y Colonialistas [1884]) (558–59).

13. As José Ricart Giralt, director of the *Revista Marítima,* pointed out in correspondence to Iradier, his journal coincides with the premises of the Exploradora: "sostiene la doctrina de que el porvenir de España está en África, dejándonos ya de la América, tan funesta para nosotros" (it maintains the doctrine that the future of Spain is in Africa, leaving behind the Americas, so fatal for us) (Iradier, *África: Viajes y trabajos* 67).

14. For an assessment of the extent to which the Franco regime made propagandistic use of philately, see Victoriano Darias:

> La monotonía, el despiste y el desprestigio filatélico de la zona colonial van a terminarse desde 1949 con una muy acertada política de emisiones impulsada por el general José Díaz de Villegas, activo africanista . . . desde su llegada a la Dirección General de Marruecos y Colonias posteriormente denominada de Plazas y Provincias africanas, quien consigue dar un giro de seriedad y belleza a los sellos coloniales mediante nuevos diseños realizados por artistas especializados que son convocados a participar en los oportunos concursos. El 24 de febrero de ese año se instituyó el "Día anual del sello colonial". . . . Consecuencia de este esfuerzo estético algunos de los sellos españoles de Guinea van a lograr galardones internacionales.

> (The philatelic monotony, loss of direction, and discredit of the colonial zone come to an end from 1949, with a very successful emission

policy promoted by General José Díaz de Villegas, an active Africanist. . . . After his arrival at the General Directorate of Morocco and Colonies, subsequently renamed African "Plazas y Provincias," who managed to give a new seriousness and beauty to the colonial stamps through new designs made by specialized artists who were invited to participate in the appropriate contests. On February 24 that year, the "annual colonial stamp day" was instituted. . . . As a consequence of this aesthetic effort, some of the Spanish stamps from Guinea would win international awards). (unpaginated)

It is within this new turn in the political use of philately for colonial propagandistic purposes that the one hundredth anniversary of Iradier's birth was marked with a series of commemorative stamps and postcards.

15. Manuel Iradier would return to the Gulf of Guinea for a second expedition in 1884, this time in the company of Spanish doctor Amado Osorio, and with the financial support of the Sociedad de Africanistas and the Sociedad Geográfica Española.

16. On the first expedition, they arrived at the island of Fernando Poo on May 16, 1875, and settled on the island of Elobey Chico on May 18, 1875, where they were stationed until their return to Fernando Poo on January 24, 1876. Manuela and Isabel resided in Fernando Poo until March 1877, and Manuel Iradier prolonged his stay until December 1877. By the time of his second expedition to Africa, in 1884, his sister-in-law Manuela had passed away: "Manolita Urquiola, que está enterrada en el cementerio de Santa Isabel de Vitoria, falleció a su vez—en 1880—a los 24 años debido a las fiebres contraídas en África" (Manolita Urquiola, who is buried in the cemetery of Santa Isabel, in Vitoria, passed away in turn—in 1880—aged 24 due to fevers contracted in Africa) (Gutiérrez Garitano, *Apuntes de la Guinea* 213).

17. Cristina Morató, in *Las reinas de África: viajeras y exploradoras por el continente negro* (aimed at a general audience), includes a chapter on "Isabel de Urquiola, a la sombra de Iradier" (Isabel Urquiola, in the Shadow of Iradier) and another one on "Mary Kingsley, la indómita Victoriana" (Mary Kingsley, the Indomitable Victorian).

18. See Gallego et al.

19. In November 1969, the director of Madrid's astronomical observatory presented a formal proposal to the Spanish administration for the establishment of a meteorological station in the island of Fernando Poo; it contained a description and type of technological instruments it should carry, the estimated cost, and its multiple benefits: "reportaría ventajas no solo a la ciencia en general sino al adelantamiento de su colonización en cuanto se refiere a su higiene, agricultura y comercio" (it would bring advantages not only to science in general but to the advancement of its colonization in terms of its hygiene, agriculture and commerce). The project did not prosper. Archivo General de la Administración, Alcalá de Henares. Fondo África, Sección 15 (4). Caja 81/06944.

20. Iradier, in his book *África: Viajes y trabajos de la Asociación Euskara la Exploradora,* volume II, includes a long chapter on meteorology, in which he describes the position of the observatory, a full list of its equipment, and its function (181-ss).

21. In a document issued on January 2, 1876, the governor of Fernando Poo informs the Ministerio de Ultramar in Madrid: "Participa haber nombrado Segundo Maestro interino de la Escuela pública a D. Manuel Iradier Bulfy Martínez . . . para que la escuela reciba todo el impulso que es de desear especialmente para la propagación de nuestro idioma en estas posesiones en donde apenas se habla otro que el inglés" (Communicates having appointed Mr. Manuel Iradier Bulfy Martínez as Second interim Teacher of the Public school . . . so that the school receives all the impulse that is to be desired, especially for the propagation of our language in these possessions where hardly any language but English is spoken) (Archivo General de la Administración, Alcalá de Henares. Fondo África 15 (4). Caja 81/06956).

22. "Acompañando Instancia de Doña Isabel Urquiola de Iradier, maestra interina de instrucción primaria, en solicitud del sobresueldo de la propietaria. Fernando Poo, 23 de octubre de 1876. Diego Santiesteban." Archivo General de la Administración, Alcalá de Henares. Fondo África, Sección 15 (4). Caja 81/06956.

23. For further details on the Presbyterian Missions at Corisco and on the coastal region of Río Muni during this period, see A'Bodjedi.

24. See Mackey and Nassau, among other examples.

25. Personal email communication with Enénge A'Bodjedi.

26. For studies on the experience of colonial mission schooling for girls, and the complex ideologies related to the teaching of domesticity in other former colonial contexts in Africa, see, for instance, Sheldon and Strickrodt.

27. According to Enénge A'Bodjedi, Elombuangani's full name was Elombuangani ya Didango (circa 1850-circa 1908) from the clan Bodikito of the Benga ethnic group.

28. As reported from oral sources collected by Enénge A'Bodjedi. Personal email communication. For the history of slavery in the island of Corisco, see Nerín.

Works Cited

A'Bodjedi, Enénge. "Las Iglesias Presbiterianas Ndowé." *Revista Oráfica* vol. 2, 2006, pp. 48–72.

Álvarez Chillida, Gonzalo. "Los Gobernadores de Fernando Poo (1858–1930)." *L'État dans ses colonies. Les administrateurs de l'Empire espagnol au xix siècle,* edited by Jean-Philippe Luis, Madrid, Colección de la Casa de Velázquez, 2015, pp. 157–66.

Bennett, Karen. "Speaking in Tongues: A Study of Mary Kingsley's Discourse in *Travels in West Africa*." *Máthesis*, vol. 10, 2001, pp. 103–26.

Blunt, Alison. *Travel, Gender, and Imperialism. Mary Kingsley and West Africa*. Guilford, 1994.

Bunn, David. "The Sleep of the Brave: Graves as Sites and Signs in the Colonial Eastern Cape." *Images and Empires. Visuality in Colonial and Postcolonial Africa*, edited by Paul S. Landau and Deborah D. Kaspin, U of California P, 2002, pp. 56–89.

Cordero Torres, José María. *Iradier*. Instituto de Estudios Políticos, 1944.

Darias, Victoriano. "El sello de correos como medio informativo. La Antigua Guinea Española en su filatelia." *Revista Latina de Comunicación Social*, vol. 4, no. 42, June 2001; http://www.revistalatinacs.org/2001/latina42jun/40darias.htm.

Fernández Cifuentes, Luis. "Travel Writing." *A Comparative History of Literature in the Iberian Peninsula*, edied by Fernando Cabo Aseguinolaza, Anxo Abuín González, and César Dominguez, John Benjamins, 2010, pp. 183–210.

Gallego, M. Cruz, Fernando Dominguez-Castro, José M. Vaquero, and Ricardo García-Herrera. "The Hidden Role of Women in Monitoring Nineteenth-Century African Weather: Instrumental Observations in Equatorial Guinea." *American Meteorological Society*, March 2011, pp. 315–24.

García Cantús, Dolores. *Abandonar Guinea: Informe de García Tudela al Gobierno de la República, 1873*. Ceiba Ediciones/Serie Documentos de la colonización, 2004.

García Tudela, Ignacio. "Informe del Gobernador de Fernando Poo, D. Ignacio García Tudela, demostrando y enardeciendo la necesidad y la conveniencia de abandonar dicha colonia y sus dependencias. Santa Isabel, 14 de diciembre de1873." Archivo General de la Administración, Alcalá de Henares. Fondo África, Sección 15 (4). Caja 81/6939.

Gutiérrez Garitano, Miguel. *Apuntes de la Guinea. Vida, obra y memoria de Manuel Iradier y Bulfy*. Ikusager Ediciones, 2011.

———. *La aventura del Muni*. Ikusager Ediciones, 2010.

Iradier y Bulfy, Manuel. *África: Fragmentos de un diario de viajes de exploración en la zona de Corisco*. Boletín de la Real Sociedad Geográfica de Madrid. Madrid: Imprenta de Fortanet, 1878.

———. *África: Viajes y trabajos de la Asociación Euskara la Exploradora. Reconocimiento de la Zona Ecuatorial de África en las Costas de Occidente: sus montañas, sus ríos; sus habitantes; clima, producciones y porvenir de estos países tropicales. Posesiones Españolas en el Golfo de Guinea. Adquisición para España de la nueva provincia del Muni*. vol. 1 [1887]. Imp y Enc de Andrés P. Cardenal y Banco España, 1901.

———. *África: Viajes y trabajos de la Asociación Euskara la Exploradora: Reconocimiento de la zona ecuatorial de África en las Costas de Occidente: sus montañas, sus ríos; sus habitantes; clima, producciones y porvenir de estos países tropicales. Posesiones Españolas en el Golfo de Guinea. Adquisición para España de la Nueva Provincia del Muni*, vol. 2 [1887]. Imp y Enc de Andrés P. Cardenal y Banco España, 1901.

———. "Exploración en territorios del golfo de Guinea: Discurso pronunciado por Don Manuel Iradier en la sesión de 25 de Mayo de 1886." *Boletín de la Real Sociedad Geográfica de Madrid*, vol. 9, 1886, pp. 25–36.

———. "Instancia de Manuel Iradier y Bulfy. Fernando Poo, 1 de enero, 1877." Archivo General de la Administración, Alcalá de Henares. Fondo África, Sección 15 (4). Caja 81/06956.

Kingsley, Mary H. *The Story of West Africa*. Horace Marshall, 1900.

———. *Travels in West Africa. Congo Français, Corisco and Cameroons*. MacMillan, 1897.

———. *West African Studies*. MacMillan, 1899.

Koczanowicz, Leszec. "Politicizing Weather: Two Polish Cases of the Intersection between Politics and Weather." *South Atlantic Quarterly*, vol. 106, no. 4, Fall 2017, pp. 753–67.

Llosa Sanz, Álvaro. "Los viajes y trabajos de Manuel Iradier en África: género e hibridismo textual en el relato de viajes en el siglo XIX." *Revista de* Literatura, vol. 67, no. 34, 2005, pp. 557–84.

Mackey, James L. *A Grammar of the Benga Language*. Mission House, 1855.

———. *Mackey's Grammar of the Benga-Bantu Language*, revised by Rev. R. H. Nassau. American Tract Society, 1892.

Majó Framis, Ricardo. *Las generosas y primitivas empresas de Manuel Iradier Bulfy en la Guinea Española, el hombre y sus hechos*. Consejo Superior de Investigaciones Científicas/IDEA, 1954.

Martin-Márquez, Susan. *Disorientations. Spanish Colonialism in Africa and the Performance of Identity*. Yale UP, 2008.

Morató, Cristina. *Las reinas de África. Viajeras y exploradoras por el continente negro*. Plaza y Janés, 2003.

Mukhopadhyay, Priyasha. Review of *Heroic Imperialists in Africa: The Promotion of British and French Colonial Heroes, 1870–1939*, by Sèbe, Berny. *Interventions: International Journal of Postcolonial Studies*, vol. 17, no. 5, 2015, pp. 771–73.

Nassau, Robert Hamill. *Crowned in Palm-Land. A Story of African Mission Life [being a Life of M. C. Nassau] with illustrations* (A Memoir of Mary Cloyd Latta Nassau). J. B. Lippincott, 1874.

Nerín, Gustau. *Corisco y el estuario del Muni (1470–1931). Del aislamiento a la globalización y de la globalización a la marginación*. L'Harmattan, 2015.

"Proposición al Ministerio de Ultramar de una estación meteorológica en la isla de Fernando Poo por el director del Observatorio de Madrid, 1869–1870."

Archivo General de la Administración, Alcalá de Henares. Fondo África, Sección 15 (4). Caja 81/06944.

Santiesteban, Diego. "Acompañando Instancia de Doña Isabel Urquiola de Iradier, maestra interina de instrucción primaria, en solicitud del sobresueldo de la propietaria. Fernando Poo, 23 de octubre de 1876." Archivo General de la Administración, Alcalá de Henares. Fondo África, Sección 15 (4). Caja 81/06956.

———. "Oficio del Gobernador Diego Santiesteban al Ministro de Marina. Fernando Poo, 1 de julio de 1875." Archivo General de la Marina "Álvaro de Bazán," Ciudad Real, Sección Expediciones, Legajo número 356.

Sheldon, Kathleen. "I Studied with the Nuns, Learning to Make Blouses." *The International Journal of African Historical Studies*, vol. 31, no. 3, 1998, pp. 595–625.

Schneider, Jürg, and Miquel Vilaró i Güell. "Fourteen Views of Fernando Poo to Save the Colony." *European Society for the History of Photography*, June 2014, pp. 1–30.

Sèbe, Berny. *Heroic Imperialists in Africa: The Promotion of British and French Colonial Heroes, 1870–1939*. Manchester UP, 2013.

Strickrodt, Silke. "African Girls' Samplers from Mission Schools in Sierra Leone (1820s to 1840s)." *History in Africa*, vol. 37, 2010, pp. 189–245.

Urquiola de Iradier, Isabel. "Instancia elevada al Rey por Isabel Urquiola de Iradier solicitando sobresueldo. Fernando Poo, 8 de septiembre, 1876." Archivo General de la Administración, Alcalá de Henares. Fondo África, Sección 15 (4). Caja 81/06956.

———. "Instancia de Isabel Urquiola de Iradier. Fernando Poo, 16 de octubre, 1876. Archivo General de la Administración, Alcalá de Henares. Fondo África, Sección 15 (4). Caja 81/06956.

Various authors. *Iradier. Conmemoración de su primer centenario*. Consejo Superior de Investigaciones Científicas/IDEA, 1956.

2

Eva Canel and the Gender of Hispanism

LISA SURWILLO

With the Treaty of Paris (December 10, 1898), Spain relinquished control over its most valuable colony to the United States. Cuba was not a party to the negotiations that ended the inter-imperial war that had begun, however, as a Cuban struggle for independence from Spain. When Cuban insurgency continued after the U.S.-Spanish peace, Washington opted for direct occupation of the island in an attempt to head off a full revolution and the eventuality of a racially diverse governance. Any pretense of Cuban independence post-1898 disappeared with the Platt Amendment in 1901 as the United States was confirmed as the island's new colonizing metropolis with the power to intervene unilaterally in Cuban affairs and, with repercussions today, to lease land for its naval bases. U.S. control of Cuba was reinforced during the Second Occupation of Cuba in 1906–09, when the secretary of war, William Taft, declared himself the provisional governor of Cuba.[1] Just five years later, the Spanish-born writer Eva Canel (1857–1932) traveled to Cuba and penned a travelogue that addressed the imperiled Spanish identity of the island. Through this endeavor, she joined a larger transatlantic conversation regarding Spanish regenerationism, Hispanism, panamericanism, and American economic and political imperialism in Spain's former colonies.

In her travel narrative, *Lo que vi en Cuba, a través de la isla* (1916), Canel addressed the personal side of Hispanism as she encountered it in Cuba. Hispanism has generally referred to the twentieth-century position held by Spanish politicians and intellectuals to maintain a claim of cultural and linguistic authority over Spain's former colonies. Often cast in terms of origins and civilization, Hispanism justified neoimperial economic and political schemes. Common people, rather than institutions, are the protagonists of her story. Laura Muñoz observes that "pareciera que lo que le interesa más es hablar de la gente común, es como si tratara de hacer un inventario de aquellas personas que de otra manera no serían conocidas" (312). Canel examined her inventory of commoners to analyze how they understood their relationship to Spain and the Spanish empire after Cuban independence and in the face of U.S. imperialism. In exploring, in print, Hispanism as manifested in the quotidian, Eva Canel engaged in the discursive battle over the historiography of Cuba post-1898, and as explained below, attempted to remake Spanish imperial identity by addressing the worst crimes of race-based slavery. That is, she conceptualized of a Hispanic identity that transcended the end of empire, but one that managed to shed the racialization brought about by the Spanish empire and its slavocracy in Cuba. The Treaty of Paris did not mark a cultural, linguistic, and economic break with Spain's neoimperial legacy in the Americas but rather one of many realignments in a much longer trajectory.[2] Her curious work invites us to reconsider the gender of the twentieth-century theorists of Hispanism.

Previous scholars have addressed the more complex aspects of the author's biography; what follows here is only a brief sketch of her life.[3] Born in a small village, Canel moved to Madrid with her mother while still young. At age fourteen the future writer married the dramatist Pedro Perillán Buxó, a now-forgotten figure who nonetheless had a long list of plays and journalistic works to his name.[4] Ideologically, Perillán Buxó leaned sharply to the left and, for political reasons, went into exile shortly after their marriage. Canel was eighteen when she followed him to the Americas, where they lived in various cities including Montevideo, Buenos Aires, and Santiago de Chile. After returning to Spain for a few short years in the early 1880s, Perillán Buxó again departed for the Americas—this time Cuba—and died there. Widowed at a young age, Canel never remarried but did return across the ocean for most of the remainder of her life. It was precisely upon becoming a widow and during her second stay in America that she began to present herself as a defender of empire. In her own words, had her husband not died, "yo habría venido a Cuba a ser lo que había sido antes; una esposa sumisa que escribía de vez en cuando sin consultarle nada y por lo cual algunas veces le ocasionaba disgustillos sin mayor importancia que le hacían mucha gracia y no los eludía" (I would have come to Cuba to be what I had been before, a submissive wife who wrote from time to time without consulting him on anything and which sometimes caused him to become mildly upset, which was inconsequential, and which he found funny and did not avoid) (10).⁵ María del Carmen Barcia Zequeira conjectures that while her political inclinations were entirely divergent from his, Canel took her husband's writerly and adventurous life as a model for her own (235). Indeed, whereas her husband had been a vocal critic of conservatism in Spain, Eva Canel became an ideologue of neoimperial Hispanism that considered Spain the rightful leader of all things cultural and economic across the Spanish-speaking world. Nevertheless, Simón Palmer judges Canel to be a prime example of a rebellious woman of the nineteenth century, not in spite of her conservative ideology, but precisely because of it: "Eva Canel se encontró defendiendo los valores que le habían inculcado desde su infancia en un lugar y en un tiempo que no correspondían, de ahí que a pesar de su ortodoxia, y precisamente por ella, fuera una rebelde" (Eva Canel found herself defending the values that had been instilled in her since her childhood in a place and in a time that did not were not the same, hence in spite of her orthodoxy, and precisely because of it, she was a rebel) ("Mujeres" 632).

Canel's life story does not follow the preferred narrative of a secretly liberal woman silenced by her husband and until recently (perhaps as a result of her conservatism) she did not enjoy the same critical interest as other women authors and travelers of her generation (see Leona Martin). In 1992, Simón Palmer deemed her to have been "olvidada" (294) while underscoring Canel's importance, evidenced by the fact that she published and lectured widely, engaging in polemical debates with a variety of Spaniards. Groundbreaking work by scholars such as María del Carmen Simón Palmer, Jean Kenmonge, and María del Carmen Barcia Zequeira, as well as studies of Hispanic women travelers, including those by Mary Louise Pratt and Adriana Méndez Rodenas, have sparked renewed attention to this unique figure, including a particularly provocative study of literary form by Beatriz Ferrús Antón.

Canel undertook her travel to Cuba in 1914, a year identified by Antonio Santamaría García and Consuelo Naranjo Orovio as pivotal to Cuban history: U.S. financial interests overtook Hispano-Cuban capitalists' investments, while the mercantile bourgeoisie, the urban middle class, and the island's workers' movement each consolidated, leading to considerable changes to society (134). In addition, Spaniards continued to emigrate at a considerable rate, and Canel saw the new residents as key to a cultural colonization of the, now, U.S. island. Moreover, Canel's defense of Spain took place as Cuba reassessed its place in the Atlantic power struggle. Canel was not alone in tackling these questions in her political writing, but she was at odds with some Spanish apologists for empire as well as the prevailing Cuban nationalist objectives. The first two decades of the twentieth century in Cuba, until about "1924 (when Gerardo Machado came to power) was [a time] of nation-building and modernization in which women actively participated" (Davies 13). Indeed, their participation was both source and evidence of modernization, "moving Cuba away from Spain and the Catholic Church towards US or French models of social development and political organization" (Davies 13). While writers and politicians across Latin America considered the growing hemispheric presence of the United States, their Spanish counterparts, too, developed an ideological response to their nation's diminished geopolitical heft. The fight for hegemony left the battlefield but remained active in the world of letters. In *The Conquest of History*, Christopher Schmidt Nowara emphasized that the idea of "Hispanism" born in the late nineteenth century was an effort by "the [Spanish] state and intellectuals to craft institutions and forms of knowledge that legitimized the continuation of Spanish rule, not least of which was the incorporation of the colonies into the archives, monuments, and narratives of Spanish history" (192). In the early twentieth century, in other words, Hispanism considered the history of the Atlantic and the former overseas colonies to be a story that Spain had the right to tell. This belief was manifest in "a politics of knowledge, largely . . . intended to reassert some sort of Spanish authority over the former colonies" (Schmidt Nowara 192). In other words, the role of the historian countered the Monroe Doctrine in a discursive sense, continuing the project of colonization by creating new epistemologies that justify Spain's control and exploitation of the Americas. The United States had a powerful role in shaping the narrative of what both the United States and Cuba were after the Spanish American war. Canel's challenge to the legitimacy of their storytelling is a unifying thread in *Lo que vi*.

Scholars of Hispanism often turn to the works of politicians such as Retana, Castelar, or Cánovas de Castillo who promoted a Hispanism of the public realm and agreed, by and large, what constituted knowledge to be wielded. Although she certainly published and ran journals that circulated in the wider public sphere, in *Lo que vi*, Eva Canel dedicated special attention to the role of private customs and friendships in maintaining Spanish cultural authority in Cuba that fell outside of institutional power, especially over emigrants from Spain. The element linking gender, private life, and the lived practices of Hispanism is friendship, and it structures Canel's *Lo que vi*. Ferrús Antón has aptly described the travelogue as "una cartografía de relaciones personales, en un mapa de contactos y afectos" (a cartography of personal relationships, in a map of contacts and affections) (226). Canel's statements on friendship appear throughout the book, anchoring her voyages and justifying her itinerary (130–31 and passim). But more than a narrative tool, the articulation of these personal ties is a textual confirmation of the bonds of Hispanism linking Spain and Cuba. Canel structured the travelogue around friendship and described her friends' gifts of lodging and the opportunity to find herself at home, literally and figuratively, in their domestic lives. In contrast, Americans from the United States are not named. Anonymous U.S. citizens appear as soldiers, tools of finance, or the instruments of politics, but they are a menace at the margins—unindividuated and unknowable. If the traditional objective of travel literature is precisely to discover the other, Canel rejects the exotic in her travel through an island that she insists is not the least bit foreign, but rather a place to recover the past and encounter a shared sense of *Hispanidad* not imposed from above but continually constituted through lived experience. The counterpoint to her emphasis on the "patria común" (common homeland) is what Laura Muñoz has identified as the "eje articulador de su discurso" (the backbone of her discourse), namely, "la censura de las costumbres y las prácticas norteamericanas en la isla" (the censorship of North American customs and practices on the island) (311). In terms of chronology, Canel charts a circuitous temporal path: regular flashbacks to colonial days allow her to assert that in spite of the U.S. occupation, Spanish residents in Cuba remain unchanged in their sentiment and habits.

Consistent with her oeuvre of travel writing—characterized, according to Caballer, by its "perspectiva femenina," *Lo que vi* explores traditions that constitute the culture Canel is examining (58). Canel emphasizes that she relates the world that she sees with a feminine eye, as opposed to what men in her place would observe (Caballer 66). This refers to the private, domestic space of households, but also to her viewpoint: unencumbered by institutional or political allegiances, she can speak freely. The curious title of this book, *Lo que vi en Cuba (a través de la isla)*, makes clear that its subject is her personal perspective of the island. The first phrase posits the existence of an objective entity to be seen in Cuba (the referent of her object *lo*), but the adverb *a través* in the second phrase situates the signified as not only visible *throughout* but also *through* the island-as-lens. Her intended readership, according to statements within the text, included both Cuban and peninsular Spaniards who needed her in order to see the truth about Cuba post-1898. Canel writes about U.S.-held Cuba in order to understand not only Spain's place in the Americas but Spain itself. The authorial power of her gaze as a writer who identified as both American and Spanish renders visible not only the ties between Spain and Cuba but also the transatlantic aspects of the modern Spanish nation that remained opaque in the peninsula. Jennifer Jenkins Wood notes that, like other good travel writers, Canel succeeds in capturing the "peculiar . . . typical, picturesque" of the lands she visited in the Americas (209). In the case of her travels in Cuba between 1914 and 1916, what Canel saw was an imperial Spain that had ceased to exist in Iberia. To a degree, Canel is a nineteenth-century imperial Spain looking to find itself.

Douglas Iverson reminds us that the reading and writing of travel narratives has been integral to the maintenance of European imperialism long after its political demise. Building upon the scholarship of academics as varied as Sara Mills, Edward Said, Mary Louise Pratt, and David Spurr, Iverson identifies the genre of travel writing after the formal conclusion of an empire—and once "the ideology of imperialism is brought into disrepute"—to be the means of reconstituting empire and its identities (202, 201). In this line, Canel writes especially for Spanish Cubans (including those Cubans who hadn't yet realized that they actually are Spanish) and reasserts, with her very presence—and their friendship with her—the legitimacy of Spanish cultural identity in Cuba.

Neither the strategic deployment of friendship among hemispheric American writers nor the political deployment of prose was new. Ronald Briggs (2) and Leona Martin (440) have analyzed the creation of informal literary societies that women formed in the late 1800s to support each others' work, networking outside of the prevailing nationalistic male literary space. Moreover, in nineteenth-century Latin America, a range of women used the novel to expound their views on the fundamental role of public morality in the political development of the new liberal republics (Briggs 2). Like other writers, such as her friend Emilia Serrano de Wilson, Canel traveled the Americas from North to South, from the United States to Chile, and developed a vast personal network along the way, but she positioned herself squarely in a transnational Hispanism that stood apart from American republican nationalisms, unlike the authors Briggs and Martin consider. Canel's person-to-person network with men and women was solidified by their shared affective ties to Spain, rather than a hemispheric intellectual project. As regards her mobility on an east/west axis, Beatriz Ferrús Antón situates Canel within a larger phenomenon in these same years of Latin American writers who traveled to Spain in search of cultural origins, while Spaniards traveled in the opposite direction in search of an identity common to metropolis and (former) colonies (222).

Canel's strategic deployment of friendship functions somewhat differently. The author presents herself as the embodiment of transatlanticism, of Spain in Cuba: her acceptance is metonymically an acceptance of Spain itself. Thus, what she sees in Cuba is only available to her. As a woman, she has access to the private lives of the friends and acquaintances that she visits and firsthand information to opine about what she considers to be the core of Spanish life. Canel emphasizes her credibility by means of a careful cultivation of a persona of spotless morality that allows her to make judgments as a woman intellectual that cross from the domestic to the political. Canel does not glorify the imperial past unilaterally, but her attention to what Unamuno had recently described as "*hechos* sub-históricos" (990) finds the aspects that fall outside of institutions but deserve curation and preservation. Her observation that imperial ties are not only political and that Cuba is still Spain paradoxically demonstrates a Romantic nationalist belief in a stable "national physiognomy"—a unique identity of a people designated "Spanish" that withstands changes on the surface (Boyd 131)— and the role of moral reform in national redemption.

The question of allegiance to Spain was not entirely one of neoimperial nostalgia. Immigration from Spain to Argentina and Cuba reached a massive scale in first decades of the twentieth century. Canel tried to make sense of the role of those Spaniards who, like her, lived in the Americas. What were the limits of their Spanishness? Could they be Cuban and Spanish? What cultural identity transcended the political rupture with Madrid and the transfer of imperial power to Washington? Canel deemed herself singularly qualified to adjudicate these questions and responded with rage when a Spanish journalist, "el Españolito" (little Spaniard), questioned her authority and suggested that Rafael Altamira was, in fact, the most qualified person to speak about Cuba. What follows is her most complete articulation of her own view of her role in the Americas, her objectivity, her intelligence, and her patriotism.

YO SOY LA ÚNICA que puede hablar: hoy soy la única que no ha tenido subvenciones porque jamás las he pedido, que no debe un pepino a ningún gobierno americano, que no ha tenido que adular por gratitudes pecuniarias, que no ha gozado sueldos del gobierno de España, como hacen correr muchos; que no ha pedido nada: ni ha tenido nada; que ha escrito voluminosos libros en honra de la patria y de los españoles, (salvo los que reputo malos) y los ha regalado para que nadie pudiese presumir que se imprimían con objeto de lucro.

Esto lo saben en todo el Nuevo Mundo y lo dirán los que no mientan: lo saben en España hombres eminentísimos, lo sabe el jefe del Estado; pues que hablen todos y digan todos ellos si algo les he pedido para mi persona ni para mi familia, y si algo me han dado. Luego soy *única* y lo digo muy alto: única en el conocimiento de los pueblos de America, de su psicología, y única en el patriotismo desinteresado.

(I AM THE ONLY ONE who can speak: today I am the only one who has not had subsidies because I have never asked for them, who does not owe a dime to any American government, who has not had to flatter for pecuniary tips, who has not enjoyed salaries from Spain's government, as many do; who has not asked for anything: nor has had anything; who has written voluminous books in honor of the homeland and of Spaniards, [except for those I consider bad ones] and who has given them away so nobody could presume that they were printed for profit.

This is known throughout the New World and will be said by those who do not lie: very eminent men in Spain know it, the head of State knows it, well, then let them all speak and say if I have asked them for something for myself or for my family, and if they have given me anything. Thus I am exceptional and I say it loudly: I am exceptional in my knowledge of the peoples of America, of their psychology, and unique in my disinterested patriotism.)

. . . .

Para que "Españolito" y otros españoles sepan dónde están los problemas hispanoamericanos es necesario que conozcan a fondo las cosas y los hombres de ambos mundos: *que sufran* en América TREINTA Y DOS AÑOS y de ellos *veintisiete* sin otro afán ni otro objetivo que el de estudiar, unificar, hacer justicia, defender a España contra insidias, injurias y calumnias, algunas escritas por esos españoles *impecables* según "*Españolito*" cuando no quiere que se les desnude y se les ponga al sol para ver si se curan de muchas lacras que afean su historia intelectual y publica. Es una lástima que muchacho tan bien intencionado se meta para juzgar al prójimo, en una sola alforja. Hay que meterse en ambas para buscar el equilibrio.

(In order for "Españolito" and other Spaniards to know where the Spanish-American problems are it is necessary for them to thoroughly know the things and the men of both worlds: *that they suffer* in America THIRTY-TWO YEARS and of those twenty-seven without any other desire or objective other than to study, unite, do justice, defend Spain against traps, insults, and slander, some written by those *impeccable* Spaniards according to "*Españolito*" when he does not want to strip them and lay them bare in order to see if they are cured of many defects that mar its intellectual and public history. It is a pity that such a well-intentioned young man becomes involved in judging his neighbor in a single sadddlebag. One must get into both to find balance) (377–78)

Claiming an unparalleled objectivity, unconstrained by state sponsorship, Canel attempts nothing less than a new history that will revive Spanish Cuba in the twentieth century.

In the first four hundred pages of *Lo que vi en Cuba—a través de la isla*, Canel sidesteps the political reasons for Cuban independence, instead insisting that in spite of a "yanqui" threat of cultural assimilation, Cuba has changed very little (especially in terms of private habits) from before 1898 and that "el carácter general es el mismo" (the general character is the same) (133). While Spanish emigrants are important to maintaining Cuba's Hispanic identity, she considers those born on the island best positioned to comprehend the U.S. menace: "Se me ocurre que los cubanos nativos van a ser los más empeñados en mantener el espíritu español porque se dan cuenta de lo que les va en ello y porque son los llamados a luchar por esa perpetuación, que es la de su propia vida" (It occurs to me that native Cubans are going to be the most determined in maintaining the Spanish spirit because they realize what is in it for them and because they are the ones called to fight for that perpetuation, that is their very existence) (134). In other words, Spanishness is cultivated independently of birthplace and is better comprehended as a spiritual Hispanism, and Cuba in the second decade of the twentieth century was the battleground over its future.

Canel feared that a U.S. narrative frame had begun to shape the way that Cubans understood their island. Haunted by the war of 1898, Canel scours the island for clues to Spanish military and discursive losses. On the recommendation of her chauffeur, she visited the "Árbol de La Paz"—a *ceiba* tree on the knoll of San Juan in Santiago de Cuba, "donde seguramente se incubó la locura del desgraciado general Toral" (where surely the madness of the wretched General Toral was incubated). She compares the commander who surrendered to the Americans unfavorably to Cortés, famously crying under the tree on the Noche Triste, but then immediately shifts from nature to narrative constructions, both visual and verbal:

> Nos bajamos del auto delante de dos cañones arquelógicos españoles y una ametralladora norteamericana que hacen de cancerberos ante una toza roja de madera. . . . Aprisionando la ceiba hay unas cuantas monumentales hojas pétreas que simulan un libro y en estas hojas completamente llenas de inscripciones, en idioma inglés, relatan *seguramente* la historia de aquella paz y de aquellas batallas y perpetúan los nombres de quienes la firmaron y quienes perecieron.
>
> (We got out of the car in front of two archeological Spanish cannons and a North American machine gun that act as doorkeepers before a red wooden stump. . . . Imprisoning the *ceiba* tree there are a few monumental stony leaves that simulated a book and in these leaves full of inscriptions, in the English language, *undoubtedly* telling the history of that peace and those battles and perpetuating the names of those who signed it and those who perished.)

—Esto está en inglés—le dije al negrito [the chauffeur]

—Sí señora: como no vienen mas que Americanos—replicó.

—Sí, pero como esta tierra es de Cuba podían haberlo escrito en los dos idiomas . . .

—Pero entonces se sabrían todas las mentiras que habrán puesto—interrumpió el chauffeur rápidamente.

—La justicia habla por tu boca—dije al inteligente negrito.

("This is in English," I said to the *negrito*

"Yes, ma'am: since only Americans come," he replied.

"Yes, but since this land belongs to Cuba they could have written it in both languages . . .

"But then all the lies they must have put would be known," the chauffeur interrupted quickly.

"Justice speaks through you," I said to the intelligent *negrito*). (*Lo que vi* 181)

Employing the diminutive term traditionally used to underscore both race and a social inferiority relative to the speaker, Canel confirms the precision of this man's understanding of public historiography.

This is the Anglophone counterhistory that she intends to halt while edifying a Spanish-centered version. Keenly aware of the importance of public monuments, Canel uses her narrative to promote the memory of General Vara de Rey and reshape knowledge of the past while proposing a physical modification to the landscape that would make General Vara de Rey present in the countryside. She reports that a landowner in Caney, where the Spanish general had died, offered to donate the land should someone wish to erect a column to the general. Canel explicitly indicates her hope that *Lo que vi* would inspire the king of Spain to do so: "[e]l coste sería una insignificancia y puede venir hecha de España" (the cost would be insignificant and [the column] could be made in Spain) (193). Canel does not mention the commemorations to the general undertaken in Spain; rather, her argument is that Spain had to ensure the construction of monuments in the Americas to narrate Cuban history from a Spanish perspective. However straightforward Canel might have intended the column to be, the meaning of her proposed monument would, of course, been continually remade by those, including women like her, who viewed it. As Tracy Anderson has argued, a consideration of gender in political commemoration (including monuments) allows us to address these sites as a point of confluence and tension among public and private space, imperial ideologies, personal loss, and individual memory (32). Canel imagined such a confluence without a corresponding tension and creation of new knowledge.

The Spain she appealed to is an idealized and reformed version of reality. Simón Palmer has assessed Canel's reception in Spain after 1898 and explained that the author was disappointed by the fact that her labors in Cuba were not celebrated in the peninsula: "Se produce entonces en ella una reacción contraria a la de la mayoría de los españoles: la reafirmación de su patriotismo y de su religiosidad" (Then a reaction contrary to that of the majority of Spaniards arises in her: the reaffirmation of her patriotism and her religiosity) ("Biografía" 300). Thus, when Canel returned to America shortly thereafter, she did so not only with a profound disappointment with Spanish politics but also, according to the same critic, "en busca de lo que su patria no le ofrece" (in search of what her homeland does not offer her) (Simón Palmer "Biografía" 300). An American in Spain, she further pursued Spain in America.

Her rediscovery of Spain in Cuba through a collection of small observations is evident in passages such as the description of the Bahía de Gibara, a major port that attracted a large number of Spanish immigrants in the nineteenth century but slowly came under the commercial control of the United States by the time Canel visited. The town was nicknamed Covadonga Chiquita on the basis of the number of Asturians residing there. Canel found

> algo de místico: en el ambiente de su vida moderna, en la tristeza de su descenso comercial, en el silencio de sus calles, flota un espiritu de dolor cristiano, dolor de ruinas jeresolimitanas; dolor que cantan con sordina, al morir en los peñascos de la costa y en las arenas de la playa, unas olas muy tímidas que llegan perezosamente, a deponer la fuerza de su origen ignoto ante las incontrastables barreras de la tierra.

> (something mystical: in the atmosphere of its modern life, in the sadness of its commercial descent, in the silence of its streets, hovers a spirit of Christian sorrow, a grief of Jerusalemite ruins; pain that they sing silently, upon dying on the coast's rocks and the sand on the beach, very shy waves that arrive lazily, to take away the strength of its unknown origin in the presence of the insuperable barriers of the Earth.) (262–63)

Upon describing her lunch among the Asturians in town, the author categorically declares, "Nuestro almuerzo no fue en Gibara, sino en Europa; no era ficción de nuestra voluntad, era función amnésica con relación al tiempo y al lugar en que nos encontrábamos" (Our lunch was not in Gibara, but in Europe; it was not fiction of our will, it was an amnesiac function in relation to the time and the place that we found ourselves) (268).

She takes the Covadoga comparison and expands its imperial dimensions, converting Gibara into the final unconquered holdout from "los hombres del Norte [sic]" (the men from the North [sic]) (265). Canel ever so playfully intimates that perhaps this town, an important port, might produce a mythical rejection of the invading culture and serve as a last holdout of Spanish spirit (the U.S. commercial presence notwithstanding):

> Las cosas caen del lado que se inclinan y si Cuba acentúa demasiado su inclinación hacia el Norte, el Norte la envolverá en sus torbellinos sin dejarle aire respirable. Que Cuba sea eternamente cubana interesa por igual a los cubanos y a los españoles que en ella viven: en segundo lugar interesa a los hispanoamericanos, a cuantos pueblos de nuestra raza pueblan el continente.
>
> (Things fall to the side they lean and if Cuba accentuates its inclinations towards the North too much, the North will envelop it in its whirlwinds leaving it without breathable air. That Cuba remains eternally Cuban equally interests both the Cubans and Spaniards who live there: secondly it interests Spanish Americans, to all those people of our race that populate the continent.) (266)

Inverting North and South, the United States' political control of the island becomes the equivalent of the so-called Muslim conquest of the Iberian Peninsula, with a mythical Spanish nation resisting assimilation. Canel writes to arrest the process of modernity and preserve a mystical past no longer (and in fact never) found in Iberia, grounded in a sense of global superiority and self-sufficiency that did not court foreign investments or entrepreneurs.

Canel dedicated significant space to discussions of gender and insisted on conservative gender roles as a form of resistance to the United States and as an avenue to rectifying racism. María del Carmen Barcia highlights the inconsistency between the author's stated views that, for example, women did not need to attend university or leave their domestic duties, with her own behavior as a public voice. This critic conjectures that Canel said what she believed each of her publics wanted to hear. While this synthesis of ideological extremes across the course of Canel's public life is plausible, given Canel's astute navigation of the publishing world, her views regarding gender are inseparable from her anxieties over Spanishness and her denunciation of the racism that Spain left in Cuba. Gender is a filter for individual identity but also for the cultural identity of the country that Eva Canel sees as in flux. In 1916, Canel's worry of assimilation into the United States was not unfounded: Texas and Florida had become states just sixty years before and progressively incorporated into U.S. culture. The author enforces traditional gender conventions in a moment of fluid cultural and political identities, when Spanish/Hispanic culture could become "Anglo-Saxon."

Canel portrays women as the practitioners of the daily life of Hispanism but also as creators of discourse through both their words and their deeds. Representative of her general outlook toward women in the public sphere was her reaction to a young woman who ran the daily paper *La Publicidad*. Canel was charmed "con la sinceridad de la joven que contaría entre dieciocho y veinte años de edad y que llevaba sobre sí el peso de una industria, aunque pequeña en sí, grande por abarcar un campo reservado a los hombres, hasta la hora presente" (with the sincerity of the young woman who was between eighteen and twenty years old and who carried the burden of an industry by herself, although small in itself, great for encompassing a field reserved for men, until the present time) (240). But Canel admonishes her to attend to her husband once she gets married and insists: "¿Pero cuando tenga usted hijos . . . ? . . . . La mujer de un hombre que puede trabajar y ganar el pan de la familia, hace bastante con criar bien sus hijos y cuidar su casa" (But when you have children . . . ? . . . . The wife of a man who can work and earn the family's bread, does enough with raising their children well and taking care of their house.) (240). Canel promotes the idea of women writers and publishers as long as their work does not disturb their tasks as wives and mothers.

Nevertheless, Canel by no means writes off married women from the realm of discourse. From among her connections of author friends, including the Baronesa de Wilson (godmother to Canel's son Eloy) and Domitila García (the Cuban writer who, in turn, had dedicated a work to her friend G[ertrudis] G[ómez de] A[vellaneda]), Canel highlights the accomplishments of Concepción Rodulfo, the Cadiz-born wife of the vice consul of Spain in Guantánamo. Rodulfo, "el ángel bueno de dondequiera que se encuentre: la criatura mas abnegada y la patriota más meretoria" (the good angel of wherever she may be: the most self-sacrificing creature and the most deserving patriot) (177) was not a writer but a socialite, yet Canel describes her patriotic charity work as analogous to her own narrative constructions of Spanish Cuba, pre- and post-1898. As discussed above, through both text and monument, the public discourse of Hispanism that found the origin of Latin American civilization in Spain claimed the right to control the historical narrative of Spanish Cuba. Canel's travelogue does just this in a straightforward manner; Concepción Rodulfo worked to counter the North American version of the War of 1898 by commissioning a pantheon for Spanish soldiers who died in the imperial wars of the 1890s. She raised all of the necessary monies for its construction and, of particular importance, managed to convince the victorious Cubans to donate "pious" amounts toward the project (199–200). Moreover, she stayed abreast of U.S. narratives regarding Cuba, lest Spanish speakers remain ignorant of the newly dominant discourse:

> La existencia de esta mujer que vive exclusivamente para su patria, sin dejar por esto de hacer donde vive todo el bien que puede, es una existencia prodigiosa. Está en su casa y está en todas partes: piensa en su tierra y hace cuanto bien puede a la tierra en que reside: aprende sola el inglés para saber lo que dice de nosotros la prensa norteamericana y traduce cuanto a su juicio, que es muy claro, nos interesa saber.
>
> (The existence of this woman who lives exclusively for her homeland, yet never failing to do all the good that she can where she lives, is a prodigious existence. She is in her home and she is everywhere: she thinks of her native land and does whatever good she can for the country in which she resides: she learns English by herself in order to know what the North American press says about us and translates all that in her opinion, which is very sound, is in our interests to know.) (241)

Concepción Rodulfo, the socialite patriot, and Canel, the writer, edified and memorialized what they considered to be heroic interventions of Spaniards in Cuba but also drew Cubans into the story of Spanish heroism, in a direct counternarrative both to the United States and to that of local patriotism that erased Spain. The young publisher of *La Publicidad*, Rudolfo, and Canel are engaged in the open debate, eighteen years after the Treaty of

Paris, as to who succeeds in telling the past and future of Spanish Cuba. Working at the margins of institutional knowledge, all three women acted from personal conviction in favor of, but not commissioned by, the state.

Literature was the field of a number of Spanish Hispanists and is a more straightforward institutional space. The importance of literature to Cuban identity comes full circle in her depiction of Santa and her role as a reader. During her visit to a rural town (Chaparra), Canel is greeted by "una mulata con todas las maneras de una señora que sabe cuáles son sus deberes" (a valiant mulata woman with all the manners of a lady who knows what her duties are) (287). Santa and Canel had met twenty-five years previously in Cárdenas, at a hotel owned by Santa's "colaborador" (collaborator) (as Canel euphemistically calls him)—a man from the same region of Asturias as Canel. But the intellectual and affective tie between the two women is not mediated by the man that they knew in common, but rather by literature. Canel, the self-proclaimed authority on Hispanist identity, values Santa as a hard worker and an ideal reader: "Santa es una mujer de alto criterio, una socia ideal para mover cualquier negocio y adelantar por medio del trabajo ordenado y metódico. Sus atenciones conmigo fueron extremadas: todavía me guardaba gratitud por mi drama *La mulata*; recordaba mi primera producción dramática como si cada ocho días asistiese a su representación" (Santa is a woman of refined taste, an ideal partner to undertake and advance any business through orderly and methodical work. Her attentions towards me were extreme: she remained grateful to me for my drama *La mulata*; she remembered my first dramatic production as if she attended its performance every week) (287–88). Canel's recollection of Santa's observation about the role of literature in the lives of Cuban women positions Canel herself as central to their present social status: "¡Las mujeres de color . . . le debemos tanto! Fue usted la primera blanca que nos dignificó en Cuba." (We women of color . . . we owe you so much! You were the first white woman to represent us with dignity in Cuba) (288).

This recollection of Santa's statement illustrates a larger argument in Canel's work. Throughout *Lo que vi* the author claims that she—and by extension Hispanism itself—is not racist. Typical of these statements is the "yo no distingo de colores: tan solo de educaciones, virtudes y culturas . . . no admito que se le mire al hombre culto y honrado el color de la cara. ¡Hay tantas almas negras con piel blanca y no las rechazamos!" (I do not distinguish among colors: only by education, virtue, and culture . . . I do not accept that the cultured and honorable man is seen by the color of his face.

There are so many black souls with white skin and we do not reject them!) (236). Her colorblindness encompasses a dismissal of the racial inequalities that she proposes for a future Hispanic Cuba.[6] Here, Canel suggests that she herself had given this singular woman (who could well be a character in her drama) the language to speak of race, marriage, and domesticity in precise terms. Her arrogance in claiming that Cuban *mulatas* needed her play in order to articulate the racial dynamics of their daily lives may appear surprising, but it is straight from the imperial handbook. She may not have given Santa the "gift" of the Spanish language, as colonizers in the Early Modern period applauded themselves for having done, but suggests that *La mulata* gave Santa and other women of color a sentimental and aesthetic framework with which to articulate their place in society.

In spite of her other statements in *Lo que vi* in support of traditional marriage, Canel contrasts Santa's industriousness, literacy, and honesty with the behavior of legally married white women (including daughters of Spaniards) in Cuba. Here, in particular, Canel reveals women's knowledge of other women's private lives to concede that at least one facet of Spanish customs had not survived political changes in the island. Canel argues that sexual practices in Cuba had become so distant from traditional Spanish habits and colonial racist ideology had become so entrenched that the institution of marriage itself had been perverted. Her evidence is Santa, a modest woman who dedicated her life to a man, helping him with his work, but, for the color of her skin, cannot become the legitimate partner of the man who loves and respects her lest society burden him with woes. Santa rejects out of hand the idea of marrying her partner, with a question "¿Para qué echar esa 'pesadumbre social' sobre un hombre tan bueno?" (Why afflict such a good man with that "social burden"?) (288) This sharp reader of Canel's play does not hide behind a theatrical morality upheld by racial claims of Spanish virtue. In contrast to Santa, Canel chastises those married white women who "suelen llevar al matrimonio un bagaje de impurezas, de prostitución clandestina o pública y no temen echar sobre el que les da su nombre 'la pesadumbre' del desprecio" (usually bring to marriage a baggage of impurities, clandestine or public prostitution, and they do not fear casting "the burden" of scorn on the man who gave them his name) (288). Canel acknowledges that the Spanish empire had raced womanhood as white and prevented virtuous women of color from being recognized as such, while simultaneously facilitating white women's deviance from strict gendered behavior. Her critique of women's actions, through her access to the circulation of private information is the clearest example of her deployment of her perspective as a woman to respond to institutions and effect change. The relationship between Canel the writer and Santa the reader is built upon a shared understanding of the social barriers that prevent women of color from attaining a "perfect" domesticity along the lines of a nineteenth-century angel of the household.

The drama to which Santa referred premiered in Havana at the Teatro Payret on Nov 10, 1893. Reviewers celebrated it as a "perfección artística" (artistic perfection) (*Pájinas*) and an "encarnación de las injusticias sociales, glorificación del amor maternal" (embodiment of social injustices, glorification of maternal love) (*El día*). Apparently antiracist in its depiction of the ways that the empire decimated gender codes, the action opens in Venezuela, where the Catalan merchant Daniel has just swindled his father-in-law, abandoned his *mulata* wife, Patria, and embarked for Barcelona with her inheritance and their young child. Twenty years pass, and Patria arrives in Catalonia to reclaim her son from the *nouveau riche indiano* who had attempted to erase his son's knowledge of his Venezuelan *Patria* and the inconvenient secrets of the American money that helped finance Catalonia's modernization. The clear heroine of the play, Patria earns the audience's approval and posits the irrevocable legitimacy of all natural mothers, independent of their race. The play underscores the crimes of the Catalans in imperialism, yet doesn't question imperialism per se, but rather the way that its racial logic destroyed the strictures of bourgeois gender roles. Once Patria's son, Luis, learns the identify of his biological mother, he definitively breaks with his father and with a sector of society corrupted by its wealth garnered through the exploitation of free blacks and the enslaved in America. As the play concludes, Luis, the white son of the *mulata* Patria, abandons Spain and departs for Venezuela.

In *Lo que vi*, Canel acknowledges and attempts to atone for the crimes of Spain's past in order to strengthen a future neoimperial moral authority over Cubans. The fact that her character, Patria, even exists is already a critique of the racial and sexual oppression that were tools of the empire. But in her portrayal of Santa's "debt" to her for *La mulata* and her own sentimental attachment to the institution of marriage, Canel demonstrates the heterosexual white bias of her particular feminism but laments that womanhood is already always gendered white—preventing women like Santa from entering a more unified Spanish identity—and blames the legacy of empire for making it so. Santa is a tool in Canel's Hispanist project. Moreover, Canel's attempt to speak for the collective "*mulatas*" and suggest that she understands their desire for inclusion in a Spanish concept of marriage anticipates Spivak's caution against the assumption of a unified perspective among subalterns and the dependence on Western intellectuals (such as Canel) to speak for a supposed collective, rather than actually listening to those they speak for. Thus, the episode with Santa serves two purposes in the overall argument of the book. First, it confirms Canel's project to shape cultural identity through narrative, drama, or monument; second, she links the issue of slavery (the stain of Spanish colonialism) to the Catalans and the continued disintegration of the empire. As *lo que vi* develops, Canel also accuses the "Catalan Block"—her term for Catalan separatists (353 and passim)—of being anti-Spanish and putting the future of the state in peril.

It slowly becomes clear that while Canel speaks to all Cubans, she is especially concerned about Catalans residing there and as she travels through the island, Canel makes it her mission to convince the Catalans she meets to support Spain. She relates as exemplary her conversation with a Catalan couple she meets on a train to Camagüey. After she convinces the fourth passenger in the car, a Cuban, of her positions vis-à-vis the Spanish government, "el simpático *noy* no se achicó por esto y entabló discusión que la acepté de grado convencida de que, estando facultada por mis antecedentes de amor a Cataluña, para cantarle las verdades, la victoria era mía" (the pleasant boy was not intimidated by this and initiated a debate that I gladly joined, convinced that, my acknowledged love for Catalonia entitled me to speak my mind, the victory would be mine) (316). Engaging with multiple stereotypes, Canel emphasizes that "un catalán que quiere ser buen español, resulta muy simpático, muy complaciente y muy patriota" (a Catalan who wants to be a good Spaniard is very pleasant, very obliging and very patriotic) (319). She lists, by name, many men and women who meet her criteria.

Canel perceived local identity and private knowledge as fundamental to forging modern Spanish identity, not merely solidifying the existing situation. Jean Kenmogne has shown that Canel developed her own regenerationist program for Spain, in accordance with the fact that the author "tenía una visión negativa y pesimista de la España de su tiempo" (had a negative and pessimistic view of the Spain of her day) (54; 56). Her rhetorical acrobatics regarding race demonstrate her particular argument that Spain needed the former colony to remake its image. Consistent with imperial and neoimperial ideology more generally, Canel emphasized that pro-Cuba and pro-Spain positions are not incompatible. Examples abound from across social strata. Here are three. Conversing with a village priest, she quickly surmises his identity:

> Es usted gallego, ¿verdad?
>
> Sí señora; ¿y usted?
>
> Casi: soy de Asturias: pero ahora en Cuba, todos tenemos la honra de ser paisanos de Colón
>
> (You are Galician, are you not?
>
> Yes, ma'am, and you?
>
> Almost, I am from Asturias but now, here in Cuba we all have the honor of being compatriots of Columbus.) (246)

Among the moneyed classes, she singles out one young woman for her dual identity: "La señorita de Mata es una criatura arrogante por su inteligencia franca y poco dúctil a los convencionalismos hipócritas: como su mamá, es cubana pero conoce bien España por haber vivido allí algunos años y ama la patria vieja al igual que la nueva" (Miss de Mata is a valiant creature for her forthright intelligence and resistance to hypocritical conventions: like her mother, she is Cuban but knows Spain well because she lived there for some years and she loves the old country as well as the new one) (328). Another friend, the capitalist Antonio Díaz Blanco, "siguió pensando en Cuba aun viviendo en España largas temporadas . . . tuvo amor para todos y fomentó en Gijón industrias y en La Habana empleaba capitales, y debiendo en su patria haber recolectado el fruto de su patriotismo" (continued thinking about Cuba even when living in Spain for long periods . . . had love for everyone and developed industries in Gijón and deployed capital in Havana, and should have reaped the fruit of his patriotism in his homeland) (161). Sentiment, argues Canel, led him to transatlantic financial ventures. Were more Spanish capitalists moved by this same affection for their *patria*, Cuba might halt the influx of U.S. finance.

Canel celebrated the overlapping identities allowed by Hispanism within the larger frame of "Spain" that contributed to the regeneration of the "patria vieja" (old country) (328) but, as noted above, she voiced particular concern over the disintegration of Spain that the "Catalan Block" represented. Her ideas were not entirely new: fifteen years before she articulated her worries regarding Catalan independence in her travelogue, she had spoken about the connections between Cuba and Catalonia at the Centre Català in Buenos

Aires. Simón Palmer explains that the author declared herself in favor of plurilingualism in the peninsula but was cautious of tying Catalonia too closely to Cuba, without the mediation of Spain. She expressed

> su desconformidad con las ideas de su admirada Pardo Bazán para quien Cuba sólo reportaba beneficios a los catalanes, que se beneficiaban de tarifas protectoras. Recuerda cómo fue un error la alianza contra la producción catalana porque aún así a los tres años estalló la sublevación, a pesar de lo cual Cataluña dió dinero para el [e]jército. La regeneración de España sólo puede venir, según Canel, de una sola idea y la unión de las regiones

> (her disagreement with the ideas of her admired Pardo Bazán for whom Cuba only produced benefits to the Catalans, who benefited from protective tariffs. She recalls how the alliance against Catalan production was a mistake because even with it the uprising erupted three years later, in spite of which Catalonia gave money to the army. The regeneration of Spain could only come, according to Canel, from a single idea and the union of the regions) ("Biografía" 300)[7]

Canel began to weave together patriotic sentiment and economic policy within the framework of fear for the collapse of a unified Spain, should Catalonia show itself to be less Spanish than Cuba.

The question was not only political and economic, but an expression of private customs and sentiments anchored in friendship. Her travel had a diplomatic impact: Cubans could voice their love for her where they may have been more reserved about the Spanish state itself. Reflecting on her visit to Guantánamo, Canel reports that she was welcomed at all of the regional social centers save one: "no me llevaron al Block Catalán porque me han dicho 'No quieren ser españoles y como sociedad extranjera no alcanza la ficción para que pueda usted visitarla.' ¡Qué pena me produjo esto!" (they did not take me to the *Block Catalán* because they told me "They do not want to be Spanish and it would be pure fantasy for you to visit it as a foreign club." What disappointment this caused me!). Canel casts the Catalan rejection of her—the embodiment of transatlantic Spanishness—as a speaker as indicative of their disinterest in dialogue with Spain. "¡Que no quieren ser españoles los catalanes de Guantánamo! ¿Pero saben lo que dicen ni lo que hacen? ¿Miden la extensión de su desprecio hacia la nacionalidad?

Felizmente no todos piensan así" (The Catalans of Guantánamo do not want to be Spanish! But do they know what they are saying or what they are doing? Do they understand the depth of their contempt towards their nationality? Happily, not everyone thinks like that) (230). Canel's vision for Spain is more imperial than national, for she promotes a Spain structured not upon a unified law, but upon unequal relations before a central imperial government and regional autonomy that would acknowledge private, local knowledge and sentiment but also solidify each area's underlying political allegiance to Spain.[8] She claims to be unable to understand the strict nationalism behind anti-Spanish sentiment. "¿Cómo puedo creer que hay catalanes que no quieren a España, que reniegan de ser españoles; que por nada ni por nadie enarbolan la bandera nacional? ¿No será un poquito de pedantesco modernismo?" (How can I ever believe that there are Catalans that do not love Spain, that vigorously deny they are Spaniards; that do not fly the national flag for anyone or for anything? Might this not be just a little bit of pedantic modernism?) (230). She concludes by underscoring the need for communities of Spaniards in the Americas to foment a cohesion lacking in the peninsula.

The narration of Cuban history, the Spanish legacy of the slave trade, and Catalan separatism are tightly braided throughout her book. Canel was deeply concerned about the responsibility for racism and how knowledge of the role played by Spaniards in the slave trade in post-1898 Cuba circulated and interfered with Spain's claim for continued cultural authority. Her travelogue attempted to reshape the prevailing discourse. A reading of *Lo que vi* deepens our understanding of neoimperialism in the early twentieth century Atlantic beyond the commonplaces of Hispanism, with Canel's denunciation of Spain's past paired with her belief in an ability to recover a moral legitimacy through the performance of disinterested objectivity and incorporation of private knowledge. Canel preached a strand of transatlantic Hispanism that was grounded in the lived experience of an imagined and improved Spain, or a "patria común" (common homeland) (Muñoz 311). Her network of female associates, writer friends, creators, and readers constituted a model set of relations that provided her with facts from within and beyond institutional knowledge that she then gave textual form. While emigration maintained Spain's foothold in sustaining cultural life in Cuba ("yo soy partidaria de que los españoles emigren" [I am in favor of Spanish emigration]) (42), Canel saw transatlantic migration as a danger to Spain if it ceded human capital to U.S.-held Cuba. She argued that Hispanist narratives and practices had the potential to prevent emigrants from becoming

Americanized while harnessing their Spanishness to solidify nationalism in the peninsula. For Canel, the continued identification of Cubans as Spaniards, as she claimed to see that they lived it in their private lives, held the key to the past and future of Spain in the island. With the perspective of a century, historians have noted that relations between Spaniards and Cubans on the island were in fact reestablished quickly and were not characterized by strife.[9] Canel is a truly transatlantic figure in terms of her biography and the topics of her fictional and nonfictional work. However, as Barcia notes, her ambiguous canonical position is the result of the fact that neither side of the Atlantic has claimed her (246).

Notes

1. For an in-depth study of this period, see Hernández.
2. See Tsuchiya and Acree.
3. See Simón Palmer (*Biografía*). Barcia Zequeiras's excellent study of Eva Canel has a series of paradoxes, in that her political and social views were conservative yet her plays and novels proposed scandalous ideas, well ahead of their time. Through a reading of Canel's biography, drawn together from her various publications, Barcia proposes a framework that comprehends Canel's praise for both Valeriano Weyler and José Martí (239)!
4. Curiously, his first play was entitled *Los negreros* (Barcia 232).
5. This and all subsequent translations by Nicole Barraza.
6. See Brown; Emirbayer and Desmond.
7. Simón Palmer refers to Canel's lecture, published as *El regionalismo de los catalanes y sus relaciones con la patria*, Tip. de *El Correo Español*, 1899.
8. Burbank and Cooper describe the political theory of global empires in much the same terms. Empires always had to "provide people—at home, overseas, and in between—with a sense of place within an unequal but incorporative polity. Resistance was a constant feature of empire" (5); Canel attempted to create this sense of place after political coercion was no longer a possibility and ever more in question in Catalonia.
9. Santamaría García and Naranjo Orovio review the reasons for the "convivencia" subsequent to 1898, highlighting the influx of Spanish immigrants, Hispanism and the accompanying fear of the United States, and the attitude of José Martí, who had emphasized that the war for independence was against Spain, not Spaniards (144). See also, Consuelo Naranjo Orovio and Antonio Santamaría García, "La tradición española en Cuba después del 98," *Rábida* 17 (1998): 67–80; Aurea Matilde Fernández Muñiz, "La presencia española en Cuba después de 1898. Su reflejo en el *Diario de la Marina* in *La nación soñada. Cuba, Puerto Rico y Filipinas*

ante el 98," coordinated by Consuelo Naranjo Orovio, Miguel Angel Puig Samper Mulero, Luis Miguel García Mora. Doce Calles, 1996, 509–18; Aurea Matilde Fernández Muñiz, "España y Cuba: ruptura y continuiad en el 98," *Casa de las Américas* 211 (1998): 78–83; and Consuelo Naranjo Orovio and Alejandro García Álvarez, "Cubanos y españoles después del 98. De la confrontación a la convivencia pacífica," *Revista de Indias* 58:212 (1998): 101–29.

Works Cited

Anderson, Tracy. "The Lives and Afterlives of Charlotte, Lady Canning (1817–1861): Gender, Commemoration, and Narratives of Loss." *South Asian Studies*, vol. 29, no. 1, 2013, pp. 31–50.
Barcia Zequeira, María del Carmen. "Eva Canel, una mujer de paradojas." *Anuario de Estudios Americano*, vol. 58, no. 1, 2001, pp. 227–52.
Briggs, Ronald. *The Moral Electricity of Print*. Vanderbilt UP, 2017.
Brown, Michael K. *Whitewashing Race: The Myth of a Color Blind Society*. U of California P, 2003.
Burbank, Jane, and Frederick Cooper. *Empires in World History: Power and the Politics of Difference*. Princeton UP, 2010.
Caballer, Mercedes. "Eva Canel, un ejemplo de transculturación in *De America: viajes, tradiciones y novelistas cortas*." *Colorado Review of Hispanic Studies*, vol. 3, 2005, pp. 57–70.
Canel, Eva. *La mulata*. Barcelona: Tip. *La Ilustración*, 1891.
———. *Lo que vi en Cuba—A través de la isla*. La Habana, La Universal, 1916.
Davies, Catherine. *A Place in the Sun*. Zed Books, 1997.
Emirbayer, Mustafa, and Matthew Desmond. *The Racial Order*. U of Chicago P, 2015.
Faber, Sebastiaan. "La hora ha llegado. Hispanism, Pan-Americanism and the Hope of Spanish/American Glory (1938–48)." *Ideologies of Hispanism*, edited by Mabel Moraña, Vanderbilt UP, 2005, pp. 62–104.
Ferrús Antón, Beatriz. "Dos modos de narrar América Latina: autobiografía y costumbrismo en Eva Canel." *Anales de Literatura Hispanoamericana*, vol. 40, 2011, pp. 219–31.
Hernández, José M. *Cuba and the United States: Intervention and Militarism 1868–1933*. U of Texas P, 1993.
Ivison, Douglas. "Travel Writing at the End of Empire: A Pom Named Bruce and the Mad White Giant." *English Studies in Canada*, vol. 29, no. 3–4, 2003, pp. 200–19.
Jenkins Wood, Jennifer. *Spanish Women Travelers at Home and Abroad, 1850–1920*. Bucknell UP, 2014.
Kenmogne, Jean. "Una escritora asturiana en América: Eva Canel." *Cuadernos Hispanoamericanos*, vol. 546, pp. 45–62.

Martin, Leona. "Nation Building, International Travel, and the Construction of the Nineteenth-Century Pan-Hispanic Women's Network." *Hispania*, vol. 87, no. 3, 2004, pp. 439–46.

Muñoz, Laura. "Reseña de *Lo que vi en Cuba* de Eva Canel. Relaciones." *Estudios de Historia y Sociedad*, vol. 30, no. 17, 2009, pp. 311–14.

"Noticias de espectáculos." *El Día* (Madrid), no. 5125, 18 July 1894, 3.

O'Connor D'Arlach, Tomás. "*La mulata*" *Pájinas literarias*. Imprenta de *La Estrella*, 1892.

Pratt, Mary Louise. *Imperial Eyes: Travel Writing and Transculturation*. Routledge, 1992.

Santamaría García, Antonio, and Consuelo Narajo Orovio. "La historia social de Cuba, 1868–1914. Aportaciones recientes y perspectivas." *Historia Social*, vol. 33, 1999, pp. 133–58.

Simón Palmer, María del Carmen. "Biografía de Eva Canel (1857–1932)." *Estudios Sobre Escritoras Hispánicas en Honor de Georgina Sabat-Rivers*, coordinated by Lou Charnon-Deutsch, Castalia, 1992, pp. 294–304.

———. "Mujeres rebeldes." *Historia de las mujeres en Occidente*, edited by Georges Duby and Michelle Perrot, Vol. 4, Taurus, 1993, pp. 629–41.

Spivak, Gayatri Chakravorty. "Can the Subaltern Speak?" *Marxism and the Interpretation of Culture*, edited by Cary Nelson and Lawrence Grossberg, U of Illinois P, 1988, pp. 271–313.

Tsuchiya, Akiko, and William G. Acree Jr., eds. *Empire's End: Transnational Connections in the Hispanic World*. Vanderbilt University Press, 2016.

Unamuno, Miguel de. "El Porvenir de España." *Obras completas*, vol. 4. Afrodisio Aguado, 1958, pp. 951–1015.

3

Gender, Race, and Spain's Colonial Legacy in the Americas

Representations of White Slavery in Eugenio Flores's *Trata de blancas* and Eduardo López Bago's *Carne importada*

AKIKO TSUCHIYA

It is only in the last decade that scholars of Iberian studies have begun to interrogate in a sustained fashion the colonialist subtext of many literary works of nineteenth-century Spain, bringing to light the ways in which the Spanish nation was shaped by empire in the economic, political, and cultural arena.[1] According to Alda Blanco, Spanish literary historiography, in an attempt to legitimize Spain as a modern European nation, has generally erased the traces of empire in discussions of nineteenth-century Peninsular literatures and cultures ("El fin" 4). Yet, as Lisa Surwillo has noted, modernity's roots are in empire and colonialism, and "literature as a space of fantasy provides a locus for imagining what was generally known but officially unacknowledged" (6). It is impossible to deny that many Spanish literary and artistic representations of the fin-de-siècle tacitly evoked imperial nostalgia, as the nation coped with the loss of its remaining colonies in the Americas and the Philippines. In fact, Blanco herself, while claiming the erasure of empire from Spanish literary history, has coined the classification "literatura del imperio" (literature of empire) to refer to works of the period that implicitly inscribe the history of empire and colonialism within their pages ("El fin").

It is well known that during the period of imperial loss in the late nineteenth century, the Spanish nation was also losing a significant sector of its population, especially from its impoverished northern regions—Galicia, Asturias, and Cantabria—through mass migration to the Americas.[2] While the male emigrant, embodied in the myth of the wealthy *indiano,* occupies a prominent place in the Spanish cultural imaginary,[3] the figure of the woman who emigrated to the New World has often been bypassed in narratives of transatlantic migration in the *fin-de-siglo* period. Although, historically, fewer than 10 percent of these emigrants from Spain to the Americas were women, with the international spotlight on "white slavery" as a rising global phenomenon at the end of the nineteenth century, Spanish writers began to address this problem in their literary works. Pardo Bazán's widely anthologized short story "Las medias rojas" (The Red Tights) (1914) perhaps best captures the desperation that drove young women, like the female protagonist trapped in a life of rural poverty in northern Spain, to abandon their homeland to pursue their dream of a new life in the Americas. The Americas appear in the young woman's imagination as "los lejanos países donde el oro rueda por las calles y no hay sino bajarse para cogerlo" (faraway lands where the streets are rolling in gold and one need only stoop down to grab it).[4] Having received an advance payment from a trafficker, she purchases a pair of red tights and prepares to embark on her transatlantic journey. Her hopes are shattered when her father discovers her plan and beats her brutally, leaving her deformed and blind in one eye, taking away her only capital—her abled and beautiful body—which would have allowed her to make a living in the New World. Tragic as this ending might be, the readers can only imagine the life of economic misery and sexual exploitation that the young woman would have suffered in the hands of her trafficker, had she made it to the New World with her beautiful body intact.

Between 1860 and 1930 sex trafficking of women occurred predominantly from Europe to the Americas, although some European women were sent to trafficking centers in different regions of Asia and Africa (Barberán Reinares 27–28).[5] The great poverty of these women, especially in rural areas in the age of industrialization, set the scene for transatlantic sexual commerce to become an actively organized global industry, facilitated by the development of new transportation and communication technologies (Barberán Reinares 8–9). The migration of men from Europe to the New World also created a demand for prostitutes where there were large concentrations of men. In turn-of-the-century Spain, both Madrid and Barcelona became major centers of international sex trafficking, with ships arriving in Barcelona and other coastal cities from places such as Poland, Russia, France, and Italy to transport women across the Atlantic. While the global sex trade provoked a political reaction both in Spain and throughout the rest of Europe, resulting in legal measures to protect women forced into prostitution against their will, these laws were ultimately unenforceable, due not only to the prevalence of clandestine sex trafficking, but also to the widespread corruption among those presumably responsible for regulating the industry. Several decades before the publication of Pardo Bazán's "Las medias rojas," Spanish writers and intellectuals had already begun to engage in a public debate on the problem of international sex trafficking (Fernández, *Mujer pública* 221),[6] giving rise to literary works such as Eugenio Antonio Flores's *Trata de blancas* (*White Slavery*) (1889) and Eduardo López Bago's *Carne importada* (*Imported Flesh*) (1891), among others.[7] Coincidentally, both authors lived abroad for an extended time in the Americas at the end of the nineteenth century: Flores spent a good part of the 1870s in Cuba, which was still a colony of Spain at the time; López Bago, for his part, emigrated to Argentina in 1888 and published *Carne importada* during his stay in the Southern Cone. That their own transatlantic crossings—their movement across different colonial contexts—influenced their literary and political writing is, therefore, not surprising.[8] While Argentina, which had been an independent nation since the early nineteenth century, undoubtedly had a different political relationship to the metropolis than colonial Cuba at the end of the century, the *representations* of these different geopolitical spaces in the works of the two Spanish authors reveal a strikingly similar colonialist mindset.

López Bago and Flores formed part of the literary school of "radical naturalism," whose objective was to take Zola's model of naturalism to its limits, inscribing marginal subjects within medical-scientific discourse and subordinating literature's aesthetic elements to positivistic analysis. At the same time, these works followed the formula of serialized fiction, resorting to sensationalistic plots and lurid representations of deviant sexuality. Thus, while the naturalist writer sought to maintain the pretense of scientific objectivity in addressing contemporary social problems, he was at the same time cognizant of the (predominantly metropolitan and male-identified) literary market to which he needed to address (and sell) his work.[9]

Flores's novel, narrated from a third-person perspective in what Luis Álvarez Castro has called a "documentary" mode (Introduction 47), gives way to a first-person account of the socially marginalized female protagonist (Pilar, subsequently renamed Estrella and Icuáa), who, after being raped by a neighbor, abandons her broken and impoverished family in a rural Spanish town and travels to Zaragoza, in hopes of finding work as a maid. There she discovers that she has been sold as a prostitute. Her narration traces her trajectory from Zaragoza to Barcelona and, eventually, across the Atlantic to Havana, where her illusion of earning a fortune is shattered when she becomes infected with syphilis and dies alone in the Hospital of Hygiene. While the editorializing voice of the omniscient third-person narrator resumes the narration at the end, for a major part of the novel he yields the narration to the female protagonist, who denounces, in first-person voice, the inefficacy and corruption of the system of regulation that permits the sexual exploitation of vulnerable women to be maintained.

For its part, López Bago's *Carne importada* is set in Buenos Aires at the turn of the century, when Argentina's capital was becoming a major center of international sex trafficking. Given Argentina's open immigration policy in the nineteenth century, the number of European immigrants to the South American nation, mostly Spaniards and Italians, reached its height in the second half of the 1880s (Fernández, *ELB* 217). From 1888 to 1890, the Argentine government even subsidized boat passages for European immigrants, encouraging the entry of "white" women into the country, some of whom would then be sold as prostitutes. Historians, as well as López Bago's own narrator, make note of the affluence of the sex traffickers, given their considerable earnings from international sexual commerce (Barberán Reinares 35; Bastia and vom Hau 477–78; *Carne importada* 158–59). López Bago's female protagonist who, like Flores's character, embarks on a journey from Barcelona to the Americas in search of better living conditions, falls victim precisely to such a trafficker. Agustina, after being raped, is brought to a brothel by her trafficker, Rodolfo; falls ill from the shock of recognizing her condition; and dies at the end of the novel. In spite of the novel's melodramatic plot, the naturalist narrator continuously defends the documentary value of his narrative, affirming that "Hay muchos Rodolfos Fick en Buenos Aires, y el personage no tiene nada de estraordinario" (there are many Rodolfo Ficks in Buenos Aires, and the character is not extraordinary in any way) (169).[10]

Returning to the problem of empire, Lisa Surwillo, in *Monsters by Trade*, has identified slavery as one of the privileged tropes of metropolitan discourse that structured the imperial narrative in significant, if sometimes indirect, ways. The term "white slave trade"—*la trata de blancas*, in Spanish—was coined to distinguish between the trafficking (and forced prostitution) of European women from that of slaves of African descent. While chattel slavery had ended officially in Cuba in 1886, by the time Flores and López Bago published their novels on transatlantic sexual commerce, fin-de-siècle discourses on both sides of the Atlantic established an analogy between the condition of slaves and that of European female sex workers in the Americas, as forms of colonial exploitation linked to the rise of global capitalism. In the words of López Bago's sex trafficker in *Carne importada*, "La trata de negros, no existe; la inmigración la sustituye" (the slave trade does not exist; immigration has replaced it) (138); and, in a similar vein, the Cuban physician Benjamín de Céspedes, in a controversial study published in 1888, a year prior to Flores's *Trata de blancas*, declared: "La prostitución era el complemento natural de la trata: ésta aportaba brazos esclavos y aquella reproducía y propagaba la generación esclava" (Prostitution was the natural complement of the slave trade; the latter provided slave labor and the former reproduced and propagated the generation of slaves) (*La prostitución* 70).[11] By explicitly linking gender oppression to slavery through the gendered and racialized trope of the prostitute's body, both Flores and López Bago expose the imperial subtext of their literary narratives.[12]

How did gender and race intersect in representations of transatlantic sexual commerce in the work of these radical naturalists? And, to restate Ann Laura Stoler's question in a different context, "In what ways were gender inequalities essential to the structure of colonial racism and imperial authority?" (42). Writers on both sides of the Atlantic considered European women who were exported to the New World for sexual slavery to be defective commodities, the dregs of European society—"los detritus de las viejas civilizaciones" (debris of old civilizations), in the words of Enrique José Varona who wrote the prologue for Céspedes's study—that have been further adulterated through their mixture with the "savage races" of Africa and Asia (Céspedes x). López Bago's narrator echoes this commonly held view in *Carne importada*: "[L]a hembra importada en América no es . . . un *producto selecto*, ni mucho menos. Generalmente es lo que se llama *un resto ó deshecho de mercancía*" (the imported female in America is not . . . a *select product*, far from the case. Generally, she is what is called the *leftover or residue of commodity*) (170). The analysis to follow will show how gender, race, and class intersect in the representation of the prostitute's diseased body, as the metaphor of "promiscuity"—quite literally meaning "indiscriminate mixture"—links female sexual deviance to racial mixture and degeneration. As Stoler has noted, colonial control was predicated on the belief in the ability to distinguish between white Europeans and their racial other(s). Within this schema, "provisional relations, based on contested classifications," such as those established by prostitution, were deemed a threat to the very structure of colonial society, as any type of mixture across race and class boundaries had the potential to undermine hierarchies on which colonialism was founded (Stoler 43). Thus, while "white" women may have been imported to the Americas to prevent sexual commerce with racial others, their migrant status, ironically, makes them "less white" in the metropolitan imagination. Moreover, racial purity was also understood to be a precondition of hegemonic masculinity,[13] as men who failed to conform to the norms of ideal masculinity were considered to be degenerate.[14]

While the racial situation in preindependence Cuba at the end of the nineteenth century was different from that of postindependence Argentina, what is noteworthy is the similarity in the use of racialized tropes to represent immigrant prostitutes in the New World, given the influx of European immigrants to both nations during this period. As Tiffany Sippial has noted, prostitution figured prominently among broader national conversations in late-nineteenth-century Cuban society, as it provided "an expedient common referent" for those concerned with defining a nascent Cuban national identity, becoming a trope for capturing class- and race-based anxieties (88).[15] It is not surprising, then, that the prostitute figure was "[p]ortrayed as either a cause or a symptom of colonial degradation" (Sippial 86) by establishing a link between deviant sexuality and racial mixture. According to Céspedes, "la meretriz de los países cálidos" (the prostitute of the warm countries) (153)—that is, the native Argentine ("criolla") prostitute—was characterized by a hysterical temperament that made her prone to what was considered sexual deviance, such as homosexuality. For their part, European prostitutes emigrated from Havana to the brothels in the interior of the island where, according to the physician, "se entregan á todo el mundo: al chino ó al negro" (they deliver themselves over to everyone: to the Chinese or the black man) (155). Interracial sexual relations between prostitutes and their clients were perceived to be a form of miscegenation, which posed a symbolic threat to whiteness, even though procreation was not an actual consequence, in a vast majority of cases. The mere possibility of racial mixture evoked fear in the Cuban cultural imaginary of the *fin-de-siglo*, in spite of the fact that following the official end of the slave trade in 1867 and the arrival of hundreds of thousands of Spanish immigrants to Cuba, the white population was rising significantly in relation to that of Afro-descendants.

Flores's *Trata de blancas* opens with an emblematic scene that foregrounds the role of prostitute as a privileged trope that reflects the Spanish nation's anxieties about imperial loss and racial degeneration at the end of the nineteenth century. As the male narrator wanders through Havana's red light district, he stumbles upon a crowd surrounding the unconscious body of the prostitute Pilar, the protagonist of the novel. Her body lies on the "suelo fangoso" (muddy ground) (74), evoking the image of filth (*fango*)—a frequent metaphor for prostitution in the literary and medical discourse of the period. In the second chapter, Pilar is transported to *la casa de socorro*, where again the narrator's gaze focuses on her body, "tumbada en la mesa, inmóvil" (lying down on the table, motionless) (92). His lengthy description of the prostitute is overtly sexualized, bordering on voyeurism, at the same time as he calls attention to her filthy and diseased body, marked by a scar from a previous injury. Most notably, as Luis Álvarez Castro notes (92n28), the narrator alludes to the symptoms of syphilis visible on the prostitute's body, "algunas manchas rojizas . . . que acaba de descubrir un practicante y cuyas manchas hace notar a su compañero, como podrían hacerlo en un anfiteatro de estudio" (some of the red stains . . . that the physician's assistant has just discovered and to which he calls his partner's attention, as they might do in a dissection hall) (92). As is typical in many of the works of radical naturalism, the gaze of the voyeur becomes indistinguishable from the medicalized gaze of the physician. Moreover, there was a common perception in nineteenth-century Spain, in spite of evidence to the contrary, that syphilis was an American virus, brought back from the New World by the explorers in the fifteenth century (P. Fernández, *Mujer pública* 226). Citing contemporary medical and literary sources, Pura Fernández shows how, in the popular imagination of the period, the "races" raised in the warmer climates of the Americas were deemed to be predisposed to greater sexual permissiveness and promiscuity (*Mujer pública* 226). It is noteworthy, in fact, that the term *race* was used rather loosely to refer to populations that were "othered" by the Europeans, including those of African, Asian, and indigenous descent. The threat of disease, particularly of a sexual nature, and of concomitant racial degeneration, was deemed to originate from spaces outside of the European metropolis.

The metropolitan gaze of Flores's narrator thus racializes prostitution and disease from the outset of the novel. That is to say, the male metropolitan subject submits the prostitute—of all races and ethnicities—to his colonizing gaze by transforming her discursively into the racial, sexual and social other.[16] As he finds himself amid a mixture of races and ethnicities, Flores's narrator, echoing Céspedes's sentiments, suggests that the most "promiscuous" among them are black, mulatto, and Chinese people.[17] Wandering through the infamous street where the brothels are located he exclaims:

"De noche aterra pasar un *placer* de esos: es más peligroso que hacer un viaje de exploración al África" (At night it's frightening to pass by those places of pleasure; it's more dangerous than to go on an exploration trip to Africa) (78), thus racializing deviant sexuality, through its identification with blackness and Africa.[18] A flashback to the protagonist's past drives home the analogy between prostitution and chattel slavery, as Pilar's new madam renames her "Estrella" (196); as we know, it was common practice for slave owners to rename the human commodity that they have purchased.[19] Back in the present moment of narration, the male narrator's gaze quickly turns to the prostitutes' attire, especially to their *pañuelos de Manila* (shawls from Manila) (81), which signal Spain's colonial history.[20] In a subsequent scene, one of the prostitutes refers to Manila as "de donde son los pañuelos y hay mucho dinero" (where the shawls are from and where there is a lot of money) (234), thus establishing an explicit connection between colonialism and capital. In Zaragoza, one of the prostitutes alerts Estrella to the daily arrival of ships to Barcelona from Spain's overseas colonies, such as Havana and Manila, alluding to the circulation of transoceanic capital in the form of the global sex trade. Upon observing the sale of one of her friends to the captain of the ship headed for Havana, she, too, expresses her desire to journey to the New World, believing, like Pardo Bazán's young female protagonist, that in America "se gana mucho dinero y se hace suerte" (you earn a lot of money and make a fortune) (260). As in the case of the historical *indianos,* the desire for upward mobility is a powerful capitalist myth that motivates many of the women aboard the ship to emigrate to the New World; yet, this myth ends up clashing violently with the reality of their transformation into commodities to be sold and discarded, that is, into products of "the gendered economic inequality created, sustained, and normalized by . . . global capitalism" (Barberán Reinares 5).

López Bago's *Carne importada*, likewise, begins by linking prostitution, race, and immigration. In the opening scene the narrator, through the eyes of one of the male officials, is witness to the mass of working-class immigrants, "el curioso espectáculo de los inmigrantes hacinados, en repugnante confusión de razas y sexos" (the curious spectacle of the pack of immigrants, in a repugnant confusion of races and sexes) (25),[21] about to embark on a journey to Argentina. Likewise, upon the female protagonist Agustina's arrival in Buenos Aires, the narrator portrays the city as a space of corruption and promiscuity, where prostitution becomes coterminous with the mixture of races and languages such that

[l]a pureza del habla de Cervantes, violada primero, prostituida después, por gentes venidas de todas partes y entregada así, marchita su belleza, flácidas las carnes á fuerza de recibir golpes y caricias, á los hijos del país, que se abrazaban con júbilo, á la que fue manceba de tantos, no de otra manera que la virilidad de un adolescente, halla ilusion sin gran esfuerzo en cualquier meretriz, idealiza la hembra, y anda enamorándose por los lupanares.

(The purity of Cervantes's language, first violated then prostituted by people who come from all over the world and, with withered beauty and flaccid flesh from blows and caresses, given over to the sons of the country who embraced each other with joy, as concubine, not different from the virile adolescents, who find easy excitement in any prostitute, idealize the female, and go around brothels falling in love.) (41)

Again, the prostitute stands as a gendered and racialized trope identified with imperial decadence, reflected in the defilement and violation of the presumably *castizo* language of the Spanish empire. During the height of the Spanish empire, on both sides of the Atlantic, linguistic *casticismo* was entangled with the notion of racial purity. The association drawn, throughout the novel, between sexual and racial purity—and, conversely, between sexual violation/violence and racial mixture—evinces how, in many colonial contexts, "sexual control has figured into the fixing of racial boundaries per se" (Stoler 45).

The construction of native Argentine identity is naturally bound to diverge from the metropolitan subject's representation of the *criollo* subject in the former colony. As William Acree has noted, Creole identity in nineteenth-century Argentina was understood to be the inverse of the original colonial term, *criollos,* referring to (white) Europeans born in the Americas with their privileged social status. By the second half of the nineteenth century, the term was "stripped of all references to Spain" and, instead, "defined what and who were 'authentically' Argentine . . . and clearly *not* European" (Acree).[22] López Bago, as a Spanish writer living in the Americas, undoubtedly configured his own image of what was autochthonous to the postcolonial nation, based on a metropolitan vision of the "native other," frequently popularized in the *novelas de folletín* (serial novels) of the times.

In this context, the Creole woman was doubly "other" owing to her gender. Like the Orientalized woman of "los países cálidos" (the warm countries) (153) associated with exotic desire in Céspedes's medical treatise, the Creole matron in *Carne importada* who takes Agustina into her brothel is sexualized, racialized, and exoticized.[23] López Bago's narrator calls attention to the matron's "labios sensuales y abultados" (sensual and bulging lips), "la pequeñez andaluza de pies y manos" (the small hands and feet, like the Andalusians),[24] associating these characteristics with her "casta indígena" (indigenous caste) (76). Seeking to expose what he perceives to be the matron's racial impurity beneath the façade of her cosmetically whitened skin, he constructs the following portrait of her: "De la mandíbula inferior saliente, propia del indio, solo quedaba algo acentuada y vigorosa la barbilla, pero con redondeces, que afeminaban, lo crudo de las líneas en el contorno . . . las herencias briosas de aquellas hembras salvajes . . . que se entregaban á los indios en las llanuras y en los bosques" (From the lower jutting jaw, typical of the Indian, only the tip of the chin was somewhat accentuated and vigorous, but with a roundness that feminized the crudeness of the lines on the edges . . . the spirited legacies of those savage females . . . who delivered themselves over to the Indians on the plains and in the forests) (77). Beyond the racial and colonialist subtext of this description, the matron's physical characterization echoes the Italian criminologist Lombroso's portrayal of the physiognomy of the criminal, and thus degenerate, woman, exemplified in the figure of the prostitute.[25] Gender, race, class, and empire intersect once again, as the narrator insists repeatedly on the vulgarity and inauthenticity of the racialized Creole woman, who imitates the "costumbres y modales" (customs and manners) of a European upper class that she has not seen firsthand and knows only indirectly through the French *feuilleton* (82). For native Argentine women to aspire to European status, through the imitation of metropolitan dress and customs, is to "depravar su organismo y emporcar la sangre" (pervert their organism and besmirch their blood) (93) and, in the case of men, to become emasculated. The Creole woman is thus identified with all that is threatening to metropolitan social norms—and, especially, to metropolitan masculinity: "la libertad peligrosa" (dangerous freedom) (91), conspicuous consumption, and sexual deviance.

The Spanish immigrant sex worker in the Americas, for her part, is the object of pathlogization for the naturalist narrator, who goes as far as to suggest that Agustina's "temperamento sanguíneo nervioso con idiosincracia genital" (nervous, hot-blooded temperament with genital idiosyncrasy) has predisposed her to become a rape victim (118). As in many of López Bago's novels, the masculine medical discourse that inscribes the prostitute's diseased mind and body exemplifies the strategy of power that Foucault has famously called the "hysterization of women's bodies" (104). Agustina's "fuerte irritabilidad nerviosa, y una hiperestesia de los sentidos" (strong nervous irritability, and an excessive sensibility) worsen after she becomes fully aware of her moral downfall, and as she lies dying at the end of the novel, she receives the medical diagnosis of "monomania melancólica suicida" (melancholic and suicidal monomania) (274, 278). As we now know, monomania, like hysteria, was one of those catchall medical diagnoses that served to pathologize behaviors—especially of women and of other marginalized subjects—that transgressed social norms. The "hysterical woman," notwithstanding her European origin, is synonymous with the new subaltern subject, reduced to a pleasure machine, a slave for the male consumer within a neocolonial economy: "es la trata, la trata de blancos, completa absoluta; brazos musculosos para las estancias, para las colonias, para el campo, para la tierra; brazos mórbidos y blancos para las bacanales, para la ciudad, para las alcobas" (it's the trade, the white slave trade, complete and absolute; muscular arms for the ranches, for the colonies, for the countryside, for the land; sickly, white arms for the orgies, for the city, for the bedrooms) (141). The narrator's denunciation of the institution of white slavery that exploits women for capital cannot be more unequivocal.

Yet López Bago's denunciation of colonialism in *Carne importada* is ironic in light of the imperial nostalgia that becomes increasingly apparent as the novel progresses.[26] By the end of the novel, Agustina, homeless and suffering from the ravages of illness, has no choice but to accept the patronage of her rapist's parents who, out of remorse for their son's actions, offer to care for the dying woman. In this fashion, López Bago's narrator articulates his neocolonial fantasy, constructing the "American" as the rapist who contaminates the metropolitan woman with disease. Based on his reading of *La tradición nacional* (1888) by the Argentine intellectual and politician Joaquín González, López Bago's narrator shares the writer's fear that the "sacred tradition" bequeathed on the colonial cities by its "illustrious founders" has been forgotten and defiled by the "revolutionary passion" of those who initiated the independence movement (146).[27] For Gónzalez (and, by extension, López Bago's narrator), the colony has the obligation to conserve the legacy of the motherland, which has been handed down to her descendants "en su forma más pura" (in its purest form) (146). That is to say, the Creole revolutionary is cast as the deviant other, who undermines the colonial legacy of the motherland, defiling her with vice and disease. Additionally, Rodolfo, the sex trafficker responsible for Agustina's corruption, is an immigrant of unknown national origin, and is also Jewish: "Supóngase aleman, ruso, húngaro, ó súbdito del Austria, pues de cualquiera de estos orígenes, son en su mayoría, los *caftens*, que regentan las casas de lenocinio" (Suppose that he's German, Russian, Hungarian or citizen of Austria, since the pimps who rule those brothels are for the most part from any of these places of origin) (158). As a foreigner and as a Jew, he is thus doubly marked by otherness.[28]

Finally, the novel's ending drives home the author's imperial nostalgia with a vengeance. As Agustina, "la infeliz espatriada" (unhappy expatriate) (281), finds herself dying in a foreign land, she spends the final moments of her life listening to popular music from her homeland and evoking memories of all that is typically "Spanish": the beauty of the landscape ("los colores del cielo español, los rios de la patria" [the colors of the Spanish sky, the rivers of the homeland] [282]), the popular festivals ("la romería de San Isidro del Campo; las ferias de Sevilla y de Valencia . . . la calle de Alcala en un día de toros" [the pilgrimage of San Isidro; the festivals of Sevilla and Valencia . . . Alcalá Street on a bullfighting day] [282]), and emblematic national spaces, such as the Puerta del Sol and the cathedrals most closely identified with the imagined nation. In spite of the imperial nostalgia, however, the novel presents the female immigrant sex worker's ultimate degradation as a direct product of neocolonial capitalism. It is also important to note that, precisely because of her Spanish/European origin—and her whiteness—her displacement and deviation from the idealized imperial nation, captured in the final pages of the novel, are meant to be all the more tragic.

As in López Bago's novel, the figure of the prostitute in Flores's *Trata de blancas* captures the racial anxieties linked to Spanish colonialism. In one emblematic scene, when Estrella and the other women who have undertaken the transatlantic journey are about to disembark in Havana, one of the men explains their situation to the women, drawing a parallel between (white) sexual slavery and chattel slavery. Before the abolition of the slave trade in Cuba, he asserts, "cogíamos en África negros, por engaños, ofreciéndoles regalos, y los traíamos aquí para venderlos" (we caught those black people in Africa, through deception, offering them gifts, and we brought them here to sell them) (288), adding that while the British beleaguered them for engaging in the slave trade, they were indifferent to the sale of women's bodies. Offended by the comparison with enslaved people of African descent, Estrella responds: "Pero nosotras no somos negras" (but we are not black) (288), affirming her racial superiority as a European subject, in spite of her status as an economically destitute woman who has been exported to the colonies. Notwithstanding Estrella's racist discourse that refuses any identification between herself and the enslaved individuals of African descent, the narrator emphasizes, once again, the economic analogy between the trafficking of immigrant women and the slavery of Afro-descendants, forcibly brought to the New World in the service of imperial capitalism.

Racial anxieties become increasingly prevalent throughout the rest of the novel. Upon disembarking the ship in Havana, what first draws Estrella's attention is the number of black people who are circulating in the public space: "lo que más me chocaba fueron los negros que en gran número circulaban por ellas [las calles]" (what most shocked me were the black people who circulated through the streets in great numbers) (297). We have already seen how the fear of sexual promiscuity is entangled with anxieties about racial mixture. While, officially, brothels in Havana were segregated according to race (Álvarez Castro 322n175), prostitutes and their clients inevitably maintained sexual relations that crossed racial boundaries. The prostitutes in the novel gossip about one of the women among them who secretly meets with a mulatto lover, in spite of the fact that "a la casa aquella no iban los negros ni los mulatos" (neither black people nor mulattos went to that house) (322). Estrella herself attributes her physical and moral degeneration to her contact with racial others and, in particular, to relations she maintains with those of African descent. In other words, the dominant metropolitan discourse of the narrator racializes the Spanish prostitute, in spite of her European origin, precisely due to her perceived contamination by the racial other—or by those who are racially ambiguous. For example, she describes her physically abusive lover as a mulatto, while confessing at the same time that "aún no estaba yo muy familiarizada con los negros y mulatos y no pude distinguir a qué raza pertenecía" (I was not yet very familiarized with the blacks and mulattos and could not discern to which race he belonged) (325). Her statement not only reveals the constructedness and fluidity of race, but also the negative cultural associations evoked by the mere idea of racial admixture. Given that the novel represents sexual and racial "contamination" as coterminous, once contaminated—both literally, by syphilis, and symbolically, through relations with the racial "other"—Estrella is forever stigmatized as both physically diseased and morally impure. Marked as a threat to both whiteness and idealized femininity, her body becomes the target of social surveillance and medical intervention.

At the end of the novel, when Estrella is taken to the Hospital de Higiene for syphilitic patients, notorious for its prison-like environment and unhygienic conditions, the omniscient narrator who resumes the narration repeatedly calls attention to the unbearable stench of the hospital ("la fetidez que despiden aquella salas" [the stench that those rooms emitted]; "inmundas escenas de esos hospitales" [filthy scenes of those hospitals] [378]) and, especially, the prostitute's diseased, foul-smelling flesh.[29] Although the association between the prostitute and the putrid flesh of the corpse has been a common leitmotif throughout the ages (Corbin 212, cited in Fuentes), the naturalist author takes this identification to an extreme, comparing Estrella's body explicitly to that of animals killed in the slaughterhouse adjacent to the hospital. The dehumanized image of the prostitute, portrayed as "aquel trozo de carne" (that piece of flesh) (385), recalls the moment on board the ship when the sailors referred to Estrella and the other prostitutes as "carne" (flesh) (277), suggesting that animal and human flesh are equivalent in their status as commodities to be sold, consumed, and discarded as waste. Of course, the title of the novel itself calls attention to the commodification—and, hence, objectification—of "foreign" flesh.

Flores brings to light the interpenetration of gender, sexuality, and race by establishing a metonymic link between the prostitute and the two men of African descent who will transport Estrella's cadaver to the medical school to be autopsied by the students. Not only does medical science strip the prostitute's body of all humanity by reducing it to "solo trozos de lo que fue" (only pieces of what it was) (387), but the metaphor of the autopsy also represents the naturalist writer's own attempt to restore social order by imposing scientific discourse on the deceased and decomposed female body. Finally, *Trata de blancas* ends with an epilogue in which an omniscient narrator informs us that the priest who tended to the dying prostitute sells Estrella's ring—her only remaining possession—for thirty *duros* and brings this sum back to her parents in Aragón. This meager sum is used to bury Estrella's mother who has also just died. Instead of bringing capital back to the metropolis for reinvestment, the emigrant woman, having invested her body—her only capital—in the colonies, fails to yield any economic return for the decaying empire.

Given the literary format of these works, we need to ask ourselves how López Bago and Flores address the problem of rendering in aesthetic form the sexual exploitation of the "subaltern" woman,[30] particularly when the narrative is focalized through the perspective of the metropolitan male subject. As Laura Barberán Reinares observes in her study of sex trafficking in postcolonial literature, "The danger of turning the trauma endured by rape victims/survivors into an erotic spectacle or an aestheticized tableau to be admired from a safe distance poses a challenge to the artist" (11). Examining these novels within the literary project of radical naturalism in Spain, we saw how the figure of the European female sex worker in the Americas served as a trope to reflect cultural anxieties about gender, race, and empire during a period of national instability and imperial crisis. Do these novels, then, ultimately do no more than to fetishize the European/white prostitute figure in an attempt to contain fears generated by subaltern subjects, especially lower-class women and the racial other? I have argued elsewhere that in López Bago's prostitution novels—and I maintain that *Carne importada* is no exception—there is a constant tension between the disciplinary function of naturalist discourse, which is to contain and eradicate the social ulcer ("llaga social") of prostitution, on the one hand, and, on the other, naturalism's voyeuristic tendencies that unwittingly transform the prostitute's body into an eroticized spectacle for the male gaze ("Taming"). In the case of *Carne importada*, it is the colonizing gaze of a metropolitan male subject. In other words, López Bago's prostitution novels presume a reader identified with a metropolitan male gaze that fetishizes the subaltern female other and sensationalizes sexual exploitation and violence, although presumably for the purpose of social critique and political denunciation. Undoubtedly, the male author's outrage is a response to the violation of innocent, white/Western European womanhood (moreover, these are very young women), recalling Estrella's protest in Flores's *Trata de blancas* that the Spanish women did not deserve to be sold like slaves, because they were "not black."

Whereas Flores's narrator, in contrast to that of López Bago, presumably gives voice to the female protagonist, who addresses her story to another female character, in the final chapter of *Trata de blancas*, it is ultimately the male physician, identified with the naturalist narrator, who leaves us with the image of the prostitute's pathologized body. For the physician, who is typically an alter ego of the naturalist writer, Estrella's body quite literally becomes an object of medical study, as he brings his gynecology students (understood, in that period, to be all male) to examine her diseased body in the Hospital of Hygiene, with the following introduction: "Grande ejemplar para estudiar el estado patológico de una mujer perdida" (great specimen to study the pathological state of a fallen woman) (380). Given the objectification of the prostitute's body under the medicalized male gaze, in these circumstances, it is difficult even to address the issue of agency of these economically destitute women who have been forcibly displaced. These novels by radical naturalists are, therefore, distinct from other works of nineteenth-century realist fiction—including those by canonical male novelists—that suggest the possibility of resistance and agency for the prostitute, especially those who actively choose street prostitution over other more "traditional" social arrangements, such as involuntary marriage or concubinage. Realist characters, such as Galdós's Fortunata and Isidora Rufete and the prostitute in Pardo Bazán's short story "Champagne," show resistive potential. However, these prostitutes do not leave the national space. López Bago's and Flores's metropolitan discourse quite deliberately perpetuates the perception of sexual danger in the (former) colonies (Barberán Reinares 26), and Western European prostitutes exported to the Americas, who engage in (social and sexual) intercourse with the racial other, become a convenient repository for this fear.

While both Flores and López Bago denounce the institution of international sexual commerce that emerged from colonialism and reaps profit from the exploitation of women, the figure of the prostitute, in the end, is reduced to a trope of otherness that captures anxieties around gender, race, and loss of empire (past and future) in the fin-de-siècle from a metropolitan perspective.[31] In both novels, the prostitute poses a threat to "racial purity and cultural identity in all forms" (McClintock 48), by rendering ambiguous the boundaries between metropolis and colony, while also transgressing racial and class boundaries.[32] Having been cast out from the metropolis as the "dregs" of civilization, these women continue to occupy a marginal—as well as ambiguous—space in (post)colonial society. As we have seen, the colonizing male gaze in these novels casts the prostitute as the embodiment of promiscuity and disease identified with racial degeneration—and, more generally, with the decline of civilization. European prostitutes in the colonies could, therefore, never really become subjects of discourse. Ann McClintock has observed in *Imperial Leather* that in a neocolonialist setting where "[b]ody boundaries were felt to be dangerously permeable and demanding continual purification," efforts to control women's sexuality arose from "acute anxiety about the desecration of sexual boundaries and the consequences that racial contamination had for white male control of progeny, property, and power" (47). In the end, both López Bago and Flores show that their denunciation of transatlantic sex trafficking is really about asserting the "male imperial body politic" (McClintock 47) in the neocolonial setting by controlling representations of "subaltern" women's sexuality.

Notes

1. Examples of book-length studies that foreground the problem of Spanish imperialism in late-nineteenth-century literature and culture include Alda Blanco's

Cultura y conciencia imperial en la España del siglo XIX (2012), Susan Martin-Márquez's *Disorientations: Spanish Colonialism in Africa and the Performance of Identity* (2008), Lisa Surwillo's *Monsters by Trade: Slave Traffickers in Modern Spanish Literature and Culture* (2014), Michael Ugarte's *Africans in Europe: The Culture of Exile and Emigration from Equatorial Guinea to Spain* (2010), and William Acree and Akiko Tsuchiya's *Empire's End: Transnational Connections in the Hispanic World* (2016). Mary Coffey and Joyce Tolliver have books in progress on the literary representations of Spanish colonialism in the Americas and the Philippines, respectively. In addition, the works of the late cultural historian Christopher Schmidt-Nowara and Josep M. Fradera have laid the groundwork for the study of empire, race, and slavery in context of the Hispanic Atlantic.

2. According to Amando de Miguel, 174,000 Spanish nationals emigrated to the New World between 1888 and 1900, a figure that grew to 400,000 between 1901 and 1910. These are official figures that include only registered passengers.

3. To point out this myth is not to imply that all emigrants to the New World returned to Spain having acquired wealth. In fact, many impoverished inhabitants of the rural north who departed for the New World with hopes of acquiring wealth were unable to return home, due to the lack of resources; many fell ill or died in the Americas. Many writers of the late nineteenth century, including Clarín, Pardo Bazán, and Pereda, took an anti-emigration stance in their literary works, often to the point of satirizing the delusion of the emigrant who abandons the homeland to "hacer las Américas" (do/make the Americas). For studies on the *indiano* figure in nineteenth-century Spanish literature and culture, see Davis, Delgado, J. Fernández, and Surwillo (129–64).

4. The use of the verb *bajarse* not only suggests the physical act of "stooping down" to grab the gold, but also the symbolic descent into prostitution in order to attain this object.

5. Victims of sex trafficking were, of course, not limited to European women. A parallel, if not identical, phenomenon at the turn of the century in the United States was its domestic slave trade industry, whereby the upper South bred slaves of African descent to supply the lower South with labor for their plantations and, later, for railroad construction (Smithers 63–82). I thank Michelle Murray for this reference.

6. For a more detailed account of the public debates surrounding white slavery in fin-de-siècle Spain, see P. Fernández (*Mujer pública* 221–30). For historical context on white slavery in Argentina and Cuba, respectively, see Guy and Sippial.

7. The widespread problem of white slavery in Europe not only captured the literary imagination, but also the attention of visual artists, such as the Valencian Joaquín Sorolla in Spain and Henri de Toulouse-Lautrec in France. Sorolla's *Trata de blancas* (1894) offers a starkly realistic portrayal of four young prostitutes sleeping in a train under the watchful eye of their Madam. Toulouse-Lautrec's *Salon de la Rue des Moulins*, created the same year, represents a group of prostitutes (again,

under the watchful eye of their Madam) in a Parisian brothel that the artist was said to have frequented. The prostitute in the foreground of the painting presumably emigrated to Argentina after being sold to a trafficker from Buenos Aires (Young).

8. According to Pura Fernández, López Bago's own experience with emigrants during his transatlantic voyage from Spain to Argentina inspired his novel (*Eduardo López Bago* 57). For his part, Luis Álvarez Castro explains the personal and political circumstances that prompted Flores to emigrate to Cuba (Introduction 15–16).

9. For a more extensive study of "radical naturalism," especially in relation to the literary market, see Pura Fernández (*Eduardo López Bago*).

10. I have maintained the original orthography and accentuation of López Bago's text, based on the edition I am using.

11. Céspedes was the former physician for Havana's Special Hygiene Section and wrote the first large-scale study of prostitution in the Cuban capital; his objective was to explain the root causes of prostitution in Havana and its impact on Cuban national identity. Like the two novelists considered here, he too could be situated in the transatlantic space, as he was a European-educated physician who returned to his native Cuba to serve as a medical inspector for Havana's Special Hygiene Section. As indicated earlier, Flores, a native of Spain, lived for an extended period of time in Cuba; López Bago, for his part, emigrated to Argentina and also spent time in Uruguay, Mexico, Cuba, and Puerto Rico.

12. As Álvarez Castro demonstrates, the crisis of gender (particularly of masculinity) in the novel is a political allegory of the struggle between metropolis (Spain) and colony (Cuba): "a twofold, antithetical nation-building process in which women forced into prostitution were conceptualized as either symbols of colonial oppression or symptoms of the metropolis's moral superiority, according to the divergent views of Cuban separatists and Spanish loyalists" ("Transatlantic Sex Trafficking" 32).

13. For a definition of the concept of "hegemonic masculinity," see Connell; and Connell and Messerschmidt. This term refers to a masculinity that "occupies the hegemonic position in a given pattern of gender relations," legitimizing the subordination of women (*Masculinities* 76). According to Connell, "Hegemony is likely to be established only if there is some correspondence between cultural ideal and institutional power"; however, it represents a normative ideal that few real men actually attain (*Masculinities* 77–79).

14. For an extensive analysis of the discourse of degeneration in relation to race and nation in fin-de-siècle Spain, see Campos et al. These authors note how discourses produced in response to the 1898 crisis attributed imperial loss to "la degeneración y pérdida de vigor del pueblo español" (degeneration and loss of strength of the Spanish people) (161). In the Cuban context, Céspedes affirms that patriotism that led to national glory was the work of the (presumably) racially pure masculine elite, "la más sana en sus costumbres, menos enervada por los vicios, mas viril y sin mezclas, por el contacto de otras razas" (the healthiest in their customs,

least weakened by vice, most virile and without mixture through contact with other races) (73).

15. Racial fears dominated the Cuban imaginary since the anticolonial insurrection of enslaved peoples in the French colony of St. Domingue, which began in 1791 and culminated in Haiti's independence in 1804. Even the insurgents in the anticolonial movement in Cuba were reluctant, during the first War of Independence, to incorporate those of African descent into the revolutionary movement, particularly since the slavery system was fundamental to the maintenance of the sugar plantations, on which the Cuban economy was based (Ferrer, "Cuban Slavery"; *Insurgent Cuba* 53).

16. As Chandra Mohanty has shown, discursive colonization is not only entangled with political and economic colonization, but also enables the latter to be sustained even after the official end of the colonial era (73–74).

17. Pura Fernández suggests that Flores entered into an implicit dialogue with Céspedes's treatise, from a "medical-social" perspective (*Mujer pública* 227).

18. Asians, likewise, are continuously stereotyped as the degenerate race; the novel depicts the Chinese as a slothful and dirty community of immigrants, many of them addicted to smoking opium (82). This stereotype, again, echoes Céspedes who, on visiting a *fumadero chino* (Chinese smoking den), portrays Asians as a "raza degenerada . . . como una plaga vegetante de hongos en un organismo podrido" (degenerate race . . . like a growing infestation of fungi in a rotten organism) (198), "una raza muerta para la civilización humana" (a dead race for human civilization) (202). It should be noted that, for the Cuban physician, all Asians are "chinos" (Chinese), whether they are from Macao, Hanoi, or Manila.

19. Subsequently, when Estrella becomes the lover of the hustler El Inglés, she is renamed, yet once again: this time, as *Icuaá* (359). Estrella's racialization through this seemingly indigenous name is significant, in light of the fact that in the second half of the nineteenth century, the Argentine state waged a series of extermination campaigns against populations of indigenous descent, the most famous of them being the "Conquest of the Desert," led by the War Minister Julio Roca in the 1870s (Hasbrouck). The extermination of the indigenous populations coincided with a state policy that promoted European immigration in order to "whiten" the population. For an analysis of Argentina's state racism and migration policies during this period, see Bastia and vom Hau, and Trinchero. One of the discursive strategies used by the state to wage a war against its own population groups was to define these subjects as foreigners (Trinchero 131). The racialization of Estrella and of the other prostitutes (including native Argentines) in the novel reflects precisely such a strategy; even those who weren't actually "foreign" were transformed discursively into "foreigners." For more on the history of indigenous genocide in Argentina, see Delrio et al.

20. As is well known, the Manila shawl was a foreign product, which originated in China and was transported to the Philippines by the Chinese merchants, only then to be "discovered" by the Spaniards (Rodríguez Collado).

21. One might wonder what groups formed a part of this "racial mixture," given that the immigrants on the boat were presumably European. Yet it is well known that a great majority of immigrants to Argentina originated from southern European countries, particularly Italy and Spain, whose inhabitants were not considered fully white (Bastia and vom Hau 479). Likewise, Eastern Europeans, particularly those of Jewish origin, were often cast as racial others in the discourses of the period (see Note 28). It was no coincidence that those marked by racial otherness were also amongst the more impoverished communities of Europe, those who had the greatest incentive to emigrate to the Americas.

22. I am retaining these connotations of the word *criollo/a*, as referring to native-born Argentines, when used in this context, and have translated it into English as "Creole." However, I am aware that the term was used differently in different contexts.

23. In Pura Fernández's words: "La tipología prostibularia también configura el personaje de la apasionada criolla, de la mujer con ascendencia americana que . . . representa a una mujer de sublime hermosura, cuya sexualidad devoradora se explica por su naturaleza americana. No hay mejor modelo literario de la mujer infame, de la *hembra depravada*, que esta tipología de la criolla seductora, fisiología movida por la ambición y el sexo desmedidos que ya incendiaba las páginas de las novelas folletinescas por entregas" (The typology of the prostitute also configures the character of the passionate Creole, the woman of American origin who . . . represents a woman of sublime beauty, whose devouring sexuality is explained by her American nature. There is no other better literary model of the dishonored woman, the depraved woman, than this typology of the seductive Creole woman, a physiology driven by excessive ambition and sex, which was already inflaming the pages of melodramatic serial novels) (*Mujer pública* 225–26).

24. As we well know, since Romanticism Andalusia has been represented in the popular imagination as Spain's orientalized "other," identified with Africa.

25. The influence of Italian criminology, and of Lombroso in particular, became widespread in Spain in the late 1880s and the 1890s.

26. For an analysis of imperial anxiety in these two works, see Álvarez-Castro ("Transatlantic Sex Trafficking"). López Bago's unabashedly colonialist stance becomes ever more apparent in his 1895 novel, *El separatista*, published in Cuba. The novel, which presents a flashback to the years of Cuba's first independence war (Ten Years' War of 1868–1878), is narrated from the standpoint of 1895, when the second war of independence broke out, coinciding also with the year in which López Bago moved from Argentina to Cuba. The novel recounts the vicissitudes of the male protagonist Lico, a separatist in favor of Cuba's independence, whose sickly, degenerate, and feminized body symbolizes the nascent Cuban nation and a threat to the Spanish empire. In this context, prostitution represented the fear not only of disease and contagion, but also of racial and class mixture, which was linked to the degeneration of the Spanish "race." The "hysterical," feminized male, in fact, became synonymous

with the Creole subject. In both of López Bago's "American" novels, prostitution is therefore a key trope through which imperial decadence becomes gendered as feminine, echoing metropolitan discourses of the fin-de-siècle. The gendering of disease and degeneration is evident in the feminization of the male bodies that the female sex workers have infected with syphilis: "los que salvaban el cuerpo, veíanse enervados, faltos de energía, extinguidos los alientos viriles, emporcada la sangre, perfumados y fláccidos los músculos en plena afeminación y en completa miseria" (those who saved their bodies saw themselves weakened, deprived of energy, their manly breath extinguished, their blood besmirched, their perfumed and flaccid muscles in full effeminacy and in complete misery) (140).

27. Álvarez-Castro, likewise, reads this family relationship as an imperial allegory, as the nostalgia for "the integrity of Argentina's old (i.e., colonial) days," set against the "immorality of the young, independent republic" ("Transatlantic Sex Trafficking" 39).

28. While there was, in fact, a significant number of Jewish sex traffickers in major transit points from Europe, especially Eastern Europe, to Latin America in the fin-de-siècle period, several critics have pointed out the tendency to exaggerate their numbers and to "orientalize them as problematic aliens," whereas the French, who also had an extensive network of traffickers, did not receive the same treatment (Las; Barberán Reinares 14, 28). As Barberán Reinares notes, many Jews were experiencing extreme discrimination—and poverty, as a consequence of their treatment (28). That López Bago would implicitly hold the Jews responsible for the ills of imperial capitalism that led to the trafficking of women evinces his complicity with anti-Semitism, prevalent in Spain since the expansion of Christianity in the Iberian Peninsula.

29. These images evoke Zola's naturalistic portrayal of the famous French courtesan Nana in the final scene of the homonymous novel, published in 1880. Nana, too, ends up as a stinking corpse, "a pile of blood and pus dumped on a pillow, a shovelful of rotten flesh ready for the bone-yard, her whole face covered in festering sores . . . her left eye entirely submerged in discharging ulcers, the other one a sunken, fly-blown black hole" (425).

30. I refer to the victims of international sex trafficking as "subaltern" subjects, in spite of their European origin, given their marginalization within metropolitan power structures, their exploitation within a (neo)colonial economy, and their identification with the global South.

31. While Argentina, unlike Cuba, has been an independent republic for more than seventy years, the imperial legacy, as demonstrated in this essay, persisted far beyond the independence of the majority of Spanish American nations in the early nineteenth century, as these writers wrote from an "awareness of a failed imperial project on the eve of its total dissolution" (Álvarez Castro, "Transatlantic Slave Trafficking" 31). The specter of colonial loss, past and future, loomed large in the imagination of metropolitan writers, especially in the late 1880s and 1890s,

as the insurrection of the revolutionaries (including many Afro-descendants) gained ground in Cuba and would culminate in the Second Independence War (1895–98).

32. In McClintock's words: "Women who were ambiguously placed on the imperial divide"—and she includes prostitutes among them—"were especially fetishized as dangerously ambiguous and contaminating" (48).

Works Cited

Acree, William G. Jr. "The Creole Circus and Popular Entertainment in 19th Century Argentina and Uruguay." *Oxford Research Encyclopedias: Latin American History*; http://latinamericanhistory.oxfordre.com/view/10.1093/acrefore/9780199366439.001.0001/acrefore-9780199366439-e-104; accessed July 20, 2017.

Álvarez Castro, Luis. "Transatlantic Sex Trafficking and Imperial Anxiety in Nineteenth-century Spanish Fiction: *Trata de blancas* (1889) and *Carne importada* (1891)." *Hispanic Review*, vol. 86, no. 1, 2018, pp. 25–44.

———. Introduction. *Trata de blancas (novela social)*, by Eugenio Antonio Flores. Institución Fernando el Católico (CSIC), 2014. 7–52.

Barberán Reinares, Laura. *Sex Trafficking in Post Colonial Literature: Transnational Narratives from Joyce to Bolaño*. Routledge, 2015.

Bastia, Tanja, and Matthias vom Hau. "Migration, Race and Nationhood in Argentina." *Journal of Ethnic and Migration Studies*, vol. 40, no. 3, pp. 475–92.

Blanco, Alda. *Cultura y conciencia imperial en la España del siglo XIX*. Publicacions de la U de València, 2012.

———. "El fin del imperio español y la generación del 98: nuevas aproximaciones." *Hispanic Research Journal*, vol. 4, no. 1, Feb. 2003, pp. 3–18.

Campos Marín, Ricardo, et al. *Los ilegales de la naturaleza. Medicina y degeneracionismo en la España de la Restauración (1876–1923)*. CSIC, 2000.

Céspedes, Benjamín de. *La prostitución en la ciudad de la Habana*. Establecimiento Tipográfico O'Reilly, 1888.

Connell, R. W. *Masculinities*. 2nd ed. U of California P, 2005.

———, and James W. Messerschmidt. "Hegemonic Masculinity: Rethinking the Concept." *Gender and Society* vol. 19, no. 6, Dec. 2005, pp. 829–59.

Corbin, Alain. "Commercial Sexuality in Nineteenth-Century France: A System of Images and Regulations." *The Making of the Modern Body: Sexuality and Society in the Nineteenth Century*, edited by Catherine Gallagher and Thomas Laqueur, U of California P, 1987, pp. 209–19.

Davis, Stacy Lynn. "'Hacer las Américas' es hacer el hombre: (Re)Constructing Spanish Masculinities in the Indianos of Benito Pérez Galdós and Emilia Pardo Bazán." Diss., Washington U in St. Louis, 2016.

Delgado, Luisa Elena. "El lugar del salvaje: Galdós y la representación del indiano." *Homenaje a Alfonso Armas Ayala*, vol. 2, Ediciones del Cabildo de Gran Canaria, 2000. 303–14.

Delrio, Walter, et al. "Discussing Indigenous Genocide in Argentina: Past, Present, and Consequences of Argentinean State Policies toward Native Peoples." *Genocide Studies and Prevention: An International Journal*, vol. 5, no. 2, 2010, pp. 138–59.

Fernández, James. "America Is in Spain: A Reading of Clarín's 'Boroña.'" *Bridging the Atlantic*, edited by Marina Pérez de Mendiola, State U of New York P, 1995, pp. 31–46.

Fernández, Pura. *Eduardo López Bago y el naturalismo radical: la novela y el mercado literario en el siglo XIX*. Rodopi, 1995.

———. *Mujer pública y vida privada: del arte eunuco a la novela lupanaria*. Tamesis, 2008.

Ferrer, Ada. "Cuban Slavery and Atlantic Antislavery." *Slavery and Antislavery in Spain's Atlantic Empire*, edited by Josep M. Fradera and Christopher Schmidt-Nowara, Berghahn, 2013, pp. 134–57.

———. *Insurgent Cuba: Race, Nation, and Revolution, 1868–1898*. U of North Carolina P, 1999.

Flores, Eugenio Antonio. *Trata de blancas (novela social)*, edited by Luis Álvarez Castro, Institución Fernando el Católico (CSIC), 2014.

Foucault, Michel. *The History of Sexuality: Volume I: An Introduction*. Translated by Robert Hurley, Random House, 1980.

Fradera, Josep M., and Christopher Schmidt-Nowara, eds. *Slavery & Antislavery in Spain's Atlantic Empire*. Berghahn Books, 2013.

Fuentes, Teresa. *Visions of Filth: Deviancy and Social Control in the Novels of Galdós*. Liverpool UP, 2003.

Guy, Donna J. *White Slavery and Mothers Alive and Dead: The Troubled Meeting of Sex, Gender, Public Health, and Progress in Latin America*. U of Nebraska P, 2000.

Hasbrouck, Alfred. "The Conquest of the Desert." *The Hispanic American Historical Review*, vol. 15, no. 2, 1935, pp. 195–228.

Las, Nelly. "White Slavery." *Jewish Women's Archive*; https://jwa.org/encyclopedia/article/white-slavery; accessed July 18, 2017.

López Bago, Eduardo. *Carne importada*. Urbano Rivero "La Maravilla Literaria," 1891.

———. *El separatista*. Edited by Francisco Gutiérrez Carbajo, Castalia, 1997.

Martin-Márquez, Susan. *Disorientations: Spanish Colonialism in Africa and the Performance of Identity*. Yale UP, 2008.

McClintock, Anne. *Imperial Leather: Race, Gender and Sexuality in the Colonial Contest*. Routledge, 1995.

Miguel, Amando de. "La emigración española a América a finales del siglo XIX y principio del XX." *Los Cuadernos del Norte*, vol. 2, 1984, pp. 7–16.

Mohanty, Chandra. "Under Western Eyes: Feminist Scholarship and Colonial Discourses." *Third World Women and the Politics of Feminism*, edited by Chandra Talpade Mohanty, Ann Russo, and Lourdes Torres, Indiana UP, 1991, pp. 51–80.

Pardo Bazán, Emilia. "Las medias rojas." *Biblioteca Virtual Miguel de Cervantes*; http://www.cervantesvirtual.com/obra-visor/cuentos-de-la-tierra--0/html/dcb42d82-2dc6-11e2-b417-000475f5bda5_2.html#I_1_; accessed July 20, 2017.

Rodríguez Collado, Mercedes. "La pieza del mes: mantón de Manila, 1850–1860." *Museo del Romanticismo*, febrero 2012; http://www.mecd.gob.es/dms/museos/mromanticismo/colecciones/pieza-trimestre/2012/piezames-febrero-2012/piezames-febrero-2012.pdf; accessed July 18, 2017.

Schmidt-Nowara, Christopher. *Empire and Antislavery: Spain, Cuba, and Puerto Rico, 1833–1874*. U of Pittsburgh P, 1999.

———. *Slavery, Freedom, and Abolition in Latin America and the Atlantic World*. U of New Mexico P, 2011.

Sippial, Tiffany A. *Prostitution, Modernity, and the Making of the Cuban Republic, 1840–1920*. The U of North Carolina P, 2013.

Smithers, Gregory D. *Slave Breeding: Sex, Violence, and Memory in African American History*. U P of Florida, 2012.

Stoler, Ann Laura. *Carnal Knowledge and Imperial Power: Race and the Intimate in Colonial Rule*. U of California P, 2002.

Surwillo, Lisa. *Monsters by Trade: Slave Traffickers in Modern Spanish Literature and Culture*. Stanford UP, 2014.

Trinchero, Héctor Hugo. "The Genocide of Indigenous Peoples in the Formation of the Argentine Nation-State." *Journal of Genocide Research*, vol. 8, no. 2, 2006, pp. 121–35.

Tsuchiya, Akiko. "Taming the Prostitute's Body: Desire, Knowledge, and the Naturalist Gaze in López Bago's *La prostituta* Series." *Marginal Subjects: Gender and Deviance in Fin-de-siècle Spain*, U of Toronto P, 2011, pp. 162–90.

———, and William G. Acree Jr., eds. *Empire's End: Transnational Connections in the Hispanic World*. Vanderbilt UP, 2016.

Ugarte, Michael. *Africans in Europe: The Culture of Exile and Emigration from Equatorial Guinea to Spain*. U of Illinois P, 2010.

Young, Richard. "Urban Identity: Buenos Aires and the French Connection." *Relocating Identities in Latin American Cultures*, edited by Elizabeth Montes Garcés, U of Calgary P, 2007, pp. 35–54.

Zola, Émile. *Nana*. Translated by Douglas Parmée, Oxford UP, 1998.

PART II

RACE, PERFORMANCE, AND COLONIAL IDEOLOGIES

4

A Black Woman Called *Blanca la extranjera* in Faustina Sáez de Melgar's *Los miserables* (1862–63)

ANA MATEOS

Introduction

Debates about slavery and emancipation crucially structured nineteenth-century discourse about the role of women in society. However, in a departure both from the early examples set by Spanish Romantic women authors and from Anglo-American women's activism in the mid-nineteenth century, in Spain, the situation of women was not generally viewed as comparable to the plight of slaves, on the grounds that Christianity had already liberated them from bondage (Burguera 173–79). Even when facing opposition and criticism for taking on public roles, as in their involvement in the abolitionist movement, Spanish women avoided "the use of images of bondage" to illustrate the social constraints that they were slowly overcoming (Partzsch 873). The idea that women had overcome slavery, it has been argued, "explain[ed] away feminist demands for equal political rights and access to the productive sector" (Aldaraca 63). One might add that it also helped to suppress discussion of women's marriage rights, that is, their ability to choose their husbands, as well as their physical vulnerability and defenselessness within marriage. The lack of marriage rights not only involved a deprivation of freedom regarding choice or action, but fundamentally invoked the largely unspoken reality of women's lack of ownership of their own bodies in marriage. In *Touching Liberty*, whose study of the intersection of abolitionist and feminist discourses will be central to this essay, Karen Sánchez-Eppler observes that, though widespread, women's lack of ownership of their own bodies was also a topic mostly avoided by nineteenth-century Anglo-American feminist activists. As an exception, the renowned American abolitionist and feminist Lucy Stone wrote in 1858 that "it is very little to me to have the right to vote, to own property, etc. if I may not keep my body and its uses, in my absolute right. Not one wife in a thousand can do that now" (qtd. in Sánchez-Eppler 23).

Despite this widespread reluctance to invoke the slave analogy, some post-Romantic nineteenth-century Spanish writers did characterize bourgeois metropolitan women in marriage in terms of slavery and thereby offered, in addition, an indirect but unmistakable critique of Spain's maintenance of slavery in its remaining overseas territories. For example, in his article "Economía y amor" (1879), Leopoldo Alas (1852–1901), author of the well-known naturalist novel *La Regenta* (1884–85), illustrates forced marriage by describing bourgeois women having to marry old *indianos*. He uses the example of "Fúcar" (301), the famous *negrero* (slave trader) of realist writer Benito Pérez Galdós's (1843–1920) novels, to suggest the slave analogy. Similarly, in *El deber cumplido* (1875), the writer, editor and activist, Faustina Sáez de Melgar (1834–1895) tells the story of a young woman forced to marry an old Spanish *indiano* who has recently returned from Cuba, in order to pay her father's debts. Several years earlier, Sáez de Melgar published *Los miserables* (1862–63), a novel that, as I propose in this essay, deploys the slave analogy through its female protagonist, Alejandrina, as a critique of both women's situation in marriage and slavery.[1]

Such an alignment of abolitionist and feminist concerns is reflective of Sáez de Melgar's lifelong commitment to the rights of both women and slaves. Though often categorized within the conservative group of women writers labeled "escritoras isabelinas" (isabelline writers)[2] or "escritoras virtuosas" (virtuous writers), regarded as instrumental in the construction of the traditionalist ideology of domesticity during the nineteenth century, Sáez de Melgar also actively sought to reform the situation of middle-class women by defending their access to the workforce and to education.[3] In recent years, she has increasingly received attention from critics for her role in abolitionism, as a member of the *Sección de Señoras de la Sociedad Abolitionista* (Ladies' Division of the Abolitionist Society) founded in 1865, as editor of her own periodical, *La Violeta* (1862–66), and as a fictional writer. As these studies have shown, while her social activism did not involve the participation of any African descendants, thereby relegating them to their status as passive recipients of white women's actions, her works of fiction nevertheless allowed for a more inclusive vision.[4]

Falling within the genre of the *folletín social*, a style of melodramatic novel that flourished during the mid-century in Spain, *Los miserables* combines an approach to social conflict inspired by Christian and utopian values, and typical of earlier Romanticism, with a descriptive style characteristic of an emerging realist movement. Like many *folletines*, *Los miserables* was first published in serial format, and it presents an improbable story full of surprising plot twists, Manichean moral dualism, and the possibility of redemption.[5] Originally born in Brazil, the protagonist Alejandrina moved to Madrid as an infant. Her mother, the *condesa de Paraná* (countess of Parana), was a Brazilian woman of color, while her father, also Brazilian, was white-skinned.[6] They went to Spain to inherit the titles of Marquise and Marquis of Blancarosa as well as properties bequeathed to them by a late relative of Alejandrina's father.[7] Soon thereafter, at the beginning of the first wave of Carlist wars (1833–1840), both of them were killed and had their titles and properties stolen by the assassins, Cristina Guanter, her husband Álvaro López (who became the new Marquise and Marquis of Blancarosa), Fray Severo, and Tragabombas. Alejandrina, twelve at the time and fearing for her life, fled Madrid in 1834 and, with the help of a young friar, Fray Benigno, returned to Brazil, where she took possession of the family's diamond mines, but then spent many of the following years in India doing missionary work.

Fifteen years later, in 1849, Alejandrina, now a young woman, returns to Spain with her cousin Lucas Mendoza and Fray Benigno to recover her aristocratic title and her property, and to root out her parents' assassins. She occupies the most luxurious palace in the center of Madrid and exhibits great lavishness. Going by the enigmatic name of "Blanca la extranjera" (Blanca the foreigner), she paints her originally white skin black to disguise herself as she secretly plans her revenge.[8] Her cousin also adopts blackface, but only in order to escape recognition by his estranged wife Guillermina. Occasionally, Alejandrina also wears the costume of a *reina negra* (black queen). While in blackface, an appearance that recalls her mother, Alejandrina also donates large amounts of her money to charity to help ameliorate the conditions of the working class. As if the plot were not complicated enough already, Alejandrina reveals that she is actually a slave to a man.[9] She explains to Guillermina that while she was traveling in India with her supporter Fray Benigno, she had to marry the chief of an indigenous tribe in India in exchange for the freedom of the friar, who had fallen captive to them. The narrator and Alejandrina describe the Indians, using imperialist categories, as primitive and uncivilized *salvajes* (savages). She does not provide much detail of her life in the Indian tribe, but she complains of being trapped in an unhappy marriage, subjected to the mandates of a man she does not love, and characterizes herself as a slave. Though her husband has allowed her to return to Spain to reclaim her property, he has also kept their daughter to ensure her return. Despite the suspense of its plot, as well as its early and direct engagement with the intersectionality of issues of gender and race, *Los miserables* remains virtually unnoticed in contemporary scholarship.

This essay explores Alejandrina's shifting racial identity through the use of blackface and argues that she enacts an interaction of nineteenth-century Spanish proto-feminism and abolitionism, both premised on the liberal ideal of the right to ownership of one's own body.[10] In particular, I view Alejandrina in blackface as representing the condition of a white woman in marriage by evoking metaphorical allusions to bondage, specifically, to the ongoing practice of slavery in the Caribbean, where it remained legal until 1886. Though the novel does not directly mention Cuba or Puerto Rico, it alludes to the continuing institution of slavery through references to Brazil as the heroine's country of origin, where slavery was abolished just two years later than in Cuba. It was indeed not unusual at the time to criticize Spain's participation in slavery and the slave trade only in terms of other countries' involvement in those practices, so as to raise awareness while avoiding Spanish censorship on the matter (Surwillo, *Monsters* 41–42).[11] The allusion to bondage slavery is further sustained by making Alejandrina the proprietor of diamond mines that she inherited from her Brazilian family, and which traditionally used slave labor.

In using bondage slavery to represent the plight of women, *Los miserables* continues, but also innovates, a tradition in Hispanic literature going back to the novel *Sab* (1841) by the Cuban-born writer Gertrudis Gómez de Avellaneda (1814–1873). Susan Kirkpatrick has pointed out that Gómez de Avellaneda "found it easier to express abolitionist sentiments . . . than to broach directly the issues of sexual inequality implied in its [*Sab*'s] structure . . . [and] was more fearful of openly representing female ambition and rebelliousness than she was of acknowledging the justice of Sab's anger with her own class and race" (158–59). While in Avellaneda's novel the male gender of the slave appears to enable the woman author to voice her own plight, it also bypasses some of the distinctive forms of oppression suffered by female slaves. In Sáez de Melgar's *Los miserables*, by contrast, the proto-feminist discourse is taken up by a woman in blackface, which suggests a solidarity across racial lines based on an idea of common womanhood. The adoption of blackface also, and perhaps unexpectedly, allows Alejandrina more freedom of speech in her crusade; for in Sáez de Melgar's fictional work, non-white women seem less constrained by some of the conventional limiting norms of behavior imposed on their white counterparts. For example, her play *La cadena rota* (1870) features a female slave giving voice to the play's feminist agenda since "la criolla . . . sigue estando subordinada a la estructura social patriarcal" (the creole woman . . . remains subordinated to the patriarchal social structure) (Tsuchiya, "Género" 125). But unlike *La cadena rota*, *Los miserables* alludes to bondage through a white woman's adoption of a different bodily appearance, thereby bringing into focus the bodily basis of bourgeois women's subjugation in marriage. As Sánchez-Eppler has convincingly argued, the rhetoric of feminism and abolitionism converged upon the common belief that women and slaves were objects of subjection for displaying a "physical difference from cultural norms of white masculinity" (15).

Beyond the critique of both bondage and marriage, the novel also proposes a common strategy of emancipation for women across racial lines, through the means available at the time to middle- and upper-class women. In particular, as Mónica Burguera has shown, philanthropy provided a venue for those women to exercise a kind of agency normally denied to them within the domestic sphere of marriage, a situation that changed little throughout the nineteenth century. Relying on accounts of philanthropy on both sides of the Atlantic, I interpret Alejandrina's philanthropic activity performed in blackface as envisioning social agency for women across racial lines.

The comparison of white women with slaves has been criticized for not capturing the particularity of the black body and, in Sánchez-Eppler's words, turning "moments of identification" into "acts of appropriation" (20). On the one hand, in *Los miserables*, to the extent that the slave analogy is deployed through a character who (albeit temporarily) exhibits the physical markers that provoke white society's racial prejudice, the "the fact of one's blackness," to use Frantz Fanon's expression, is made visible, not hidden (54). On the other hand, the fact that Alejandrina is merely performing blackness, and doing so from the perspective of a white subject, recalls Kirkpatrick's observation, that Avellaneda's *Sab* "colonized the mulatto's subjectivity to suit her own purpose" (158). Moreover, the novel's proposal of a common emancipatory strategy through philanthropy seems to presuppose a metropolitan ideal of female respectability, and even to reinforce racial hierarchy. This essay, while acknowledging these important limitations, will for the most part explore the productive aspects of Alejandrina's performance.

Performing the Slave Analogy

Alejandrina is the only woman in *Los miserables* who both finds herself in an unwanted marital relationship and identifies herself as a slave. The other two relevant female characters in the novel, Guillermina and Cristina, represent alternative models of womanhood of the time. The upper-class Guillermina, happily dedicated to raising her son and adopted children, stands for the traditional domestic woman. Her husband Lucas Mendoza fled political persecution in Spain for Brazil, but did not return when the threat subsided, neglecting his wife and son for more than a decade.[12] Though abandoned by her husband, of whose whereabouts she is ignorant, Guillermina longs for his return. At the end of the novel, she decides to take him back when he returns and expresses repentance for his past neglect. By contrast, the working-class Cristina is critically portrayed in the terms characteristic of the deviant woman, who uses her beauty to seduce wealthy men and move up the social ladder. Cristina's behavior is driven by her desire to overcome her working-class origins, a goal that she tries to achieve by engaging in romantic relations with wealthy men outside marriage. After several unsuccessful liaisons, she ends up marrying Don Álvaro López, a cousin of Alejandrina's father. She and her husband assassinate Alejandrina's parents, and thereafter she takes up the title of Marquise of Blancarosa. Cristina's subversion of traditional bourgeois norms of female propriety appears as an expression of a character that is considered "evil" through and through, leading her to assassinate and steal. The novel's condemnation of the free-spirited and working-class Cristina, and its praise of the modest Guillermina, does not, however, imply its unequivocal endorsement of the traditionally obedient domestic woman. The novel places Alejandrina between the decisiveness of Cristina and the submissiveness of Guillermina by having her both abide by the institution of marriage and react against some of the practices associated with it, such as the deprivation of women's ownership of their own bodies.

The novel's critique of Alejandrina's marital situation starts off by placing her marriage in "pagan" India, which she describes in primitive terms. This reference to a distant culture serves to identify the practice of enslaving women with paganism, thereby echoing the traditional belief, prevalent in nineteenth-century Spain, that Christianity had liberated women from slavery. At the same time, Alejandrina's situation was not atypical among middle-class women of the time, who were regularly given to unwanted husbands, were tied to unhappy marriages and faced the threat of losing custody of their children if they dared leave their spouses.[13] In highlighting aspects of Alejandrina's marriage that would seem most familiar to a bourgeois female readership, *Los miserables*' reference to a *salvaje* husband draws upon an imperial imaginary of an alleged Western and Christian superiority and simultaneously evokes the subjection of bourgeois women in the domestic realm in metropolitan Spain. The conflation of imperial and domestic ideology echoes Anne McClintock's thesis that "the cult of domesticity was not simply a trivial and fleeting irrelevance, belonging properly in the private, 'natural' realm of the family" but rather "an indispensable element of both the industrial market and the imperial enterprise" (5). In particular, the appeal to an uncivilized territory captures the liberal bourgeois idea of the domestic as a remnant of the original state of nature, where women remained under the subjection of patriarchy and were excluded from the rule of law. According to classical liberalism, the public sphere of equal citizens emerged through a social contract from a state of nature, where inequality had prevailed until then (Pateman 1–2). Carole Pateman has convincingly shown that the inequality of the state of nature, though supposedly eradicated from the social sphere, was nevertheless purposefully maintained within the domestic one, where women were treated as legal minors and had limited property rights; men presented themselves as equal to one another in the social sphere, but made themselves masters in their own families (2). Thus, the defining characteristics of Alejandrina's domestic life, placed in a land outside civilization, metaphorically express the private sphere as a remnant of the original state of nature.

Alejandrina's adoption of blackface when she returns to Spain further emphasizes women's exclusion from civil society and their lack of ownership over their bodies. She takes on the appearance of the race subjected to slavery, thereby expressing the situation of women through the analogy of slavery, but also brings out a new racial regime that was being consolidated at the time. In doing so, she uncovers a society that increasingly gives importance to modern racial categories constructed on perceived physical traits, instead of just following centuries-old criteria of societal organization based primarily on genealogy, in particular, on Muslim, Jewish, or African heritage. This newer racial regime, as Susan Martin-Márquez explains, gained prevalence in the second half of the nineteenth century with the advent of allegedly more scientific accounts of racial difference (39–50).

The novel does not directly invoke the ancestry of the Spanish characters in order to classify them racially, but it does point to certain societal changes that might help to explain the weakening of the old regime. Indeed, it depicts a society in which economic development, the civil wars between Carlists and liberals, and the resultant political exile have made it difficult to reliably determine lineages and, in consequence, have destabilized the formerly rigid statutes of social division and enabled new social mobility across classes. In *Los miserables* we thus find characters experiencing social mobility because no observable traits or known ancestry tie them to distinct social groups. Individuals originally from the lower classes, such as Cristina Guanter, have easily become part of the upper classes amid the political turbulence, while others, born into the aristocracy, are unaware of their social origins and are raised in lower-class families. Moreover, the very fact that the characters nowhere consider the ancestry of Alejandrina to determine her racial identity is an indication of a broader dynamic in liberal Spain, that of downplaying its ethnic diversity based on its Semitic past. Spain's first liberal Constitution (1812) sought to unify Spaniards and Americans of European descent as a racially homogenous group (Galván Rodríguez 26).[14] Drafting that constitution in 1811, Agustín Argüelles described Spanish society as homogenous like the rest of Europe, a characterization that, as Lisa Surwillo points out, was employed "in a racial rather than purely social sense" ("*Don Álvaro*" 53) and that, at least on the surface, seemed to set aside Spain's old anxiety about not being European enough due to its Semitic heritage.[15] At the same time, this self-ascribed homogeneity was built upon a new type of segregation, as the 1812 Constitution excluded from citizenship its population of sub-Saharan African-descent (Galván Rodríguez 27 and 49).[16]

Los miserables combines the new racial exclusions expressed in the 1812 Constitution of Cadiz with the increasing relevance given to physical markers in the second half of the century, and presents a unifying discourse of "whiteness" directly based on skin color. Indeed, it is their newfound and shared "whiteness" that allows for the Spanish characters' above-mentioned social mobility. Likewise, the new prominence of the racial difference constructed on the basis of skin color, between Spaniards and colonial populations of color, represented by Alejandrina and Lucas Mendoza in blackface, creates insurmountable social barriers.

The role of skin color in Spain's new racial regime is underlined in the automatic reactions of the Spaniards when they see Alejandrina in blackface for the first time. Without having met her before, and having assumed from her adopted name (Blanca) that she is a white woman, they accept her invitation to her luxurious palace in Madrid. Very much to their surprise, the guests find a wealthy black woman instead: "El marqués y D. Severo retrocedieron con espanto, quedando asombrados al ver que la elegante dama era una negra" (The Marquis and D. Severo recoiled with horror, shocked to see that the elegant lady was a black woman) (2: 65).[17] Those characters seem to naturally associate wealth with whiteness, insofar as they are taken aback and react negatively to a black woman occupying an upper-level social position. Alejandrina addresses, and objects to, some of the racist comments and reactions by explaining the irrelevance of skin color in determining moral character or social status: "—En vuestro rostro se ve pintada la sorpresa; ¿os admira mi color? les preguntó. . . . —Nada tiene de particular; habéis encontrado acaso lo que no esperabais: una negra, que se llama Blanca y que posee inmensas riquezas para premiar la honradez" ("Your face has a look of surprise; does my skin color shock you?" she asked them. . . ." It is nothing out of the ordinary; perhaps you have found what you were not expecting: a black woman who is called Blanca and who owns immense riches as a reward for her honesty") (1: 412). Despite Alejandrina's efforts to contest racial prejudices, the two characters are immediately identified by their skin color as belonging to a distinctive and different race: The Spanish characters characterize Alejandrina as "negra," (black woman) and her cousin Lucas Mendoza as a "doctor negro," (black doctor) placing both of them within the "raza de esclavos" (race of slaves) (1: 25; 1: 135; 1: 192).

The increasing significance of skin color as a criterion for social distinction had previously enabled Alejandrina, who is of mixed race, but has inherited her father's skin color and hair, to pass for white: "la marquesa era morena con cabellos negros como el terciopelo, y Alejandrina blanca y rubia como el oro" (the marquise was dark with hair black like velvet, and Alejandrina white and blond like gold) (1: 89). In several passages, the novel draws a contrast between her appearance and her mother's, and emphasizes that she has taken after her father alone in skin color. "Usted recuerda las facciones de Alejandrina? —Sí; era rubia, blanca con ojos y cejas negras como el terciopelo, semejantes a los de su madre; solo que la blancura y el dorado color de la cabellera habíalo sin duda heredado de su padre.... —Es verdad, no puede ser ella [*la condesa de Paraná*]" ("Do you remember Alejandrina's features?" "Yes; she was blonde and white with eyes and eyebrows as black as velvet, similar to those of her mother; only she had, without doubt, inherited her whiteness and her hair's golden color from her father."... "It's true, it can't be her [the countess of Parana]") (1:163–64). Although Alejandrina has inherited some of her mother's features, it is her skin color that fundamentally determines her racial type. Thus, when—and only when—Alejandrina paints her face black, she adopts her mother's racial identity.

The role of skin color in determining racial identity is especially significant in the case of Lucas de Mendoza, who also purposefully paints his face black, in this case, to avoid being identified by his estranged wife, Guillermina. The latter cannot recognize the black doctor as her husband, despite noticing that their facial features are identical, as we read on several occasions:

> [recordó] las facciones, todos los rasgos característicos de su marido, y murmuró para sus adentros: —Si este hombre no fuera negro, le creería mi marido.
>
> ([She remembered] his features, all the characteristics peculiar to her husband, and muttered to herself: "If this man were not black, I would believe he was my husband.") (2: 296)
>
> —¡Oh! ¿yo no sé qué es esto! ¡cada día encuentro más semejanza entre las facciones de mi marido y las de ese hombre! Sólo me confunde su negra tez.
>
> ("Oh! I do not know what this is! Each day I find more resemblance between the features of my husband and those of that man! Only his black complexion confounds me.") (1: 431)
>
> —¿Ya se han reconocido? —No, señor; le cree verdaderamente un negro.
>
> ("Have they already recognized each other?" "No sir; she truly believes he is a black man.") (2: 130)

This anecdote suggests, furthermore, the significant role of racial constructions in determining or even transforming one's identity.[18] Some of the novel's characters also judge him on the basis of pejorative associations with his adopted skin color. For example, some question his expertise and even consider him a witch doctor:

>—¿Y qué particularidad ha notado usted en este sabio médico? le preguntó Blanca.
>
>—Nada más que una, su color, ¡qué lástima!

("And what peculiarity have you noticed in this wise doctor?" Blanca asked him. "Nothing but one, his color, what a pity!") (1: 117)

>—Jesús! ¡qué cosa tan rara! . . . ¿será V. hechicero y como algunos que he conocido? . . .
>
>—¿Tú has conocido hechiceros? . . . la interrumpió el doctor; eso sí que es más raro. —¡En las novelas digo! si no me ha dejado V. concluir, exclamó Zoa.
>
>—¡Ah! . . . ¿en las novelas? . . . bien; ¿y me parezco yo a ellos?

("Jesus! What a strange thing! . . . might you be a witch doctor like some I have known?" . . . "Have you met witch doctors?" . . . interrupted the doctor; "that is certainly most strange." "In the novels, I mean! You did not let me finish the sentence," Zoa exclaimed. "Ah! . . . in the novels? . . . Okay; and do I look like them?") (1: 335)

Similarly, Alejandrina is deemed socially and morally inferior on the basis of her blackface by both "good" and "bad" characters, according to the novel's ideological model, revealing the pervasiveness of racism. For example, one of the former, Idelmaro, comments: "Ella se lo merecía, es hermosísima; no tiene más falta que el color de su tez demasiado moreno" ("She deserved it, she is very beautiful; her only flaw is that her complexion is too dark") (1: 141). Nevertheless, only the characters presented as evil, Fray Severo and Cristina Guanter, express especially harsh negative reactions to Alejandrina's appearance in blackface. For example, Cristina remarks: "—¡Conque Blanca la Estranjera es una hija de esa raza de esclavos! . . . —Justamente: yo la he visto por mis propios ojos; es negra. —¡Quién lo había de decir! . . . cualquiera se la imagina un ángel, un ser celestial . . . Quién sabe si será un demonio" (" 'So Blanca la Estranjera is a daughter of that race of slaves!' . . . 'Exactly: I have seen her with my own eyes; she is black.' 'Who would have said it! . . . everyone imagines that she is an angel, a heavenly being . . . who knows whether she might be a demon' ") (2: 25).

The novel highlights perceived bodily markers at the root of those prejudices through the continuous references to the dark color of her skin, and by making Alejandrina and Lucas Mendoza not perform the caricatured roles traditionally associated with black people, as was customary of white actors performing in blackface in theater (Lane 18–50). Alejandrina presents herself to Madrilenian society as an extremely wealthy woman acquainted with European manners, who displays the most exquisite luxury and counts on the assistance of many servants. It is only a superficial physical appearance that stands between the Spaniards and the two Brazilians, and which grounds the prejudices against them. Moreover, both characters become black and even acquire new identities in the eyes of Spanish society, simply by painting their skin. Thus, by distancing those characters from stereotypical racially inflected behaviors and by having them elicit different reactions depending on their appearance, the novel singles out skin color alone as the basis for racism and enslavement; and by treating skin color, for these characters, as something temporary and contingent, it reveals racist attitudes as contingent as well, not based on any intrinsic distinctions among people. Moreover, in line with certain sociological accounts of racial formation that emerged in the 1980s, the novel presents race as a construction meant to serve a specific social, and often economic, agenda.[19]

Such an understanding of race seems to lie behind Alejandrina's conception of her own racial identity. As the combination of her adopted appearance and her adopted name suggests, Alejandrina seems to be far from adhering to any particular racial identity, placing herself rather outside of such categorizations. In switching between appearances, she is characterizing racial formation as a social construction contingent upon different agendas. When asked with which race she identifies herself most, she answers that she chooses among different appearances according to her goals and plans: "—Entonces el verdadero color de V. ¿cuál es? pues recuerdo haberla visto en el vapor cuando vinimos del Brasil, blanca y rubia, morena después, y negra hoy. —Mi color natural es el primero; pero yo adopto el que mejor conviene al desarrollo de mi plan de venganza" ("Which, then, is your true color? Because I remember having seen you on the steamboat when we were coming from Brazil, white and blond, later dark and now black."

"My natural color is the first one; but I adopt the one that best suits the development of my plan for revenge") (1: 409).

As for the Spanish characters, the novel configures their racial biases around their economic interests. Cristina Guanter, her husband Álvaro López, Tragabombas, and Fray Severo murder Alejandrina's parents so as to acquire their wealth and property, and in particular, Cristina and Álvaro then take up the titles of Marquis and Marquise of Blancarosa, which, respectively, Alejandrina's father had inherited from a Spanish relative of his and her mother had acquired through marriage. Cristina and Álvaro took up the aristocratic titles, which contain a clear allusion to whiteness, by literally eliminating the Americans. Alejandrina, years later, returns to Spain in blackface and under the name of *Blanca la extranjera*, another allusion to whiteness.

Alejandrina's adoption of blackface also challenges traditional gender roles, such that it brings together abolitionist and feminist discourses; in particular, this racially constructed idea of the body becomes the site where efforts to emancipate women and slaves converge. Though it owes its idealist impulse to Romanticism, *Los miserables* can be read as a critical response to the gender discourses implicit in the figure of the vengeful hero in Spanish Romantic drama of the 1830s, such as Martínez de la Rosa's *La conjuración de Venecia* (1834), Duke of Rivas's *Don Álvaro o la fuerza del sino* (1835), García Gutierrez's *El trovador* (1836), and Hartzenbusch's *Los amantes de Teruel* (1837). Despite being set in different periods and places, these plays share the general plot of a hero attempting to seek revenge and gain social recognition, a storyline similar to that of *Los miserables*. *Los miserables*, I suggest, replays this structure while contesting these plays' gender discourses in at least two important ways. First, instead of a hero we have a heroine who undertakes the task of restoring the family's honor. Second, if in the Romantic plays the hero identifies with the fatherly figure and dismisses the mother—who is barely, if at all, mentioned, as Labanyi has pointed out (15–21)—in *Los miserables* Alejandrina renders her mother visible by adopting a physical appearance that is reminiscent of the late *condesa de Paraná*. It is rather Alejandrina's father who remains invisible and plays no role in the story, the physical appearance she has inherited from him having literally been painted over. Labanyi further points out that in the Romantic plays, the cancellation of the social role of the mother took on a racial meaning by making the mother racially alien, for example, the Inca princess in *Don Álvaro* or a Roma woman in *El trovador* (17). In *Los miserables*, too, the feminine figure is racially marked, though here, her differentiation serves the opposite goal. When Alejandrina takes on the appearance of her black mother, her body becomes the site where social exclusion—based on gender as well as race—is contested.

In this context of challenging traditional gender roles, Alejandrina's act of reclaiming stolen properties has a specific emancipatory significance that might have resonated with the female readership at that time. Spain's nineteenth-century legal system regulated women's inheritances and dowries, in principle, to endow women with some security and protection from a husband's economic or physical abuse.[20] In general, and despite small variations in regional laws, women were the proprietors of their dowries and of money and property inherited from their families. By law, husbands could manage and administer these assets only with their wives' authorization, and on the condition that they not squander them. A husband's misuse or mismanagement could be grounds for dissolution of the marriage, and thus for his loss of access to his wife's body. Conversely, a wife's accusation of physical abuse could also lead to dissolution of the marriage and, in turn, would impede his access to her assets.[21] But despite being proprietors of their assets, wives had no legal standing to manage them, for example, to sell or rent properties or invest money. Legally, they were treated as minors, a provision that most often rendered the husband the only possible administrator of such assets. Thus, in practice, the dowry served primarily to make a potential bride more attractive to a man. The fact that a husband, more often than not, gained control over his wife's property was exemplified by the extent to which "un matrimonio sin dote resultaba bastante problemático, hasta el punto de que las fundaciones para dotar a las doncellas sin recursos era una práctica corriente desde hace siglos" (a marriage without dowry turned out to be quite problematic, to the point that foundations for endowing maidens without means with dowries had been common practice for centuries) (Ortego Agustín 189).

The ambiguity of bourgeois women's ownership of property mirrors their relationship to their own bodies. Indeed, we should not underestimate the link between owning property and owning one's own body in liberalism. John Locke explains in the *Second Treatise of Government* that one's right to own property is premised on one's right to self-ownership (13–14). The fact that white women figured as owners of property but were not allowed to exercise that ownership thus also reflected their conflicted relation to their own bodies. This ambiguous situation of a woman's relationship to her body, both in economic and sexual terms, is directly exemplified in an important passage of *Los miserables*, where Alejandrina dresses up as an exotic black queen, a *reina negra*, wearing arm-bracelets embedded with diamonds: "Había tenido el capricho de disfrazarse de negra, y tenía su hermoso cutis admirablemente teñido de un negro lustroso y aterciopelado. Vestía un vaporoso traje de crespón blanco, que dejaba en descubierto sus brazos y su cuello, en los que ostentaba un collar y unos brazaletes de brillantes de un valor incalculable" (She had had the whim to disguise herself as a black woman, and she had her beautiful complexion admirably dyed with a lustrous and tantalizing black. She wore a sheer dress of white crepe, which left her arms and neck bare, on which she displayed a necklace and diamond bracelets of incalculable value) (1: 405).

While Alejandrina is engaged in this little performance, Tragabombas, now one of the spectators, expresses his desire to possess the *reina negra* by marrying her: "—¡He aquí una negra que yo haría con gusto mi esposa! se fue diciendo Tragabombas ¡Y qué no valen los brillantes que lleva encima! . . . ¡cuernos de vaca! ¡constituyen una fortuna . . . ¡quién los pillara!" ("Here is a black woman whom I would gladly make my wife!" Tragabombas went on saying. "And how expensive are the diamonds she is wearing! . . . holy cow! They are worth a fortune . . . who could get them!") (1: 413). If the characterization of the black queen as a wife presents marriage as a form of slavery, Alejandrina's representation of the *reina negra* turns symbols endowed with a meaning of enslavement into symbolic acts of self-assertion. In principle, the slave-bracelets embedded with diamonds signal the *reina negra*'s body as property, given that, in the pictorial depictions of slavery, bracelets repeatedly served to characterize their bondage;[22] moreover, diamonds were traditionally mined by slaves and, in this particular context, they are also the source of the wealth Alejandrina has inherited from her family. Tragabombas, one of the assassins of Alejandrina's parents, automatically perceives the economic meaning of the queen/slave body when he links its possession with the acquisition of the precious gems that she is wearing, bringing up the parallel between slavery and marriage in the overlap of the sexual and the economic. He hints at the sexual dimension involved in the ownership of female slaves, who were far more vulnerable than male slaves to sexual exploitation at the hands of their masters. Through that allusion, Tragabombas's remarks further point to the conflation of the corporeal and the economic in marriage, and of the roles of master and husband.

When in blackface, Alejandrina's body is identified as a member of the "race of slaves," which further serves to reveal her lack of agency over her own body in marriage. At the same time, she makes a symbolic attempt to claim ownership over her body by appearing in Madrid as a wealthy owner of diamond mines. When she performs as a *reina negra,* Alejandrina makes a further demonstration of symbolic self-ownership. The diamonds adorning her body present the female body as an object of desire and possession. But insofar as the diamonds are merely objects of display, which the spectators are denied the possibility of possessing, Alejandrina the "esclava" wife asserts ownership of her own body. The fact that Alejandrina makes this symbolic demonstration by performing in blackface and as a woman of color reflects the fact that it was often easier for white women to voice their dissatisfaction in marriage indirectly, by adhering to other social groups' demands that also reflected theirs. And yet, these comparisons, as scholars have pointed out, always run the risk of turning a blind eye to the privileges enjoyed by white women. *Los miserables* manifests some awareness of Alejandrina's conflictive position as a white woman, whose wealth was produced by slaves in the diamond mines of Brazil. Her decision to adopt a black appearance when she comes back from Brazil, and not to identify herself with her white color, may be understood in light of that conflict as a symbolic denial of the entitlement of the white side of her ancestry to the profits of slavery. Furthermore, in doing so, she symbolically relates blackness, not only to being owned but also to the act of owning.

We must, however, keep in mind that all these symbolic gestures of self-ownership in Madrid take place when Alejandrina has already married and surrendered herself to the will of her "*salvaje*" husband and has become, in her own words, an *esclava,* in order to save the life of her supporter Fray Benigno, who had fallen prisoner to the Indian tribe. Like another famous slave, the Cuban Sab of Gómez de Avellaneda's novel, who gives up his much-wanted freedom to fulfill his beloved's desire, Alejandrina has given up her freedom for the sake of someone else's happiness. By renouncing their own interests, both Alejandrina and Sab instantiate a pattern common in sentimental narratives about women and slaves. According to Lou Charnon-Deutsch, sentimental fiction established that it is typically women—and the same could be said of slaves—who "ought, for the sake of preserving society, to be self-sacrificing, nurturing, humble and long-suffering" (47) and that women's decisions always involve "some form of feminine self-cancellation, acquiescence, subservience," as a voluntary form of slavery (57). Charnon-Deutsch further characterizes this sacrifice as "masochism" (70), insofar as, despite the cost and suffering involved, it led to the attainment of a sense of happiness and pleasure, which were believed to be associated with a virtuous life. Sybille Fischer has interpreted the character of Sab as an example of a general type in abolitionist texts: the submissive slave who relinquishes his or her freedom to ensure his or her master's happiness (114–20).

In *Los miserables*, Alejandrina, torn between the liberal impulse to exercise agency over her own body and the desire to satisfy someone else's needs, opts for the latter. However, whereas sentimental narratives depict women's and slaves' sacrifice of individual interests as a path to their self-realization and fulfillment, and ultimately to happiness, Alejandrina's decision to help her friend leaves her longing for her individual agency. Her performance in blackface, and especially as a *reina negra*, to claim the right to self-ownership is thus an expression of her frustration and loss. And all these efforts to claim ownership of her own body in marriage remain merely symbolic, in that they will have no effect on the conditions of her marriage to a man who is keeping her daughter as a guarantee of her return.

Philanthropy as a Transatlantic Strategy of Gender and Racial Emancipation

Besides such symbolic assertions of self-ownership, Alejandrina also participates in social strategies of agency that were actually developed by women at the time, both white and black. As scholars of modern Spain have extensively noted, philanthropy became one of the most important venues enabling well-to-do women to transcend the confines of the traditional domestic sphere in a way that was also sanctioned by the liberal establishment. Starting in the 1820s, when the first laws regulating women's participation in charities were passed, upper-class and aristocratic Spanish women devoted themselves to helping the working class ameliorate their social situation in a variety of ways. By appealing to their distinctive femininity, characterized by compassion and care, attributes traditionally used to justify their confinement to the domestic sphere, those Spanish women were able to justify and even demand such incursions into a social sphere that had been originally defined according to the alleged superior rational nature of men (Burguera 186). *Los miserables* further evokes the participation of affluent women of color in philanthropy already taking place at the time on the British Caribbean island of Barbados, which, as Melanie Newton has shown, afforded those free women of color a degree of social agency. When *Los miserables* was published, slavery was still in place in the Spanish Caribbean, which was also heavily segregated. Nevertheless, by evoking the practices already occurring in the British Caribbean, *Los miserables* presents philanthropy as a transatlantic model of womanhood with the potential to reach across racial divisions, albeit by clearly maintaining class differences.

Alejandrina, again in blackface, employs her own wealth in charitable activities to improve the living conditions of Madrid's poor, showing a wealthy woman of color asserting herself as a social agent assisting others in the public sphere, thereby contesting not only women's traditional confinement to the private sphere, but also racist presuppositions about those of African descent as lacking agency. Her philanthropic activity therefore not only reveals an abstract solidarity based on similar social circumstances but also performs an embodied act of racial integration. In doing so, she goes beyond the actions of white Spanish female abolitionists at the time, including Sáez de Melgar herself. Despite positioning themselves against slavery, these women did not involve, or encourage the involvement of, free people of color living in Madrid in their own activism, even though there were women of color in Madrid protesting against slavery at the time. Henriette Partzsch, in her work on Sáez de Melgar's periodical *La Violeta*, published in the early 1860s, notices that women's abolitionist activism, while reacting against slavery, also promoted "an infantilized and homogenized image of black people, reducing them to recipients of their charitable efforts" (871).[23] By contrast, in becoming a leading agent in Spain's social development through her philanthropic activity, Alejandrina in blackface represents a woman of color exercising, rather than passively receiving, compassion and care.

At the same time, such a model is not devoid of problems. First, Alejandrina's philanthropy, given that it depends on wealth acquired from diamond mines, exhibits strong parallels with the charitable activities of nineteenth-century *indianos* returning from Cuba.[24] The Spanish *indianos* became wealthy in all sorts of activities connected directly or indirectly to sugar production, which was dependent on slave labor. Some of the wealthiest *indianos* even participated directly in the most lucrative business of all, the kidnapping, transport, and illegal sale of Africans as slaves in Cuba, as numerous studies in recent years have shown.[25] One powerful historical example of the connection between philanthropy and slavery was the Marquis of Manzanedo, a man characterized by writers and historians as the "representante de los negreros en España" (representative of the slave traders in Spain) (Espadas Burgos 286). Though originally a poor peasant from Northern Spain, Manzanedo amassed an incredible fortune in his years in Cuba through slavery and the slave trade, and in Madrid he unambiguously and forcefully defended the interests of pro-slavery factions. His wife, Maria del Carmen Hernández Espinosa, meanwhile, diverted her husband's wealth to all sorts of philanthropic activities in Spain (Cruz del Amo 271–77). It is crucial to keep in mind that behind her disguise, Alejandrina too is a white (though of mixed heritage) woman practicing philanthropy with wealth gained through slave labor.

Alejandrina's involvement in charitable activities not only enacts the general pattern of *indianos* practicing philanthropy upon their return from Cuba with profits from a slave-based economy, but also, insofar as she herself is identified with the race of slaves, brings to the foreground the particular type of oppression at the root of this philanthropy. Alejandrina's coloring of her skin directly and openly expresses the economic connection between slavery and philanthropy that the humanitarian goals of philanthropy helped conceal. For philanthropy's laudable goals enabled *indianos* to construct a public image diametrically opposed to the figure of the cruel and barbarian *negrero*, who places profit above moral costs; their philanthropy undoubtedly helped silence public discussions regarding the despicable origins of their wealth. In the particular example of Maria del Carmen Hernández, hardly an isolated case of an *indiano*'s wife using money gained overseas for charity, the connection between charity and slavery further reveals the incongruous position of some Spanish upper-class women, who could assert their own, often philanthropic, social agency thanks to their wealth acquired through exploitation.[26]

This is not the only reason why the novel's use of philanthropy might send a mixed message. In her work on Barbados, Melanie Newton further argues that philanthropy, while allowing affluent women of color to exercise social agency, also promoted a certain model of womanhood associated with charitable activities in Europe, which prescribed "piety, purity, submissiveness" (237–38). Having those women engage in philanthropy was, then, echoing Foucault's idea of discipline, a productive way of regulating behavior through a social practice associated with respectable European women (Newton 232). As a tool for implementing a certain type of womanhood among former female slaves, philanthropy further helped "Europeanize" the British Caribbean during the postemancipation period, enabling the metropolis to continue to assert its values and way of life in its colonies. From this perspective, it would appear that Alejandrina, a woman in blackface from the Americas, adopts a model of social behavior in agreement with what was expected from a respectable woman in Spain at the time. Though discriminated against for her darker skin color, she finds a way of assimilating herself to Spain's cultural and social paradigm by embracing its sanctioned model of bourgeois female behavior. The seemingly conciliatory image of a white woman in blackface assisting others as a model of integration across racial lines thus contains significant historical contradictions and fissures symptomatic of a liberalism founded upon imperial and capitalist practices.

Conclusion: Only Skin-Deep?

If the novel's presentation of philanthropy as a transatlantic model of emancipation involves a certain ambiguity, does such ambiguity extend to other aspects of its protagonist, Alejandrina, and her behavior? On the one hand, Alejandrina exhibits solidarity with those in the greater Spanish territory of African descent, by making them visible, by exhibiting their agency, and by denouncing racial prejudice. Furthermore, she claims to view race as a construct in service of certain social agendas; she is certainly willing to manipulate her racial identity to achieve her own ends. On the other hand, in private Alejandrina seems to show a partiality for the racial identity she enjoyed before adopting blackface.

Even though Alejandrina adopts her mother's appearance in public, she reverts to her original appearance in her more intimate quarters. While this is clearly to be expected from a woman who is actually of pale complexion, she obsessively furnishes her living quarters in white, down to the smallest detail:

> Todo era blanco; los sillones de terciopelo, las paredes de damasco, las colgaduras de los balcones, la alfombra del pavimento. . . . Los marcos de los espejos también eran de una madera blanquísima con incrustaciones de nácar. La mesa de mármol, sobre la cual se veían infinidad de frascos con esencias y pomadas, estaba a la derecha; a la izquierda y velado por colgaduras de encaje se veía un precioso baño de una blancura deslumbradora.
>
> (Everything was white; the velvet armchairs, the damask walls, the drapes of the balconies, the rug on the floor. . . . The frames of the mirrors too were made of a very white wood with mother-of-pearl inlays. The marble table, on which an infinite number of bottles with essences and ointments could be seen, was on the right; on the left and veiled by lace drapes a beautiful bath of a dazzling whiteness could be seen.) (1: 108)

She even arranges to have two blond and blue-eyed servant girls, dressed in white clothes and pearls:

> Para que nada dejase de ser armónico y bello en tan romántico tocador, las camareras eran dos hermosísimas jóvenes, rubias como el oro, con azulados ojos y labios de coral. Vestían trajes de balista blancos, y tenían los cabellos recogidos en redecillas de felpilla, salpicadas de perlas. . . . Una cortina de terciopelo blanco cubría aquella puerta, impidiendo que penetrase aire, y vedando al propio tiempo a las del guardarropa que dirigieran la vista al interior del gabinete donde su señora se desnudaba.
>
> (So that nothing departed from harmoniousness and beauty in such a romantic dressing room, the maids were two beautiful young women, blond like gold, with blue eyes and coral lips. They wore white suits of batiste,[27] and had their hair gathered in chenille hairnets, dotted with pearls. . . . A white velvet curtain covered that door, keeping the air from penetrating, and at the same time preventing those in the cloakroom from directing their gaze to the interior of the sitting room where their lady was undressing.) (1: 108)

The fact that Alejandrina obsessively furnishes her intimate quarters in white, especially the bathroom, where she cleans off the black paint, suggests that she remains in the grip of a racist ideological connection between white skin and bodily purity.[28] Moreover, the notion of bodily purity had, for the nineteenth-century woman, an unmistakable sexual dimension tied to the ideal of female respectability. As Akiko Tsuchiya states, sexual discourses and practices functioned to determine a woman's normative status, since "female deviancy and sexuality were conflated in the nineteenth century through a linkage between deviancy and the female body" (*Marginal Subjects* 14).

Alejandrina, who presents herself in blackface, exhibits solidarity with slaves, and contests racial prejudices expressed by Spaniards against those of African descent, as well as the foundation of racism more generally, needs to be surrounded by whiteness in her intimate quarters. This need seems to undermine her claim to stand outside of racial categories, as if she, for her own part, were racially neutral. More generally, her expressed attitudes notwithstanding, Alejandrina seems to reproduce certain aspects of the racial hierarchy she denounces. With this, perhaps, the novel can be seen as underscoring the impact of socially established racial attitudes, especially for those who stand to benefit from them, such as the white-skinned Alejandrina.

At the end of the novel, Alejandrina unmasks her parents' assassins and turns them over to the authorities to be prosecuted and to have their usurped titles and properties returned to her. In appealing to the authorities, Alejandrina, as an American and, in particular, as a mixed-race person, affirms the right of Americans, including those of African descent, to equal protection under Spanish law. As a wife, she claims the right to own property and, through that, to the ownership of her own body. She further does so in blackface, presenting Afro-Hispanic women as rightful agents of transformation within the social sphere, albeit by assimilating them into the model of female respectability imposed by the metropolis. Alejandrina's gesture renders the black body visible through the merging of abolitionist and feminist concerns, even though that ultimately means silencing the voices of those suffering the enslavement she is protesting against.[29]

Notes

1. The plot of *Los miserables* bears no resemblance to that of Victor Hugo's famous *Les miserables*, whose first part was published in April 1862.

2. "Isabelline" refers to the period encompassing the rule of Queen Isabel II (1822–1868). All subsequent translations into English are my own.

3. For a view of Sáez de Melgar as a traditionalist, see Sánchez Llama.

4. Henriette Partzsch comments on the racial exclusions in Sáez de Melgar's social activism (877) but Akiko Tsuchiya's analysis of Sáez de Melgar's *La cadena rota* reveals a much more complex attitude toward the inclusion of those of African descent in her fictional work ("Género" 121–28).

5. The Madrid periodical *La Iberia* (June 15, 1863) advertises *Los miserables* as being for sale in serialized format at the offices of *La Violeta*, the Madrid-based periodical directed by the author. In *La Correspondencia de España* (November 5, 1862) we read that the serialization would begin in November 1862 and run through the following year.

6. The novel repeatedly describes Alejandrina's mother as "morena" (dark), a term used at the time to describe people of color, while it underlines the "blancura" (whiteness) of her father's skin. Guillermina characterizes the late Marquise's skin color as a fault: "La marquesa, que era una bellísima americana, sin más defecto que su color moreno, casi bronceado" (The Marquise, a beautiful American woman, had no other flaw but her dark, almost tanned, skin color) (1: 62).

7. The name "Blancarosa" combines the words for white ("blanca") and pink or rose ("rosa").

8. "Blanca" is an adjective meaning "white."

9. "En medio de este fausto que me rodea, en medio de esta atmósfera al parecer de felicidad y de bienandanza, mi corazón vive muriendo, mi pensamiento está siempre fijo en otras regiones donde hay seres que me llaman y á los que me encadena un lazo indisoluble, formado por la más increíble fatalidad. Me juzgas libre y soy esclava" (Amid this splendor that surrounds me, amid this atmosphere of feigned happiness and prosperity, my heart lives dying, my thoughts are always fixed to other regions, where there are beings calling me and to whom an insoluble bond, formed out of the most unbelievable misfortune, fastens me. You judge me to be free and I am a slave) (2: 115).

10. Alejandrina's strategy also aligns with the nineteenth-century Hispanic tradition of white actors painting their faces black in theater, as distinct from the *caricaturist* practice of blackface followed in the United States during the same period. Jill Lane has argued, for example, that in nineteenth-century Cuban theater, white actors' use of blackface to represent characters of African descent served not so much to caricature, but rather, to critique racist constructions. In Spanish theater, too, black characters were also played by white actors, a circumstance that, according to Mercedes Vidal Tibbits, "no connotaba el carácter bufo, caricaturesco y ridiculizante asociado con el uso de actores cómicos con la cara pintada de negro ('blackface') en muchas obras de teatro norteamericanas del siglo XIX y principios del XX" (did not have the comic, caricaturing, and mocking connotation associated with the use of comic actors in blackface in many north-American plays of the nineteenth and early twentieth centuries) (3).

11. The imperial displacements that we see in *Los Miserables*, which mentions only colonial territories that were never possessed by Spain (i.e., India and Brazil), might also be thought of as extending responsibility for imperialist practices to other nations.

12. More evidence that Brazil functions as a kind of stand-in for Cuba in the novel is that some Carlist supporters (like Lucas Mendoza) were deported to Cuba as political prisoners, for example, Antonio Eugenio Flores (1852–1908), son of the well-known *costumbrista* writer Antonio Flores (1818–65).

13. Only the short-lived 1870 Spanish law gave the *patria potestad* or custody to the mother (Cruz del Amo 172).

14. In the debates during the drafting of the 1812 Constitution, geographical origin predominated over perceived phenotypical features as a criterion of ethnic differentiation: members of the commission distinguished between the populations of European and African origin. Participants also employed the old terminology of the "*casta*" (caste) rather than "*raza*," (race) though they often referred to colonial Spaniards of sub-Saharan-African descent by their perceived skin color, as "*morenos*" (dark) or "*pardos*" (brown). At the same time, they did not invoke Spain's Semitic heritage as a criterion for racial classification. If a unified sense of European ancestry was put forward in 1812, Spaniards and Latin Americans later delineated the so

called *raza latina* (Latin race), which was meant to differentiate certain populations of southern European origin from northern Europeans (see Gabilondo).

15. The relevance and role of Spain's Semitic past in shaping its modern national identities in nineteenth-century Spain is a complex issue. Martin-Márquez argues that, while during the first half of the nineteenth century and, especially, in the Romantic plays of the 1830s, Spanish intellectuals attempted to recover and celebrate Spain's diversity and Semitic heritage, during the second half they clearly attempted to tie Spain's identity to an alleged Christian and non-Semitic past. By contrast, Joshua Goode argues that the late nineteenth century witnessed the emergence in Spain of an idea of race that celebrates racial mixing (32–75).

16. Article 22 of the 1812 Constitution states that the population of sub-Saharan African descent could be granted citizenship by the Spanish Parliament only through extraordinary service to the nation.

17. Cristina also says: "—Solo salgo para asistir a fiestas tan espléndidas como la que esta noche ofrece la condesa negra. Tragabombas se sonrió con malicia al escuchar el dictado de negra" ("I only go out to attend such splendid parties as the one given by the black countess tonight." Tragabombas grinned with malice when he heard blackness mentioned) (2: 42). When Tragabombas mentions that the mixed-race woman "—Se la juzga una diosa, y se la adora como a una criatura celestial" ("is deemed a queen and adored like a heavenly creature") (2:42), Cristina responds in disbelief: " '—¿A pesar de su negrura?' . . . murmuró la marquesa mordiéndose los labios con estremecimiento colérico. '—A pesar de todo, señora' " ("Despite her blackness?" . . . murmured the marquise, biting her lips with an angry shudder. "Despite everything, my lady") (2: 42).

18. I owe this observation to Michelle Murray.

19. The origin of a sociological understanding of race can be traced back to Robert Miles's "Apropos of the Idea of 'Race.' "

20. In nineteenth-century Spain the legal regulation of wives' economic situation was complicated due to the enforcement the old civil code of the *Leyes de Toro* until 1889, and the existence of small variations according to *leyes forales* (regional laws). I have followed the detailed historical studies conducted by Maria Ángeles Ortego Agustín and Maria Cruz del Amo.

21. It should be added that even slaves, in principle, could take legal action against their masters for excessive violence, a model of slavery that, as Daylet Domínguez explains, was based on Alfonso X's *Las siete partidas,* and intended to provide the slave with some rights to property and physical integrity (270 note 10). I thank Lisa Surwillo for discussion of the parallelisms between laws condemning use of excessive violence against women and slaves.

22. The use of arm-bracelets to express the enslaved condition of individuals is often found in nineteenth-century Orientalist paintings depicting slaves in harems to express enslavement. It also can be found in some reproductions of Josiah Wedgwood's famous medallion of a kneeling black man asking for freedom.

23. Ironically, the racial views of those abolitionist movements shared important features with some pro-slavery discourses, insofar as they depicted the slave as in need of the master's protection and care, and thereby, as Daylet Domínguez puts it, continued to follow the "logic of slavery" (265). As Domínguez explains, the Countess of Merlín, in her infamous *Los esclavos en las colonias españolas* (1841), tells of slaves who, despite having gained their freedom, decide to remain under their master's servitude as an expression of gratitude for their protection and care, proposing a "humanitarian" view of slavery.

24. Surwillo provides several examples of *negreros* employing their wealth in charitable activities upon their return to Spain, which appears to have been a common practice: "These *americanos* went to Cuba not to civilize the colony, but to modernize and civilize outlying areas of the metropolis" (*Monsters* 159).

25. For recent discussions, see the essays in Rodrigo y Alharilla and Chaviano López.

26. The following fascinating detail underlines the extraordinarily ambiguous position of upper-class white women within the imperial network. Lisa Surwillo has noted that Antonio López, another famous nineteenth-century Spanish slave trader, "paid off debts and founded a shipping line for smuggling slaves" with the dowry of his Cuban wife, Luisa Brú Lassús (*Monsters* 149).

27. I have not been able to make sense of the transmitted text, "balista" ("ballistic"), and have translated as if "batista" were intended.

28. As scholars have noted, the modern concern for hygiene arrived in Spain from northern Europe in the late eighteenth century and became consolidated in the mid-nineteenth century with the medical writers Mateo Soane (1791–1870) and his disciple Felipe Monlau (1801–1871) (Burguera 83–98, 293–303). At first, hygienic efforts were focused on the working classes but later spread to middle-class domestic households. Anne McClintock, through her analysis of nineteenth-century advertisements for the British soap Pearl, has further shown the interplay of hygienic practices, sexuality, and race (207–31).

29. This type of inclusion through assimilation seems to be a general pattern in Spanish abolitionist texts, though its manifestations vary according to gender. Commenting on the Spanish literary depictions of male Afro-Cubans fighting in favor of the liberal cause, Lisa Surwillo writes: "It is clear in this literary version of the facts that slaves' actions were crucial, even as it assimilates, reshapes, and silences the actual motivations of the rebellious Afro-Cubans (slaves and free) into a European liberal story of social change" (*Monsters* 65).

Works Cited

Alas, Leopoldo. "El amor y la economía." *Revista de Asturias*, no. 19, 1879, pp. 300–302.

Aldaraca, Bridget. *El Ángel del Hogar: Galdós and the Ideology of Domesticity in Spain.* U of North Carolina P, 1991.

Blanco, Alda. "Escritora, feminidad y escritura en la España de medio siglo." *Breve historia feminista de la literatura española (en lengua castellana),* edited by Iris M. Zavala, vol. 5, Anthropos, 1998, pp. 9–38.

Burguera, Mónica. *Las damas del liberalismo respetable.* Madrid: Cátedra, 2012.

Charnon-Deutsch, Lou. *Narratives of Desire: Nineteenth Century Spanish Fiction by Women.* Pennsylvania State UP, 1994.

La Correspondencia de España (Madrid), 5 Nov. 1862.

Cruz del Amo, María. "La familia y el trabajo femenino en España durante la segunda mitad del siglo XIX." Diss., Universidad Complutense de Madrid, 2008; http://eprints.ucm.es/8148/1/T30558.pdf; accessed June 20, 2018.

Domínguez, Daylet "En los límites del discurso esclavista: Retórica abolicionista, afectos y sensibilidad en *Los esclavos en las colonias españolas* de la condesa de Merlín." *Cuban Studies,* vol. 45, no. 1, 2017, pp. 252–72.

Espadas Burgos, Manuel. *Alfonso XII y los Orígenes de la Restauración.* Madrid: CSIC. 1975.

Fanon, Frantz. *Black Skin, White Masks.* Grove, 1967.

Fischer, Sibylle. *Modernity Disavowed. Haiti and the Cultures of Slavery in the Age of Revolution.* Duke UP, 2004.

Gabilondo, Joseba. "Genealogía de la 'raza latina.' Para una teoría de las estructuras raciales hispanas." *Revista Iberoamericana,* vol. 75, no. 228, 2009, pp. 795–818.

Galván Rodríguez, Eduardo. *La Abolición De La Esclavitud En España: Debates Parlamentarios, 1810–1886.* Dykinson, 2014.

Goode, Joshua. *Impurity of Blood; Defining Race in Spain 1870–1930.* Louisiana State UP, 2009.

La Iberia (Madrid), 21 June 1863.

Lane, Jill. *Blackface Cuba, 1840–1895.* U of Pennsylvania P, 2005.

Kirkpatrick, Susan. *Las Románticas: Women Writers and Subjectivity in Spain, 1835–1850.* U of California P, 1989.

Labanyi, Jo. "Liberal Individualism and the Fear of the Feminine in Spanish Romantic Drama." *Culture and Gender in Nineteenth-Century Spain,* edited by Lou Charnon-Deutsch and Jo Labanyi, Clarendon Press, 1996, pp. 8–26.

Locke, John. *Second Treatise of Government: An essay concerning the True Original, Extent End of Civil Government.* Edited by Richard H. Cox, Wiley-Blackwell, 1982.

Martin-Márquez, Susan. *Disorientations: Spanish Colonialism in Africa and the Performance of Identity.* Yale UP, 2008.

McClintock, Anne. *Imperial Leather.* Routledge, 1995.

Miles, Robert, "Apropos of the Idea of 'Race' . . . Again." *Theories of Race and Racism: A Reader,* edited by Les Back and John Solomos, Taylor and Francis, 2009, pp. 125–43.

Newton, Melanie. "Philanthropy, Gender, and the Production of Public Life in Barbados, ca. 1790–ca. 1850." *Gender and Slave Emancipation in the Atlantic World*, edited by Pamela Scully and Diana Paton, Duke UP, 2005, pp. 225–46.

Ortego Agustín, María Ángeles. *Familia y Matrimonio en la España del siglo XVIII: Ordenamiento Jurídico y Situación Real de las mujeres a través de la Documentación Notarial.* Dissertation, Universidad Complutense de Madrid, 1999; http://biblioteca.ucm.es/tesis/19972000/H/0/H0048101.pdf; accessed June 20, 2018.

Partzsch, Henriette. "Violets and Abolition. The Discourse on Slavery in Faustina Sáez de Melgar's Magazine *La Violeta* (Madrid, 1862–66)." *Bulletin of Spanish Studies*, vol. 89, no. 6, 2012, 859–74.

Rodrigo y Alharilla, Martín, and Lizbeth J. Chaviano López, eds. *Negreros y esclavos. Barcelona y la esclavitud atlántica (siglos XVI–XX)*. Icaría, 2017.

Sáez de Melgar, Faustina. *El deber cumplido*. Imprenta de Pedro Núñez, 1879.

———. *Los miserables de España o secretos de la Corte*. Imprenta Hispana de Vicente Castaños, 1862–63.

Sánchez Llama, Íñigo. *Galería de escritoras isabelinas. La prensa periódica entre 1833 y 1895.* Cátedra, 2000.

Sánchez-Eppler, Karen. *Touching Liberty: Abolition, Feminism, and the Politics of the Body.* U of California P, 1997.

Surwillo, Lisa. *Monsters by Trade: Slave Traffickers in Modern Spanish Literature and Culture.* Stanford UP, 2014.

———. "Speaking of Race in *Don Álvaro*." *Revista Hispánica Moderna*, vol. 63, no. 1, 2010, pp. 51–67.

Tsuchiya, Akiko. *Marginal Subjects: Gender and Deviance in Fin-de-siècle Spain.* U of Toronto P, 2011.

———. "Género, asociacionismo y discurso antiesclavista en la obra de Faustina Sáez de Melgar." *No hay nación para este sexo. La Re(d)pública transatlántica de las Letras: Escritoras españolas y latinoamericanas (1824–1936)*, edited by Pura Fernández, Iberoamericana Vervuert, 2015, pp. 111–30.

Vidal Tibbits, Mercedes. "El hombre negro en el teatro peninsular del siglo XIX." *Hispania*, vol. 89, no. 1, 2006, pp. 1–12.

5

Colonial Imaginings on the Stage

Blackface, Gender, and the Economics of Empire in Spanish and Catalan Popular Theater

MAR SORIA

Blackface is a nineteenth- and twentieth-century transnational theatrical practice amply studied by critics of Cuban and U.S. cultural productions. However, little has been said on the role of such racial impersonation in the Spanish context despite—or precisely because of—the fact that it is still present on Spanish stages and streets.[1] Focusing on fin-de-siècle theatrical production in Spain, this chapter investigates how the comical staging of blackface in *género chico*—mass-produced one- and two-act plays—served to reinstate the metropolis' superiority over Cuba in the Spanish and Catalan national imaginaries, thus forging a sense of national self.

In this vein, *género chico* blackface can be analyzed as a transatlantic example of what Jill Lane in *Blackface Cuba, 1840–1895* defines as "ImpersoNation," or the theatrical performances across the American hemisphere that "link racial and gender impersonation to the development of racialized national discourses" (16). From this perspective, through *género chico* blackface,

> white actors step into the social skin of others and instantiate the assumed separation of body and subjectivity for nonwhite subjects, a separation fundamental to slavery and to military conquest, enabling the continued production and maintenance of racial difference itself. (16)

Following Eurocentric assumptions about racial difference, *género chico* blackface performance imposed a colonialist and racist perspective by possessing and (re)creating the voice and body of the Other.² In contrast to the serious tone of dramas and tragedies, the comical tone of *género chico* would predispose spectators to perceive the staging of blackface as utterly amusing. By resorting to a distorted version of the Spanish language, exaggerated bodily and facial gestures, a mocking tone of voice, and artificially darkened skin, *género chico* blackface ridiculed black people. The derision of black people exhibited in these performances reinforced the European hegemonic division between colonizer and colonized, a division based, as Edward Said notes, on the assumption that colonized people and women were reliant on their instincts and closer to nature while the European colonizer—male and white—was associated with mind and reason (206–208).³ Furthermore, because the staging of *género chico* blackface relied on the (re)creation of racial hierarchies that imagined black people as inferior to whites, the racial impersonation integral to blackface buttressed the economic foundations of the Spanish empire built upon the slavery system. In this respect, it is important to note that Madrid and Barcelona—the main beneficiaries of the flow of capital from the Cuban plantation system (Rodrigo y Alharilla 235)—were the two key locations in which *género chico* was staged in Spain. Following Walter Mignolo's assertion that "there is no modernity without coloniality" ("Coloniality" 39), it would not be incorrect to state that the economic accumulation resulting from the Spanish colonial enterprise supported, at least in part, the emergence and great success of this modern theatrical form. Considering that the public attending these performances in the metropolises of Barcelona and Madrid included the upper-middle classes (Versteeg 92) whose wealth was often linked to colonial commerce and investment, it is logical that *género chico* plays offered a positive portrayal of these social classes' socioeconomic interests and racial identity.

Género chico blackface, as the two plays analyzed in this essay demonstrate, thus contributed to the portrayal of the white race not only as superior to nonwhite races, but also as the universal norm. In fact, the construction of white and black people in *género chico* corresponds to what Richard Dyer has noted as the main characteristic of white imperialist discourse. For this critic, whites construct their own race as invisible in contrast to other races. This is so because whites have assumed that their racial identity corresponds to a disembodied and universal conceptualization of race and, as such, whites see themselves simply as "the human race" (3). In contrast, black people are "reduced (in white culture) to their bodies and thus to race" (14). Furthermore, Dyer notes that in order to build a sense of self, those who see themselves as white depend on the often-negative representation of the nonwhite (24). Therefore, *Género chico* blackface, like other white-centered discourses, resorts to the representation of the nonwhite as unintelligent and/or sexual in order to define the white man as intelligent and skillful.

By constructing whites and nonwhites in this manner, *género chico* blackface (re)produced and strengthened what Aníbal Quijano identifies as the coloniality of power of the European colonial enterprise, the conflation of practices and knowledge that supported the European exploitation of the colonized. In particular, *género chico* blackface reinforced what Quijano defines as "a Eurocentric perspective of knowledge" (534) and Mignolo describes as the "epistemic colonial difference" ("The Geopolitics" 85). According to this Eurocentric episteme, race was defined as the "naturalization of colonial relations between Europeans and non-Europeans" (Quijano 534–35). While Europeans defined themselves as white and rational and therefore, as superior, they coded the phenotypic traits of the colonized as the biological manifestation of their natural inferiority and difference. As a result, nonwhites were regarded as "objects of study, consequently bodies closer to nature. In a sense, they became dominable and exploitable" (Quijano 555). From this perspective, blackface sustained the epistemic logic of coloniality, contributing in this manner to the production of the Eurocentric and hegemonic knowledge that validated the colonial enterprise.

Borrowing from Saidiya V. Hartman's analysis of nineteenth-century U.S. minstrelsy in *Scenes of Subjection: Terror, Slavery, and Selfmaking in Nineteenth-century America*, I suggest that the comical and sensual embodiment of blackness in *género chico* responds to the "economy of enjoyment" in which "the bound black body, permanently affixed in its place, engenders pleasure . . . obtained from the security of place and order and predicated on chattel slavery" (31).[4] In dialogue with other theatrical representations across the Atlantic, I demonstrate how the performance of *género chico* blackface entailed the appropriation, colonization, and commodification of the black body for the amusement of a European white audience. The performance and reception of blackface in Spain, however, responds to that country's particular national and historical context. Unlike in the United States or Cuba, by the late eighteenth century the black population living in Spain was very small (Lipski 1; Graullera Sanz 181). Thus, the representation of black people in nineteenth-century blackface did not serve to maintain power hierarchies and racial differences within the country's population, as in the U.S. and Cuban cases—a fact that also explains the limited number of Spanish plays featuring blackface, in contrast to these other two countries.[5] Blackface, however, allowed Spaniards to imagine themselves as citizens of a white imperial nation, and thus as part of the desired European imperial elite formed by nations such as Great Britain, France, and Germany, with the right to exploit what they perceived to be the lower races. What blackface brings to the fore, thus, is that like other European nations, Spain's nation-building project rested on the idea that "the 'nation' in Europe was mainly constituted of one ethnicity, articulated as 'whiteness'" (Mignolo, "Introduction" 157).

In the context of nineteenth-century Spain, the term *raza* (race), "[e]xtremely flexible in its meaning," carried multiple meanings as Joshua Goode explains in his *Impurity of Blood: Defining Race in Spain* (4). According to Goode, *raza* referred not only to particular biological traits that defined a group of people, but also to the innate spiritual attributes of Spanish citizens that led them "to act, think, and feel in a particular way" (4–6). In contrast to other colonial nations such as England, France, and the United States, Spain promoted racial hybridity as a way to create affinity and unity when regional, class, and political discord undermined national cohesion (13). However, historian Antonio Feros also notes that, in the colonies, "[r]acial mixture, justified *a posteriori* as a mechanism of assimilation, was in reality a product of the exploitation of colonial subjects and of their subjugation" (284). Colonial miscegenation was promoted in order "to improve the African and indigenous peoples through biological mixing with the superior Europeans" (Smith and Nalbone 3). As Ada Ferrer suggests, this idea was "premised on the agency of Europeans and the passivity of the other" (*Insurgent Cuba* 4), an idea that hints toward Spain's gendered understanding of racial differentiation shared by other European colonial powers in the nineteenth century, as Berndt Ostendorf has demonstrated. For Ostendorf, European imperialism was "in tune with a geopolitical gender ascription in the anthropology discourse of the Enlightenment: Europe was always regarded as the masculine continent, the colonial world as feminine" (117–18). Since race was perceived as the biological, cultural, and personal features "transmitted across the generations" (Goode 7), colonial discourse often associated the phenotypes of the colonized—such as skin color or hair types—with an inferior race with backward cultural customs and an abhorrent sexuality: nonwhite people were seen either as feminized or excessively sexual. By conflating skin color and race, colonial imperialism established a social hierarchy that demonstrated white people's superiority.

In Spain, as in other European countries and among the white elite in colonial Cuba, those defined as the black race—people of African descent with black skin—were considered to occupy the bottom of the racial hierarchy. Especially in Cuba, where the state and the elites feared black rebellion and demand for equality, a racist discourse that degraded black people predominated throughout the nineteenth century.[6] For instance, David Sartorious notes how politicians and intellectuals in Cuba grew increasingly reluctant to see the positive influence of African culture in Cuba when, by 1840, the total black population surpassed the white (171). Ferrer also indicates how the colonial elite and its supporters' fear of the black population was widely accepted in the 1890s despite the significant increase in the numbers of whites living in Cuba. Even within the insurgent movement, "black mobilization . . . also created anxieties" (*Insurgent Cuba* 112).

The cultural reaffirmation of Spain as an empire in *género chico* was particularly crucial during the second half of the nineteenth century, when Spain's image as an international power was in decline. Domestic sociopolitical instability, the emergence of the remaining colonies' pro-independence movements, and increasing pressure from other colonial nations destabilized the economic and cultural base of Spain's self-perception as an empire. Specifically, the problematic relationship between Cuba and the metropolis took center stage in the Spanish imaginary since the island had become a major source of wealth, imperial pride, and anxiety for the metropolis. This island was not only a lucrative market as the world's major exporter of sugar, but it also ranked as the greatest purchaser of African slaves in the nineteenth century (Ferrer, "Cuban Slavery" 154). Indeed, Cuba's abundant resources, natural beauty, and strategic military and commercial location made the island a much-desired imperial possession (Pierpaoli 470).

However, the intensification of Cuban nationalist sentiment, exemplified by numerous uprisings and civil conflicts throughout the century, threatened political and economic control of the metropolis over the island. Because radical Cuban nationalism was founded on the idea of an independent nation without racial divisions, conservative sectors of Spanish society, such as protectionist associations, the Liga Nacional, and the Círculos Hispano-Ultramarinos, perceived the Cuban and Spanish abolitionist agendas as a direct danger to Spain's colonial interests (Schmidt-Nowara, "National

Economy" 622). Spanish pro-slavery opinion claimed that the abolition of slavery was antipatriotic (Martínez Carreras 76; Schmidt-Nowara, "National Economy" 626) and would bring about the Africanization of the island and its subsequent loss as a colony (Arroyo Jiménez 142).[7] Most importantly, because many prominent Spanish businessmen, merchants, and investors relied on the slave trade in Cuba, pro-slavery Spaniards saw the continuation of this practice as essential to their economic interests (Schmidt-Nowara, "Spain" 63).[8] With such strong economic and political investment in the island, Spain became the last European country to legislate and officially abolish slavery in its colonies in 1886 (Martínez Carreras 77).[9]

The heated debate on slavery and its abolition intensified during the second half of the nineteenth century, driven by the growth of antislavery sentiment at home and abroad.[10] Although Spain had abolished the slave trade (but not slavery) in 1820, its involvement continued informally. However, the consolidation of abolitionist ideology in many Western countries at the time, the international pressure to stop the slave trade, and the abolition of slavery in the United States after the Civil War contributed to shape Spain's public opinion against this inhumane practice (Arroyo Jiménez 127–28; Schmidt-Nowara, "Spain," 57). Thus, in the 1850s and 1860s, an increasing number of Spanish politicians, economists, and writers alike opposed the institution of slavery. The growing strength of such a line of thought sparked the creation of the Spanish Abolitionist Society (Sociedad Abolicionista Española) in 1865 and the anti-abolitionist Ladies' Society (Sociedad de Señoras) in 1868 under the direction of popular poet Carolina Coronado. Thanks to their public and educational work, by 1881 Spain was "una sociedad ya muy sensibilizada" (a society already highly aware) about the evils of slavery (Martínez Carreras 77).

Antislavery sentiment also permeated the Spanish literary realm. Theater in particular functioned as an effective platform to educate a broad audience on the abolitionist cause. Throughout the nineteenth century, several dramas appeared with a clear antislavery message such as Wenceslao Ayguals de Izco's *Los negros* (1836), Ángel Maria de Luna and Rafael Leopoldo Palomino's *Haley o el traficante de negros* (1853), Luis Blanc y Navarro's *Romper cadenas* (1873), and Faustina Sáez de Melgar's *La cadena rota* (1879). Yet the popular *género chico* usually voiced pro-slavery views, portraying black people as lazy, sensual, stupid, and animalistic.[11] Such is the case of the Catalan comedy *Las Carolinas* (1886) by librettist Antoni Ferrer i Codina and the *zarzuela*—one- or two-act musical play—*La perla cubana* (1890) by José Jackson Veyán. Set in two different geographical locations (Barcelona and La Habana respectively), each play presents a seemingly opposing ideological agenda regarding slavery. Whereas *Las Carolinas* seems to advance abolitionist and anticolonial ideas, *La perla cubana* strongly advocates for slavery and colonialism. However, a more detailed analysis of these two plays unveils that, even though the Catalan play appears to embrace the abolitionist cause, the comical staging of blackface mocking black Cuban men ultimately configures a superior Spanish masculinity as the benchmark of empire during key moments of its decline.

As Aaron Clark and others have pointed out, the *género chico* was a crucial vehicle for the creation of nationhood in Catalonia.[12] Although *género chico* is often associated with Madrid and the portrayal of typical Spanish customs and people, the genre was actively cultivated in Barcelona (Clark 80). Hence, many of the *zarzuelas* and *sainetes* (one- and two-act plays) that premiered in Madrilenian theaters would soon be staged in the Catalan capital with great success. However, moved by a growing nationalist sentiment, Catalan playwrights also aimed to create an autochthonous theatrical form portraying *costumbrista* or everyday life scenes of their homeland in their mother tongue.[13] One of the first authors to adapt the *género chico* to the Catalan stage was the applauded Catalan playwright and journalist Antoni Ferrer i Codina (1837–1905) with numerous dramas, *zarzuelas,* and one- and two-act comedies (Blanco García 182). Such is the case of *Las Carolinas,* a one-act bilingual comedy, in which Ferrer i Codina portrays the exploits of Emilio, a violinist and womanizer living in Barcelona.[14]

In the play, Emilio, a womanizer, rushes through a balcony into the living room of an upscale apartment at night. Soon thereafter, the audience learns that he is escaping from Don Simón, the husband of his last romantic conquest, Carolina. Realizing that he has entered someone else's apartment by mistake, Emilio hides in the chimney. Then, the people living in the apartment, Don Ramón and his daughter, also named Carolina, make an appearance talking about the imminent arrival by ship of Don Ramón's protégé, a runaway slave from a Cuban plantation that, not coincidentally, is also named Carolina.[15] Once Don Ramón's daughter is alone, she discovers Emilio, with whom she is madly in love. Fearing her father's anger against the intruder, Carolina asks Emilio to pass as the black Cuban protégé, Domingo, since Emilio's face and hands are now black with the soot from the chimney. The disguise proves effective since Don Ramón, who has misplaced his glasses, warmly welcomes the false fugitive. After some comic misunderstandings, the story ends when Emilio unveils his true identity and Don Ramón accepts him as his future son-in-law.

First staged in February 1886 (eight months before the abolition of slavery in Cuba), *Las Carolinas* illustrates the current debates on slavery in the peninsula and the island. Don Ramón, as a pro-abolitionist, rejoices upon reading the news in the newspaper about the possible end of slavery:

> Oh! Felicitat! Los insurrectos sembla que tornan á treurer el nas. La paz del Zanjon no haurá sigut més qu'una tregua.—Ara será la definitiva y vindrá'l triunfo de la civilisación contra la barbarie. . . . Crech qu'al fín veuré realistat el meu ideal. No en va s'aixeca en la capital del Nort-América l'estatua de la llibertat iluminant al mon. Els negres serán libres.[16]

> (Oh! Happiness! It seems that the insurgents have shown up again. The peace of Zanjón will not have been but a truce. —Now it will be the final one and the triumph of civilization over barbarity will come. . . . I believe that I will finally see my ideal come true. Not for nothing the Statue of Liberty rises in the capital of North America enlightening the world. Black people will be free.) (10)[17]

Don Ramón's comments reflect the greater visibility of Cuban supporters of independence who had become "more outspoken in their demands for abolition and reform concessions" in the early 1880s (Corwin 310). Don Ramón believes that the abolition of slavery is a precondition for civilization, asserting that the United States is an example of a modern democratic country that contrasts with the backward and absolutist Spain.[18] In fact, his perception of Spain as barbaric because of its involvement in the slave trade echoes Spanish and American abolitionist opinions that considered the slave trade and slavery as backward practices (Surwillo 201; Gould, *Barbaric Traffic* 3–4). Thus, he claims: "Ya ha passat el temps del absolutisme, de la desigualtat de rassas. Igual será l'amo que l'esclau, gracias als autonomistas" (The time of absolutism, of racial inequality has passed. The master and the slave will be the same, thanks to the supporters of independence) (17). However, he also points out that as a result of this antislavery, pro-independence movement, "la isla acabará per ser una provincia del North-América" (the island will end up being a province of North America) (17), echoing Spanish conservative opinion, which considered antislavery supporters unpatriotic and at the service of foreign interests (Martínez Carreras 76).

Interestingly, Carolina reminds him of the origins of the family's fortune: "la va adquirir el teu papá comprant y venent esclaus en la Isla de Cuba" (your father acquired it by buying and selling slaves on the island of Cuba) (10). The play's association between a Catalan family and the slave trade is not merely anecdotal.[19] As Fradera suggests, "La burguesia catalana havia tingut des de finals del segle XVIII in fins a l'abolició definitiva una adhesió sense fissures a l'esclavitud i al tràfic d'esclaus. Actitud, d'altra banda, que no era merament intel.lectual, sinó pràctica, perquè s'havien dedicat reiteradament a l'una i altra" (The Catalan bourgeoisie had had since the end of the eighteenth century until the definitive abolition of slavery uninterrupted support of slavery and of slave trafficking. This was an attitude that was not merely intellectual but practical, because they had repeatedly dedicated themselves to both) ("Miquel Biada" 29). Specifically, Zeuske and García Martínez note that "after 1820 Catalans—along with some merchants from Cadiz, France, and the United States—controlled the Cuban slave trade" (206). For instance, historians Josep María Fradera, Martín Rodrigo y Alharilla, and José Antonio Piqueras give numerous examples of prominent Catalan businessmen whose involvement in the slave trade allowed them to amass fortunes and, in some cases, even obtain aristocratic titles awarded by the Spanish monarchy, who, as Piqueras states, was also directly implicated in the slave trade (112–13).[20] Thanks to their economic wealth, these men occupied prominent political and social positions in Catalonia, becoming major investors in the industrial, commercial, financial, and urban development of Spain and Catalonia (Piqueras 105–108; Rodrigo y Alharilla 229). It is not surprising then that, as the well-known historian of Barcelona Robert Hughes argues, "[b]ig businessmen in nineteenth-century Barcelona believed in slavery and saw no reason to deny it" (415), a fact that Fradera and Surwillo corroborate. Fradera describes how in 1841 the Catalan Junta de Comerç (Board of Commerce) organized a committee led by prominent Catalan businessmen involved in the slave trade such as Joan Illas i Ferrer, Josep Xifré, and Jaume Torrents to fight against a British proposition to end slavery in Cuba and Puerto Rico ("La participació catalana" 130–31). Similarly, Surwillo notes that in 1876, "men of finance and industry signed "the largest petition in Spain against colonial reforms," including the abolition of slavery (168).

Acknowledging his family's involvement in the slave trade, Don Ramón feels ashamed of his father's fortune that he now enjoys: "M'horrorisa el pensar que tot lo que tinch es producto d'aquet ilicit y repugnan comers"

(I'm horrified to think that everything I possess is a product of that illicit and repugnant commerce) (10). For that reason, he desires to "contribuir á la emancipació dels esclaus; per més que passi plassa de mal espanyol" (contribute to the emancipation of slaves; despite being seen as a bad Spanish patriot) (10). Don Ramón, despite risking being considered a traitor to the nation for supporting Cuba's independence and its pro-abolitionist agenda, has volunteered to receive Domingo, the slave who has escaped from a plantation, also named Carolina. The Catalan man feels that his shame can be alleviated only by "la simpatía y apoyo á aquella rassa desheredada" (the empathy and support of that disempowered race) (11).

On first appearance, when Don Ramón reads in the newspaper about the possible abolition of slavery, his enthusiastic reaction—his daughter is alarmed at his shouts of joy—as well as his sympathetic speech suggest his belief in racial equality. Don Ramón's reaction to the news that he has just read in the newspaper: "Pero, papa . . . qué son aquets crits?" (but, papa . . . what are those shouts?) (10)—and his sympathetic speech point to his belief in racial equality. However, his ensuing comments, both disconcerting and racist, about Domingo undermine his pro-abolitionist stance. For instance, in preparation for Domingo's arrival, Don Ramón asks his daughter to purchase and cook the food that he assumes the Cuban runaway likes, including their two pet parrots: "plátanos, pinyas y cassabe, que'ls hi agrada molt, y avuy per obsequiarlo mataràs els dos lloros y'ls farás amb arrós. . . . Jo encarregaré á la Riba dos ó tres sarrións de cocos" (bananas, pineapples and cassava, which they like a lot, and today to treat him you'll kill the two parrots and will make them with rice. . . . I will order two or three baskets of coconuts at Riba) (11). The presence of these products in Barcelona's stores attests to the transatlantic commercial exchange established between metropolis and colony, especially during the second half of the nineteenth century.[21]

Whereas cassava is an ingredient in traditional Cuban bread and pineapples and coconuts are native to the island, eating parrots is not part of the Cuban diet. However, Don Ramón affirms that "els negres's moren per l'arrós de lloro" (blacks die for rice with parrot) (11). By assuming Domingo's culinary preferences, Don Ramón constructs the black Cubans from a Eurocentric and imperialist point of view. As Aníbal Quijano states, the foundational myth of European colonial power "involved a cognitive model, a new perspective of knowledge within which non-Europe was the past, and because of that inferior, if not always primitive" (552). This idea is substantiated in *Las Carolinas*, since in the play subjects of African descent are considered primitive and barbaric because they eat the animals commonly held as pets in the West. Consequently, hearing about this culinary practice, Carolina exclaims disparagingly: "Vaya un caprixo! pobres bestias!" (What an insane idea! Poor animals!) (11). In this manner, the assumed culinary otherness of black Cubans serves as an empire-building narrative, intended to humorously sublimate the white audience's fear of the black race by establishing the empire's culture as superior and normative. Furthermore, Don Ramón understands Domingo's blackness as a negative trait that, curiously, can be transcended also through food. Accordingly, Don Ramón instructs his daughter to cook with foods such as cod with milk because "aixó'ls aclareix el color" (that lightens their color) (11).

Emilio's passing as black points in the same direction. In addition to his physical appearance in blackface, Emilio performs the black Cuban through his speech. Curiously, Emilio was a volunteer soldier in Cuba, which made him familiar with the slaves' way of speaking Spanish: "vaig ser voluntari de Cuba y vaig aprendre el parlar bossal dels negres de las hisendas (I was a volunteer in Cuba and learned the *bozal* language of the blacks from the *haciendas*) (19–20). Using his own version of *bozal*, "Domingo" describes to Don Ramón his experience as a slave and his escape from the Cuban hacienda: "Yo, mi amitu, sé bosá. Mi taita vendé prun túnicu museringa capatá tiu Juruco," (I, my master, know bozal. My father sold me very early to the overseer uncle Juruco) and "Brube jato tiu Jurucu. Sobá culito mí. Mucho pegá. Monte cojé. Játa jojó" (Brube jato uncle Jurucu. He hit my butt) (21).[22] Kristina Wirtz's and Jill Lane's observations regarding the representation of *bozal* in Cuban literature and *teatro bufo* are pertinent to the study of slave speech representation in Spanish *género chico* plays. Drawing on the work of linguistic anthropologists Susan Gal and Kathryn A. Woolard, Wirtz states that in nineteenth-century Cuba, "[l]anguage ideologies and, particularly, notions about how different social groups spoke Spanish were certainly intertwined with racial and national imaginaries, creating mutually reinforcing notions about accents and social identifications" (275). In this fashion, the written and theatrical representation of *bozal* did not reflect the actual black Cuban speech but functioned as a way of racializing the nation through "a cultural performative, conjured into existence through repeated performances" that operated "against the very interest of the alleged speakers" (Lane 48). In *Las Carolinas*, the distorted representation of black Cuban speech—the linguistic otherness that presented Spanish and Catalan as familiar languages to the audience—responds to an imperialist discourse that imagines black people as ridiculous, less intelligent and civilized than whites, thus justifying their socioeconomic subjugation. In fact, the term *bozal* was also used during this time to define "those who were simple, idiot, or inane" (Serna 97). Domingo's autonomy as a runaway slave is tempered by a narrative discourse replete with nonsensical and humorous-sounding words that serve to infantilize him.

Furthermore, by stating that Domingo's father was the slave trader who sold him to the plantation master, Emilio's criticism of slavery becomes an individual problem, placing the blame on a heartless father instead of a well-established socioeconomic system—the Spanish slave trade—from which whites obtained the greatest financial benefits. Similarly, in order to convince Don Ramón that Emilio is the black slave, Carolina asks the young man to sing a *tango* with her while she plays the piano. The tango sung by Emilio and Don Ramón's daughter emphasizes the erasure of the colonial institution of slavery. The inclusion of the sensuous *tango* in *Las Carolinas* attests to the great popularity of this Caribbean musical form, the protean and symbiotic nature of *género chico,* but also to the logics of empire governing the transatlantic cultural exchange.[23] The fact that the author's stage directions state that "En lugar de este tango puede cantarse el de la zarzuela 'Cádiz' u otro" (This tango could be replaced by another tango from the zarzuela "Cádiz" or another one) (20) highlights this idea. Any tango featuring a couple of "negritos" singing sensually would satisfy an audience craving a tamed exoticism. Thus, in the play's tango, Emilio and Carolina adopt the voices of two black Cuban lovers. Yet their seemingly innocent flirtatious musical exchange unveils a less romantic story: the history of human exploitation and trafficking at the hands of white Europeans and North Americans.

Describing their exotic and black African origins, the couple sing in a duet:

> En Congo luango
> yo soy nacido,
> y tú eres negra
> carabalí.
>
> (In Congo Luango
> I was born,
> and you are a black woman
> carabalí.) (20)

As John K. Thornton and Hugh Thomas have observed, the Loango region (present-day Republic of Congo) provided many slaves to the Atlantic slave trade (Thornton 848; Thomas 365). Similarly, "'*Carabalí*' is an African tribe, whose name was used as a form of surname to distinguish between slaves with the same first name" (García Rodríguez 25). In particular, "Slaves designated Carabalí in Cuba were those shipped from the ports of the two cities of Calabar and the neighboring city of Bonny, in modern-day Nigeria" (Wirtz 186). Additionally, the meaning of the tango's title "El cimarrón" makes reference to fugitive slaves who often settled in independent communities, although the term "first referred to feral cattle who ran wild in the hills of Hispaniola" (Klein 112). In this respect, it is worth noting how both *cimarrón* and *bozal* reflect the capitalist ideology of the empire behind chattel slavery. Indeed, "Bozal" is a Spanish word first used in Spain and its colonies to refer to untamed cattle (Serna 97). Later on, the word also identified "black people of African origin recently removed from their country (and) persons not expressing themselves properly in Spanish" (Serna 97). From this perspective, both terms show how slavery created false equivalences between humans and cattle as living property, whose escape meant the owner's loss of profit.

If the play resorts to racist humor and a musicalized romantic duet to erase any serious critique of slavery, the true Domigo's complete absence from the stage easily eliminates the only first-person account of slavery in the play.[24] In contrast, Emilio's voice dominates the narrative. His monologues open and close the representation, providing the venue to inspire the audience's sympathy for the womanizer. In his extensive opening monologue, the Catalan Don Juan perceives his love affair with Don Simón's wife as the invasion and conquest of another man's most valuable possession: "ja profanava aquell santuari matrimonial" (I defiled that matrimonial sanctuary) (8) and "reyna d'aquell castell" (queen of that castle) (8). This association, however, also showcases the interrelation between gender, nationalism, and imperial power. From the very beginning, Emilio compares his amorous affairs with the conquest of other nations. As he says, "no ha hi res que fassi tanta por com un marit quan se li hi invadeixen'ls estats" (there is nothing so scary as a husband when his estates are invaded) (7), a statement that is quite meaningful when considering that cuckolded Don Simón is the only Spanish-speaking character in the play.

Indeed, in *Las Carolinas* women are presented as men's possessions. This explains why Don Ramón, although in favor of the emancipation of slaves, is against women's liberation, as he reminds his daughter the first time she tells him she loves Emilio:

Don Ramón: El cor ja li dono, pero á tú no t'haurá.

Carolina: Pots ben proclamar la llibertat.

Don Ramón: Dels negres.

(Don Ramón: I give him your heart, but he won't have you.

Carolina: You can well proclaim freedom.

Don Ramón: Of blacks). (12)

Furthermore, for Don Ramón an economically independent woman is unthinkable. When Carolina proposes to Don Ramón that he give away his shameful fortune and live off her piano lessons, Don Ramón rejects the proposition outright: "Ah! no! aixó no . . ." (Oh! no! not that . . .) (11).

Furthermore, Emilio closes the play emphasizing the relationship between his womanizing masculinity and imperial desire by comparing his romantic conquests, both named Carolina, to the Caroline Islands, a Spanish colonial territory in the Pacific:

> Fugia de Carolinas
> com el diable de la creu
> y haguera dat per cap preu
> fins las d'allá á Filipinas.
> Pero cambiant la fortuna
> els papers en pochs instants,
> faig com van fé 'ls alemans;
> á la fí me'n quedo una.
>
> (I was fleeing the Carolinas
> like the devil from the cross
> and would have paid any price
> for going from there to the Philippines
> Because of fortune changing
> the roles in an instant,
> I do what the Germans did;
> in the end I keep one.) (27)

Indeed, the Caroline Islands had been the center of public attention in Spain the year before the staging of the play. Driven by his desire to expand the German empire, Otto von Bismarck claimed the possession of the Spanish islands in 1885 (Elizalde Pérez-Grueso 159). After various standoffs and negotiations, the Pope, serving as mediator in the conflict, granted the islands' sovereignty to Spain and the right to their economic and commercial exploitation to Germany (Rey Vicente and Canales Torres 28). In the same agreement, Spain also ceded the Marshall Islands to the Germans upon payment of four and a half million dollars (28).[25] Thus, having to choose between Don Simón's wife and Don Ramón's daughter, Emilio's decision making parallels that of the Germans, who, despite not officially possessing one group of islands (Las Carolinas), were able to obtain another (the Marshall Islands).

Emilio's marriage to Don Ramón's daughter is thus presented as both an imperial and an economic conquest, especially considering that he accepts marrying her when he learns that her inheritance—her value in the marriage market—amounts to "trescents mil duros" (three hundred thousand *duros*) (19). The representation of the female protagonist as an imperial conquest—a metaphor also deployed in Jackson Veyán's *zarzuela*, as explained below—illustrates the role of gender in the configuration of imperialism and the coloniality of power. In her study of the intersectionality of gender, class, and race in the construction of British imperialism, Anne McClintock observes that "gender dynamics were, from the outset, fundamental to the securing and maintenance of the imperial enterprise" (7). McClintock further argues that according to the Enlightenment epistemology that informed European colonialism, "the imperial conquest of the globe found both its shaping figure and its political sanction in the prior subordination of women as a category of nature" (24).

Decolonial theorists such as María Lugones, Freya Schiwy, and Mignolo have also noted the phallic and heterosexual character of the colonial enterprise, calling attention on how gender imaginaries have permeated the coloniality of power ("The Coloniality of Gender "11–12; 276; "Coloniality" 49). Schiwy, for instance, has noted how "[t]he gendering of colonial imaginaries has operated as a means of rendering European masculinity through Othering" (275). For his part, Mignolo observes that the coloniality of power "was founded in two embodied and geo-historically located pillars: the seed for the subsequent racial classification of the planet population and the superiority of white men over men of colour but also over white women" ("Coloniality" 49). Indeed, the representation of Carolina, Don Ramón's daughter, corroborates what Lugones describes as the role assigned to European bourgeois woman in the coloniality of gender. Carolina is thus not depicted as Emilio's "complement, but as someone who reproduce[s] race and capital through her sexual purity, passivity, and being homebound in the service of the white, European, bourgeois man" ("Toward a Coloniality of Gender" 743). Therefore, Don Ramón's daughter, domestic and sexually pure, is to pass colonial wealth to (white and male) deserving hands. Since Carolina's inheritance originates in the slave trade, the play places Emilio, a good patriot who fought for Spain's sovereignty over Cuba, as the direct beneficiary of the Spanish economic exploitation of the island. The title of the play further highlights the link between gender, coloniality, and race. *Las Carolinas* refers not only to the Spanish colonies in the Pacific Ocean but also to the hacienda plantation in Cuba from where the slave has escaped and to the women Emilio romantically conquers.

Despite the superficial antislavery rhetoric of *Las Carolinas*, the performance of blackface in Ferré i Codina's play reproduces the same imperial ideologies that frame the unabashedly racist zarzuela *La perla cubana*.[26] Written by the popular zarzuela librettist José Jackson Veyán and music composer Gaspar Espinosa de los Monteros in 1890, this one-act comic zarzuela narrates the story of Roberto, a young Spaniard living in Cuba who is about to lose his family's country villa in La Habana. Debt-ridden, Roberto's only option is to marry an ugly rich Cuban heiress. As a present for his future wife, Roberto has bought two Cuban slaves, Perla and Chimbo. However, his budding and passionate love for beautiful light black-skinned Perla makes him unsure about his imminent marriage. Despite the insistence of Don Carmelo—the heiress's wealthy uncle—that Roberto sign the marriage contract, the young Spaniard finally chooses Perla over his fiancée, demonstrating in this way his preference for true love over money and seemingly over racial difference. Once Perla verifies Roberto's love for her, the false slave unveils her real identity as Doña Concha, Roberto's moneylender, and Chimbo's as Concha's brother Juan, and confesses that brother and sister have pretended to be slaves to find out whom Roberto truly loves. The zarzuela ends with the prospect of a happy union between the rich biracial woman and the Spaniard and, therefore, between Cuba's natural and economic wealth and Spanish colonial enterprise.

In *La Perla*, as in *Las Carolinas*, *género chico* blackface relies on theatrical conventions such as the caricature of the black character's speech and physical appearance to represent racial otherness and to establish the inferiority of black subjects to whites. Jackson Veyán's staging of racial difference corresponds to a transnational and transhistorical perception in the West that associated blackness with the ugly and the deformed. According to Tudor Parfitt, "In Europe, for hundreds of years, being black, Jewish, sickly, and ugly became almost conterminous. Black Africans . . . became the paradigm of the extreme 'other' and the 'ugly race'—a sort of missing link between true humanity and the orangutan" (7–8).[27] As portrayed in *La perla cubana*, Chimbo not only speaks a "deformed" version of Spanish, but his unsightly and misproportioned physiognomy is constructed in negative correlation with what is perceived as white people's physical traits. In this manner, Chimbo's physical appearance, interaction, and dialogue with the other characters function to ridicule black men while boosting the play's comicality with racial stereotypes. For instance, Chimbo describes his nose as a "josico . . . chancho" (a wide snout) (8), a physical trait often associated with apes.[28] His black skin color is associated with dirt, an idea emphasized in the diegesis of the play by a white actor's use of blackface paint. Thus, when Juan sees his own painted face in the mirror, he exclaims: "(Debo estar) como el carbon . . . ¡Bueno estás, Juanito! Bonita cara tienes para hacer *Entre mi mujer y el negro*" (I look like coal. . . . You look good, Juanito! A pretty face to act in *Entre mi mujer y el negro*) (8). Juan makes reference to this highly successful zarzuela written by Luis de Olona in 1859 because one of the main characters, a black slave who is in love with his mistress, is continuously portrayed as ugly and grotesque.[29] By making reference to this black male character, Juan reinforces his perception that his blackened face is ugly and abnormal. In addition, Juan's intertextual reference attests to the endurance—*La perla cubana* was staged thirty years after Olona's zarzuela—of a widely accepted racist discourse in Spain that rendered black people intellectually and aesthetically inferior. Through this type of negative representation, *género chico* blackface, like nineteenth-century U.S. minstrelsy, "offered a way to play with collective fears of a degraded and threatening—and male—Other while at the same time maintaining some symbolic control over them" (Lott 13).

The connection Juan makes between coal and blackness also points to a common perception in Western culture in which this mineral was associated with dirt.[30] Another example of the association between black skin and dirt takes place when Don Carmelo approaches the *mulata* Perla and she exclaims: "Cuidado, no se manche la mano; como soy de color" (Look out, do not dirty your hand with my color) (10).[31] From this perspective, being black was seen as being tainted and, thus, abnormal.[32] In contrast, white skin color was naturalized as an ideal by Europeans. As Dyer demonstrates, in Western culture whiteness symbolizes "moral and also aesthetic superiority," because white is constructed as a sign of beauty, purity, and cleanliness (70). Therefore, Juan's and Perla's comments reinforce the white supremacist idea that "[t]o be white is to have expunged all dirt, faecal or otherwise, from oneself: to look white is to look clean" (Dyer 76). Symbolically, the connection between dirt and race is further emphasized through blackface makeup, which is presented as an unnatural state for whites who have to stain their faces to resemble a black person. Thus, Juan states: "Tú, al menos, como eres morenita, no has tenido que embadurnarte la cara; pero yo, embetunado hasta las orejas . . . ¡y con unos sudores que paso! Ni aun llorar puedo por no despintarme" (You, at least have not had to smear [whiten] your face; but I've smeared myself from ear to ear . . . and when I sweat! I cannot even cry for fear of smudging) (21).[33] Blackface performance is humorous because a white man passing as black is artificial, farfetched, and temporary, as demonstrated in the white characters' metatheatrical observations about the artificial character of blackface makeup.[34]

In order to exploit this racial personification on the stage, *La perla cubana* insists on the performative and theatrical aspect of blackface. For instance, Roberto shows surprise when Chimbo leaves a black stain on his hand after the slave kisses it when begging for his life.[35] In this fashion, Juan, a high-class "caballero" (gentleman) (20), is very offended because Roberto and Don Carmelo treat him "como á un negro" (like a black man) (21) when he passes as Chimbo. Precisely because a classist and racist society expects black people—but not upper-class white people—to be mistreated, a gentleman passing as black and being treated as such on stage is shocking and amusing for the audience. The comedy further normalizes the debasement of black people by making Chimbo speak "en negro" (in black) (26) or in a Spanish that, like Domingo's *bozal* in *Las Carolinas*, renders the character ridiculous and dumb. Also, following the same ideological pattern, Roberto and Don Carmelo continuously debase Chimbo with their insults.[36] For instance, the slave is described as unintelligent—"imbécil" (moron) (7) and "estúpido" (stupid) (8, 11, 19), but he is also equated to someone lacking moral values: "canalla" (scoundrel) (10) and "bergante" (rascal) (20). The black slave is further dehumanized when Roberto and Don Carmelo compare him to an "animal" (animal) (7) and an "orangután del demonio" (devil's orangutan) (10). These terms used in the play are intentional, since the association between apes and what was perceived as the black race by Europeans, common at the time in scientific texts, echoes discourses of racial difference that endorsed white supremacy and justified the economic subjugation of black people (Soria 52).

Nevertheless, in contrast to *Las Carolinas*, *La perla cubana* goes a step farther in normalizing violence against male slaves. If *Las Carolinas* mostly focuses on ridiculing the qualities of the character in blackface, *La Perla* normalizes the verbal and physical violence against the black slave on stage. For instance, Roberto, full of spite for Chimbo because he often prevents the Spaniard from being alone with Perla, threatens to shoot him—"Te voy a matar. (Coge la pistola.)" (I'm going to kill you. [Takes the gun]) (8)—or beat him to death—"Ya le tengo yo pronosticado que ha de morir de un golpe" (I predict that he is going to die from one blow) (11)—and break his bones—"Voy a romperte un hueso" (I'm gonna break one of your bones) (18). On different occasions, Roberto also kicks him with animosity while insulting him: "Toma, imbecil [*sic*]. (Dándole un puntapié)" (Take this, you idiot. [Kicking him]) (7) and "Vete al infierno [Dándole un puntapié]" (Go to hell. [Kicking him]) (12). Even Don Carmelo, who does not own Chimbo, kicks the slave, an action to which Roberto responds with encouragement: "Muy bien hecho; nada, duro con él" (Well done. That is it, let him have it) (11). Kicking the slave is so central to the intended comic effect of the play that it becomes the focus of Juan's solo song:

> Si cepillo su ropa,
> si le rizo el tupé,
> siempre le estoy mirando
> á la punta del pié.
> Y al volverme de espalda,
> por más que echo á correr,
> me da siempre las gracias
> con la punta del pié.
> ¡Chimbo infeliz!
> ¡Chimbo infeliz!
> Con qué punta tan dura
> te apuntalan *aquí*.
>
> (If I brush his clothes,
> if I ruffle his toupee,
> I'm always looking
> at his feet.
> And when I turn away,

no matter how fast I run,
he thanks me
with a kick of those feet.
Unhappy Chimbo!
Unhappy Chimbo!
With what a hard shoe tip
they prop you here.) (21; my emphasis)

The music, the lyrics, and the bodily performance accentuate the comical intent of the song: a well-off gentleman with a good education—"artista de primor" (a fine artist) (20)—receives numerous kicks in the rear from his fake owner when passing as a slave. In particular, the actor's gesture of pointing at his rear—"aquí" (here)—while singing the last line must have caused the audience's laughter.

However, the comical performance of physical violence on stage holds a more perverse connotation: the scene familiarizes and normalizes violence against black men's bodies for the audience's pleasure. Studying the undetected forms of violence and domination in the everyday practices of enjoyment in nineteenth-century U.S. society, Saidiya Hartman suggests that the normalization of violence derives from the idea that slaves, due to their "emotional resources, animal needs, and limited affections," were naturally predisposed to endure violence (35). The same idea about black people's ability to withstand violence was also present in Spain. For instance, the first Spanish encyclopedia, the *Enciclopedia Moderna*, published between 1851 and 1855 and which aimed to instruct "la gran masa del pueblo" (the masses) (Mellado, "Prólogo" v), specified that black people were more indifferent to pain than whites because of their inherently enduring constitution ("Negros" 536).

Interestingly, physical and verbal violence are both absent in the representation of the female slave in the play. Instead, Perla, as representative of the female gender, is portrayed as inherently deceitful and flirtatious as she defines herself: "Para fingir, las mujeres, y sobre todas, yo. ¿Cuántas mentiras no habrán dicho mis ojos por capricho ó conveniencia?" (Women are good at faking; I'm the best at it. My eyes have lied many times for a whim or for convenience) (9). More importantly, Perla embodies palatable female black otherness, the *mulata*, the racialized and gendered other, which the playwright controls and dominates through her theatrical sexualization. Thus, Perla notices in her song to Roberto how her skin color scares white men:

> El verme morenita
> les causa miedo,
> sin saber lo que guardo
> dentro del pecho . . .
>
> (When they see that I am dark-skinned
> they are frightened,
> without knowing what I keep
> in my chest . . .) (18)

Yet her sexualization through the sensuous lyrics, music, and the actress's suggestive movements nulls any possible threat in reality. Instead of being depicted as aggressive like her black-skinned brother, Perla is portrayed as a charming "morenita" (18)—a dark woman with a light complexion—who attracts Roberto with her sensual and delightful personality and beauty. In fact, the use of the diminutive "-ita" when she describes herself as "morenita" points to her self-infantilization and, thus, to her representation as an unthreatening Other. Consequently, Roberto is not scared but attracted to her:

> tu cara
> no me dá miedo;
> verla junto á la mía
> és cuanto quiero.
>
> (your face
> does not frighten me:
> I just want it
> close to mine.) (18)

In fact, unlike Chimbo, she is not portrayed as black because, as explained above, black skin was normally associated with the ugly. She is not depicted as white either because, on stage, she and the actress playing her would have to wear blackface makeup to pass as a slave. Thus, given the end-of-the-century idea of female beauty—a white woman—in Europe as well as the spectators' familiarity with the comic tone of *género chico*, the black makeup would conceal the actress's attractiveness on stage and, as in Chimbo's case, would make the character comical to the audience, impeding their perception of Perla as a sensual character. In fact, as the zarzuela's title and her name both suggest, the female slave is compared to a pearl, a precious gem, whose native Cuban beauty acquires marketable qualities in the hands of imperial capitalism. Therefore, Roberto states that he has bought her precisely because "la llaman la Perla cubana" (they call her the Cuban Pearl) (6), and Don Carmelo, noticing her value, asks Roberto to sell her to him: "¿quieres venderme tu Perla?" (do you want to sell me your Pearl?) (13).

Even more interesting is the fact that Perla also depicts herself as a commodity in her flirtatious conversations with Roberto and Don Carmelo. When Don Carmelo laments that he cannot buy her because Roberto claims there is no money to purchase her, she replies "Eso prueba que valgo muy poco" (That proves I am not worth much) (14). However, soon thereafter, she admits her monetary value acknowledging that "he sido una adquisición muy cara" (I have been a pricey purchase) (15). Perla's casual comments on her monetary value actually normalize and naturalize her enslaved status. Her performance idealizes female slavery, obliterating the horrors suffered historically by real enslaved women. For instance, when she describes the person who sold her to Roberto, she defines him as "el encargado de mi venta" (the one in charge of selling me) (15) instead of "el negrero" (the slave trader), which glosses over the inhumane economic exchange between Roberto and the slave trader and which is at odds with the usual representation of the slave trader in nineteenth-century literature, as Lisa Surwillo notes (10).[37] Furthermore, Perla equates being an actual enslaved person and being a metaphorical slave to love. When Roberto frees Perla after she gives him the sum of money he paid for her, she claims: "Ahora me ha hecho el señor más esclava que nunca" (16).[38] She also states that she cannot abandon her master, "siendo el señor tan Bueno . . . (Con mucha zalamería.) . . . ¡Tan simpático!" ([because] he has been so good . . . [In a flattering tone] . . . So nice) (16). Perla's idealized account of her captivity contradicts the experiences of a majority of enslaved women in nineteenth-century Cuba.[39]

The fact that Doña Concha's slave status is not real but just a performance can explain Perla's idealization of the life of slavery. However, Doña Concha's unquestioning acceptance of Roberto's physical violence toward Chimbo shows that the high-class *mulata* is aware of the hardships of being a slave and perceives them as normal. In this sense, Doña Concha's European ancestry and economic status override the history of slavery inscribed in her skin color. This complex entanglement of color and class explains why Roberto's treatment of Chimbo does not deter Doña Concha from loving the Spaniard. Furthermore, the heroine's unconditional love for Roberto reinforces the audience's sympathy for the Spanish character, especially when, at the end of the story, he follows his heart by choosing Perla instead of his rich fiancée.

The play, indeed, portrays Roberto favorably from the very beginning. In his opening monologue and song, he describes himself as a shrewd entrepreneur—"Me llaman Roberto el diablo / por mi genio emprendedor" (They call me Roberto the devil for my business skill)—and a confident and fearless man: "En el mundo no hubo obstáculos / que no los venciera yo" (There has not been a hurdle / I have not been able to jump) (6). Roberto indeed exhibits the qualities associated with white imperialist masculinity in Western culture at the time. According to Eurocentric assumptions, the white man was positioned at the top of the racial and gender hierarchy as a symbol of his perfection and closeness to God. In contrast to women and other races, the white man stood out for his rational and intangible qualities that conformed his spirit. As Dyer remarks, apart from courage and determination, one of the main qualities of the white man's spirit was his enterprising nature that configured him as the natural leader of humanity's progress (31). According to this idea, Roberto is a natural modern entrepreneur with the energy and willpower that will keep not only his economic situation afloat but also that of Spain, as a representative of that nation. In fact, if there is a character who really benefits economically at the end of the play, it is Roberto.

Another positive trait that the play associates with Roberto is the fact that he strictly follows the traditional Spanish code of honor. Although the possession of these qualities seems to be shadowed by his intense desire for women—"Pero ante unos ojos lánguidos, / me postro como un melón" (But facing those drooping eyes / I become as soft as a melon) (6)—it is actually his womanizing nature that presents the character as familiar and endearing to the audience. Indeed, Roberto is presented as a pleasant Spanish Don Juan, a well-known character, with a curious twist. In his opinion, color is no detriment to a woman's beauty since his desire for women transcends racial boundaries:

> Me gusta una niña cándida,
> pero más me gustan dos;
> y si son de rostro angélico
> nunca reparo en color.

> (I like an honest girl,
> but I like two of them better;
> and if their face is angelic
> I do not care about color.) (6)

However, what seems to be a description of a nonracist heterosexual desire, actually reflects Roberto's masculinist view of women that corresponds to that of the stereotypical Spanish lover or Don Juan. Thus, his womanizing Spanish masculinity, described in the play in a positive light, would have been familiar and pleasing to a Spanish audience. Yet, despite his apparent nonracist sexual drive, Roberto realizes that his love for a penniless *mulata* would affect his social image in Cuba, as implied by his rhetorical question: "¿por qué no estaré yo en España, donde lo moreno es lo que priva?" (why am I not in Spain, where dark skin is everything?) (7). He humorously reiterates this idea associating his love for a dark woman with his dark fate: "¡Enamorado de una mulata, y arruinado! . . . ¡No puede darse porvenir más obscuro!" (In love with a mulata, and ruined! . . . What a dark future!) (20). Roberto's fate, however, changes when, at the end of the play, Perla reveals her true identity as Roberto's high-class moneylender, Doña Concha de Almeida. Although still a *mulata*, she bears the title "Doña," which suggests her inscription within respectable upper-class Cuban society, whereas her last name, "de Almeida," hints at her Spanish origins. Additionally, because Spain, like Brazil, understood miscegenation as a positive strategy to whiten the darker races and secure the superiority of the white race (Smith and Nalbone 3), the romantic union between Doña Concha and Roberto would be seen in a positive light.[40]

By marrying Roberto as Doña Concha, the *mulata* will perform an act of love, assuming her subservient role as the wife and giving all she possesses to her future Spanish groom. Thus, Roberto's possession of Doña Concha's exotic body and immense wealth through marriage functions as a trope for the colonization of Cuba by a masculine imperial Spain. Indeed, the association between Cuba and Perla is evident in the *mulata*'s flirtatious song to Roberto:

> Fueron mi cuna las puras olas;
> fué el sol de Cuba mi ardiente sol;
> fué mi alimento la *guanabana*
> y el aguacate y el marañón.

(The pure waves were my crib;
it was Cuba's sun that warmed me;
my nourishment was guanabana
and avocado and cashews.) (17)

By describing herself as a pearl born and nourished by Cuba's natural landscape and resources, the slave represents herself as an exotic virgin body ready to be colonized. In this sense, Perla symbolizes the sensual but "innocent, tropical Cuba" also portrayed in nineteenth-century Cuban theater (Lane 124). However, instead of being "rescued from the lascivious Spanish imperialist" (Lane 124), as in Cuban plays, Perla is portrayed as a gem to be colonized. The playwright's choice of name for the *mulata* character, "Perla," further underscores this idea. Because of its great natural resources and strategic location, Cuba was known as the Pearl of the Antilles among imperial powers such as the United States, England, and Spain (Pierpaoli 470). Even the character's real name, "Doña Concha," is symbolic, since her name (*concha*) is connected to her name as a slave "Perla." In this fashion, when the Spaniard marries Doña Concha he will still find the Pearl of the Antilles at his disposal. Roberto stands as a representative of white colonial masculinity since he possesses the white spirit that powered the imperial enterprise through the conquest and domination of space embodied by the Cuban *mulata*.

End-of-the-century *género chico* plays in Spain negotiated the colonial relationship between Cuba and the metropolis by demonstrating the inferiority of the colonial subject and Cuba's need to submit to metropolitan control (Soria 59–60). Following this idea, if the performance of blackface in Cuba and the United States contributed to defining the nation in racial terms (Lane 16), this theatrical impersonation in Spanish *género chico* was used to define the imperial national body as a familiar white and masculine body in opposition to the female and black other. Indeed, the two male protagonists are portrayed as opportunistic, promiscuous, and physically attractive, traits associated with the character of Don Juan, the well-known epitome of Spanish masculinity. As Roberta Johnson points out, after José Zorrilla's *Don Juan Tenorio* (1844) debut, "the figure increasingly became associated with national values" serving as a site of expression of diverse and at times conflicting ideas of Spanish national identity (111).[41]

In *Las Carolinas* and *La Perla cubana*, the figure of Don Juan transcends national boundaries to become the symbol of a new imperial Spain anchored in gender and racial hierarchies hinged to colonial ideologies. The happy marriage between the protagonists in both plays not only provides the customary felicitous ending of *género chico* plays, but it also symbolizes men's possession of women according to nineteenth-century law and the transfer of Cuban wealth into Spanish hands. In this sense, if romance can serve to reconcile ideological contradictions in national narratives, as Doris Sommer suggests in *Foundational Fictions, Las Carolinas* and *La Perla cubana* follow a trend within *género chico* in which "romantic alliances secure dominant racial, class, and gender hierarchies to prescribe imperial imaginings of the ideal relationship between metropolis and colony" (Soria 46). Ultimately, the mockery of Domingo's and Chimbo's characters through blackface, the sexualization of the *mulata,* and the association of women with the colonies serve as counterpoints to render Emilio and Roberto the successful protagonists of both plays. Therefore, the production, staging, and consumption of blackface and blackness in Spain respond to a white Spanish imaginary's desire to control and contain the fear when confronted with otherness. By reimagining the other that Spanish colonial enterprise had brought to the imperial "home," *género chico* reinforced Spaniards' imagined community based on a familiar sense of nationhood, while justifying the socioeconomic and ideological underpinnings of the Spanish empire.

Notes

1. The 2014–15 season at the Catalan National Theater dedicated to the *sarsuela* featured a white singer in blackface in the staging of *La Legió d'Honor* (1930). See pictures at www.tnc.cat/es/per-comencar-zarzuela. Following the Metropolitan Opera in New York, the Royal Theater of Madrid decided to eliminate blackface in Shakespeare's *Othello* in 2016. Blackface is also a common practice in the Three Wise Kings parade in Spanish cities on January 5. In this festivity, a white actor in blackface embodies King Baltasar.

2. I understand race not as biological phenomenon but as a cultural construct contingent on the sociohistorical context in which the term is used. Therefore, I see race "as a method of structuring society according to a supposedly natural order of difference and hierarchy that includes some in the racial fold and excludes many others" (Goode 4). Accordingly, I also find the conflation of race and color dependent on specific historically bound cultural beliefs. As Susan Gubar states, "[R]ace and color are not immutable categories but classifications with permeable boundaries" (247).

3. The depiction of black people and women as inferior was also a common feature in nineteenth-century minstrelsy in the United States (Lott 16; Toll 88).

4. The comical performance of blackface on the stage unveils similar transatlantic theatrical conventions founded on imperial ideology. As Catherine M. Cole remarks, "The colonial experience is certainly central to any consideration of the global economy of blackface, as the form both traveled and found fertile soil throughout the circuits of empire" (225).

5. In Cuba, blackface played a major role in the cultural production of the time, since it tapped into long-standing racial anxieties of the white population. According to Louis Pérez, the fear of slave rebellion and racial conflict among creoles was predominant throughout the century (79, 94).

6. For instance, David Sartorious notes how politicians and intellectuals in Cuba grew increasingly reluctant to see the positive influence of African culture in Cuba when, by 1840, the total black population surpassed the white (171). Ada Ferrer also indicates how the colonial elite and its supporters' fear of the black population was widely accepted in the 1890s despite the significant increase in the numbers of whites living in Cuba. Even within the insurgent movement, "black mobilization . . . also created anxieties" (*Insurgent Cuba* 112).

7. I use the term *pro-slavery* to refer to those who supported slavery but who did not necessarily join the anti-abolitionist movement. Similarly, not all antislavery supporters were explicitly abolitionists. Furthermore, Cuban and metropolitan antislavery ideology also differed, since in Spain, "abolitionists sought to reconstruct Spanish colonial hegemony on the basis of free labor" (Schmidt-Nowara, *Empire*, 126).

8. Spanish and Cuban slavery supporters did not share the same economic interests. According to Schmidt-Nowara, "While colonial slave-owners advocated free trade, metropolitan producers and defenders of colonial slavery categorically opposed free trade because protected Spanish and Antillean markets were essential to their prosperity" (*Empire* 57).

9. Indeed, Pamela Beth Radcliff notes that, from 1780 to 1867, 780,000 slaves were transported to Cuba, "virtually the same number sent to all of Spanish America between the sixteenth and eighteenth centuries" (30). In Puerto Rico, slavery was abolished in 1873.

10. The debate on such a controversial topic reached high levels of confrontation not only among the associations involved but also in the streets. Martínez Carreras observes that, in addition to numerous public demonstrations, there were also revolts in the streets of Madrid in 1872 (76).

11. See Soria's "Domesticating Cuba" and Vidal Tibbits's "Relaciones interraciales."

12. Nation-building processes in Spain and Catalonia differ greatly because Catalonia has been historically subjected to the political and administrative control of Castile and Madrid since the fifteenth century. Unlike Spain, in the nineteenth century Catalonia became a "nation without state" (McRoberts 2). However, as

seen later in this essay, Catalonia's flourishing economy benefited greatly from the exploitation of the colonies. Thus, despite the evident political and cultural differences in the Spanish and Catalan nation-building projects, imperial designs fueled their respective nationalist imaginaries.

13. The First and Second Catalanist Congresses (1880 and 1883 respectively), the Memorial de Greuges (1885), a statement of grievances "denouncing Castile's oppression of Catalonia, the formation of the Lliga de Catalunya (League of Catalonia) in 1887, the publication of the Bases de Manresa in 1892, and the Compendi de Doctrina Catalanista (Compendium of Catalinist Doctrine) in 1895, during the same era as that of the plays analyzed here, exemplify the consolidation of Catalan nationalism (McRoberts 24–26).

14. To counteract the resurgence of Catalan and Basque nationalism, the Spanish government issued the 1867 Royal Order that forced Catalan and Basque playwrights to write parts of their plays in Spanish. As a response, Catalan authors often included a grotesque character speaking in Castilian (Navarra Ordoño 26). Curiously, the only character that speaks Spanish in *Las Carolinas* is the cuckolded Don Simón. His portrayal as a man who lacks control over his domestic affairs can be read as a metaphor of an emasculated Spain.

15. Ferrer i Codina's decision to name the two female characters and the plantation "Carolina" further exemplifies the association between gender, slavery, and colonialism in the play.

16. The Peace of Zanjón marked the end of the Ten Years' War (1868–1878), Cuba's first war for independence. It reestablished Cuba as a Spanish colony, freed the slaves who had fought in the conflict, and promised future reforms (Pérez 96–97). Soon thereafter, in August 1879, the Little War took place for a year.

17. All the translations are mine.

18. Don Ramón is obviously idealizing the United States here, since racial inequality continued after the abolition of slavery in the country.

19. When Don Ramón tells his daughter of his intention to help Domingo escape slavery, he also mentions that he is aware that Domingo's slave owner "[es] trova á Barcelona" (is in Barcelona) (11). The presence of Domingo's slave owner in Barcelona hints at Catalonia's role in the slave trade. Similarly, the fact that the fugitive slave is supposed to come in a trading ship—"[el] San Roque"—from Cuba also emphasizes the existence of these transatlantic economic connections between Catalonia and Cuba.

20. Francisco Martí Torrens, Juan Güell i Ferrer, Josep Xifré, Salvador Samà i Martí, Joan Illas i Ferré are some of the names of the Catalans involved in slavery and the slave trade. Although many of the Catalans became involved in the trade once they migrated to Cuba, Maluquer de Motes reminds us that the slave trade was also operational in Barcelona (109).

21. Cuban pineapples gained great popularity in Spain, especially in Catalonia where industrialists such as Isidro Soler marketed the fruit in innovative ways (Fernández Prieto 257).

22. The tango in the highly popular *zarzuela Cádiz* (1886) also portrays slave speech in a similar humoristic and derogatory way.

23. In end-of-the-century Spain, the terms *tango* and *habanera* were used indistinguishably. See Sánchez Sánchez for a historical account of this musical form in Spain and Guerrero Fernández for an overview of the influence of Cuban music on nineteenth-century Spanish *zarzuela*.

24. The absence of Domingo's voice in *Las Carolinas* contrasts with slave narratives in the United States, which relied on the slave's voice to humanize him/her, and were a vital element of the abolitionist movement. In the nineteenth-century United States, Philip Gould states that slave narratives "self-consciously stage scenes of speaking and wield tropes of utterance to counter the constant prospect of being silenced" ("The Rise" 20).

25. The crisis sparked a strong nationalist response among different sectors of Spanish society, including irate public demonstrations in Madrid where protesters attacked the German embassy (Elizalde Pérez-Grueso 54; Del Rey Vicente and Canales Torres 27). In Barcelona, the public patriotic demonstration was widely supported by groups of different political alliance, from Republicans to supporters of Catalan autonomy, and attracted as many people as the demonstration in Madrid (Rodrigo y Alharilla 349–50). In the play, Emilio mentions how his watch was stolen at "la manifestació per lo de las Carolinas" (at the demonstration for Las Carolinas) (9).

26. Although this *zarzuela* was first staged in 1890, it was written thirteen years earlier, as shown in Jackson Veyán's correspondence with music composer Francisco Asenjo Barbieri ("Sr. D. Asenjo Barbieri" 668). This would explain why *La Perla* still portrays slavery as a common practice in Cuba four years after its abolition. At the same time, it also hints at the fact that the abolition law did not eliminate racial and pro-slavery mentality in the metropolis.

27. For other accounts on the connection between ugliness and black people, see Bindman et al. and Young.

28. Mellado's *Enciclopedia* states that the physical appearance of black people, such as their "nariz ancha y aplastada" and their bodily shape, point to "una modificación de la especie humana . . . que se asemeja al orangután" (519).

29. For a more detailed analysis of Olona's *zarzuela* and the representation of this black character, see Soria's "Domesticating Cuba." The fact that Jackson Veyán includes an intertextual reference to Olona's play attests to the enduring and negative influence of this *zarzuela* in the construction of the attitude toward black people in the Spanish popular imaginary.

30. Mellado's encyclopedia describes the skin color of black people as "aceitoso y sucio" (oily) with a "tinte carbonado" (carbon-like dye) (536). The author goes even farther to claim that their skin color is actually an "escrecion de carbono superabundante [*sic*]" (superabundant excretion of coal) (537).

31. In end-of-the century Spain and Cuba, the phrase "de color" was used by colonial authorities to refer to black and mixed-race people derogatorily (Ferrer, *Insurgent Cuba* 11). In this sense, the association between skin color and race was

culturally determined. In fact, as Ferrer notes, the phrase was not used to describe "Chinese and Yucatecan contract laborers, who were generally classified in censuses as white" (n. 205).

32. In *Las Carolinas*, Emilio's coal blackface is also seen as dirt that he tries to clean unsuccessfully. After washing his face in water, he discovers that he is dirtier than before: "Ja dech estar net. . . . Batua'l dimoni. Encara m' he enmascarat més" (I must be clean now. . . . What the devil? I have made myself even dirtier) (16).

33. Juan's metareferential comment also illustrates the practical issues that white actors faced when performing blackface.

34. Referring to the U.S. context, Lott comments on the fact that early minstrelsy audiences believed in the racial authenticity of blackface performance (8). However, this author also states that the interplay between blackface as mask and as authentic representation of race and its association with "irony toward the fakes and belief in them make the task of gauging audience response a dizzying one" (9).

35. *Las Carolinas* also exploits this performative aspect when Lino notes that while Domingo's face is black his hands and ears remain white (22).

36. While Don Carmelo's and his niece's race is not made explicit in the *zarzuela*, it can be assumed that they are either Spaniards or *criollos*, since they belong to the Cuban elite and no mention is made of their skin color.

37. According to Lisa Surwillo, the slave trader in Spanish fiction symbolized "the monstrous form of the state: an imperiled empire, complicit with Black Legend stereotypes, but within the capitalist framework that enabled the empire to flourish" (10).

38. One of the play's inconsistencies is that Roberto never questions how Perla, being a slave, has access to such a considerable sum of money.

39. Masters and overseers often subjected female slaves to brutal physical and psychological abuse. Actual female slaves' legal denunciations and testimonies can be found in García Rodríguez.

40. See Telles for an account of the use of miscegenation as a "whitening" strategy in Brazil.

41. Indeed, the influence of Zorrilla's play—itself inspired by Tirso de Molina's drama *El burlador de Sevilla y convidado de piedra* (1630)—on *Las Carolinas* and *La Perla cubana* is not surprising, considering that Zorrilla's version became "one of the key plays—if not the key play—of the nineteenth century" with numerous theatrical renditions and parodies (Gies 286).

Works Cited

Arroyo Jiménez, Paloma. "La Sociedad Abolicionista Española, 1864–1886." *Cuadernos de Historia Moderna y Contemporánea*, vol. 3, 1982, pp. 127–49; revistas.

ucm.es/index.php/CHMC/article/view/CHMC8282110127A/1260; accessed May 15, 2017.
Ayguals de Izco, Wenceslao. "Los Negros." *El cancionero del pueblo: colección de novelas, cuentos y canciones originales en prosa y verso*, vol. 3, Wenceslao Ayguals de Izco, 1843, pp. 107–207; archive.org/stream/elcancionerodel3v4aygu#page/n3/mode/2up/search/negro; accessed May 15, 2017.
Bindman, David, and Henry Louis Gates, eds. *The Image of the Black in Western Art*. Harvard UP, 2011.
Blanc, Luis, et al. *Romper cadenas*. Teatro de Novedades, 1873.
Blanco García, Francisco P. *La literatura española en el siglo XIX*. Vol. 3, Madrid, Sáenz de Jubera, 1894.
Burgos, Javier de. *Cádiz*. Composed by Federico Chueca and Joaquín Valverde, R. Velasco, 1897.
Clark, Walter Aaron. *Enrique Granados: Poet of the Piano*. Oxford UP, 2006.
Cole, Catherine M. "American Ghetto Parties and Ghanaian Concert Parties: A Transnational Perspective on Blackface." *Burnt Cork: Traditions and Legacies of Blackface Minstrelsy*, edited by Stephen Johnson, U of Massachusetts P, 2012, pp. 51–72.
Corwin, Arthur F. *Spain and the Abolition of Slavery in Cuba, 1817–1886*. U of Texas P, 1967.
Dyer, Richard. *White*. Routledge, 1997.
Elizalde Pérez-Grueso, María Dolores. *España en el Pacífico, la colonia de las Islas Carolinas (1885–1899): un modelo colonial en el contexto internacional del imperialismo*. CSIC, 1992.
Fernández Prieto, Leida. *Cuba agrícola: mito y tradición (1878–1920)*. CSIC, 2005.
Feros, Antonio. *Speaking of Spain: The Evolution of Race and Nation in the Hispanic World*. Harvard UP, 2017.
Ferrer, Ada. "Cuban Slavery and Atlantic Antislavery." *Slavery and Antislavery in Spain's Atlantic Empire*, edited by Josep M. Fradera and Christopher Schmidt-Nowara, Berghahn, 2013, pp. 134–57.
———. *Insurgent Cuba: Race, Nation, and Revolution, 1868–1898*. U of North Carolina P, 2005.
Ferrer i Codina, Antoni. *Las Carolinas*. Francisco Badía, 1903.
Fradera, Josep María. "Miquel Biada i l'esclavitud a Cuba." *Fulls del Museo Arxiu de Santa María de Mataró*. 1982, pp. 29–33. Revistes Catalanes amb Accés Obert (RACO); www.raco.cat/index.php/FullsMASMM/article/view/115217/144091.
———. "La participació catalana en el tràfic d'esclaus (1789–1845)." *Recerques*, no. 16, 1984, pp. 119–39. Revistes Catalanes amb Accés Obert (RACO)' www.raco.cat/index.php/Recerques/article/view/137618/241428.
———, and Christopher Schmidt-Nowara. *Slavery and Antislavery in Spain's Atlantic Empire*. Berghahn Books, 2013.

García Rodríguez, Gloria. *Voices of the Enslaved in Nineteenth-Century Cuba: A Documentary History*. U of North Carolina P, 2011.

Gies, David Thatcher. *The Theatre in Nineteenth-Century Spain*. Cambridge UP, 2005.

Goode, Joshua. *Impurity of Blood: Defining Race in Spain, 1870–1930*. Louisiana State UP, 2009.

Gould, Philip. *Barbaric Traffic: Commerce and Antislavery in the Eighteenth-Century Atlantic World*. Harvard UP, 2009.

———. "The Rise, Development, and Circulation of the Slave Narrative." *The Cambridge Companion to the African American Slave Narrative*, edited by Audrey A. Fisch, Cambridge UP, 2007, pp. 11–27.

Graullera Sanz, Vicente. *La esclavitud en Valencia en los siglos XVI y XVII*. CSIC, 1978.

Gubar, Susan. *Racechanges: White Skin, Black Face in American Culture*. Oxford UP, 2000.

Guerrero Fernández, Aimée. "Presencia cubana en la zarzuela española." *Revista de Musicología*, vol. 28, no. 1, June 2005, pp. 443–54.

Hartman, Saidiya V. *Scenes of Subjection: Terror, Slavery, and Self-Making in Nineteenth-Century America*. Oxford UP, 1997.

Hughes, Robert. *Barcelona*. Random House, 1993.

Jackson Veyán, José. *La perla cubana*. Composed by Gaspar Espinosa de los Monteros, R. Velasco, 1890.

———. "Sr. D. Asenjo Barbieri." 11 August 1877. *Documentos sobre música española y epistolario*, edited by Emilio Casares, vol. 2, Fundación Banco Exterior, 1988, p. 668.

Johnson, Roberta. *Gender and Nation in the Spanish Modernist Novel*. Vanderbilt UP, 2003.

Klein, Martin A. "Cimarron," *Historical Dictionary of Slavery and Abolition*. Rowman and Littlefield, 2014, p. 112.

Lane, Jill. *Blackface Cuba, 1840–1895*. U of Pennsylvania P, 2005.

Lipski, John M. *A History of Afro-Hispanic Language: Five Centuries, Five Continents*. Cambridge UP, 2005.

Lott, Eric. "Blackface and Blackness: The Minstrel Show in American Culture." *Inside the Minstrel Mask: Readings in Nineteenth-Century Blackface Minstrelsy*, edited by Annemarie Bean et al., Wesleyan UP, 1996, pp. 3–34.

Lugones, Maria. "The Coloniality of Gender." *Worlds and Knowledges Otherwise*, vol. 2, Spring 2008, pp. 1–17; globalstudies.trinity.duke.edu/wp-content/themes/cgsh/materials/WKO/v2d2_Lugones.pdf; accessed September 15, 2017.

———. "Toward a Decolonial Feminism." *Hypatia: A Journal of Feminist Philosophy*, vol. 25, no. 4, Fall 2010, pp. 742–59.

Luna, Angel María de. *Haley, o, el traficante de negros: drama en cuatro actos, en prosa*. Francisco Pantoja, 1853.

Maluquer de Motes, Jordi. "La burgesia catalana i l'esclavitud colonial: modes de producció i pràctica política." *Recerques*, vol. 3, 1974, pp. 83–116.

Martínez Carreras, José U. "La abolición de la esclavitud en España durante el siglo XIX." *Esclavitud y derechos humanos: La lucha por la libertad del negro en el siglo XIX*, CSIC, 1990, pp. 63–77.

McAllister, Marvin Edward. *Whiting Up: Whiteface Minstrels and Stage Europeans in African American Performance*. U of North Carolina P, 2011.

McClintock, Anne. *Imperial Leather: Race, Gender, and Sexuality in the Colonial Contest*. Routledge, 2013.

McRoberts, Kenneth. *Catalonia: Nation Building without a State*. Oxford UP, 2001.

Mellado, Francisco de Paula. "Negros." *Enciclopedia Moderna: Diccionario universal de literatura, ciencias, artes, agricultura, industria y comercio*, vol. 1, Establecimiento de Mellado, 1854, pp. 519–44.

———. Prólogo. *Enciclopedia Moderna: Diccionario universal de literatura, ciencias, artes, agricultura, industria y comercio*, vol. 1, Establecimiento de Mellado, 1854, pp. v–xix.

Mignolo, Walter. "The Geopolitics of Knowledge and the Colonial Difference." *The South Atlantic Quarterly*, vol. 101, no. 1, 2000, pp. 57–96.

———. "Introduction: Coloniality of Power and De-colonial Thinking." *Cultural Studies*, vol. 21, no. 2–3, pp. 155–67.

———. "Coloniality: The Darker Side of Modernity." *Modernologies: Contemporary Artists Researching Modernity and Modernism*. Edited by Sabine Breitwieser. Museu Dar Contemporani de Barcelona, 2009.

Molina, Tirso de. *El Burlador de Sevilla*. Edited by Carmen Becerra Suárez, AKAL, 2008.

Mora Alzinelles, Víctor, and Lluís Capdevilla Vilallonga. *La legió d'Honor*. Composed by Rafael Martínez Valls, 1930.

Navarra Ordoño, Andreu. *La región sospechosa: La dialéctica hispanocatalana entre 1875 y 1939*. U Autònoma of Barcelona, 2012.

Ostendorf, Berndt. "Creole Cultures and the Process of Creolization: With Special Attention to Louisiana." *Louisiana Culture from the Colonial Era to Katrina*. Louisiana State UP, 2008, pp. 103–35.

Parfitt, Tudor. *Black Jews in Africa and the Americas*. Harvard UP, 2013.

Pérez, Louis A. *Cuba: Between Reform and Revolution*. Oxford UP, 2014.

Pierpaoli, Paul G. "Pearl of the Antilles." *The Encyclopedia of the Spanish-American Wars: A Political, Social, and Military History*, edited by Spencer C. Tucker, vol. 1, ABC-CLIO, 2009, p. 470.

Piqueras, José Antonio. *La esclavitud en las Españas: Un lazo transatlántico*. Catarata, 2011.

Quijano, Aníbal. "Coloniality of Power, Eurocentrism, and Latin America." *Nepantla: Views from South*, vol. 1, no. 3, 2000, pp. 533–80.

Radcliff, Pamela Beth. *Modern Spain: 1808 to the Present*. Wiley and Sons, 2017.

Rey Vicente, Miguel Del, and Carlos Canales Torres. *Breve historia de la Guerra del 98*. Ediciones Nowtilus S.L., 2010.

Rodrigo y Alharilla, Martín. "From Periphery to Centre: Transatlantic Capital Flows, 1830–1890." *The Caribbean and the Atlantic World Economy*, edited by A. B. Leonard and David Pretel, Palgrave Macmillan UK, 2015, pp. 217–37; *link.springer.com*, doi:10.1057/9781137432728_10; accessed May 15, 2017.

Sáez de Melgar, Faustina. *La Cadena rota*. Edited by Eduardo Pérez-Rasilla Bayo, Asociación de Directores de Escena de España, 1998.

Said, Edward. *Orientalism*. 1979. Vintage Books, 1994.

Sánchez Sánchez, Víctor. "La habanera en la zarzuela española del siglo diecinueve: Idealización marinera de un mundo tropical." *Cuadernos de Música, Artes Visuales y Artes Escénicas*, vol. 3, no. 1, 2006–2007, pp. 4–26.

Sartorious, David. *Ever Faithful: Race, Loyalty, and the Ends of Empire in Spanish Cuba*. Duke UP, 2013.

Schmidt-Nowara, Christopher. *Empire and Antislavery: Spain, Cuba, and Puerto Rico, 1833–1874*. U of Pittsburgh P, 1999.

———. "National Economy and Atlantic Slavery: Protectionism and Resistance to Abolitionism in Spain and the Antilles, 1854–1874." *Hispanic American Historical Review*, vol. 78, no. 4, 1998, pp. 603–29.

———. "Spain and the Politics of the Second Slavery." *The Politics of the Second Slavery*, edited by Dale W. Tomich, State U of New York P, 2016, pp. 57–81.

Schiwy, Freya. "Decolonization and the Question of Subjectivity." *Cultural Studies*, vol. 21, n. 2–3, 2007, pp. 271–94.

Serna, Juan M de la. "Bozal." *The Historical Encyclopedia of World Slavery*, edited by Junius P Rodriguez, ABC-CLIO, 1997, vol. 1, p. 97.

Smith, Jennifer, and Lisa Nalbone. "Introduction." *Intersections of Race, Class, Gender, and Nation in Fin-de-Siècle Spanish Literature and Culture*. Routledge, 2017, pp. 1–22.

Sommer, Doris. *Foundational Fictions: The National Romances of Latin America*. U of California P, 1993.

Soria, Mar. "Domesticating Cuba: Romantic Liaisons and Imperial Power in Spanish Zarzuela." *Intersections of Race, Class, Gender, and Nation in Fin-de-siècle Spanish Literature and Culture*, edited by Jennifer Smith and Lisa Nalbone, Routledge, 2017, pp. 24–45.

Surwillo, Lisa. *Monsters by Trade: Slave Traffickers in Modern Spanish Literature and Culture*. Stanford UP, 2014.

Telles, Edward E. *Race in Another America: The Significance of Skin Color in Brazil*. Princeton UP, 2004.

Thomas, Hugh. *The Slave Trade: The Story of the Atlantic Slave Trade: 1440–1870*. Simon and Schuster, 2013.

Thorton, John K. "Loango: Slave Trade." *Encyclopedia of African History*, edited by Kevin Shillington, vol. 3, Fitzroy Dearborn, 2005, pp. 847–48.

Toll, Robert C. "Social Commentary in Late-Nineteenth-Century White Minstrelsy." *Inside the Minstrel Mask: Readings in Nineteenth-Century Blackface Minstrelsy*, edited by Annemarie Bean et al., Wesleyan UP, 1996, pp. 86–110.

Tucker, Spencer, editor. *The Encyclopedia of the Spanish-American and Philippine-American Wars: A Political, Social, and Military History*. ABC-CLIO, 2009.

Versteeg, Margot. *De fusiladores y morcilleros: el discurso cómico del género chico, 1870–1910*. Rodopi, 2000.

Vidal Tibbits, Mercedes. "Relaciones interraciales en el teatro peninsular del siglo XIX." *Biblioteca Virtual Miguel de Cervantes*; www.cervantesvirtual.com/obra-visor/relaciones-interraciales-en-el-teatro-peninsular-del-siglo-xix-0/html/018cd96e-82b2-11df-acc7-002185ce6064_3.html#I_0; accessed May 15, 2017.

Wirtz, Kristina. *Performing Afro-Cuba: Image, Voice, Spectacle in the Making of Race and History*. U of Chicago P, 2014.

Young, Robert. *Colonial Desire: Hybridity in Theory, Culture, and Race*. Routledge, 1995.

Zeno y Gandía, Manuel. "Influencias del clima en las enfermedades del hombre." *Memorias leídas en la Sociedad Anatómica Española*, Julián Peña, 1873, pp. 77–91; reader.digitale-sammlungen.de/resolve/display/bsb11037702.html. Bayerische StaatsBibliothek digital; accessed May 15, 2017.

Zeuske, Michael, and Orlando García Martínez. "La Amistad: Ramón Ferrer in Cuba and the Transatlantic Dimensions of Slaving and Contraband Trade." *Slavery and Antislavery in Spain's Atlantic Empire*, Berghahn Books, 2013, pp. 200–28.

Zorrilla, José. *Don Juan Tenorio: drama religioso-fantástico en dos partes*. Antonio Yenes, 1846.

PART III

GENDER AND COLONIALISM IN LITERARY AND POLITICAL DEBATES

6

Becoming Useless

Masculinity, Able-Bodiedness, and Empire in Nineteenth-Century Spain

JULIA CHANG

Gender is a matter inherent to the modern state, and the military has long served as an organization for curating masculinity. On September 30, 1842, *La Junta Directiva de Sanidad Militar* (Sanitary Corps Board of Directors) published the newly approved medical criteria for military conscription in Spain.[1] The document stipulates: "Son *inútiles* para el servicio militar los mozos que tengan ó padezcan los defectos físicos ó enfermedades comprendidas en el cuadro" (Those considered useless for military service are the young men who possess or suffer from the physical defects or illnesses included in the table) ("Reglamento" 211; emphasis mine).[2] Among the many "physical defects" that would disqualify someone from military conscription, "[p]érdida completa del *miembro viril* ó de ambos testículos" (total loss of the virile member or of both testicles) is perhaps the most salient (Article 11; emphasis mine). The process of making ordinary men into soldiers entailed identifying, quite literally, the *virile members* of the state.[3] Engendering the ideal male was a central issue for the military in nineteenth-century Spain. As Michael Iarocci explains, "It is difficult to imagine a more self-consciously 'masculine' institution within the nineteenth-century-gendered division of labour and social space" ("Virile Nation" 191).[4]

It is important to recall the stakes of this biopolitical battleground. The military's investment in gender norms had particular implications for the projects of colonialism it helped sustain. The Spanish state sought out virile, able-bodied men largely in the service of war. In fact, colonial uprisings, American wars of emancipation, and new imperial endeavors drove the need for military conscription in Spain throughout the nineteenth century. Esteban Rodríguez Ocaña describes the significant role that medicine played vis-à-vis the military and its colonial projects. He writes:

> La situación colonial exagera determinados aspectos de la relación medicina-público, en términos de conceder autoridad (en el sentido de poder coactivo) a los profesionales cuando tratan con población autóctona, pero que no son exclusivos de ella: ocurre en el ámbito militar, donde los agentes sanitarios poseen un grado y pueden, por lo tanto, disponer sobre todos los sujetos con grado inferior a ellos, comenzando por los soldados de tropa, naturalmente.
>
> (The colonial situation exaggerates certain aspects of the relationship between medicine and the public, in regard to granting authority (in terms of coercive power) to professionals when they are dealing with a native population, but this is not exclusive to a colonial situation: It also occurs in the military sphere, where health workers are commissioned and can, therefore, outrank subjects with inferior standing, beginning with infantry soldiers, naturally.) (Rodríguez Ocaña 297)

What I hope will become clear over the course of this essay is that the military is where gender works most clearly in the service of colonialism. Empire has not only entailed the policing of bodies in the colonies, but it has also directly impacted the gendering of Spain's national citizenry. Soldiers' bodies—inspected by military doctors—become the visible projection of Spanish imperial power in the colonies. This power, I argue, is predicated on the intersection of gender and able-bodiedness. Yet, while Spanish military power depends on its able-bodied men, nowhere else is masculinity more important and yet more fragile.

Richard Cleminson and Francisco Vázquez García have commented that Spain's lack of virility was blamed for the loss of its American colonies in the first half of the nineteenth century (*Hermaphroditism* 18). Later, in the aftermath of colonial defeat, a collective sense of impotence exacerbated concerns around the virility of the nation's men. The so-called Disaster of

1898 ignited biopolitical concerns that led the military to seek a racial explanation for Spain's military defeat. "The military's Sanitary Corps," Joshua Goode explains, "entrusted with the mission to identify the 'useful Spanish soldier,' took as its mission the improvement not of colonized peoples, but of soldiers who seemed unable to control or conquer them" (125). In contrast with other European nations, such as France, England, and Germany, which deployed racial theories for the purposes of governing their colonies in a "more modern and efficient manner," the Spanish military applied such theories of race domestically (Goode 122). Racial management took place in the "context of military retrenchment" and concerned "not the colonized other, but the deficient Spaniard who did not measure up to other European or U.S. Forces" (Goode 123). Thus, for example, in the early-twentieth-century anthropologists Federico Olóriz and Manuel Antón sought to define the "useful Spaniard" (Goode 123) and General Weyler, the minister of war, well known for his development of concentration camps in Cuba, sponsored an anthropological study of the "useful Spanish man" to serve in the military (Goode 129). In 1911, Luis Sánchez Fernández, doctor and super-inspector of the *Sanidad Militar* (Sanitary Corps), presented an extensive study on the useful Spaniard from a medical standpoint at a conference in Granada sponsored by the *Asociación Española para el Progreso de las Ciencias* (Spanish Association for the Advancement of Science). As so many "useful" Spaniards were sacrificed in colonial wars, regenerating "el español útil" (the useful Spaniard) became key to reviving the Spanish nation in the wake of its colonial failures.

Examining medicine and narrative fiction, this essay probes the process of engendering the masculine ideal of *el útil* (the useful), alongside his counterpart, *el inútil* (the useless). Engaging with feminist and queer approaches to disability as well as Foucault's theories of disciplinary power and biopolitics, I unpack the concept of utility in the context of Spain's imperial anxiety in the nineteenth century. In so doing, I demonstrate how ability operates as a powerful and expansive cultural narrative that intersects with gender, sexuality, beauty, and, more tacitly, race. These identificatory categories are all crucial components to the production of the soldier as an extension of imperial power, just as they produce "the useless." This essay is comprised of four main sections. Section one, "The Colonizer," critically engages with decolonial feminist scholarship and proposes a nuanced understanding of how colonialism and gender intertwine by looking at the production of the colonizer rather than just the colonized. From there I turn to the figure of "el soldado español" (The Spanish Soldier), a romantic image of the Spanish soldier, contrasted with the bleak historical reality of the military in the nineteenth century. Next, I examine the concept of uselessness. Bringing disability studies into conversation with Michel Foucault's theorization of "utility," I interrogate the criteria that rendered men *inútil* (useless). In the final section, "El cojito," (The Little Cripple) I extend my analysis of utility to Benito Peréz Galdós's *Aita Tettauen*—a historical novel that features a young boy with a physical disability who becomes enamored with the military in the midst of the Spanish-Moroccan War.

The Colonizer

Argentine philosopher María Lugones has been one of the key figures in laying the groundwork for decolonial feminism, a school of thought that treats gender as "a colonial concept and a mode of organization of relations of production, property relations, of cosmologies and ways of knowing" (186). Lugones explains that the Spanish and Portuguese imposed a gender system in the Americas that eradicated indigenous cosmologies and alternative forms of social organization. Moreover, the gender binary and compulsory heterosexuality functioned differently for Europeans and colonial subjects: it dehumanized colonized people by rendering them animalistic, while making middle- and upper-class white women mere reproducers of their race (201). Lugones refers to these effects as the "dark" and "light" sides of colonialism, respectively. This gender system, Lugones insists, which takes the white European male as its norm, originated "during the Spanish and Portuguese colonial adventures and became full blown in late modernity" (206).

Decolonial feminism revises what Peruvian sociologist Aníbal Quijano has termed the "coloniality of power"—a concept that points to the colonial matrix from which modern Eurocentric power extends, ultimately outlasting the project of colonialism itself. The coloniality of power, Quijano elaborates, hinges on the axes of racial classification and the control of labor power (533). Building on this concept, Lugones advances a notion of "the coloniality of gender," trenchantly arguing that gender "was constitutive of the coloniality of power as the coloniality of power was constitutive of it" (202). From this intersectional perspective, gender, heterosexuality, and race function together to buttress European colonization and capitalism. This framework holds critical promise for decolonial feminist scholarship and responds to two major theoretical shortcomings: (1) the reductionist or complete absence of gender as an analytic in decolonial and postcolonial scholarship; and (2) the taken-for-granted universality of white women's subject position in certain feminist analyses of patriarchy.[5] While the coloniality of gender certainly proves fruitful for understanding how gender and sexuality operated in the service of Western colonial domination, it also runs the risk of construing a monolithic image of the Spanish/Portuguese/European male, who appears to occupy a uniform and stable position within gendered colonial relations.

As the editors of this volume have noted, the Spanish empire has received scant critical attention from feminist postcolonial scholars. Thus, even as Spain comes to stand in for the Colonizer writ large, the specificity of Spanish colonial projects remains understudied in critical approaches to Western colonialism, appearing marginal to the text as passing mentions and footnotes. Lugones's narrative, for one, depicts the colonizer in broad strokes: he is a white European male who appears immune to the forces of history and processes of subjectivation. In reality, however, the Spanish male's relationship to whiteness remained contested for about as long as the categories "European" and "white" have held political purchase—arguably throughout the modern colonial period.[6] The well-known saying "Africa begins in the Pyrenees," for example, attests to Spain's peripheral European status and questionable whiteness in the eyes of its northern neighbors.[7] Susan Martin-Márquez has commented on the internalization of this belief in the nineteenth century, noting that "many intellectuals in Spain had come to believe that their nation's fall into decline had to be attributed to some essential characteristic of Spaniards" (175). Indeed, the history of Spanish imperial decline and the power plays among competing Western empires heavily influenced the widespread perception of Spain's national decadence and racial inferiority.[8]

In the context of Spain's colonial defeat, medical doctors, anthropologists,[9] and fiction writers including Benito Pérez Galdós, Emilia Pardo Bazán, and Leopoldo Alas alike scrutinized its male population. Consequently, the Spanish male body became a spectacular site of impotence and emasculation on the national and global stage. In the first half of the century, Spanish defeat in the American wars of independence was attributed to the Spaniards' lack of virility. And in *fin-de-siglo* Spain, concern around the vitality of the Spanish race, in direct relation to its failed colonial projects, loomed large among the Spanish intelligentsia. Thus, if we are to treat the Western gender system as constitutive of the coloniality of power and vice versa, then we should attend to its productive forces on both sides of the Atlantic. For, as the Algerian writer Albert Memmi has shown, colonialism produced the oppressor and the oppressed: "The bond between the colonizer and colonized is thus destructive and creative. It destroys and re-creates the two partners of colonization into colonizer and colonized" (89).

What interests me, and what remains underdeveloped in current approaches to gender and Western colonialism, are the ways in which coloniality of gender underwrites the production of the *colonizer*. How do gender, race, and sexuality work through this destructive/creative bond? In order to address this question, we must begin with a more nuanced examination of the Spanish colonizer, whose maleness (and whiteness) cannot be taken for granted. Scholars have thoroughly documented how the female body served as a site of anxious inquiry for medical doctors, while masculinity and medicine remains understudied.[10] Woman, in the nineteenth century, undoubtedly stood as a sign of pathology. As Catherine Jagoe explains, "El varón es la pauta del cuerpo sano, desde la cual se mide al sexo femenino" (The male is the standard for the healthy body, against which the female sex is measured) (307). Yet while medical doctors may have rendered the male body the *ideal* figure of health, in reality doctors (acting as agents of the state) regularly scrutinized the youth male population. They did so, moreover, with the specific aim of determining who would be fit to secure the nation and its colonial territories. Cleminson and Vázquez García write that "[o]ne consequence of the ongoing colonial wars of the nineteenth century was regular call-ups to the army. The legal doctor's duty was to certify the male-ness of the conscript" (*Hermaphroditism* 19).

If military masculinity operated as expression of imperial power, it was an ideal that Spaniards, particularly in the nineteenth century, continually struggled to achieve. Acknowledging the fragility of this imperialist gender ideal does not negate the fact that gender operated as a technique of domination in the Americas and elsewhere. Instead, my hope is to shed light on simultaneous operation of gender as an expression of imperial might *and* as a tool of colonization. These entwined processes of subjectivation and dehumanization attest to the pervasive, inescapable force of gender within projects of colonialism. Yet, even as a soldier's virility stands in as a sign of male colonial potency, he is not indestructible—he is vulnerable to the emasculating ravages of war.

El soldado español

In nineteenth-century Europe, the soldier exemplified the ideal citizen. Alan Forrest, commenting on postrevolutionary France, argued that "[v]irile and heroic values associated with the military became increasingly merged with the ideal of the citizen" (122). "Full citizenship," Forrest writes, "implied an acceptance of the duty to serve, and a willingness to sacrifice oneself for the cause of the community" (112). The same was true in Spain. Geoffrey Jensen explains that, in the nineteenth century, Spain saw the emergence of the liberal-romantic notion of the "citizen solider" whose *contribución de sangre* (blood contribution) was expected in exchange for constitutional rule (22). What is more, the soldier stood as a symbol of national unity during a century fraught with civil wars and cantonal rebellions. Military historian Captain Francisco Villamartín claimed in his book *Nociones del arte militar* (1869) that war produced "el soldado español" (97). Acknowledging the racial and regional differences that had long divided Spain, he writes: "provincialistas en la paz, españoles en la guerra" (provincialists during peacetime, Spanish during war) (99, qtd. in Jensen 29). We can trace this romantic notion of war in Benito Pérez Galdós's *Episodios Nacionales*. In his analysis of *Trafalgar*, Michael Iarocci argues that "[b]y fusing a coming-of-age narrative with the representation of the nation at war, Galdós has foregrounded the nexus between the assumption of an adult male gender identity, on the one hand, and the emergence of nationalist ideology, on the other" (193). Even in the wake of Spain's defeat in the Battle of Trafalgar, then, the productive force of war endures. For one of its "rhetorical effects," writes Iarocci, "is to 'produce' men, regardless of the outcome of battle . . . rendering the male citizen of the idealized state" (196).

These romantic images of the virile citizen-soldier appear quixotic, however, when contrasted to the bleak historical reality of the Spanish military. Despite the liberal-romantic call to defend the nation, there were men who simply refused serve. Those who avoided conscription could hardly be blamed. Many did so because of the dire conditions in the colonies under which soldiers fought. Carolyn Boyd notes, for example, that Spanish troops in the Americas "were outnumbered, neglected, and unpaid" and "fought a losing battle against insurgency and disease," thus making conscription highly unpopular in the 1820s (68). The latter proved to also be true in the second half of the century, when disease ravaged Spanish troops in North Africa. In the introduction to *Higiene militar* (1909), Martín Salazar cites the Spanish-Moroccan War (1859–60) as one of the most important military campaigns of the nineteenth century after the American colonial wars (10). Salazar writes that of the fifty thousand soldiers deployed nineteen thousand fell ill and an additional three thousand died from illness (10). These numbers were exponentially higher in Cuba. In an 1897 publication, entitled *La salud del europeo en América y Filipinas*, medical doctor Víctor Suarez Capalleja exclaims: "¡Ojalá se hubiese abrigado más á nuestros soldados y tal vez hoy estaría terminada la guerra de Cuba, abismo donde se consumen tantos millones y, lo que importa más, donde se pierde gran parte de la flor y esperanza de nuestra duchada patria!" (If only our soldiers were better protected maybe today the War in Cuba would be over, a hell where millions are consumed, and even more importantly, where a significant proportion of our best and brightest, the hope for the future of our country, are lost) (196). According to Stanley Payne, many troops deployed to Cuba never even made it to the battlefield. By one account, 49,000 Spanish soldiers were hospitalized for noncombat illnesses during the last ten months of 1895. This number reached a staggering 232,000 in 1896 and 231,000 in just the first half of 1897 (Payne 76). Payne explains, "Such figures were not made public during the war, but the grotesquely high mortality rate in the Spanish Army during peacetime was a matter of common knowledge to many. It eventually became impossible to disguise the realities of the Cuban campaign" (76).

In addition to these conditions, social class played a decisive role in determining conscription. Geoffrey Jensen points out that the Spanish military was comprised largely of men from the lower classes.[11] This is because any male had the right to hire substitutes or make payments to avoid military service. The *quintas* (conscription), as it was called, was an "unjust system of conscription that subjected the working classes to involuntary and inhuman servitude while permitting the middle and upper classes to purchase their way out of service" (Boyd 76). By 1883 this practice generated an estimated 77 million pesetas yearly from such payments (48). During the Restoration period, the price for draft redemption was set at a hefty sum of 1,200 pesetas and the majority of young men who purchased their way out of military service came, not from the aristocracy, but the bourgeoisie (Payne 48). This fact challenges the treatment of the bourgeois male as the exemplary modern citizen in Spain. Fernando Puell has argued that by 1868, there were large numbers of peasants and urban workers that comprised military recruits precisely because their families could not pay substitutes (210). Furthermore, they were conscious of the fact that they were "el único colectivo que aportaba hombres para a la milicia" (the only collective that supplied men for the militia) (Puell 210). In sum, although the military as an institution was intended to manufacture the citizen-soldier, in reality, it generated national ambivalence and gender trouble.

Los inútiles

The nineteenth century witnessed the rise of the biopolitical state, of which medicine and hygiene formed a key part.[12] Ricardo Campos Marín explains that, in the particular case of Spain, liberal revolution and industrialization expanded medicine's political and social jurisdiction:

> [L]os cambios en la medicina . . . tuvieron una proyección político-social de primer orden. En las nuevas circunstancias, medicina y estado estrecharon sus lazos. El médico como experto en la salud de los seres humanos reclamaba la acción del estado, y éste, como responsable del bienestar de sus ciudadanos, buscaba el consejo del médico sobre las medidas a adoptar. El proceso final no fue lineal ni simétrico y estuvo sometido a frecuentes desencuentros, pero la consecuencia de este continuado diálogo fue la extensión de la medicina a los más variados campos de la actividad humana, dejando sentir su presencia en ámbitos como la asistencia, la reforma social, la higiene y la lucha contra las epidemias.
>
> (Changes in medicine . . . had a socio-political impact of great consequence. Under these new circumstances, medicine and the state strengthened ties. The doctor, as an expert in the health of human beings, demanded the state act, and the state, responsible for the well-being of its citizens, sought the advice of the doctor regarding which measures to adopt. The final process was neither linear nor symmetrical and was subject to frequent disputes, but the result of this continuing dialogue was the expansion of medicine into the most varied fields of human activity, allowing its presence to be felt in areas like charity, social reform, hygiene, and the fight against epidemics.) (*Curar y gobernar* 14)

Similarly, Anne Gilfoil has argued that "[a]s a form of medical policing, hygiene's imperative was the regulation of biological and social relations, and its champions were the members of the medical profession" (37). Hygiene and legal medicine, both invested in social order, promoted ideas of sexual difference that were intolerant to gender ambiguity.[13] They upheld what Thomas Laqueur has termed the "two-sex model," a binary system that rendered hermaphroditism a thing of the past. In the case of Spain, Catherine Jagoe explains that prior to the eighteenth century, women were not seen as morphologically different than men (308).[14] Citing the Spanish translation of Jean-Jacques Rousseau's *Émile*, Jagoe asserts that idea of sexual difference intensified as French texts in translation made their way to the Peninsula (310).

Curating military masculinity in this context figured as part of a larger project of managing the national population. In nineteenth-century Spain there was a "need to seek out pathological and dissident strains in the national body" (Cleminson and Vázquez García, *Hermaphroditism* 18). Such "dissident strains" often encompassed those that experienced social, political and economic inequality (including prostitutes, criminals, and alcoholics) and were deemed " 'ilegales de la naturaleza' y, consecuentemente, de la sociedad" (criminals against nature, and therefore, against Society) (Campos Marín et al. x). In the case of those labeled "useless" by the military, we see how colonialism impacted the "administration" of sex in the metropolis. Doctors, by conducting these medical exams in accordance with the criteria of the *Sanidad Militar,* determined not only which men would have the capacity for combat, but also which individuals were sufficiently able-bodied and appropriately masculine to uphold and represent imperial power. The very medical discourse that produced "useful men" also, inevitably, produced the useless. The military, in conjunction with medicine, acted as a large scale and particularly powerful sorting mechanism that normalized (or pathologized) all those that were examined in accordance with a gendered understanding of ability. These very operations that separated the population (soldiers/useful men) from this excess (the useless) are exemplary of how the "technology of sex" enables the regulation of populations through what Michel Foucault terms biopower (*History of Sexuality* 146).

In contradistinction to sovereign power, biopower was concerned with the management of life (rather than the taking of life) and entailed "distributing the living in the domain of value and *utility*" (144; emphasis mine). Biopower, Foucault explains, "has to qualify, measure, appraise, and hierarchize, rather than display itself in its murderous splendor; it does not have to draw the line that separates the enemies of the sovereign from his obedient subjects; it effects distributions around the norm" (144). In the case of the military, the norm—or, to be more precise, the ideal—regulates the economy of utility through which the human body becomes an object of discipline and, in turn, a "body-weapon, body-tool, body-machine complex"—for the purpose of colonial war (*Discipline and Punish* 153).

Tellingly, the soldier figures as an exemplary subject of the disciplines. "[T]he solider," Foucault writes, "has become something that can be made; out of a formless clay, an inapt body, the machine required to be constructed" (135). By enabling the relation of "docility-utility" to coalesce through a system of constant coercion and surveillance, disciplinary power "[gets] rid of the peasant and [gives] him the air of a soldier" (135). The more docile they are, Foucault contends, the more useful they become. Vázquez García demonstrates that as early as the seventeenth century, the Spanish state sought out ways to increase men's utility ("utilidad") specifically for military conscription.[15]

But, as we have already seen, not all men can be made into soldiers. So, who are the useless? And what does it mean to be rendered useless by the state? The military medical exams served as checkpoints during which doctors discerned which members of the nation were not only able-bodied, but also medically male. While disciplinary power appears to have a totalizing reach—anyone ("formless clay") can be made into soldier—the existence of "the useless" renders this assertion false. In fact, in 1910 Luis Sánchez Fernández makes this point explicitly: "La conocida frase de que para hacer guardias y pelar patatas cualquiera sirve, es un error de los pueblos poco militares" (The well-known saying that to keep watch and peel potatoes anyone will do, is an error of nonmilitary peoples) ("El Reclutamiento" 22). In sum, disciplinary power has its limits. "Los inútiles," those who fail to meet the medical criteria of the *Sanidad Militar* or those permanently injured while serving in the military, cannot be reformed. They occupy the outside of the docility-utility relation. The military criteria for utility, then, produce excess and insufficiently gendered bodies that remain excluded from direct participation in colonial war. These useless bodies are, in turn, exempt from the life-affirming force of biopolitics.

While the notion of utility lends itself to the concept of ability, a cursory look at the requirements for military conscripts shows that physical ability—narrowly defined—is not the only requirement for military deployability. In 1842, the *Sanidad Militar* published the medical criteria for military recruits, which (as I indicated at the start of this essay) included the presence of both testicles and the so-called virile member. Those who lacked male genitalia or failed to meet other requirements were designated "inútiles" ("Reglamento" 210). Acting on behalf of the state, legal-medical doctors helped curate the ideal male while also cataloguing insufficiently gendered individuals, as well as those with physical and mental disabilities. Some notable examples of the "defects" include article 3, "Falta total de las orejas" (Total lack of ears); article 4, "Pérdida de la totalidad de la nariz" (Loss of the entire nose); article 8, "Alopecia permanente, ó caida de los cabellos completa, sin esperanza de renovación posterior" (Permanent alopecia or complete hair loss without hope for later regrowth); article 12, "Falta completa de un miembro" (Total lack of a limb); and article 21, "Pérdida de sustancia de un labio que no se puede remediar con la operación" (Substantial loss of the lip that cannot be mended with surgery) ("Reglamento" 210–11).

What these criteria reveal is that ability—defined solely in terms of physical capacity—does not equal utility. Disability, scholars have shown, is an expansive and subjective category. Garland-Thomson, for one, defines disability as a "pervasive cultural system that stigmatizes certain kinds of body variations," which "like femaleness, is not a natural state of corporeal inferiority, inadequacy, excess, or a stroke of misfortune" ("Feminist Disability Studies" 5). Therefore, we ought to examine the concept of the "useless" as a particular iteration of disability, which Garland-Thomson defines as "a culturally fabricated narrative of the body, similar to what we understand as the fictions of race and gender" ("Feminist Disability Studies" 5), and one that takes shape through or against interlocking notions of gender, sexuality, and ability. In this vein, while seemingly irrelevant to one's capacity to serve in the military, male virility nonetheless proves central to military utility. The importance placed on genital certainty and virility shows the discursive capaciousness of disability as an identificatory construct. The marriage of male sexuality and ability illustrates Robert McRuer's claim that "compulsory heterosexuality is contingent on compulsory able-bodiedness, and vice versa" (2). Moreover, if "disability cancels out the sexuality" as Rosemarie Garland-Thomson contends, then here the reverse is true: nonsexuality cancels out able-bodiedness (19). Put simply, the lack of male genitalia renders one "useless."[16]

In addition to virility, beauty figures as an important, and perhaps surprising, feature of utility—evidenced by disqualification based on hair loss and facial disfigurement.[17] These are not obvious requirements for able-bodiedness but are necessary for the production of male beauty and overall "aesthetic competence" (Serlin 155). In other words, men's physical appearance, or male beauty, to be more precise, has as much to do with the successful performance of their masculinity as their physical strength and dexterity. As Rosemarie Garland-Thomson has demonstrated, disability has historically been "defined as much by appearance ("form") as by any limit on function" (*Extraordinary Bodies* 7, qtd. in Schweik 15). "Normalcy and beauty" she argues, "are twin ideologies" ("Feminist Disability Studies" 11).

Male beauty, in other words, underwrites the notion of military utility. As such, the soldier's appearance works as a form of social control and proves crucial to gender as an expression of imperial power. As we will see in the following section, there is a strong aesthetic component that underwrites the production of military masculinity, upholding the fantasy of "perfect, public bodies," to borrow Tobin Siebers words (198, qtd. in Schweik 15).

El cojito

The entwinement of disability, masculinity, and empire comes into clear view in Benito Pérez Galdós's *Aita Tettauen*, a historical novel set against the backdrop of the Spanish-Moroccan War (1859–60). Published in 1905 after the so-called Disaster of 1898, the novel's opening lines are steeped in melancholy, as the narrator describes the cyclical rise and fall of empire: "Antes de que el mundo dejara de ser joven, y antes de que la Historia fuese mayor de edad, se puede advertir y comprobar la decadencia y ruina de todas las cosas humanas. . . . Decaen los imperios, se desmedran las razas, los fuertes se debilitan y la hermosura perece entre arrugas y canas" (Before the world stopped being young and before History aged, the decadence and ruin of all human things could be perceived. . . . Empires fall, races deteriorate, the strong are weakened and beauty perishes among wrinkles and gray hair) (97). These grandiose proclamations and sweeping rhetoric foreground the centrality of racial fitness, ability, and beauty to imperial glory. They register, quite explicitly, what Alda Blanco refers to as "nineteenth-century imperial consciousness" (6–7). What this description obscures are the simultaneous subjugation and dehumanization of the colonized on which Spain's imperial glory is predicated. Indeed, the narrator curiously speaks of imperialism in the abstract ("decaen los imperios") rather than point to the specificities of Spanish empire. He then seamlessly transitions to describing Lucila as allegory—again without having to explicitly discuss Spain's American colonies. Even as the text tells a story of empire, then, it also occludes a historical account of Spanish colonialism.

In the same breath, the narrator introduces the first character, Lucila Ansúrez, who, in her youth embodied "aquel primoroso renuevo del árbol celtíbero" (that exquisite renewal of the Celtiberian tree) (97) and possessed an "aspecto heléncio" (Hellenic look) as though she had been transported from "la edad homérica" (the Homeric age) (98). Instead of embodying "the timeless, eternally legitimate" quality of female political allegory (White

244), the now "withered" beauty stands for Spain's fallen imperial status: "En fin, echando por delante estas retóricas, os dice el historiador que la hermosura de la sin par Lucila, hija de Ansúrez, se deslucía y marchitaba, no bien cumplidos los treinta años de su existencia" (In short, setting idle words aside, the historian will tell you that the beauty of the unequalled Lucila, daughter of Ansúrez, faded and withered, not yet reaching thirty years of existence) (97). The melancholic imagery speaks to Sara L. White's argument that feminine allegories get twisted and corrupted in crucial political moments (233). The narrator's bloated, misogynist language couches Lucila's appearance in racialized terms: he emphasizes her whiteness by pointing to her Celtic-Iberian origins and Hellenic beauty. This conforms with scientific racial discourse of the nineteenth century that led Spaniards to disavow Semitic and African roots and, instead, affirm their whiteness by emphasizing, for example, Celtic and Iberian heritage (Martin-Márquez 42, 46). Acknowledging the Ansúrez family's notable racial lineage makes explicit the biopolitical stakes of this family's spectacular decline in the context of Spain's lost empire. That is, Spain's imperial failures correlate with the nation's crisis of racial decline.

The narrator points to Lucila's marriage "sin glorias ni afanes" (with neither troubles nor fanfare) (98) and her first pregnancy as the catalyst of her physical deterioration: "A poco de casarse dio Lucila en engordar, con gran regocijo de su esposo el bueno Halconero, que a menudo la pesaba . . . y celebraba triunfante las libras que en cada trimestre iba ganando aquel lozano cuerpo. ¡Adiós, ideal; adiós, leyenda; clásicas formas, adiós!" (Shortly after getting married Lucila got heavier, to the great delight of her husband, the good Halconero, who weighed her frequently . . . and celebrated the triumphant pounds that healthy body gained each trimester. Farewell, ideal; farewell, legend, classic forms, farewell!) (98). Halconero celebrates his wife's pregnant form, but the narrator, from his postimperial vantage point, views it with disdain ("¡Adiós, ideal!") (Goodbye, ideal!) as if her growing body were a sign of decadence rather than fertility.[18] Vicente's birth ironically heralds the enfeeblement and decline of empire, and soon after, we learn that the handsome primogenitor, who inherited the "todos los rasgos étnicos de los *autrigones*" (all of the ethnic traits of the Autrigones) (the Autrigones being one of the first peoples to populate Spain), permanently injures his legs (99). While disability remains an overlooked feature of the novel, it permeates the story of race and empire that unfolds from the first chapter.[19]

Vicentito initially "se criaba *como un rollo de manteca*" (grew *like a roll of lard*); however, at the age of three he becomes emaciated, and in 1859, the year Spain declared war on Morocco, the seven-year-old boy now has "el rostro como un ángel" (the face of an angel) but "torcido y desaplomado el cuerpo" (a twisted and collapsed body) (99). The narrator recounts that, after a fall from a toy horse, the young boy grew a tumor in his leg, which the doctors in his small town unsuccessfully removed. Unable to walk, he is given the name "el cojito." Here reproduction begets degeneration. That Lucila's pregnancy propagates feebleness and premature decrepitude evokes the discourse of degeneration that emerged in the last decades of the nineteenth century, intensifying after 1898. As Campos Marín et al. argue: "Cuestiones como la disminución de la talla, el aumento de nacimientos de niños enclenques y raquíticos, la predisposición a las enfermedades, etc., . . . se relacionarán en el ocaso del siglo XIX con la degeneración y la herencia" (Questions such as decreases in height, the increase in births of sickly and rickety children, the predisposition towards illnesses, etc., . . . would, in the twilight of the nineteenth century, be associated with degeneration and heredity) (161). It is significant that this story of decadence takes on gendered contours—such as Lucila's withered beauty and Vicentito's wounded masculinity. These perversions of gendered norms register a concern that circulated within discourses of degeneration—speaking to the "the popular perception that society as a whole was moving toward gender indifferentiation [which] posed a threat to the bourgeois masculine establishment" (Tsuchiya 16). Susan Martin-Márquez explains that theories of degeneration in Spain, which she argues emerged in the decades prior to 1898, correlated racial degeneration with emasculation (176). Similarly, Cleminson and Vázquez García note that the regenerationist discourse that emerged after the so-called Disaster of 1898 expounded on the importance of virility and traditional gender roles:

> The understanding of masculinity as expressed in regenerationist texts can be seen . . . to hinge on two basic interpretations. On the one hand, decadence is seen as the result of a general process of "devirilization" and effeminization of the population. On the other, the "ills of the nation" are represented as the result of a battle between the powers of masculinity and the weaknesses of femininity. The solution of such a state of affairs is predicated on the restoration of masculinity over and above feminine values. ('*Los invisibles*' 177)

Disability and gendered perversions become bodily inscriptions of racial degeneration.[20]

Vicentito represents, adopting Lee Edelman's words, "futurity's fragile figure," which is in dire need of saving; but because of his disability, I argue, he cannot be saved.[21] If Lucila's morphing pregnant body appears as the monstrous deformation of her classic beauty, her son's disability only further extends the tragedy of their degenerative lineage. In both cases, bodies bear the somatic signs of degeneration, thereby emblematizing the narrator's legendary opening words: "Decaen los imperios, se desmedran las razas, los fuertes se debilitan y la hermosura perece entre arrugas y canas" (Empires fall, races deteriorate, the strong are weakened and beauty perishes among wrinkles and gray hair). Martin-Márquez has argued that "Galdós's narrator encourages us to read the prematurely aged and incapacitated Vicentito as symbolic of a Spain that is ill prepared for, but nonetheless enthralled with, the prospect of war" (125). Indeed, war becomes the spiritual analgesic for Vicentito and a "fallen" Spanish empire.

Perfectly timed with Isabel II's declaration of war against Morocco, the sadness that follows Vicentito's fall morphs into an intoxicating obsession with his opposite: the military, the epitome of virile able-bodiedness. Lucila, in a plea to convince her husband to relocate the family to Madrid exclaims: "El ejército es su delirio" (The army is his delirium) and "lo que más le gusta y enamora . . . es ver soldados en artilleros" (what he likes the most and is enamored of . . . is seeing soldiers with their artillery) (100). Vicente's younger siblings also take on this obsession:

> Pilarita y sus hermanos Bonifacio y Manolo contagiados de los gustos del primogénito, despreciaba toda clase de juguetes para consagrarse al militar juego, aprovechando el material de guerra desechado por Vicente: cañones, tropa y oficialidad de cartón o de estaño, banderolas, espada de palo y morriones de papel. La niña desmintiendo su sexo apacible, era la más brava en las marchas, en las escaramuzas y refriegas, que algún día le valieron solfas de Lucila en semejante parte.

> (Pilarita and her brothers Bonifacio and Monolo, infected by the tastes of the primogenitor, spurned all types of toys to devote themselves to military games, taking advantage of the war material tossed aside by Vicente: cannons, cardboard or tin soldiers and officers, banners, stick swords and paper helmets. The little girl, eschewing her mild-mannered sex, was the bravest during the marches, in the skirmishes and scuffles, that some days earned them spankings from Lucila, applied to the usual place.) (131)

The pervasive emotions of colonial war, however, know no bounds as Pilarita becomes improperly gendered by this imperial contagion. Commenting on this passage, Ian Russell asserts that

> [f]rom the beginning, Galdós frames the greater narrative arc of the novel with the early failures of gender ideals and racialized boundaries represented in these children. Gender is mixed-up: the boy is lame and inactive, while his younger sister causes consternation for being aggressive and butch. Likewise, the supposedly pure Spanish race is conflated with the decrepit body. (630)

Vicentito's disability, like Lucila's ugliness, becomes a marker of degeneration—showing the extent to which able-bodiedness, from the perspective of empire, implicitly underwrites racial vigor.

Swayed by the rehabilitative promise of war, Halconero concedes to Lucila's pleas and decides to move the family to Madrid: "Hemos de dar al niño satisfacciones de *su gusto militar* para que se le pongan los espíritus en aquel punto de alegría que ha de ayudar a las potencias corporales. . . . Bien dijo quien dijo que alma lleva cuerpo" (We had better satisfy the boy's taste for the military to raise his spirits to that height of happiness that ought to restore his bodily strength. . . . Well said whoever said that the soul carries the body) (101). Halconero's rationale evinces Foucault's claim that by disciplining the soul, the body can be made useful. "The soul," writes Foucault, "is the prison of the body" (*Discipline* 30). By consuming spectacular displays of military might and imperial power Halconero believes that reviving Vicentito's spirit can somehow rehabilitate—in other words, discipline—his disabled body. But such a feat is pure fantasy. The consumption of military spectacle provides only temporary alleviation for Vicentito, just as it does for the Spanish nation. The Spanish-Moroccan War, widely regarded as part of O'Donnell's efforts to revive the country following Spain's defeat in the American colonies, did not result in new colonial territory but instead brought "the government a brief respite from political conflict during the patriotic euphoria that followed" (Boyd 76). Martin-Márquez has argued that while many historians reference O'Donnell's speech in which he expressed his intention to restore Spain's honor through the war, many Spaniards, including Isabell II, hoped Spain would acquire new colonial possessions and were thus disappointed by the outcome (55). "For many," she writes, "the war had done much to incite, but little to satisfy, the desire for conquest in Africa" (55).

The family moves to a tower on *la calle Mayor* (Main Street) where Vicentito can watch the colorful troops marching in uniform. The child's parents explain: "En Madrid verás pasar batallones con música, escuadrones de caballería tocando los carlines, y artillería con cañones y todo" (In Madrid you will see battalions parading by with music, cavalry squadrons fingering their silver coins, and artillery with cannons and all) (101). The image below, a photograph of O'Donnell leading troops through the Puerta del Sol in 1860, shows an ebullient scene similar to the one Galdós depicts in the novel—the street jam-packed with troops and a throng of civilians. Much like Vicentito who "sacó medio cuerpo por la ventanilla" (stuck half his body out the window), the troops here are surrounded by dozens of eager onlookers hanging out of windows and balconies (101).

What is striking here is the significance placed on the aesthetic form from the start of the novel. We begin with the loss of Lucila's beauty, and then move on to Vicentito's visibly disabled body—which, the novel suggests, must be repaired through the arousing pleasures of sight. Vicentito needs to *see* the military to in order to satisfy his *gusto militar* (taste for the military). Vicentito's father provides his son with a stereoscope of battle scenes from French colonial campaigns in Algeria that, according to Martin-Márquez, were the very images the Catalan painter Mariano Fortuny was encouraged

Figure 6.1. O'Donnell junto a las tropas de la Campaña de África pasando por la Puerta del Sol en 1860 (O'Donnell with troops from the African campaign passing through Puerta del Sol in 1860).

to view before painting *Battle of Tetuán*—serving as "another indication of the profound impact of visual technologies on the reality and representation of the conflict" (125).²² It is not only that the war is widely depicted and visualized by a hungry public, but that military aesthetics take on an erotic sensibility, as evinced in Vicentito's remarks that "Estos soldados son los más guapos que he visto" (These soldiers are the most handsome ones I have ever seen) (112). When Lucila expresses surprise in reaction to this comment he retorts, "Madrita, también a ti te gustan los militares . . . no me digas que no. . . . Bien conozco que te gustan picarona" (Mommy, you like military men too . . . don't tell me that isn't true. . . . I know very well that you like them you naughty woman) (112). Here the young Vicentito alludes to his mother's not-so-secret attraction to soldiers. In this sense, their shared "gusto militar" (taste for the military) quickly becomes erotic in nature. As Vicentito evaluates the troop's "aesthetic competence" (Serlin 12), it becomes clear that military utility is not only about battle, but also about the aestheticization of war. That is, the public performance of imperial power—handsome soldiers marching in uniform—seduces a vulnerable public that eagerly consumes these visual displays. Representations of Spanish masculinity thus prove to be just as important as winning the war, demonstrating that military utility hinges on the interplay between male beauty, masculinity, and able-bodiedness.

Patriotism reaches a fever pitch in the novel, and Juan Santiuste, a family friend and possible former suitor of Lucila, volunteers for conscription. Vicentito is thrilled to be so close to the soon-to-be soldier, who promises to send letters describing the battle scenes of *Tetuán*. While Juan is hailed a future hero, Halconero, the child's father becomes emasculated, realizing that he is no longer cut out for war. In a fit of tears, he utters: "Tú vas, Juan, y yo no. . . . Yo *inútil*, yo . . . trastoviejo . . . tú gloria, yo estropajo. . . . Abrázame . . . te quiero . . . ¡Viva España" (You are going, Juan, but not me. . . . Me useless me . . . an old piece of junk . . . you glory, me rubbish. . . . Give me a hug . . . I love you. . . . Long live Spain!) (142; emphasis mine). Father and son now unite as two useless members of the nation. And as if to permanently seal his useless fate, Halconero suffers a sudden fall that eventually leads to his death. The narrator notes: "El niño cojo, que arrimado al balcón había presenciado el accidente y caída de su padre" (The crippled boy, who clinging to the balcony had witnessed his father's accident and fall) (143). Halconero, on his deathbed, evokes the unifying force of Villamartín's "soldado español" (Spanish soldier) (97) when he states "pienso yo que se juntarán las de toda España para ir a esa guerra"

(I think troops from all over Spain will unite to join this war) (102). The nation, therefore, clearly needs colonial war to sustain its nation-building project. Vicentito, now fatherless, relies even more on Juan and the war to enliven his spirits and those of the fallen nation. Galdós anticipated that such ends could be achieved, as the following quote illustrates, through the relationship of docility-utility. The narrator explains:

> Fueron los españoles a la guerra, porque necesitaban gallear un poquito ante Europa, y a dar al sentimiento público, en el interior, un alimento sano y reconstituyente. Demostró el General O'Donnell gran sagacidad política, inventando aquel ingenioso saneamiento de la psicología española. Imitador de Napoleón III, buscaba en la gloria militar un medio de integración de la nacionalidad, un dogmatismo patrio que *disciplinara* las almas y las hiciera más *dóciles* a la acción política.
>
> (Spaniards went to war, because they needed to peacock a bit for Europe, and by exteriorizing that feeling, it became, internally, a healthy and restorative nourishment. General O'Donnell demonstrated great political wisdom, inventing that ingenious healing of Spanish psychology. An imitator of Napoleon III, he sought in military glory a means of solidifying nationality, a patriotic dogmatism that would *discipline* souls and make them more *docile* to political action.) (132–33; emphasis mine)

The term *gallear* (to peacock)—a masculine display of power—is an especially apt image when read in juxtaposition to the "niño cojo" whose body prevents him from "strutting" about. Here, Galdós masterfully illustrates O'Donnell's need for this conspicuous war to reconstitute the nation's *esprit de corps*. Reading this passage in Foucauldian terms, patriotism operates as a force that effectively disciplines souls, rendering them docile and therefore useful to the nation and its imperial endeavors.

Juan, once in *Tetuán* (Tetouan), questions his patriotic duty as he bears witness to violence: "Yo te aseguro que al ver en estos días el sinnúmero de muertos destrozados por las balas, no he sentido más lástima de los españoles que de los moros" (I can assure you that upon seeing in these days those countless bodies destroyed by bullets, I haven't felt more compassion for the Spanish than for the Moors) (185). Thereafter, he has nightmarish visions of Vicentito's funeral procession and Lucila in mourning. Awake but hallucinating, Juan defensively cries out:

Yo no le he matado, Luci . . . ¿Cómo había de matarle yo, que tan de veras le quiero? . . . Lo que hay, Luci, es que se ha venido abajo el castillo de la epopeya, y si al caer todo ese matalotaje quedó Vicentito enterrado entre los escombros, no es culpa mía, Luci . . . Luci, no es culpa mía . . . ¡Vicente entre las ruinas! . . . Pero ¿qué culpa tengo? . . . Yo no derribé el castillo vetusto . . . se cayó él solo . . . porque quiso caerse . . . Yo no he sido, Luci. . . .

(I didn't kill him, Luci . . . ¿How would I have killed him, if I love him so truly? . . . What it is, Luci, is the castle of the epic feats has crumbled, and if when all of that mess fell down Vicentito got buried among the rubble, it isn't my fault, Luci . . . Luci, it isn't my fault . . . Vicente among the ruins! . . . But what fault do I have? . . . I didn't knock down the ancient castle . . . it fell by itself . . . because it wanted to fall. . . . It wasn't me. . . . Luci . . .) (240)

Here, the weight of a crumbling empire falls on the shoulders of the ambivalent soldier who has turned his back on his patriotic calling. The image of "el cojito" buried in the ruins of empire haunts the psyche of the perfect male-citizen-soldier who is rendered utterly vulnerable when sent off to war. Juan fails to rescue the ailing imperial nation, perhaps out of refusal to become disabled in combat and therefore useless himself. While the military turned the virile members of the nation into soldiers, they also undermined the life-affirming force of biopolitics by sending its useful population off to war. The useful have the "honor" of being exposed to death while the useless, cast aside as excess bodies, ironically have the right to live. While being declared useless by military doctors may have been life-affirming, survival seemingly entails the exclusion from the humanizing category of gender.

Conclusion

By exploring the concept of utility, and its entwinement with gender, ability, and sexuality, I have demonstrated the ways in which colonial wars in the nineteenth century necessitated the "administration" of sex in the metropolis. Debunking the myth of a uniform and stable image of the Spanish colonizer, this essay shows that the coloniality of gender has powerful effects on both sides of the colonial divide. While gender clearly functions as a technique of colonial domination, it also undermines expressions of Spanish imperial power. Gender, alongside sexuality and able-bodiedness—the latter being most undertheorized within Iberian studies—are the metrics by which the population is sorted and organized around a norm. This is particularly true for the male youth population who were routinely labeled as "useless" if they failed to meet the medical requirements for normative masculinity. Such metrics become ever more crucial during times of colonial crisis and defeat.

The military, in seeking out the useful in the service of empire, ultimately engages in a self-defeating biopolitical project: one that bestows on its best men—that is, virile, able-bodied, and aesthetically competent men—the right to live, while dramatically increasing their chances of dying. The soldier's beauty, able-bodiedness, and virility, therefore, always remain subjected to corruption and death via combat, illness, and disease. These risks inherently render military masculinity an unstable and fragile expression of imperial power. This ironic turn challenges the understanding that biopower functions through an invariant, stable division that condemns some to death while letting others live. The discourse of regeneration that surged after 1898, with a particular focus on the military, responds to the belief that useful Spaniards—that is, virile and able-bodied soldiers—were rendered especially vulnerable by the projects of colonialism that they served.

Contrary to romantic patriotic narratives of colonial war and military service, many men, mainly the bourgeoisie, actively resisted shedding blood for the nation. Those who did so understood the risks of becoming disabled, killed, and therefore emasculated in war. The useless, on the other hand, excluded from direct participation in colonialism by the state, proved to be wasteful to empire as they were not virile, abled-bodied, or medically verifiable men. Sánchez Fernández disparagingly refers to them as "residuo que gravita sobre el trabajo de los útiles" (dregs that weigh down the work of the useful) and "peso muerto" (dead weight) (*El hombre español útil* 2). What we have here are various iterations of the so-called useless that amount to a crisis of masculinity: men deemed useless by the state, soldiers rendered useless in war by disease and combat,[23] and bourgeois males who refused to realize their masculine potential. A look at the production of the useless in nineteenth-century Spain sheds light on the intricate ways in which gender as a technique of colonialism, alongside ability, aesthetics, race, and sexuality, unwittingly produces "the useless" as excess bodies that fail to be disciplined. Thus, for those who fail to inhabit the norms delineated by the state, gender proves to have a dehumanizing effect on both sides of the Atlantic and the colonial divide. Ultimately, the Spanish empire required masculinity and yet this very requirement undermined the colonial enterprise it was meant to uphold. In turn, the military became a potentially self-defeating biopolitical institution that exposed the soldiers to physical incapacitation and death, rendering the useful Spaniard an easily corruptible ideal.

Acknowledgments

Research for this essay was made possible with the Humanities Research Grant from the Society for the Humanities at Cornell University. I would like to also thank my research assistants Matías Borg Oviedo and Kelly Moore for helping me in the final stages of the manuscript.

Notes

1. The *Sanidad Militar* formed after the death of Fernando VII at the start of the Carlist Wars (Rodríguez Ocaña 296). It consisted of a small group of medical doctors that assessed conscripts, treated soldiers in the field, and staffed military hospitals. This is also the body that published the official criteria for military conscription.

2. All translations are my own.

3. Richard Cleminson and Francisco Vázquez García examine the 1842 *Reglamento* (Regulation) in their essay "The Hermaphrodite, Fecundity, and Military Efficiency: Dangerous Subjects in the Emerging Liberal Order of Nineteenth-Century Spain." Commenting on the virility requirement, they argue: "Clearly, in order to be a reliable, efficient soldier, it was necessary to possess all the male parts in functioning order" (78). That virility be necessary for military conscription merits further discussion since it does not obviously ensure physical ability.

4. Tellingly, the Spanish military's requirement of virility remained in place until March 2009 when the *Ministerio de la Presidencia* (Ministry of the Presidency) removed the phrases "falta total de pene" (complete lack of a penis) and "ausencia de ambos testículos" (absence of both testicles) from its list of disqualifications, thereby allowing transgender individuals to enlist for the first time (Gonzáles).

5. Lugones is responding to feminist philosophy and what she calls "white feminist theory and practice" (187).

6. See Martin-Márquez for a discussion on whiteness and racial panic in nineteenth-century Spain (39–60).

7. Michael Ugarte notes that this phrase was attributed to Alexandre Dumas and "was put forth not coincidentally with the Napoleonic invasion of Spain at

the commencement of the nineteenth century, indicating a rivalry between the two empires: one on the wane, the other on the path to glory" ("The Spanish Empire on the Wane" 179).

8. For an analysis of Spain's peripheral geopolitical relationship within modern Europe, see Iarocci's *Properties of Modernity*. For further discussion on the Northern European orientalization of Spain, see Charnon-Deutsch, Fernández Cifuentes, Flesler, Hooper, and Tofiño-Quesada.

9. Felipe Ovilo Canales—hygienist and historian—was one of the leading doctors of the *Sanidad Militar* and active in the regenerationist movement. While not directly involved in military medicine, Pedro Mata i Fontanet is another well-known medical figure who advanced the ideas of legal medicine, which concerned the sexing of bodies. In anthropology, Ángel Pulido, Federico Olóriz, and Manuel Antón examine the Spanish male, and in particular the soldier, in their writings on racial decline. See Joshua Goode for an extensive discussion of Pulido, Olivo, Olóriz, and Antón (121–205).

10. There is a growing body of scholarship on masculinity in modern Spain. See Joseba Gabilondo, Mark Harping, Collin McKinney, and Zachary Erwin. See also Cleminson and Vázquez García (*'Los Invisibles*') for an analysis of masculinity in relation to male homosexuality in nineteenth- and early-twentieth-century Spain.

11. The living conditions of the urban and rural poor, of course, impacted potential recruitment process and, in turn, had important implications for access to affirmative biopower. Luis Sánchez Fernández correlates wealth to height in his study of the useful Spaniard: "Se han observado en muchos países que la *riqueza* y el bienestar elevan la talla, atribuyéndose á la mejor alimentación, á la vida cómoda y á los cuidados higiénicos, y llega a la diferencia á 6 cm. de ventaja en los ricos sobre los pobres" (It has been observed in many countries that *wealth* and well-being increases height, being attributed to better nourishment, a comfortable lifestyle and careful hygiene, and reaching a six centimeter advantage of the rich over the poor) ("El hombre español útil" 13).

12. See Vázquez García's *La invención del racismo* (*The Invention of Racism*) for an extensive history of the emergence of biopolitics and racism in Spain.

13. Vázquez García observes that in seventeenth-century Spain the nascent biopolitical state was already concerned with issues related to maleness such as effeminacy ("afeminamiento") and sodomy (*La invención del racismo* 126).

14. Here Jagoe references Huarte de San Juan's *Examen de ingenios* (*The Examination of Men's Wits*) (1575), which, in the Galenic tradition, treats woman as "un hombre al revés, con los órganos genitales metidos para adentro" (an inside out man, with the genital organs shoved inside) (307).

15. Vázquez García demonstrates that the Bourbon reforms created a taxonomy of the poor ("los indigentes") with of aim of determining which men could be made useful for the military: "Reaparece la división establecida según criterios de utilidad, prescribiendo el uso de los vagabundos para fines militares, pues era

propósito de Ensenada armar un poderoso Ejército y una formidable Marina, que devolvieran a la monarquía española el protagonismo en la escena internacional" (The divide based on criteria of usefulness reappears, prescribing the use of vagabonds for military purposes, as it was Ensenada's intent to arm a powerful Army and a formidable Navy, so that the Spanish monarchy would again assume the role of protagonist on the international stage) (*La invención del racismo* 77).

16. I understand the term *nonsexuality* to encompass the lack of virility signaled by the absence of the virile member and/or testicles. The prefix "non" indicates a negation of normative sexuality (from the perspective of the Sanitary Corps). This term should not be confused with asexuality, which broadly refers to the lack of interest in sexual activity.

17. Goode discusses the ways in which beauty becomes a central component in military applications of racial science in the twentieth century. See chapter 6, "Recruiting the Race: Military Applications of the Racial Mix" (121–42).

18. It is important to acknowledge Lisa Surwillo's observation that discussions of Spanish empire and fiction tend to focus on the "discourse of decline, loss, or more importantly disaster" (6–7). While important, these analyses, Surwillo contends, obscure the ways in which "Cuba and other territories were not simply part of a culture framed in decadence but also constitutive of modernity and the nation as it evolved in the nineteenth century" (7). In the case of *Aita Tettauen*, Galdós appears to infuse his narrative with the intensified post-1898 discourse of degeneration, even as he seems keenly aware of the ambivalent ways in which colonialism buttressed the project of the modern nation.

19. A number of critics have commented on Galdós's treatment of race and empire in *Aita Tettauen*. Kathleen Davis treats this novel as medium of cultural transference, allowing readers to see the Spanish-Moroccan War from a critical, rather than a nostalgic, vantage point. Álvaro Ayo explores the colonial ambivalence that uniquely characterizes Spanish-Moroccan relationship as one that is at once "fraternal" and "fratricidal" (230). Ayo contends that Galdós advances a modern understanding of race—one that construes the Spaniard as hybrid, mixed, and unstable (230). For his part, Michael Ugarte engages with this notion of hybrid identity and argues that Galdós gives the subaltern African a voice through a kind of literary ventriloquism ("Galdós and África").

20. For further reading on theories of degeneration in Spain, see Huertas, Campos Marín, and Fuentes Peris ("'La Mala Vida'"), and Campos Marín et al. (*Los ilegales de la naturaleza*). See Pick for an in-depth discussion on degeneration in nineteenth-century Europe.

21. In his book *No Future*, Lee Edelman argues that the pervasive figure of the male child symbolizes a politics that espouses a reproductive, heterosexual temporality—what he calls "reproductive futurism" (21). The child requires protection precisely because he represents this precious future, while the queer operates as a future-negating force. Edelman uses the term "futurity's fragile figure" specifically

in reference to Tiny Tim, the disabled child in Charles Dickens's *A Christmas Carol* (45). Thus, there is an obvious parallel here in that both Vicentito and Tiny Tim are "crippled" and garner the sympathies of the reader.

22. Martin-Márquez presents an extensive discussion on the importance of vision in *Aita Tettauen*. In particular, she engages with the relationship between panoramic vision and colonial power (established by scholars such as Mary Louise Pratt), noting how Galdós complicates the notion of visual domination by subjecting it to the machinations of colonial ambivalence (127).

21. Puell reports: "Entre 1886–1898 fallecieron, durante el tiempo que realizaban su servicio militar en la Península, 12,448 soldados y 52,135 de los que se licenciaron regresaron a sus casas inútiles para realizar cualquier actividad laboral" (Between 1886 and 1898, a total of 12,448 soldiers perished while completing their military service in the Peninsula and 52,135 of those discharged returned home useless for any kind of labor) (229). This number does not appear to include any soldiers stationed abroad.

Works Cited

Ayo, Álvaro. "The War Within: National and Imperial Identities in Pérez Galdós's *Aita Tettauen*." *Hispanic Research Journal*, vol. 6, no. 3, October 2005, 223–36.

Blanco, Alda. *Cultura y conciencia imperial en la España del siglo XIX*. Universitat de València, 2012.

Boyd, Carolyn. "The Army and Politics in Spain, 1808–1874." *Spanish History Since 1808*, edited by Adrian Shubert and José Alvarez Junco, Oxford UP, 2000, pp. 64–79.

Campos Marín, Ricardo. *Curar y gobernar: medicina y liberalismo en la España del siglo XIX*. Nivola, 2003.

Campos Marín, Ricardo, José Martínez Pérez, and Rafael Huertas García-Alejo. *Los ilegales de la naturaleza: medicina y degeneracionismo en la España de la Restauración (1876–1923)*. CSIC, 2000.

Chamberlin, J. Edward, and Sander L. Gilman, eds. *Degeneration: the Dark Side of Progress*. Columbia UP, 1985.

Charnon-Deutsch, Lou. "Exoticism and the Politics of Difference in Late Nineteenth-Century Spanish Periodicals." *Culture and Gender in Nineteenth-Century Spain*, edited by Lou Charnon-Deutsch and Jo Labanyi, Clarendon, 1995, pp. 115–28.

Cleminson, Richard, and Francisco Vázquez García. "The Hermaphrodite, Fecundity, and Military Efficiency: Dangerous Subjects in the Emerging Liberal Order of Nineteenth-Century Spain." *Bodies, Sex and Desire from the Renaissance to the Present. Genders and Sexualities in History*, edited by Kate Fisher and Sarah Toulalan, Palgrave Macmillan, 2011, pp. 70–86.

———. *Hermaphroditism, Medical Science and Sexual Identity in Spain, 1850–1960.* U of Wales Press, 2009.

———. *"Los Invisibles": A History of Male Homosexuality in Spain, 1850–1939.* U of Wales Press, 2007.

Cleminson, Richard and Teresa Fuentes Peris. "'La Mala Vida': Source and Focus of Degeneration, Degeneracy and Decline." *Journal of Spanish Cultural Studies*, vol. 10, no. 4, Dec. 2009, pp. 385–97. *Taylor & Francis Online*; http://dx.doi.org/10.1080/14636200903400173.

Davis, Kathleen. "Sons of Adam: Cultural Transference in Galdós' *Aita Tettauen*." *Bulletin of Spanish Studies*, vol. 82, no. 5, 2005, 641–54. *Taylor & Francis Online;* http://dx.doi.org.proxy.library.cornell.edu/10.1080/1475382052000344183.

Edelman, Lee. *No Future: Queer Theory and the Death Drive.* Duke UP, 2004.

Erwin, Zachary. "Fantasies of Masculinity in Emilia Pardo Bazán's *Memorias de un solterón.*" *Revista de Estudios Hispánicos*, vol. 46 no. 3, 2012, pp. 547–68.

Flesler, Daniela. *The Return of the Moor: Spanish Responses to Contemporary Moroccan Immigration.* Purdue UP, 2008.

Forrest, Alan. "Citizenship and Masculinity: The Revolutionary Citizen-Soldier and His Legacy." *Representing Masculinity: Male Citizenship in Modern Western Culture*, edited by Stefan Dudnik, Karen Hagemann, and Anna Clark, Palgrave Macmillan, 2007, pp. 111–30.

Foucault, Michel. *Discipline and Punish: the Birth of the Prison.* 2nd ed., Vintage Books, 1995.

———. *The History of Sexuality.* Vintage Books, 1990.

Gabilondo, Joseba. "Histéricos con casta: masculinidad y hegemonía nacional en la España de fin de siglo (para una arqueología feminista, torcida, marxista, poscolonial, y posnacional del noventaycohismo)." *Sexualidad y escritura (1850–2000)*, edited by Raquel Medina and Barbara Zecchi, Anthropos Editorial, 2002, pp. 120–61.

Garland-Thomson, Rosemarie. *Extraordinary Bodies: Figuring Physical Disability in American Culture and Literature.* Columbia UP, 1997.

———. "Feminist Disability Studies." *Signs*, vol. 30., no. 2, 2005, pp. 1557–87, *JSTOR*; www.jstor.org.proxy.library.cornell.edu/stable/10.1086/423352.

Gilfoil, Anne W. "Doctor vs. Priest: Urban Planning and Reform in Vetusta. Leopoldo Alas's *La Regenta*." *Decimonónica: Revista de Producción Cultural Hispánica Decimonónica*, vol. 6, no. 1, 2009, pp. 34–45.

Gonzáles, Miguel. "El Ejército admite que los transexuales se alisten." *El Pais,* March 6, 2009; elpais.com/diario/2009/03/06/sociedad/1236294003_850215.html.

Goode, Joshua. *Impurity of Blood: Defining Race in Spain*, 1870–1930. Louisiana State UP, 2009.

Harpring, Mark. "Gossiping and Hysterical Manolo Infante: Traditional Gender Role Crossing as Political Metaphor in Galdós's 'La Incógnita.'" *Hispania*, vol. 90, no. 1, 2007, pp. 1–9, *JSTOR*; www.jstor.org/stable/20063434.

———. "Homoeroticism and Gender Role Confusion in Pardo Bazán's *Memorias de un solterón*." *Hispanic Research Journal*, vol. 7, no. 3, 2006, pp. 195–210.

Hooper, Kirsty. "Reading Spain's 'African Vocation': the Figure of the Moorish Priest in Three *Fin de Siglo* Novels (1890–1907)." *Revista de Estudios Hispánicos*, vol. 40. no. 1, 2006, pp. 175–99.

Huertas, García-Alejo R. *Locura y degeneración: psiquiatría y sociedad en el positivismo francés*. CSIC, 1987.

Iarocci, Michael. "Virile Nation: Figuring History in Galdós' *Trafalgar*." *Bulletin of Spanish Studies*, vol. 80, no. 2, 2003, pp. 183–202, *Taylor & Francis Online*; dx.doi.org/10.1080/14753820302027.

———. *Properties of Modernity: Romantic Spain, Modern Europe, and the Legacies of Empire*. Vanderbilt, UP 2006.

Jagoe, Catherine. "Sexo y género en la medicina del siglo XIX." *La mujer en los discursos de género: textos y contextos en el siglo XIX*, edited by Catherine Jagoe, Alda Blanco, and Cristina Enríquez de Salamanca, Icaria, 1998, pp. 305–39.

Jensen, Geoffrey. *Irrational Triumph: Cultural Despair, Military Nationalism, and the Ideological Origins of Franco's Spain*. U of Nevada Press, 2002.

Laqueur, Thomas. *Making Sex: Body and Gender from the Greeks to Freud*. Harvard UP, 1992.

Lugones, M. "Heterosexualism and the Colonial/Modern Gender System." *Hypatia*, vol. 22, no. 1, 2007, pp. 186–209. *Project MUSE*; muse.jhu.edu/article/20639.

Martin Márquez, Susan. *Disorientations: Spanish Colonialism in Africa and the Performance of Identity*. Yale UP, 2008.

McKinney, Collin S. "Men in Black: Fashioning Masculinity in Nineteenth-Century Spain." *Letras Hispanas*, vol. 8, no. 2, 2012, pp. 77–94.

———. "Pogonology, Phsyiognomy, and the Face of Spanish Masculinity." *Modernity and Epistemology in Nineteenth-Century Spain: Fringe Discourses*, edited by Ryan A. Davis and Alicia Cerezo Paredes, Lexington Books, 2017, pp. 61–88.

Memmi, Albert. *The Colonizer and the Colonized*. Beacon Press, 1965.

McRuer, Robert. *Crip Theory: Cultural Signs of Queerness and Disability*. New York UP, 2006.

"O'Donnell junto a las tropas de la Campaña de África pasando por la Puerta del Sol en 1860." 1860. Photograph. *Biblioteca Nacional*, Madrid.

Payne, Stanley G. *Politics and the Military in Modern Spain*. Stanford UP, 1967.

Pérez Galdós, Benito. *Aita Tettauen*. Edited by Francisco Márquez Villanueva, Akal Ediciones, 2004.

Pick, Daniel. *Faces of Degeneration: a European Disorder, c. 1848–c. 1918*. Cambridge University Press, 1989.

Puell de la Villa, Fernando. *El soldado desconocido: de la leva a la "mili," 1700–1912*. Biblioteca Nueva, 1996.

Quijano, Aníbal. "Coloniality of Power, Eurocentrism, and Latin America." Translated by Michael Ennis, *Nepantla: Views from South*, vol. 1 no. 3, 2000, pp.

533–80. *Project MUSE*; muse.jhu.edu/article/23906.
"Reglamento aprobado por S. A. el Regente del Reino para la declaración de exenciones físicas del servicio militar." *Boletín de Medicina, Cirugía, y Farmacia: Periódico Oficial de la Sociedad Médica General de Socorros Mutuos*, 30 Sept. 1842, pp. 209–16; hemerotecadigital.bne.es/issue.vm?id=0003046920.
Rodríguez Ocaña, Esteban. "La medicina en busca de público: España, siglos XIX y XX." *História, Ciências, Saúde-Manguinhos*, vol. 13, no. 2, 2006, pp. 295–301; dx.doi.org/10.1590/S0104-59702006000200006.
Russell, Ian. "Dressing Up Anxiety and Pleasure: Cultural Drag in Galdós's *Aita Tettauen*." *Revista de Estudios Hispánicos*, vol. 50, no. 3, 2016, pp. 629–51. *Project MUSE*; doi:10.1353/rvs.2016.0050.
Salazar, Martín. "Introducción: Valor de la higiene en el ejército." *Higiene militar: lecturas para oficiales*, directed by A. Cabeza Pereiro. Colegio de Huérfanos de la Guerra, 1909, pp. 1–20.
Sánchez Fernández, Luis. "El Reclutamiento." *Higiene militar: lecturas para oficiales*, directed by A. Cabeza Pereiro. Colegio de Huérfanos de la Guerra, 1909, pp. 21–67.
———. "El hombre español útil para el servicio de las armas y para el trabajo; sus características antropológicas á los 20 años de edad." *Acta de congreso de Granada, June, 1911*, Asociación española para el progreso de las ciencias.
Schweik, Susan M. *The Ugly Laws: Disability in Public*. New York UP, 2009.
Serlin, David Harley. "Crippling Masculinity: Queerness and Disability in U.S. Military Culture, 1800–1945." *GLQ: A Journal of Lesbian and Gay Studies*, vol. 9 no. 1, 2003, pp. 149–79. *Project MUSE*; muse.jhu.edu/article/40805.
Siebers, Tobin. *Disability Aesthetics*. U of Michigan Press, 2010.
Suarez Capalleja, Victor. *La salud del europeo en América y Filipinas y del repatriado y criollo en Europa, ségun el sistema Kneipp: higiene y aclimatación*. Pedraza, 1897.
Surwillo, Lisa. *Monsters by Trade: Slave Traffickers in Modern Spanish Literature and Culture*. Stanford UP, 2014.
Tofiño-Quesada, Ignacio. "Spanish Orientalism: Uses of the Past in Spain's Colonization in Africa." *Comparative Studies of South Asia, Africa and the Middle East*, vol. 23, no. 1, 2003, pp. 141–48.
Tsuchiya, Akiko. *Gender and Deviance in Fin-de-siècle Spain*. U of Toronto Press, 2011.
Ugarte, Michael. "The Spanish Empire on the Wane: Africa, Galdós, and the Moroccan Wars." *Empire's End: Transnational Connections in the Hispanic World*, edited by Akiko Tsuchiya and William G. Acree Jr., Vanderbilt UP, 2015, pp. 177–90.
———. "Galdós and África: A Spaniard Speaks for the Subaltern." *Diasporic Identities within Afro-Hispanic and African Contexts*, edited by Yaw Agawu-Kakraba, and Komla F. Aggor, Cambridge Scholars Publishing, 2015, pp. 85–94.
Vázquez, García F. *La invención del racismo: nacimiento de la biopolítica en España, 1600–1940*. Akal Ediciones, 2009.
Villamartín, Francisco. *Nociones del arte militar*. D.P. Montero, 1869.

White, Sarah L. "Liberty, Honor, Order: Gender and Political Discourse in Nineteenth Century Spain." *Constructing Spanish Womanhood: Female Identity in Modern Spain,* edited by Victoria Lorée Enders and Pamela Beth, State U of New York P, 1999, pp. 233–58.

7

From Imperial Boots to Naked Feet

Clarín's Views on Cuban Freedom and Female Independence in *La Regenta*

Nuria Godón

> A Cuba libertad tienen que darle
> Adelardo y su gente;
> con justicia la pide ella impaciente
> y si no se la dan, debe tomarla.
>
> (To Cuba freedom should be granted
> by Adelardo and his people;
> with justice Cuba asks for it impatiently
> and if it is not granted, Cuba should take it.)
>
> —Leopoldo Alas (Clarín), *"A Cuba"*

Two months after the first shot was fired in the Ten Years' War (1868–1878)—the first of three conflicts between the Spanish metropole and forces fighting for Cuban independence—Leopoldo Alas, also known as Clarín (1852–1901), published a poem entitled "A Cuba" ("To Cuba") in the journal *Juan Ruiz*. The poem describes a Cuba deserving of "libertad" (freedom), and willing to take it even if not granted: "y si no se la dan, debe tomarla" (and if it is not granted, Cuba should take it).[1] Clarín's advocacy of freedom may seem confusing in view of his other work, as he had defended the unity of the Spanish national territory, both in and outside of the Iberian Peninsula. However, the contradiction was not really that stark. His defense of national unity established parallels between lands outside of and in the Iberian Peninsula, as he compared the island of Cuba to other autonomous communities, such as Galicia and Catalonia, where independence movements were also growing. According to Clarín, "Cuba será para los cubanos, sin dejar de ser española, como Galicia es para los gallegos y Cataluña para los catalanes" (Cuba will be for Cubans, without ceasing to be Spanish, just as Galicia is for Galicians and Catalonia for the Catalans) (Alas, *Paliques* 563). For this reason, Noël Valis warns of a need to interpret the term *freedom* in this poem within its historical context: "Hay que entender con cuidado el matiz ideológico que lleva el vocablo 'libertad' en aquellos tiempos. En los 90 Clarín abogaría por la autonomía cubana, respecto a sus intereses económicos y comerciales, pero sin romper políticamente con la madre patria. Autonomía sí, independencia, no" (One must carefully understand the ideological nuance that the word "freedom" carried in those times. In the nineties Clarín would advocate for Cuban autonomy with respect to its economic and commercial interests, but without breaking away politically from the motherland. Autonomy yes, independence, no) (24).[2] Thus, common usage of the word *libertad* did not always imply a complete break with the metropole in either the 1860s or the 1890s.

The concept of "libertad" in this context suggests not only freedom of Cuba from the metropole, but of slaves from their masters. For Clarín, the analogy, free citizen (still subject to the laws of the nation in which a person resides) is to slave as autonomous territory is to colony, applies. The issue would have been evident to readers following the Cuban independence movement; during the first two conflicts—the Ten Years' War (1868–1878) and the Little War (1879–80)—the abolition of slavery was proposed by the metropole, along with Cuban autonomy, not from altruism, but as a strategy to fight against the independence movement and keep the island an integral part of the Spanish nation. This strategy aimed to make enough concessions to allow Spain to retain some control over its colonies. Christopher Schmidt-Nowara in *The Conquest of History* argues that the Spanish state was able to articulate a broadly based national project with colonialism at its core by elaborating a fraternal vision of colonial rule in the Americas (3). On another occasion, he has also noted that the promise of fraternity rested on the call for the immediate abolition of slavery in Cuba and in Puerto Rico (Schmidt-Nowara, "From Slaves" 178).[3]

At the outset of the Ten Years' War there was no clear division between abolitionists and those who were content to allow slavery to continue. Clarín's poem criticizes the politics of the Spanish overseas minister, Adelardo López de Ayala, who signed the decree on "Libertad de Vientres" ("Freedom of Wombs") in 1868 (Díaz y Pérez 501) to gradually end slavery in Cuba. In other words, rather than calling for an immediate end to slavery, as the Spanish Abolitionist Society demanded, this decree prolonged it. The "Libertad de Vientres" was approved by passing the Moret Law (1870), which, as Rebecca Scott has underscored, changed the legal status of many individuals, without changing their actual situation (347).[4] Likewise, Clarín, aware of the difference between the official position of Spain and its real position, denounced the hypocrisy of the law, noting that it would effectively prolong slavery. Indeed, this first measure of gradual emancipation and all subsequent steps toward abolition would permit slavery in Cuba for eighteen more years until its definitive abolition in 1886. It would also, as Lisa Surwillo emphasizes in her book *Monsters by Trade*, feed the simultaneously illegal (human trafficking) and lucrative transatlantic slave trade (3).[5] Taking into account the historical context, Clarín's verses in "A Cuba" (To Cuba) can be understood to urge Spain to embrace full abolition and offer Cuba autonomy and true freedom by ending slavery immediately: "con justicia la pide ella [Cuba] impaciente" (with justice Cuba asks for it impatiently) (Valis 24). The poem illustrates Clarín's early antislavery stance and his defense of colonial autonomy. As he would suggest in *Paliques*, the desire for colonial independence emerged from the lack of colonial autonomy and the continuation of slavery, which was being abolished in a gradual—rather than immediate—fashion (*Paliques* 419 and 549).[6]

In his early texts Alas used the image of violent insurgents—"barbarie impía" (impious savagery) (Valis 35)—to justify revenge—"que a la venganza fía" (that calls for revenge) (Valis 35)—whereas, on the eve of decolonization, he warned that using extreme violence against rebels would turn the defense of territorial unity into an act of savagery.[7] With the tropes of fraternity and friendship (an integral part of Spanish discourses on colonialism and Spain, which problematically conceived of its colonization as an act of love and friendship through *mestizaje*—a mixture of Spaniards and Cubans through reproduction) and the assumption that "we are all Spaniards," he suggested, for instance, that in Cuba's war "we" are not savage, even though some insurgents are (*Paliques* 563). Clarín also warns against perpetuating the Black Legend, an overly negative depiction of the colonizer focused on the narrative of Spanish cruelty. His comment suggests that abuses of power led to the failure of the colonizers' civilizing and domesticating mission and may have, instead, actually generated savagery in the colonized: "[los conservadores] no acababan de impedir ciertas atrocidades de que habla todo el mundo" ([conservatives] did not stop preventing certain atrocities about which everybody talks) (*Paliques* 563). In contrast, the defense of the principles of freedom and autonomy would support both harmony and hierarchy. In sum, the three main objectives of Clarín's political positioning are: to give Cuba autonomy; to temper all desire for independence on and outside of the Iberian Peninsula; and to maintain Spanish sovereignty over the island (García San Miguel 282; Lissorgues 51).[8]

In his prologue to the second edition of *La Regenta*, Benito Pérez Galdós, one of the most canonical Spanish realist/naturalist writers, addresses how the loss of the overseas territories may have influenced Clarín's masterpiece. In this regard, for the purposes of this study, it is important to take into consideration Surwillo's contention that the nation was newly constructed through the discourses of "home" and domesticity and that issues of political and colonial liberation play out through the portrayal of the family in the metropole (72).[9] Taking into account the aforementioned deliberations on the Cuban insurgent forces and the inscriptions of empire in the metropole, this study analyzes how Clarín intervened in the debates over the Cuban conflict through his depiction of slavery, advocacy for the autonomy of the island, and rejection of independence.[10] In his writings, Clarín problematizes the paradigm of the metropole and its colonial daughters by weaving together different metaphorical family ties, including the marital, filial, and fraternal. Particularly in *La Regenta* (1884–85), Clarín displays gender and sexuality (understood as both organizing principles of society and an instrument of hierarchical domination) as axes of the same matrix of colonial power that he observes in the Cuban conflict.

In *Local Histories/Global Designs*, Walter Mignolo explains that the colonial matrix, built on the relationships of domination/subordination and superiority/inferiority, infuses modern discourses of mastery. Departing from Anibal Quijano's idea of coloniality of power—which examines the structure of power through the concept of racial hegemony—Mignolo establishes the connection between modernity and coloniality by demonstrating how the categories of gender, sexuality, social class, race, and colonialism share a common paradigm of power.[11] By looking into the intersections of Clarín's gender and colonialist discourses, this chapter posits that his views on the organization and distribution of power (published in newspapers over the period of the three Cuban conflicts) demonstrate how he condemns different forms of slavery and advocates the formerly denied autonomy of both women and the colonies, while simultaneously safeguarding patriarchal and metropolitan sovereignty. It is important to emphasize that this chapter does not question that the desires for female and colonial independence have different driving forces and motivations. Instead, it demonstrates that Clarín's discourses on both women and colonies illustrate a common paradigm of power and reflect the intersectionality of gender, sexuality, social class, race, and colonialism.

The feminist decolonial critic María Lugones's arguments in "Heterosexualism and the Colonial Modern System" also help to explain the intersections of gender and colonialism by building on Quijano's formulation of the coloniality of power as manifested both in the nineteenth century and in today's global capitalist society. Her study shows the problems of separating race, gender, class, and sexuality into different categories, as such a separation fails to acknowledge the simultaneity of multiple systems of oppression. Furthermore, as Lugones posits that all control over sex, subjectivity, and authority is articulated around coloniality, "'coloniality' does not just refer to 'racial' classification. It is an encompassing phenomenon, since it is one of the [—one might say synonymous—] axes of the system of power" ("Heterosexualism" 191). Lugones's critique of Quijano was precisely of his overlooking how coloniality of power implicated gender relations from the beginning of colonialism until the present.

In the context of fin-de-siècle discourses of domination, Clarín's *La Regenta* advocates a more balanced distribution of power. The narrative focuses on Ana Ozores (*La Regenta,* or the judge's wife) in Vetusta, a Spanish provincial city closely modeled on the real city of Oviedo, in Asturias. Seeking to avoid an arranged marriage to the vulgar *indiano* (local returning from Cuba) Frutos Redondo, Ana marries Víctor Quintanar, a local official who treats her kindly but is more interested in Golden Age theatre than in his wife. Quintanar's refusal of conjugal relations leaves Ana sexually unsatisfied, leading her to feel a strong attraction for her husband's treacherous friend Álvaro Mesía. Afraid of adultery, she turns to religion, seeking moral refuge in the Magistral, a power-hungry local priest. The Magistral, unlike Víctor, is aware of the amorous conflict that Ana suffers. He struggles to win her over from Álvaro, who is his political rival, and ultimately falls in love with her. The novel also portrays the Magistral's relationship with two other women. Olvido, a wealthy single woman, is an *indiano*'s daughter who is unable to find a suitor who measures up to what she thinks she deserves and becomes smitten with her handsome confessor. And Obdulia, a widow, tries to add the Magistral to her long list of sexual conquests. Her history of casual encounters with charcoal makers, coachmen, street vendors, bourgeois men, marquises, and priests forces the Magistral to maintain a distant relationship with the promiscuous and undisciplined penitent. The Magistral's relationship with each one of these women also functions as a trope for different responses to his desire for territorial control. The first part of this chapter examines Alas's literary masterpiece as a commentary on colonial and female autonomy within the dynamics of domination and subordination. The second part reveals the way in which the erotization of these dynamics downplays the impact of insurgent forces.

The trope of domination has an overwhelming presence in *La Regenta*. The opening of the novel introduces the Magistral as a greedy priest with dreams of territorial control. His desire for domination is revealed in a scene in the belfry of the cathedral, from which he gazes down on Vetusta through a spyglass, identifying and describing what he sees as if to possess the inhabitants of the provincial town. As he looks down on the land, his focus is on how he can exercise power over each region and use it to enrich himself: "Don Fermín contemplaba la ciudad. Era una presa que le disputaban, pero que acabaría por devorar él solo. ¡Qué! ¿También aquel mezquino imperio habían de arrancarle? No, era suyo . . . ¿Qué habían hecho los dueños de aquellos palacios viejos y arruinados de la Encimada que él tenía allí a sus pies? ¿Qué habían hecho? Heredar. ¿Y él? Conquistar" (Don Fermín gazed down upon the city. Others wanted to wrest this prey from him, but he alone was going to devour it all. What? Was even this wretched empire to be snatched from his grasp? No; it belonged to him. . . . What had ever been achieved by the owners of those ancient, decrepit residences in the cathedral quarter, La Encimada, down there at his feet? Yes, what had they done? They had inherited. And he, what had he done? He had conquered) (19; Rutherford 29).[12] Beyond this scene, the opening chapter highlights three areas of interest: La Encimada, the old city where the nobles dwell; La Colonia (also seen as "América abreviada" and "la Vetusta novísima" ["little America" and "modern Vetusta] [24; 33–34]), where the *indianos* reside, that is, the "residential districts for the new rich, who have made their money in national trade in Cuba" (Labanyi, *Gender* 210–11); and El Campo del Sol, the industrial outskirts and home of the working class.

The scope of the Magistral's gaze allows the reader to visualize the urban expansion that had required the demolition of the old city wall around La Encimada to open a space for industrial and colonial transformations of the city: industrial, with the outlying factories, and colonial, with hotels and "mansions" (*casonas*). The contributions of luxury hotels and *casonas* to modern Spanish architectural culture (whose opulence recalls Paez's

Hotel in *La Regenta*) are, as Surwillo has shown, legacies of colonialism of which fin-de-siècle writers were aware. Among them, Surwillo has indicated how Clarín ridicules the triumphal story and fortunes some "*indianos*" brought back to the peninsula and displayed in their neighborhood homes in a provincial city in northern Asturias when describing La Colonia as: "dazzling with vibrant colors, and steely reflections, like some birds from a South American jungle, or a savage Amerindian woman adorned with feathers and ribbons of clashing color . . . inopportune displays of stone; sham solidity, vociferous luxury. The city of an emigrant's dreams" (quoted in *Monsters* 134).

The priest's imperial vision conveys the analogy between the domination of these territories and of his three daughters of confession, while associating each daughter with a territory: Ana Ozores, married to the retired Judge of Vetusta and living in La Encimada; Olvido Páez, the second-richest *indiano*'s only daughter, who resides in La Colonia; and the merry widow Obdulia Fandiño, well known for her scandalous attire and the heavy, harsh-sounding pounding of her heeled boots. Obdulia's undisciplined behavior mirrors the defiant attitude held by residents of Campo del Sol, where "[n]o era que allí [el Magistral] no tuviera ninguna influencia, pero la tenía menos" (it was not that he was without influence among the workers, but he influenced only a minority) (23; 33). By feminizing the object of imperial conquest, Clarín presents Ana as territory to be conquered; Olvido portrays the legacies of colonial servitude; and Obdulia embodies the threat of the independence movement in the Spanish colonies through portrayals linked to degeneration.

The colonial matrix of power in which gender and colonial discourses intersect in the desire to control women and geographical territories is not limited to the Magistral's imperial vision and to the religious context; it also permeates the civil sphere. The analogy between love and territorial conquest becomes evident when Víctor Quintanar, the retired judge, admiringly associates the majestic gestures of the actor playing the seductive conqueror in Zorilla's *Don Juan Tenorio* with imperial power once displayed in Cuba:

[S]e acercó a ella [to Ana] el buen Quintanar diciéndole al oído con voz trémula por la emoción:

—¿Verdad, hijita, que es un buen mozo? ¡Y qué movimientos tan artísticos de brazo y pierna! . . . Dicen que eso es falso, que los hombres no andamos así . . . ¡Pero debiéramos andar! y así seguramente andaríamos y gesticularíamos los españoles en el siglo de oro, cuando éramos dueños del mundo; esto ya lo decía más alto para que lo oyeran todos los presentes. Bueno estaría que ahora que vamos a perder a Cuba, resto de nuestras grandezas, nos diéramos esos aires de señores y midiéramos el paso . . .

[I]n a voice trembling with emotion he whispered into her ear:

"He is a handsome fellow, is he not, my child? And such artistic movements of the arms and legs! People say that it is artificial, that men do not really walk in that way. But men should! And no doubt we Spaniards did walk and gesticulate in that way in the Golden Age, when we were masters of the world." (Here he raised his voice so that the others should hear him.) "But now that we are on the point of losing Cuba, all the remains of our former grandeur, it would be a fine thing for us to stride about and give ourselves such lordly airs." (374)

Taking into account the mention of Cuba, Pérez de Ayala reads the use of Zorrilla's drama in *La Regenta* "as a ritual observance and celebration of the nobility of the past. . . . [I]t also serves to unify the Hispanic community in its resurrection of the past cultural, economic, and political triumph" (quoted in Mandrell, "Nostalgia" 50). Reading this specific passage within the framework of the loss of the Spanish empire, one may also deduce from Quintanar's commentary that the judge believes that neither delusions of grandeur nor weak and naive management from the metropole will help to maintain the unity of Spain. This dynamic plays out in the text. Víctor is totally naive about Álvaro Mesía's flirtation with Ana and does not realize that it will end in the loss of his wife's honor (and of his own, as well). This happens because, according to Mandrell, in a passage full of irony, Víctor is unable to perceive Álvaro Mesía's own parody of Don Juan as he tries to seduce Ana during the play. Álvaro emulates the myth with "prosaica imaginación del petimetre" (his prosaic fop's imagination) at a time when, as the seducer observes, "El don Juan de Zorrilla ya solo servía para hacer parodias" (by now, Zorrilla's *Don Juan* was only good for parodying) (quoted in Mandrell, *Don Juan* 135). Álvaro represents only a ridiculous imitation of the Spanish myth, rendered deplorable by fleeing from Vetusta after causing the retired judge's death and abandoning Ana after his eventually successful seduction of her.

Ana, too, creates her own reading of the play. She assigns herself great prominence as a character and considers herself the true protagonist (DuPont, *Realism* 211). She compares herself with the Commander's daughter in the play, cloistered at home, sexually unsatisfied, and yearning for the seducer to penetrate walls and to appear miraculously in her room. Ana develops the image of the protector she had already seen in Álvaro; she imagines him killing Frutos Redondo (the *indiano* who first came to her aunts with a marriage proposal for Ana eight years ago) and stealing her away. Although Ana envisions adultery as liberation during the play, she is reluctant to imagine herself as an adulterer. As Biruté Ciplijauskaité notes, it is important to highlight that, right after the play, Ana conceives of adultery in terms of usurpation of honor: "¿Sucumbiría ella como doña Inés, caería en los brazos del don Juan loca de amor? No lo esperaba; creía tener el valor para no entregar jamás el cuerpo, aquel miserable cuerpo que era propiedad de don Víctor sin duda alguna" (Would she succumb like Doña Inés, would she fall maddened by love into the arms of Don Juan? She didn't think so. She believed she had the strength never to surrender her body, that miserable body which was, without any doubt, the property of Don Victor) (356; 378–79).

Until the moment in which Vetusta discovers Ana's adultery, she is without a doubt the most prized territory of the city, "perla de Vetusta" (pearl of Vetusta) (558; 590), "fortaleza inexpugnable" (impregnable fortress) (132; 141). These textual metaphors enable the allegory of Ana as Cuba since, as Gertrudis Gómez de Avellaneda and José Martí remind us, Cuba—the so-called *perla* del mar (pearl of the sea) (Gómez de Avellaneda, *Antología* 29) and *perla* de las Antillas (pearl of the Antilles) (Martí, *Contra* 12)—was also a source of power imagined by the imperial community as forever loyal to the Spanish state. That being said, Ana has her own imagination and desires. She is conscious of her beauty (102) and, after a conversation with her aunts, of her exchange value, as well (99). Her good friend Frígilis nonetheless notes that Ana is a "mina de oro en un país donde nadie sabe explotar las minas de oro" (a gold mine in a country where nobody knows how to work gold-mines) (108; 117), but her true problem is her lack of autonomy, to which she feels unentitled. When she seeks a way to escape the arranged marriage with Frutos Redondo, she thinks, "[q]uería emanciparse; pero ¿cómo? Ella no podía ganarse la vida trabajando: antes la hubieran asesinado las Ozores: no había manera decorosa de salir de allí a no ser el matrimonio o el convento" (She wanted to liberate herself, but how? She could not work for her living—the Ozores sisters would sooner kill her than allow that to happen—and so there was no decorous way out, other than marriage or the convent) (103; 111).

Ana is not the only one aware of the sociopolitical impediments to the pursuit of emancipation, as this passage echoes Clarín's own thoughts on the need for sociopolitical change to avoid such situations. The author's views on women's rights, as on Cuban freedom, were moderate rather than revolutionary.[13] As Jo Labanyi has shown, Clarín defended women's autonomy, believing that they should marry for love and not see themselves obligated to do so for money, but he completely rejected the emancipation of women (224). Ana's beliefs echo advocacy for women's greater autonomy while still rejecting full female emancipation: when she faces the prospect of marriage and feels a desire for emancipation, she immediately disregards it as reckless. For her family, female emancipation is a dishonorable option and, therefore, she completely dismisses the idea.

Furthermore, Clarín ridicules Frutos Redondo, a wealthy *indiano* who is ready to conquer the city by buying the best of everything and getting married to the prettiest woman in Vetusta: "Vio a Anita, le dijeron que aquella era la hermosura del pueblo y se sintió herido de punta de amor. Se le advirtió que no le bastaban sus onzas para conquistar aquella plaza. Entonces se enamoró mucho más" (He saw Anita, was told that she was the beauty of the town, and felt the prick of love's arrows. He was warned that his dollars were not sufficient for the conquest of this fortress, and this made him fall much more deeply in love) (110; 118–19). The safeguarding of the honor of the nation and the family shows a common paradigm of power, which reinforces the entanglements between conceptualizations of the colony and of women. In his journalistic writings, Clarín critically notes that "muchos *incondicionales* entienden por integridad de la patria las ventajillas que sacan los *indianos* de que se considere Cuba como país conquistado" (Many loyal supporters understand "integrity of the country" to mean those benefits that *indianos* receive as a result of Cuba being considered a conquered land) (*Paliques* 563).[14] For the most part, society overlooks abusive behaviors in Cuba, but as Surwillo says, "in literary works the immorality of the slave trade was rarely in doubt" (10). Redondo's treatment of Ana as potential conquest echoes these abuses through his unlawful political and economic activities. When the protagonist's aunts approach her with a marriage proposal from the boorish *indiano,* Ana rejects it by locking herself in her room. She resists submitting to the *indiano,* whose successful business in Havana comes from "buscar negros al África y comprarlos y venderlos a espaldas de la ley" (searching for Negroes in Africa and buying and selling them behind the back of the law) (420; 446).

At the beginning of the second Cuban conflict, in October 1879, and on the occasion of the encounter between the Spanish leader Antonio Cánovas del Castillo and the German leader Otto von Bismarck, Clarín denounces this "monstrous form of the state" by sarcastically accusing Cánovas del Castillo of solving Spanish economic problems by being: "proteccionista y negrero. A los blancos no les dejo comerciar con sus cosas pero sí con los hombres. Hay que respetar los derechos adquiridos . . . por los que no tienen derechos y a los que tienen el derecho de comerciar hay que cobrárselo; de ahí los derechos de aduana" (protectionist and slave trader. I do not allow white people trade with their belongings but (I do) with human beings. Acquired rights must be respected . . . for those who do not have rights and to those who have the right to trade, there must be a fee; hence the custom duties) (*Paliques* 56). In order to protect the integrity of the Ozores family, that is, to enable its economy to flourish, Ana's aunts become moral accomplices in a figurative *trata* with the slave trader. However, Ana, as a nonconformist woman, rejects a union based not on companionship, but on economic interest, illegal trafficking, and violent acts. She resolves to maintain her family's honor without submitting to the whims of the *indiano* from Matanzas, a Cuban province whose association with brutal and violent killings should not go unnoticed. She writes a letter to her friend Frígilis, who had already introduced her to another suitor, Víctor Quintanar. In doing so, Ana escapes from the violent *indiano* slave trader and marries the lenient (but paternalistic) Judge Quintanar.

Initially, Ana accepts condescending treatment from a husband more than twice her age. Ultimately, however, Víctor's paternalism becomes a burden for Ana. His filial love for "Anita," as he habitually infantilizes her, fails to satisfy Ana's desire to be loved and to have children. Víctor's filial attitude reflects the limitations of Spanish nationalist views on Cuban liberation: a desire to maintain both unity and authority. In discourses on Cuba, some abolitionists, such as Rafael María de Labra, advocating for the autonomy of Cuba, call for the further strengthening of the relationship with the colonies through biological and cultural ties, namely, through *mestizaje*.[15] This *mestizaje* is envisioned as placing both groups on an equal footing. Clarín, too, suggests that cultural and biological kinship should produce unity. For him, the colonies should not be treated as minors but as adults with responsibility, like all Spaniards. Part of the problem, according to him, is rooted in the word *madre-patria* (motherland), which feeds the metaphor of filial dependency (*Paliques* 419): "Sí, ese es el error; los cubanos no son nuestros hijos, son nuestros hermanos; somos nosotros mismos, son—somos—los Pérez, Fernández, González castizos que fueron—fuimos—a Cuba hace cuarenta, cien, doscientos, trescientos años" (Yes, that is the error; the Cubans are not our offspring, they are our brothers, they are we ourselves, they are—we are—authentic Perezes, Fernandezes, Gonzalezes, they—we—who went to Cuba forty, one hundred, two hundred, three hundred years ago) (*Paliques* 419). In this manner, Clarín promotes the fusion of colonizers and colonized through *mestizaje*, advocating the idea of a biological and cultural basis for national unity.

Víctor reduces Ana precisely to such an infantile state, with his paternalistic and condescending treatment. This being said, the fact that Olvidito Páez, the infantilized daughter of a rich Vetusta *indiano*, maintains a status in which "La servían negros y negras y un blanco, su padre, el esclavo más fiel" (She was waited on by Negroes and Negresses and one white man, her father, who was her most faithful slave) (260–61; 276), demonstrates how Clarín complicates the depiction of filial relationships regarding autonomy and responsibility. The connotations of slavery evoked by the two black domestic servants are here ironically transferred to the figure of the father. Unlike Francisco Páez, who works hard to find a way for Olvido to fit into Vetusta society and serve in the process of nation building, Víctor fails to uphold these colonial ideals. Throughout the text, Víctor undermines the main strategies that Antonio Feros has traced in his study of the genesis of the Spanish colonial narrative. The historian identifies a Spanish master imperial narrative, whose aim was to serve the process of nation building through religious, cultural, and biological programs (113). Víctor is not interested in any religious program; he lacks the will and the ability to engage Ana in a cultural program based on Spanish myths of the Golden Age; he denies his wife the possibility of having children, so no biological program; and he is unable to understand that his wife is being seduced by Álvaro and indoctrinated by the Magistral. All of the above leaves Víctor without arguments to legitimize the imperial narrative in his family.

In contrast, the Magistral makes use of a religious program to guide and manipulate Ana, not as his daughter of confession, but as the soul sister that Ana wants to be. When Ana writes to him announcing her "afán de no ser ingrate . . . [and her] voluntad firme de hacerme buena" (resolution to become a good woman . . . [and her] determination not to be unthankful) (449; 476), the Magistral quickly perceives the confidence he instills in her through the spirit of fraternity. From father confessor, he becomes a soul bound by fraternity: "recibí más pronto amparo de Dios por mano de quien quisiera llamar mi padre y prefiere que no le llame si no hermano mío; sí, hermano mío, hermano muy querido, me complazco en llamárselo" ([I] was sooner succoured by God when He sent me the man whom I would like to call my father but who prefers me to call him my brother. Yes, my brother—my dearly beloved brother. It fills me with joy to address you thus) (449; 476). There is also a moment when the priest "pensaba lo mismo que la Regenta: que había hecho un hallazgo, que iba a tener un alma hermana" (His thoughts were similar to those of the judge's wife: he believed that he had made a great discovery, that he was going to have a soul sister) (221; 231) "Una mujer deslumbrante de hermosura por alma y cuerpo, que en una hora de confesión le había hecho ver mundos nuevos, le llamaba ahora su *hermano mayor querido*, se entregaba a él, para ser guiada" (A woman whose soul and whose body were of dazzling beauty, who in an hour of confession had made him see new worlds, now called him her beloved elder brother, and gave herself to him, to be led) (455; 483).

The spirit of fraternity is traced through a sense of protection and belonging to a single community that Ana conceives of as *"supravestustense"* (346). This phrasing echoes the idea of the superiority of nations that Antonio Cánovas del Castillo affirms in his *Discurso sobre la nación* (1882). Such "supra-nations" are "expansivas, absorbentes, que sobre sí han tomado el empeño de llevar a término la ardua empresa de civilizar" (expansive, absorbing, those who have made the effort to accomplish the arduous undertaking of civilizing) (131) and "están bastante más cerca de la fraternidad entre sí, porque no se niegan, a lo menos, el respeto recíproco" (they are much closer to fraternity among themselves, because they do not deny each other, at least, mutual respect) (110). Thus, for both characters, fraternity means an "hallazgo," (discovery), a sense of community that unifies people from different territories. Gender hierarchy remains in place; the "hermano mayor del alma" (elder brother's soul) is responsible for guiding his sister's soul toward the harmony that both of them seem to experience during a summer full of erotic suggestions of spiritual and fraternal love. This relationship, while not truly egalitarian, at first seems far more fulfilling to Ana than those with Redondo and Víctor. The dream of kinship is not built on self-sacrifice, but on joy, sensuality, and eroticism; as Maite Zubiaurre and Eilene Powell have observed in the introduction to their edition of *La Regenta*, these traits are the main elements in the construction of Ana's character (xiii–xv).

Ana's fantasy portrays fraternity as blissful, but this promise of bliss is ultimately shattered by her symbolic enslavement in the Holy Week procession. Instead of allowing Ana to walk at his side, the Magistral forces her to walk barefoot in front of all of Vetusta. He abuses the confidence offered by his sibling's soul, displaying her "como un triunfador romano a una esclava" (like a Roman victor with a slave) (560; 593), humiliating her and denying her autonomy. Ana does not feel part of a *supravetustense* community in her slavish walk. The promise of spiritual siblinghood does not lead to an egalitarian relationship. Likewise, enslavement denies any promise of equality between the metropole and the colonies. Promises are not sufficient to guarantee true communion. Instead, the colonies need liberty and autonomy to overcome the abusive control of "[la relación] metropolitana y colonial, que tanto favorece los instintos de tiranía, de explotación" (the metropolitan and colonial relationship, that favors so much the instincts of tyranny, of exploitation) (Paliques 419). In this passage, the colonies' lack of autonomy, linked to enslavement, highlights the binaries of metropole-colony, colonizer-colonized. Clarín's response to Cánovas del Castillo's question, "whether Spain, having already lost 'su gloria de otros siglos'" (its glory of centuries gone by), should become part of "ese corto número de naciones superiores" (that small number of superior nations) (Blanco, "Spain" 9), rejects discourses of total superiority in support of proofs of fraternity, liberty, and renegotiation of rights. In this sense, the Magistral, blinded by a desire for superiority, is unable to perceive that the abuse, enslavement, and betrayal of fraternity would eventually result in Ana's abandonment of him as spiritual master, demonstrating that abuses based on discourses of superiority will not lead to love, or to territorial governance. The priest's tyranny corroborates what Ana had thought earlier: "El Magistral no era el hermano mayor del alma, era un hombre que debajo de la sotana ocultaba pasiones, amor, celos, ira" (He wasn't her elder brother, her soul brother, he was a man hiding passions—love, jealousy, anger—under his soutane) (532; 563).

Clarín manifests similar concerns in his approaches to both Ana and Cuba. He warns that the enslavement and the threat (or feeling) of being enslaved may result in revolutionary desire for emancipation, whereas the paternalistic attitude toward them (women-colonies) can lead to frustration and, later on, to disloyalty. Alternatively, approaching them with a fraternal attitude not only enhances equality, autonomy, and sense of belonging to a single community, but also safeguards the power hierarchy by offering a sense of protection.

If Clarín's narrative about Ana is consistent with the need for female/colonial autonomy in order to achieve familial/national harmony, Obdulia Fandiño embodies the threat of independence of the Cuban insurgents, seen as "hijos de España extraviados" (stray children of Spain) (*Paliques* 419). The accusation is linked to what he understands to be misbehaviors that lead to national degeneration. Obdulia's initial characterization appears through the memories of Saturno Bermúdez, the risibly incompetent antiquarian and historian of Vetusta, who recalls a letter he had received from her:

> un billete perfumado de su amiguita Obdulia Fandiño, viuda de Pomares . . . ¿Qué era aquello? O. F. decían dos letras enroscadas como culebras en el lema del sobre . . . una mujer despreocupada, tal vez demasiado; Era una original. . . . En cierta ocasión ella había dejado caer el pañuelo, un pañuelo que olía como aquella carta, y él lo había recogido y al entregárselo se habían tocado los dedos y ella había dicho: "—Gracias Saturno" Saturno, sin don. (31)

> (A perfumed note from his friend, the young widow Obdulia Fandiño. What a thrill! He delayed opening the mysterious letter until after he had taken his soup. Why not dream a little? What could it be? O. F. said two letters, intertwined like snakes, in the crest on the envelope . . . this lady was very free and easy, perhaps excessively so—even capricious. . . . On another occasion she dropped her pocket-handkerchief, scented with the same perfume as the letter, and he picked it up, and when he gave it back to her their fingers touched, and she said, "Thank you, Saturn." Just "Saturn," without the formal "Don.") (41–42)

Obdulias's letter, its scent, and the handkerchief inflame Saturno's fantasies. The handkerchief echoes the dynamics of courtly love, in which a devoted admirer cherishes a token given to him by his lady. However, the chivalric allusion clashes with the dense scent of the "billete" (bill/note) associated with the prostitutes in the previous scene, when "[Saturno salía] a olfatear el vicio, el crimen, pensaba él, crimen en que tenía la seguridad de no caer, no tanto por esfuerzos de la virtud como por invencible pujanza del miedo que no le dejaba nunca dar el último y decisivo paso en la carrera del abismo. Al borde llegaba todas las noches" ([Saturno was going] to catch a whiff of vice, of crime as he conceived it—crime that he was certain he would not commit, less because of the striving of virtue than because of the invincible power of the fear which never allowed to him to take the final decisive step into the abyss. He reached its brink every night) (30; 40).

Even when Obdulia tries to avoid such interpretations (instead of asking for a date, the widow requests a planned visit to the cathedral for some family members returned from Havana), the antique "expert" continues reading the note as a seductive overture. With this hope, Saturno meets Obdulia in the cathedral. Once there, he becomes obsessed with her scandalous attire and the noise produced by "El taconeo irrespetuoso de las botas imperiales, color bronce, que enseñaba Obdulia debajo de la falda corta y ajustada" (the disrespectful clatter of the bronze-colored imperial boots which Obdulia displayed under her tight, ankle-length skirt) (36; 46). In contrast to Ana's bare feet, silence, and lack of autonomy in the procession, Obdulia profanes the ecclesiastical body, penetrating it noisily with her heels. Obdulia's outfit denotes a subversive act: "la falda de raso, que no tenía nada de particular mientras no la movían, era lo más subversivo del traje en cuanto la viuda echaba a andar. Ajustábase de tal modo al cuerpo, que lo que era falda parecía apretado calzón ciñendo esculturales formas" (The widow's satin skirt, unremarkable so long as it was stationary, was the most subversive part of her costume as soon as she began to walk. It was such a close fit that it looked like a tight pair of trousers, clinging to statuesque forms) (33; 46). She conceives of herself, through fashion, as a primordial being. In her performance of excess, she inflames others' desire for her body—a form of objectification that, far from being a simple abdication of agency, facilitates her desire for dominance. As Tsuchiya asserts, fantasy has a productive and foundational role, allowing marginal subjects to generate new spaces of subjectivity and desire (*Marginal* 215).

Obdulia's boots are an especially significant aspect of her self-presentation. Sonia Núñez Puente observes the unusual attention that the new feminine footwear attracted in the nineteenth century, when boots acquired their fetishistic connotation, becoming a symbol of sexuality and dominance (11). The specific style of boots chosen by Clarín, "imperial boots," reinforces Obdulia's staging of empowerment and conquest within a colonial/imperial narrative, making visible—and reinforcing—the connections among gender, sexuality, and imperialism. Saturno recites the names of kings who resisted Muslim conquest during a period in which they took control of most of the Iberian Peninsula; as he attempts to do so, however, he becomes confused by Obdulia's outfit. By associating Obdulia's imperial boots with the Reconquest of the Iberian Peninsula, the text posits Saturno's body as a site of resistance against domineering female forces. The battle between Saturno (Vetusta's male virginal body) and Obdulia (whose Arabic name means "one who makes life enjoyable" but also "servant of God") ends with the victory of male authority. Despite Obdulia's protecting her feet with female imperial boots, her fear of mice (or desire to play cat and mouse) ultimately undermines her performance of power:

> [Obdulia] dio un chillido y se agarró a don Saturno que, patrocinado por las tinieblas, se atrevió a coger con sus manos la que le oprimía el hombro; y después de tranquilizar a Obdulia con un apretón enérgico, concluyó de esta suerte: . . . creció tanto su fama, que presto se vio siendo emporio, y gozó hegemonía, digámoslo así, sobre las no menos santas iglesias de Tuy, Dumio, Braga, Iria, Coimbra, Viseo, Lamego, Celeres, Aguas Cálidas *et sic de coeteris*. . . . —¡Amén!—exclamó la lugareña sin poder contenerse; mientras Obdulia felicitaba a Bermúdez con un apretón de manos, en la sombra. (36)

> ([Obdulia] screamed, and clung to Don Saturn who, encouraged by the gloom, felt bold enough to grasp between his hands the hand which pressed his shoulder. After soothing Obdulia with an energetic squeeze, he concluded: . . . "its renown so grew that it found itself betimes to be a great emporium, and indeed to enjoy hegemony, as one might say, over the no less Holy Churches of Tuy, Dumio, Braga, Iria, Coimbra, Vizeu, Lamego, Celeres, Aguas Cálidas, *et sic de coeteris*. . . . "Amen!" exclaimed the countrywoman, unable to restrain herself, while Obdulia congratulated Bermúdez by pressing his hand in the dark.) (47)

Obdulia's humorous display of fear allows Saturno to reestablish authority, concluding his recital with the victory of male territorial hegemony. Hence, Clarín's narrator gives victory to male hierarchy, vanquishing Obdulia's stomps, while allaying anxieties produced by female desires of empowerment.

The fact that Obdulia is linked in Saturno's imagination to Moorish forces within the context of imperial narratives shapes her character as an exotic other, that must be either expelled from the Iberian Peninsula or merged with the dominant culture. Confronting Saturno's imagination, the Magistral, rather than visualizing Obdulia as the other, accepts her as daughter of confession due to "exigencias sociales" (social requirements) (221; 233). He embraces Obdulia in a modern nation-building project as a supplement in order to enhance his resources of power: "Su autoridad, que era absoluta casi, no conseguía sujetar aquel azogue que se le marchaba por las junturas de los dedos. . . . A pesar de esta cordial antipatía, siempre estaba afable y cortés con la viuda. . . . La urbanidad era un dogma para el Magistral lo mismo que para Bermúdez, pero sacaban de ella muy diferente partido" (In spite of his virtually absolute authority he could not subdue her: like a ball of quicksilver she kept slipping from his grasp. . . . In spite of this cordial dislike, he was always affable and courteous to the widow. . . . Urbanity was a dogma for the canon theologian as it was for Bermúdez, but they put it to very different uses) (34; 44–45). Obdulia increases the enviable Magistral's battalion of daughters of confession in the church's fights for power even if, as Pérez Galdós commented about Obdulia, "sea forzoso admitir en ellos [los batallones] para hacer bulto *lo peor de cada casa*" (it is necessary to admit into them [the battalions] *the worst of each household* in order to achieve the need) (xiv). Obdulia's erotic configuration as a deviant subject implies the need to control her in the face of emergent feminism, and serves as an apology for imperialism in light of the independence of the colonies. In this sense, like those *extraviados* working in El Campo del Sol, who form a crucial part of the transformed city of Vetusta, the Magistral reinserts Obdulia into a national project of containing and neutralizing her invasive potential.

Social class hierarchy also intersects with gender in the context of fin-de-siècle discourses of domination. The narrator's analogous characterization of the merry widow and the workers in the industrial outskirts represents the subversion of ecclesiastical power. Both Obdulia and the workers (in spite of having different interests) unsettle power hierarchies through their strident noises, dense smells, and undisciplined and defiant behavior. For the Magistral, in El Campo del Sol, "los rebeldes . . . escuchaban con la boca abierta a los energúmenos que les predicaban igualdad, federación, reparto, mil absurdos, y a él no querían oírle cuando les hablaba de premios celestiales. . . . El Campo del Sol se les iba" (the rebels . . . listened open-mouthed to hotheads preaching equality, federalism, redistribution of wealth and a thousand other absurdities, yet who would not listen when he talked of celestial rewards. . . . El Campo del Sol was slipping from the Church's grasp) (23; 33). The Magistral retains his influence over Obdulia by keeping her as daughter of confession, even as she challenges him and, by extension, the religious institution. In such a manner, facing the cathedral, El Campo del Sol displays "chimeneas delgadas, largas como monumentos de una idolatría" (Those tall, slender chimneys were monuments of idolatry) (23; 33). These chimneys confront, parodically, the feminine spires of the churches, insulting the churchgoers with the whistling of the machines—"[silbidos] burlescos, silbidos de sátira, silbidos de látigo" (a mocking whistle, a satirical whistle, the whistle of a whip) (23; 33). In a similar way, Obdulia's pounding footsteps, strident laughter, dense perfume, and provocative attire disturb the sacred atmosphere of the basilica. This parallelism becomes apparent in the Magistral's reaction, as he runs into the widow at the cathedral:

> [cuyas carcajadas] llenaron el ambiente, profanado ya con el olor mundano de que había infestado la sacristía desde el momento de entrar. . . . Aquella señora entendía la devoción de un modo que podría pasar en otras partes . . . pero en Vetusta no . . . proponía rifas católicas, *organizaba* bailes de caridad, novenas y jubileos a puerta cerrada, para las personas decentes . . . ¡mil absurdos!. (34)

> ([Obdulia Fandiño's laughter] filled the air, which had already been profaned by the worldly perfume with which she had saturated it from the moment she had entered the sacristy. . . . That lady understood religion after a fashion which may be acceptable elsewhere . . . but not in Vetusta . . . she proposed Catholic raffles, wanted to organize exclusive charity balls, novenas and jubilees for people of quality—a thousand of absurdities!) (43–44)

Obdulia's alternate way of understanding and practicing religion indicates her subversive intentions to defy political and ecclesiastical power through what was referred to as the democratic "mania of equality" (Moscoso, *Promesas* 28). Drawing on Richard Robert Madden's and Charles Ollier's writings, Javier Moscoso explains that, for these authors, among others, "la manía de la igualdad, que en 1870 pasó a denominarse *morbus democraticus*, hundía sus raíces en el deseo inmoderado de elevarse por encima del propio origen, hasta destruir las instituciones políticas y eclesiásticas" (the mania of equality, that in 1870 was called *morbus democraticus*, was rooted in the immoderate desire to rise above one's own origin, to the point of destroying political and ecclesiastical institutions) (28). Like them, Alas expressed the fear of social degeneration through the usurpation of power, raising anxieties over the potential threats to bourgeois hegemony.[16] Obdulia deploys this "immoderate" desire as a female deviant subject, whose flamboyant behavior and urge to conquer are condemned by bourgeois morality. Her understanding of religion is less concerned with promises of heavenly salvation than with equal rights: "Para la Fandiño la religión era esto, apretarse, estrujarse, sin distinción de clases ni sexos" (For Obdulia this was what religion was all about, pressing up against each other, squeezing each other, without any distinctions of class or sex) (503; 532–33).

In the narrator's description, Obdulia's attempts to usurp power are not limited to the cathedral; her *morbus democraticus* also extends to the possessions displayed in the Marquis of Vegallana's kitchen: "Por toda la provincia tenía esparcidos sus dominios el Marqués, en forma de arrendamientos que allí se llaman caseríos, y a más de la renta, que era baja, por consistir el lujo en esta materia en no subirla jamás, pagaban los colonos el tributo de los mejores frutos naturales de su corral, del río vecino, de la caza de los montes" (The marquis's dominions were scattered all over the province in the form of rented rural properties. In addition to the rent, which was small, because never raising the rent is a luxury which an aristocratic landlord can enjoy, each tenant paid Vegallana the tribute of the finest produce of his farmyard, the nearby river and his hunting expeditions) (160–61; 170). On the one hand, the metaphor of the peasant as "colono" makes Clarín's repudiation of *caciquismo* (abusive control) clear, condemning the fact that "para muchos, la integridad de la patria consiste en que, en Cuba, no pierdan su predominio los ricachos constitucionales" (for many people, the integrity of the country consists of, in Cuba, the rich constitutionals not losing their predominance) (*Paliques* 549). Likewise, in *La Regenta*, he denounces the abuses of the *ricachos* (the well-off). In both texts, these abuses lie in the quest for hegemony and territorial gain, which Clarín allegorically situates in the kitchen. In the aforementioned *Palique* published in 1897, Clarín concludes: "Cuba se pierde . . . como *se pierde* la carne del puchero con estos calores: Desde el momento en que no se puede *comer*, ni sirve para hacer caldo . . . gordo" (Cuba goes to pot . . . just as the meat for the stew gets ruined with such heat: once it becomes inedible it's not even useful for indulging oneself in a fatty broth) (*Paliques* 549). He thus criticizes the arguments of those opposed to granting autonomy to Cuba. In *La Regenta*, the identification between loss of sovereignty and the cooking pot in the Marquis's kitchen, where the best nourishments from the provincial colonies are sent, can be understood in relation to the imperial state.

Clarín presents Obdulia's invasion of the kitchen as a transgressive act. Pedro, the chef in charge of maintaining an order we come to see is unwittingly androcentric, ironically considers women and kitchens as antithetical terms, like liberty and government. Indeed, he loses control when Obdulia occupies his kitchen, placing her hands into the same dough he is kneading. Furthermore, when "Obdulia se acercó al dignísimo Pedro y sonriendo le metió en la boca la misma cucharilla que ella acababa de tocar con sus labios de rubí (este rubí es del cocinero). . . . Pedro llegó a donde pocas veces; a consentir que las criadas de la casa intervinieran en los asuntos de los negros pucheros de hierro" (Obdulia came up to him and, with a smile, slipped into his mouth the same spoon which has just been caressed by her ruby lips [the "ruby" is the chef's]. . . . Pedro even went to the extraordinary length of permitting the servants girls to participate in the activities surrounding the black iron casseroles) (163; 173). Pedro's total loss of control over his cooking pots is linked to the sexual emancipation of the merry widow, and her interference in masculine control through the assertion of her sexual agency. Obdulia's provocative gesture becomes an important tool of conquest when she penetrates Pedro's mouth with the spoon. However, the free indirect speech also reveals Pedro's desire to acquire what seems to him to be a precious stone. In the end, Obdulia's disruptive action only helps female servants to take their place in the kitchen, as expected, based on normative gender roles.

Chapter 8 of *La Regenta* serves as a preamble to Clarín's vision of how female sexual agency and empowerment can degenerate into barbarous behaviors. While Alvaro Mesía thinks that there is not a single strong woman on earth (145), he maintains a conversation with Paco Vegallana about preparing a romantic *donjuanesca* conquest of Ana. Once they arrive at the Marquis's palace, they find:

> una hermosa cabeza de mujer, cubierta con un gorro blanco de fantasía, apareció en una ventana al otro lado del patio que había en medio de la casa . . . manos de muñeca, mostraban, levantándolo por encima del gorro, un pollo pelado, que palpitaba con las ansias de la muerte; del pico caían gotas de sangre.
>
> Obdulia, dirigiéndose a los atónitos caballeros, hizo ademán de retorcer el pescuezo a su víctima y gritó triunfante: —¡Yo misma! ¡he sido yo misma! ¡Así a todos los hombres! (147)
>
> (A beautiful female head wearing a fancy white hat appeared at a window on the other side of the courtyard around which the

> house was built . . . hands of a china doll held up above the hat a plucked chicken, still quivering in its death-throes, blood dripping from its beak.
>
> Obdulia, turning toward the speechless gentlemen, made to twist her victim's neck, and cried in triumph: "All by myself! I did it all by myself! That's what I do to all the men!") (157)

It is noteworthy that throughout the novel, the young male seducers are called *pollos*, in the colloquial sense of a young conqueror; the peacock refers to the Magistral, and the Vetustan rooster to Álvaro. Both Álvaro and Paco had sexual encounters with Obdulia in the past. After being conquered and left behind by Álvaro and Paco, Obdulia calls for the extermination of men and, in her fantasy, confronts masculine sexual potency, comically holding the *pollo* tightly and showing a desire to wring his neck, in a symbolic act of castration. Obdulia's satirical transformation into a black widow doll signals her incipient female emancipation. In spite of the objectification of this comic *femme fatale*, the violence of the scene presents the image of a savage tyranny set in motion by Obdulia's explosion of resentment, which links female liberation to barbarism.

Obdulia's characterization, with its emphasis on sexual liberation, competitive desires, and barbarism allows Clarín to locate the corruption of power on both sides of the Atlantic: in the metropole, represented by the political forces that abuse Ana and Cuba; and in the colony, represented by the desire for emancipation. However, the desire for emancipation is reduced to a simple decorative archetype, a chimera. After all, the illusory control Obdulia evokes through her clothing and footwear becomes insignificant, in light of the public reaction to Ana's costume during the Holy week procession:

> ¡El pueblo entero pendiente de los pasos, de los movimientos, del traje de Ana, de su color, de sus gestos! . . . ¡Y venía descalza! ¡Los pies blanquísimos, desnudos, admirados y compadecidos por multitud inmensa!" Esto era para la de Fandiño el bello ideal de la coquetería. Jamás sus desnudos hombros, sus brazos de marfil sirviendo de fondo a negro encaje bordado y bien ceñido; jamás su espalda de curvas vertiginosas, su pecho alto y fornido, exuberante y tentador, habían atraído así, ni con cien leguas, la

atención y la admiración de un pueblo entero, por más que los luciera en bailes, teatros, paseos y también procesiones. (558)

(The eyes of the whole town riveted on Ana's steps, her movements, her clothes, her color, the look of her face! And she was barefoot! Her feet, naked and as white as white, admired and pitied by the immense crowd!" For Obdulia Fandiño this was the perfect ideal of coquetry. Her own naked shoulders, her ivory arms acting as a background for clinging black embroidered lace, her back with vertiginous curves, her bosom, high and strong, exuberant and tempting, had never attracted in this way or in anything like this way the attention and admiration of an entire town, however much she had displayed them in ballrooms, theatres, promenades and processions.) (590)

The fascination that Ana produces reduces Obdulia to the unessential. Her envy makes her wish to conquer Ana, who is the object of all gazes enjoying her religious enslavement. Obdulia's admiration of Ana provokes in her a "lujuria bestial, disparatada, inexplicable por lo absurda. Sentía Obdulia en aquel momento así . . . un deseo vago . . . de . . . de ser hombre" (crazy, brutal lust, so absurd as to be inexplicable. Obdulia felt a vague desire . . . to . . . to . . . to be a man) (558; 591). The widow's homoerotic desire makes clear her feeling of impotence within the social order, while highlighting the perversity implied in female/colonial liberation. Furthermore, Ana's admired status confirms that in order to attain the category of feminine idol, Obdulia must give up her sexual power and accept her status as colonized subject.

Clarín's masterpiece and journalistic writings exemplify how, within Spanish fin-de-siècle cultural production, the defense of the family and national unity is interwoven into two narratives, the imperial and the patriarchal, sharing the colonial system of power that shapes Clarín's views on gender and colonialism. Taking into account Clarín's antislavery position and his advocacy of Cuban and female autonomy, *La Regenta*'s representation of power illustrates the complexities of freedom and subjection in the call for women's greater autonomy and a better distribution of territorial authority, while rejecting the full emancipation of either women or the territories. Clarín denounces, on the one hand, colonial corruption and the moral complicity of those who directly or indirectly support any kind of slavery.

On the other hand, he represents independence as savage and degenerate. He defends Cuba's political autonomy but not its sovereignty, and he does the same for women. In both cases, Clarín associates total sovereignty with acts of barbarism, while making evident the disparity between promises, fears, and reality.

Notes

1. Subsequent translations from the text are mine.
2. The Ten Years' War ended with the Peace of Zanjón, in which the assimilation of Cuba with the metropole is described as if Cuba were a province of Spain (Dardé, "América" 410). However, the island was not granted autonomy until November 1897.
3. According to Schmidt-Nowara, the Spanish Abolitionist Society, along with the Spanish republicans who supported it, reinforced the image of a transatlantic Spanish nation and showed a frustrated but significant effort by the political Left to translate the process of emancipating slaves, in its various stages, into a democratic, multiracial, and imperial project ("From Slaves" 178). Alas is among those republicans who supported the emancipation of slaves, as well as a multiracial imperial project.
4. As Arthur Smith pointed out, the "Libertad de Vientres provided for liberty of all slaves born on that date or thereafter. The second most important provision of the Moret Law granted freedom to all slaves over 65 years of age (later amended to 60). Other important provisions declared the freedom of all slaves confiscated from slave ships, of all slaves who had served under the Spanish flag in the Cuban insurrection and of slaves not legally included in the census registrations of Puerto Rico and Cuba" (218).
5. Surwillo explains, "The transatlantic slave trade was carried out by *negreros*—slave ship captains—but this same word was also use to describe the capitalists who financed and masterminded slaving expeditions to Africa and then managed the smuggling of contraband men and women onto the island. These businessmen created huge fortunes and vast networks of influence that extended across insular (Cuba) and peninsular Spain" (3).
6. My analysis will place the poem "A Cuba" in dialogue with Clarín's journalistic pieces on Cuba, which intervene more directly in debates about independence.
7. In Clarín's early texts, insurgents were not part of the metaphorical family; rather, they were individuals who put the family in danger. Clarín's elegy "A la muerte de Gonzalo Castañón" (1870) praises an Iberian writer and politician in Cuba, whose assassination was linked to the pro-independence movement (Valis 29). In that work, the poetic voice encourages brave Cubans to defend themselves against the *barbarie impía* (pro-independence movement) that oppresses Cuba. As

Schmidt-Nowara has shown, the Spanish republican press that followed the war in Cuba provided its readership with images of bestial violence to represent the Cuban rebels ("From Slaves" 178). Clarín brings this image in his verses to Castañón, showing his rejection of insurgents by depicting them as uncivilized barbarians lacking spirituality. In contrast, his vision of courageous Cubans, meaning the rest of the island's population, as "hermanos," (siblings), suggests the sense of fraternity that he will defend in advocating Cuban autonomy.

    8. Historical studies on how the Spanish republican press addressed the Cuban conflict in relation to the process of national/imperial narrative building have been recently put in dialogue with other theoretical and literary approaches to the inscriptions of empire in Spanish cultural production. These new approaches analyze the cultural impact of the conflict on discourses of domesticity, while questioning some of the premises of the imperial narrative, and result in revisionist volumes such as *Empire's End*, co-edited by Akiko Tsuchiya and William Acree Junior. In this anthology, authors demonstrate that the end of empire, rather than occurring at the close of the Spanish American War of 1898, was a process that covered practically the entire nineteenth century and even had ramifications (both real and symbolic) beyond it (*Empire* 3).

    9. In examining the role of Cuba in relation to slavery, race, gender, and colonialism in Galdós's novels, Surwillo shows that Galdós reconfigures the paradigm of metropole and colonial daughters as one of marriage.

    10. References to colonialism not only permeate Alas's masterpiece, but they are also found in many of his short stories, among them, "Adiós Cordera," "Superchería," "En el tren," and, in greater detail, in "Boroña," "El Rana," "La contribución," and "El sustituto." All of these works intertwine representations of colonialism with discourses of race, gender, and class.

    11. According to Quijano: "What is termed globalization is the culmination of a process that began with the constitution of America and colonial/modern Eurocentered capitalism as a new global power. One of the fundamental axes of this model of power is the social classification of the world's population around the idea of race, a mental construction that expresses the basic experience of colonial domination and pervades the more important dimensions of global power, including its specific rationality: Eurocentrism. The racial axis has a colonial origin and character, but it has proven to be more durable and stable than the colonialism in whose matrix it was established. Therefore, the model of power that is globally hegemonic today presupposes an element of coloniality" (533).

    12. Thanks to John Rutherford, readers have an English translation of this Spanish masterpiece. All subsequent English translations of *La Regenta* follow the edition by Rutherford.

    13. Clarín calls for a renegotiation of power to achieve women's greater autonomy, while rejecting their full emancipation in different arenas, including education. Although I do not address the topic of education in my essay, the

debate on women's education provides another clear example of Clarín's thoughts on gender and colonialism. Clarín supports women's education for specific professions that, in his view, were appropriate for women. However, he also opposes what he called "la educación *hombruna* de la mujer" (the manly education of a woman) (*Paliques* 381), which other writers, Emilia Pardo Bazán among them, called "la emancipación intelectual de la mujer" (women's intellectual emancipation) (*Paliques* 381). In other words, he opposes women's access to many forms of higher education and to careers he felt were inappropriate for them: "Pero figúrese que . . . quisieran ser médicas, abogadas, periodistas, ingenieras, catedráticas, etc., etc." (But imagine that . . . [women] might want to become doctors, lawyers, journalists, engineers, professors, etc., etc.) (*Paliques* 381). Facing Pardo Bazan's criticism, Clarín declares: "es muy hacedero llamar frívolo, superficial, anticuado, misoneo [sic] á quien se opone a la *emancipación intelectual* (!) [sic] de la *mujer*" (It is very easy to call frivolous, superficial, antiquated, misogynistic anyone who opposes women's *intellectual emancipation* [!]) (*Paliques* 381).

14. In *Monsters by Trade*, Surwillo explains that "the concept of national integrity was reinvigorated in the second half of the nineteenth century as part of the patriotic discourse of empire and the economic policy of protected markets" (73–74).

15. See Labra's reasoning in "La autonomía colonial en España" and *La crisis colonial de España (1868–1898)*.

16. *La Regenta* offers a gallery of ambitious female workers. In fact, ambition appears as the cause of social degeneration, and a significant threat during the Restoration period. Lawrence Rich has analyzed the intersections between women and the working class in *La Regenta*, revealing a potential threat to bourgeois hegemony and the author's implied fear of social degeneration ("Fear").

Works Cited

Alas, Leopoldo. *Cuentos*. Ed. Ángeles Ezama. Crítica, 1997.

———. *Cuentos*. Ed. José María Martínez Cachero. Libertarias, 1998.

———. *Paliques*. Hemeroteca Municipal de Madrid, 2003.

———. *La Regenta*. Ed. John Rutherford. Penguin Classics, 1984.

———. *La Regenta*. Ed. Maite Zubiaurre and Eilene Powell. Stockcero, 2012.

Blanco, Alda. *Cultura y conciencia imperial en la España del siglo XIX*. Publicacions de la Universitat de València, 2012.

———. "Spain at the Crossroads: Imperial Nostalgia or Modern Colonialism?" *A Contra Corriente. A Journal of Social History and Literature in Latin America*, vol. 5, no. 1, 2007, pp. 1–11.

Cánovas del Castillo, Antonio. *Discurso sobre la nación: Ateneo de Madrid, 6 de noviembre de 1882*. Biblioteca Nueva, 1997.

Ciplijauskaté, Biruté. *La mujer insatisfecha: Adulterio en la novela realista*. Edhasa, 1984.

Dardé, Carlos. "América en la conciencia española de la Restauración 1875–1902." *Menéndez Pelayo. Cien años después. Actas del Congreso.* Universidad Internacional Menéndez Pelayo, 2015, pp. 407–34.
DuPont, Denise. *Realism as Resistance: Romanticism and Authorship in Galdós, Clarín, and Baroja.* Bucknell UP, 2006.
Feros, Antonio. " '*Spain* and America: *All Is One.*' Historiography of the Conquest and Colonization of the Americas and National Mythology in Spain.1892–c.1992." *Interpreting Spanish Colonialism: Empires, Nations, and Legends*, edited by Christopher Schmidt-Nowara and John M. Nieto-Phillips, University of New Mexico Press, 2005, pp. 109–35.
Gómez de Avellaneda, Gertrudis. *Antología poética.* Ed. Mary Cruz. Letras Cubanas: 1983.
Labanyi, Jo. *Gender and Modernization in Spanish Realist Novel.* Oxford UP, 2000.
Labra, Rafael María. "La autonomía colonial en España." *Discursos.* Madrid, 1892, pp. 85–90.
———. *La crisis colonial de España (1868–1898): Estudios de Política palpitante y discursos parlamentarios.* Madrid, 1901.
Lissorgues, Yvan. "España ante la guerra colonial de 1895 a 1898: Leopoldo Alas (Clarín), periodista, y el problema cubano." *Hommage à Juan Marinello et Nöel Salomon: Cuba, les étapes d'una libération, Actes du Colloque Internacional.* Université de Toulouse, 1978, pp. 47–76.
Lugones, Maria. "Heterosexualism and the Colonial/Modern Gender System." *Hypatia*, vol. 22, no. 1, Winter 2007, pp. 186–209.
Mandrell, James. *Don Juan and the Point of Honor: Seduction, Patriarchal Society, and Literary Tradition.* Pennsylvania State UP, 1992.
———. "Nostalgia and the Popularity of Don Juan Tenorio: Reading Zorrilla through Clarín." *Hispanic Review*, vol. 56, no. 1, Winter 1991, pp. 37–55.
Martí, José. *Contra España.* Ed. Andrés Sorel. Txalaparta, 1999.
Mignolo, Walter. *Local Histories/Global Designs: Coloniality, Subaltern Knowledges, and Border Thinking.* Princeton UP, 2000.
Moscoso, Javier. *Promesas incumplidas. Una historia política de las pasiones.* Taurus, 2017.
Núñez Puente, Sonia. "Cuerpos fragmentados: Ana Ozores Emma Bovary y el fetichismo." *Transitions: Journal of Franco-Iberian Studies*, vol. 2, 2006, pp. 6–34.
Pérez Galdós, Benito. "Prólogo." *La Regenta*, de Leopoldo Alas, Clarín, Fernando Fé, 1901, pp. v–xix.
Quijano, Anibal. "Coloniality of Power, Eurocentrism, and Latin America." *Nepantla: Views from the South*, vol. 1, no. 3, 2000, pp. 533–80.
Rich, Lawrence. "Fear and Loathing in Vetusta Coding Class and Gender in Clarín's *La Regenta.*" *Revista Canadiense de Estudios Hispánicos*, vol. 25, no. 3, 2001, pp. 505–18.

San Miguel, Luis García. *El pensamiento de Leopoldo Alas, Clarín*. Centro de Estudios Constitucionales, 1987.

Schmidt-Nowara, Christopher. *The Conquest of History. Spanish Colonialism and National Histories in the Nineteenth Century*. U of Pittsburgh P, 2006.

———. "From Slaves to Spaniards: The Failure of Revolutionary Emancipations in Spain and Cuba, 1868–1895." *Illes i Imperis*, vol. 2, 1999, pp. 177–90.

Scott, Rebecca. "La dinámica de la emancipación y la formación de la sociedad post-abolicionista: el caso cubano en una perspectiva comparativa." *Esclavitud y derechos humanos: la lucha por la libertad del negro en el siglo XIX*, edited by Francisco de Solano and Agustín Guimerá, Consejo Superior de Investigaciones Científicas, 1990, pp. 345–52.

Smith, Arthur. "The Spanish Abolition Law of 1870: A Study in Legislative Reluctance." *Revista de Ciencias Sociales*, vol. 4, no. 1, 1960, pp. 215–35.

Surwillo, Lisa. *Monsters by Trade. Slave Traffickers in Modern Spanish Literature and Culture*. Stanford UP, 2014.

Tsuchiya, Akiko, and William G. Acree Jr., eds. *Empire's End. Transnational Connections in the Hispanic World*. Vanderbilt UP, 2016.

———. *Marginal Subjects. Gender and Deviance in Fin-de-Siècle Spain*. U of Toronto P, 2011.

Ugarte, Michael. "The Spanish Empire on the Wane: Africa, Galdós, and the Moroccan Wars." *Empire's End. Transnational Connections in the Hispanic World*, edited by Akiko Tsuchiya and William G. Acree Jr., Vanderbilt UP, 2016, pp. 177–90.

Valis, Noël. "En busca de una incomprensión histórica: El joven Leopoldo Alas y la cuestión cubana." *Letras Peninsulares*, vol. 5, no. 1, 1992, pp. 23–39.

Zubiaurre, Maite, and Eilene Powell. "Introducción." *La Regenta* by Leopoldo Alas, Stockcero, 2012, pp. vii–xlix.

8

Dalagas and *Ilustrados*

Gender, Language, and Indigeneity in the Philippine Colonies

JOYCE TOLLIVER

Language, indigeneity, and the secular power of the Catholic Church have always been at the heart of Spanish colonialism, and, as historians have amply documented, the entanglements of these issues are nowhere as complex as in the Philippines.[1] What is less frequently acknowledged is that gender performance and expectations were also tightly intertwined with issues of indigeneity and of language policy, and that this intersection was at the heart of both the Spanish colonial regime and the resistance to that regime in the Philippines. Raquel A. Reyes and Megan C. Thomas have both made crucial contributions to our understanding of the performance of bourgeois masculinity that was at stake in the campaigns of the anticolonialist *Ilustrados* of the late 1880s and 1890s, but little has been written about the role played by notions of femininity and of the intersections between the norms of performance of Filipina gender and of indigeneity.

In this study, I offer a preliminary exploration of how the nationalist rhetoric of the Filipino male intellectuals who led the reformist Propaganda movement employed linguistic choices that drew doubly on discourses of indigeneity and of sexual purity in their appeals to bourgeois Filipinas as co-creators of the emerging Philippine nation. My analysis of José Rizal's "Message to the Young Women of Malolos" (1889) and Pedro Paterno's "La dalaga virtuosa" (1910) traces the national leaders' consistent invocation of an idyllic, pan-Philippine indigenous identity, whose unity and perfection depended paradoxically on modern Catholic notions of female sexual purity. In both texts, I argue, language policy issues are centrally at stake in the imagination of Philippine identity.

Ironically, it is within the context of their putative support for Philippine women's education that each writer exhorts his female audience to contribute to the making of the modern Philippine nation by embodying sexual purity. The incarnation prescribed by Rizal is that of a virginal, self-sacrificing mother, while Paterno imagined the post-1898 Filipina as a pious maiden. Rizal's essay, written in Tagalog, took the form of an open letter to a group of twenty young women who had approached Governor General Valeriano Weyler, in person, to present a formal petition for the establishment of a Spanish-language school for women in the town of Malolos. Paterno's tale forms part of *Aurora social* (*Social Dawn*), his trilogy of Spanish-language writings that he intended for use in Philippine schools—about a decade after the U.S. government had decreed that all public school instruction must be given in English.[2]

In order to reach a preliminary understanding of the complex interactions of gender, language, religion, and indigeneity in the Philippine colonial era, it is essential to understand something about the particularities of the Spanish colonization of the Philippines. The vast archipelago's remoteness from the Peninsula and its great linguistic and ethnic heterogeneity presented serious challenges to colonization through religious conversion, and to the imposition of Spanish as a national language and lingua franca. While government officials tended to stay for only short terms in the Philippines, Spanish friars sent by their respective orders might serve as village friar curates for many years. Beginning in the late eighteenth century, Spanish friars were assigned to serve as permanent parish priests in the Philippines, which gave them a new degree of autonomy from their Church superiors as well as considerable political control in the villages (Schumacher 14–15). Vicente Rafael explains that the power of the friars was such that they often undermined the authority of the representatives of the Crown in the Philippines. He thinks of the friar as a sort of "double agent, simultaneously enacting and limiting, enabling while challenging the absolutist vocation of the king's supernatural sovereignty" (*Motherless* 25).

Since the friars were charged with overseeing the local schools, they held complete control over the implementation of public education in the Philippines. Rather than educate Filipinos in Spanish, as the law demanded, they limited the teaching of Spanish to the ecclesiastical context, and provided a rudimentary education in the bits and pieces of the vernacular languages they had managed to learn.³ Some historians, such as Keith Whinnom, explain the practice of limiting the teaching of Spanish to Church-related vocabulary in practical terms: since the friars stayed in the archipelago long enough to learn the vernacular languages, they simply found it easier to teach in those languages than to teach the locals a second language (Whinnom 160–61).

Yet it was no coincidence that the withholding of access to the Spanish language also gave the friars iron control over the colonized peoples of the Philippines. As Nicanor G. Tiongsen states, in fact, "the friars derived their power from the lack of a common language between the government and the natives" (162). This de facto rule by friars, or *frailocracia*, became an essential element of colonial power in the Philippines: the order by friars melded the rule of God and the rule of Spain in one figure, and, significantly, in one language—Spanish. Spanish colonial rule in the Philippines depended crucially on this metonymic association among the Spanish language, Spain, and the Church.⁴

The abuses of the local populations perpetrated through the *frailocracia* became a central target of the first leaders of the Philippine anticolonial movement, the self-named *Ilustrados* (Enlightened Ones). These economically privileged young men came from the small minority of elite Filipinos who had been educated in Spanish. Nearly all of them lived in Spain for an extended period; and their anticolonialist periodical *La Solidaridad* was published, from Barcelona and from Madrid, in Spanish. They generally used Spanish to communicate among themselves, partly because they did not all share the same vernacular languages. Most of the *Ilustrados* published their essays and other works primarily in Spanish. This linguistic choice allowed them to reach a broader audience of intellectuals, both in the archipelago and in the Peninsula, while also signaling their membership in a cultural elite. Through their choice to publish and speak in Spanish, the *Ilustrados* signaled that they were speaking both to *peninsulares* and to fellow Filipino elites, rather than to the members of any one of the many vernacular linguistic communities in the archipelago.

The polyglot physician José Rizal (1861–1896), known across the archipelago and the Peninsula as the author of the anticolonialist novels *Noli me tangere* (1887) and *El filibustero* (1891), was acknowledged as the primary spokesperson of the *Ilustrados* during his own time. He became the martyred national hero shortly after the Spanish government had him executed for treason following a sham trial, in 1896. Rizal had consistently advocated for the assimilation of the Philippine peoples into the Spanish nation and opposed the nascent Philippine movement for independence, but his biting exposés of the abuses of the colonial government and of the Church were perceived to represent a threat to colonial hegemony.

On the other hand, other members of the *Ilustrados,* such as Pedro Paterno, would go on to play prominent roles in the Philippine Revolution and in the Philippine-American War.[5] Paterno (1857–1911) remained on the periphery of the group of Philippine reformists that Rizal had led: other *Ilustrados,* such as Graciano López Jaena, Marcelo del Pilar, and Rizal himself, shunned Paterno for the flamboyant and fanciful image he painted of himself as a *maginóo,* or descendant of ancient Philippine nobility, as well as for his shifting political alliances, which were widely interpreted as motivated by opportunism. After he helped to negotiate the 1897 Pact of Biak-na-bato, which marked the failed end of the Philippine Revolution, Paterno was denounced as a sellout, a charge that came to define his legacy. Renato Constantino called Paterno "the broker of the betrayal of the revolution" (Reyes, "'Treasonous'" 89). Paterno's voluminous publications on Philippine indigeneity have been largely overlooked by scholars today, as they were even during Paterno's time (Mojares 98). Nevertheless, Portia Reyes has argued compellingly that they deserve to be considered seriously as important contributions to the history of Philippine nationalism (Reyes, "'Treasonous'").

For the *Ilustrados,* a key moment in the struggle for a democratic Philippine nation came in December 1888, when a group of twenty young women from the city of Malolos formally requested that the Governor General establish a Spanish-language school for women in their town. To those familiar with Spanish colonialism in Latin America, it might seem mystifying that the Malolos women had to petition the Governor General to establish a school in the language of the colonial power, after nearly three centuries of Spanish colonial domination. But in fact, in marked contrast to the American colonies, Spanish never really took root in the Philippines. The 1903 U.S. Census estimated that only 1.6 percent of "the civilized population" of the Philippines had received secondary education in any language; for women, the figure was seven-tenths of 1 percent (Pardo de Tavera 41). Erin P. Hardacker documents the overwhelming logistical obstacles to implementing the free education in Spanish that was mandated in 1863, including a dearth of qualified teachers and the fact that the vast majority of those not belonging to the cultural elite spoke a local language natively. But it is also clear that the status of Spanish as the language of both political and ecclesiastical power, combined with the strong incentive for the friar curates to withhold this linguistic access to power from the native populations, made it unlikely that the multiple royal decrees ordering the establishment of Spanish-language public schools would be implemented.

The petition of the women of Malolos, then, forced the hand of the Crown, obliging it to choose between its own laws, on the one hand, and, on the other hand, an informal system of government that allowed the colonial government bureaucracy to wash its hands of any practical responsibility for the day-to-day workings of colonial rule. The petition also directly threatened the control of the friar curates. Not only were the women demanding secular Spanish-language education, but they were demanding that it be provided to women, thus enabling their access to political power. The women's claim to a legal right to an education—threatening on its own terms—was intertwined with their open defiance of the iron-clad control imposed by the friars, who had come to represent the combined abuses of colonialism, racism, and sexism.[6] In the first place, the women refused to allow the town's friar curates to act as their intermediary with the Governor General, in an overt challenge to the *frailocracia*. They refused to allow the friars to vet their letter or, indeed, even to see it, in spite of the friars' demand to be informed of its contents (Tiongson 173).[7]

Weyler arrived in Malolos on the morning of December 12, 1888. He inspected some schools and ordered that fines be imposed for noncompliance with the education decrees. He then announced that, after a lunch break, he would meet with any villager who wished to register a complaint about any school in the town. All twenty of the women appeared at the appointed hour, bearing the signed petition, and, resisting the friars' interference, managed to personally deliver the document directly to the Governor General. Their petition was originally denied, and rumors circulated that one of the friar curates, alarmed by the Maloleñas' audacious threat to his control, had pressured Weyler not to establish the school (De los Santos 31). But after several weeks during which the women and their supporters tirelessly campaigned for the school, the request was finally approved. López Jaena and other *Ilustrados* celebrated the news of the approval as a major victory, and López Jaena praised the Maloleñas as heroines for the reformist cause (López Jaena, "Amor" 14).

At this point, the *Ilustrado* Marcelo Del Pilar contacted his friend José Rizal, who was carrying out research at the British Library, and urged him to write an open letter to the women who had signed the petition. For Del Pilar, this was a golden opportunity to piggyback on the Malolos women's initiative in support of the *Ilustrado*'s own anticolonial cause. It was at Del Pilar's urging that Rizal chose Tagalog as the medium for his message. Del Pilar gave no rationale for his suggestion that Rizal switch to his first language for this crucial essay, and Rizal demanded none.[8] In any case, Rizal followed the advice of his friend, and wrote the letter in Tagalog. In spite of the overtly political function of the essay, it was not translated to Spanish for publication in *La Solidaridad*, the *Ilustrados*' journal. In fact, it would not be translated to Spanish during Rizal's lifetime, and it was not even published in the original Tagalog until 1902. Fourteen years passed between the time of its original publication and its translation to Spanish.[9] Today, the letter is most commonly read in the English translation, under the title, "Message to the Young Women of Malolos" (1961).[10]

It is significant that, when Del Pilar approached Rizal about writing the letter to the Maloleñas, Rizal was immersed in his preparation of the first modern edition of Antonio Morga's 1609 *Sucesos de las Filipinas* (*History of the Philippines*). The Rizal edition of Morga would come to play a foundational role both in the recovery of early colonial discourse about the Philippines and in the creation of a modern national discourse on Philippine indigeneity. In his copious annotations to Morga's *Sucesos*, Rizal argues for the existence of a pre-Hispanic indigenous Malayan golden age in the Philippines. Drawing on Morga's depiction of a thriving pre-Hispanic culture, Rizal used his annotations to argue that the weaknesses of the late colonial Philippines were caused by the corrupting influence of the Spanish religious orders, which destroyed the peaceful and industrious communities that comprised the pre-Hispanic Malayan civilization. When Rizal paused his work on Morga to write the open letter to the women of Malolos, he undoubtedly had both indigeneity and the abuses of the friar curates very much on his mind.

His evocation of a golden age of indigeneity in his letter to the Maloleñas, however, would take a new turn with the introduction of the evocation of a time when both the Islas Filipinas (that is, the Islands) and the Filipinas (that is, the Philippine women) were unadulterated, pure, and uncorrupted. That is, in appealing to female indigeneity, he imposes a gendered hierarchy on the idyllic communitarian vision of the pre-Hispanic Malayan civilization he had constructed through his reading of Morga. By projecting the gender hierarchy of the colonizers onto the idyllic nonmodern civilization he invokes, Rizal ironically recolonizes that civilization.[11]

In his open letter, Rizal praises the efforts of his *compatricias* (female compatriots), but then goes on to set out the limitations of women's role in the anticolonialist movement. This pattern of damning by faint praise is established from the beginning, when he compares the twenty courageous women with most of the Philippine women he has known. Most Filipinas, he says, are like "plantas marchitas sembradas y criadas en las tinieblas, cuyas flores carecen de perfume, cuyos frutos no destilan savia" (faded plants, sown and reared in the darkness) ("A las compatricias" 27; "To My Countrywomen" 26). He allots far more space to discussing the flaws of most Filipinas than he does to his praise of the Malolos women, preferring to focus his attention on the dangerous submissiveness to the authority of the friars that he sees in most Filipinas. In fact, he claims that Asia is less advanced than the Western world because of the unquestioning servitude of Asian women ("A las compatricias" 28; "To My Countrywomen" 27).

Whatever egalitarian humanism informs Rizal's arguments is undercut by his reliance on the traditional notion that the primary social value of women's education is that educated women make better wives and mothers. In fact, following this conservative rationale, Rizal considers Philippine women almost exclusively in terms of their potential to produce sons who will be productive citizens: "Sois las primeras en influir en la conciencia del hombre. . . . No espere el pueblo honor, ni prosperidad mientras eduque tuertamente al niño, mientras sea esclava e ignorante la mujer que ha de vigilar los pasos del hijo" (You [women] . . . are the first to influence the consciousness of man. . . . The people cannot expect honor or prosperity so long as they will educate their children in a wrong way, so long as the woman who guides the children in his first steps is slavish and ignorant) ("A las compatricias" 28; "To My Countrywomen" 27). In elevating women's maternal role over the development of individual women's minds, Rizal propagates the discourse of female subservience expressed in nineteenth-century European and Philippine conduct manuals, and of Philippine publications such as Father Modesto de Castro's conduct manual, *Ang Pagsusulatan ng Dalawang Binibini na si Urbana at si Feliza*, which was contemporaneous to and echoed Sinués's *El ángel del hogar* (Tiongsen 212–35).

Given that the Malolos women were requesting the establishment of a school that would offer *Spanish*-language education, it seems curious that Rizal completely skirts the issue of language. The Marxist historian E. San Juan suggests that, in writing his response to the Maloleñas, Rizal was scarcely concerned with making a statement about Spanish-language education for women. In fact, San Juan dismisses the seriousness not only of Rizal's concern with women's access to Spanish-language education, but even of the petitioners' request itself: "Rizal urges the use of rational analysis and judgment in all activities—not just in learning Spanish, which for the Malolos women was really a pretext to have access to the mentoring wisdom of Teodoro Sandiko, Rizal's progressive compatriot" (67).[12] San Juan's claim regarding the motivation of the signatories is both dismissive of the Maloleñas's intellectual engagement and oddly flattering to Sandico, especially since he also claims that it was Sandico himself who wrote the petition. On the other hand, San Juan's observation about the relative importance that Rizal gives to the language issue is very important. Indeed, while Rizal speaks of the need for education in general, he never mentions the question of access to the language of political, civic, and ecclesiastical power. While the Maloleñas foreground the issue of access to Spanish, Rizal keeps it firmly in the background of his essay. In this sense, it is worthwhile to examine in greater depth the ramifications of his choice to respond to the petition in Tagalog rather than in Spanish, the language in which the petition was written.

José Rizal was born in Calamba, less than a hundred kilometers from Malolos, and Tagalog was his first language. He learned some Spanish as a young boy from his mother, and all of his secondary school studies at the Ateneo in Manila were in Spanish (Guerrero 50–55). Nearly all his published essays and literary works were written in Spanish, and he regularly carried out correspondence with his fellow Philippine reformists in that language.[13] It is possible that Del Pilar and Rizal assumed that the women who signed the petition would find it easier to comprehend Tagalog than Spanish, but, as Del Pilar pointed out to Rizal, all of these women belonged to the *principalía*, the region's economic and cultural elite, to whom Spanish was accessible (Kalaw 120). In that context, Del Pilar and Rizal may have considered it symbolically powerful to write the letter, not in the language used by the peninsular friar curates to impose the Church's rule, but rather in the indigenous language that united the reformist leader with the Maloleñas.

But in writing to his female compatriots in their shared vernacular language, Rizal was simultaneously supporting and undermining Spanish-language education in the Philippines: if Spanish was the language of the colonial government and of the Church, it was a weapon that all Filipinos should learn how to wield. On the other hand, true Philippine community would be built through the language, not of the oppressor, but of the oppressed. In exhorting his female compatriots to lead other members of their sex out of their ignorance and subservience, he chooses not to address them in the priests' language. This choice could be interpreted as ideologically symbolic, but at the same time, it meant that the essay would need to be translated to Castilian before it could be shared with the metropolis.

It is not clear why Rizal's open letter was not translated to Spanish immediately, particularly given that the petition of the Malolos women was praised in *La Solidaridad*. While we have no record of what motivated the editors of *La Solidaridad* to bypass an opportunity to publish one of the Rizal's most stinging condemnations of the frailocracy, it is clear that the use of Tagalog framed it explicitly as a communication from one member of an indigenous group to another. We might be tempted to consider this choice, and *La Solidaridad*'s choice not to translate it, as decolonial gestures, similar to María Lugones's decision not to translate the aymara terms she uses in "Toward a Decolonial Feminism":

> To [translate] would enable you to understand what I am saying, but not really, since I cannot say what I want to say having translated the terms. So, if I do not translate and you think you understand less, or do not understand at all, I think that you can understand better why this works as an example of thinking at the colonial difference. (758)

And yet, when Rizal writes to the "*dalagas*" in Tagalog, he places himself in the same position of authority as the local priests who would keep the Philippine population—particularly the female Philippine population—in a position of passive recipients of his wisdom. Raquel Reyes succinctly summarizes the attitude toward women's advancement evinced by Rizal and his fellow *Ilustrados*: "Filipino women, they were convinced, had in future to take direction not from the Spanish friars but by [*sic*] the legitimate figures of moral authority and arbiters of moral rectitude, bourgeois patriots such as themselves" (139).

As a leader of the anti-friar reform movement, Rizal clearly had a vested interest in defending the desirability of education for the people of the Philippines, whether male or female. Yet the type of education he had in mind for his sister Filipinas was based on mid-nineteenth-century European models of women's education, whose primary goal was to ensure that the nation's mothers would raise sons who would grow up to be loyal, productive citizens. While the European cult of maternity draws a thick veil over the very existence of women's sexuality, Rizal offers an extended commentary on the questionable sexual reputation that Philippine women had developed in the Peninsula. Rizal claims that this bad reputation dates back at least to Sinibaldo de Mas's 1842 *Informe secreto* (Secret Report) on the Philippines, which was written for the Spanish government. He cites Mas's claim that, once male *peninsulares*—including friars—return to the Peninsula, they snicker and guffaw over the alleged licentiousness of Philippine women. As Lugones suggests, the association of sexual promiscuity with colonized populations rendered those populations less than human, since "the behaviors of the colonized and their personalities/souls were judged as bestial and thus non-gendered, promiscuous, grotesquely sexual, and sinful" (743). Given this logic, one might expect that an anticolonial leader would protest the charges leveled by Mas, and by the friars, as hypocritical, false, deeply offensive to the dignity of local women, and thus a direct affront to all Philippine people. Instead, Rizal's response is that the same charge of sexual looseness might also be leveled against peninsular women:

> Cada vez que oímos o leemos cosas de ese jaez nos preguntamos unos a otros: ¿las españolas son todas de la madera de María Santísima, y las filipinas precitas todas? Creo que, si se han de ajustar cuentas en materia tan delicada, tal vez . . . pero debo abandonar esto, que no soy confesor, ni trashumante peninsular con vara para lastimar la honra de nadie. Arrinconaré esto, y hablaré de los deberes de la mujer. ("A las compatricias" 29)
>
> (Every time we read or hear anything of this kind we ask each other: Are the Spanish women all cut after the pattern of the Holy Virgin Mary and the Filipinas all reprobates? I believe that if we were to balance accounts in this delicate question, perhaps. . . . But I must drop the subject, because I am neither a confessor nor a Spanish traveler and have no business to take away anybody's good name. I shall let this go and speak of the duties of woman instead.) ("To My Countrywomen" 28)

While apparently presenting a defense of the chastity of *most* Filipinas, in using the phrase "nos preguntamos unos a otros" (we ask each other), Rizal participates in exactly the sort of insolent disrespect he claims to disparage.

He goes on to suggest that, if Filipinas are to correctly raise their sons as patriots, they must first develop—or, rather, recover—these virtues. In sum, they must return to their earlier "pristine" state, which, he implies, they have lost because of their subservience to the friars:

[p]or espesa que sea la niebla que envuelva a nuestro pueblo, pondré diligencia suma en disiparla con la hermosa luz del sol, que fulgirá aunque ligeramente. No sentiremos fatiga si vosotras nos ayudais; ayudará también Dios . . . ; volverá a su pristino estado el nombre de la mujer filipina, de quien ahora sólo se echa de menos propio criterio: que buen natural tiénelo de sobra. ("A las compatricias" 29)

([h]owever dense the mist may be that befogs our people, I will make the utmost effort to have it dissipated by the bright rays of the sun, which will give light, though they may be dimmed. We shall not feel any fatigue if you will help us; God, too, will help to scatter the mist. . . . He will restore to its pristine condition the fame of the Filipina, in whom we now miss only a criterion of her own, because good qualities she has enough and to spare. ("To My Countrywomen" 27)

Rizal asks for the aid of the Maloleñas, as if they had not already dramatically advanced the anticolonialist, pro-education movement when they presented their petition directly to Weyler. He (and God) will be the ones working to bring the Philippines out of the shadows so that his female compatriots can return to their supposed former brilliance. Raquel Reyes does not overstate the case when she concludes that, in the efforts of Rizal and his *Ilustrado* colleagues to "sever the bonds between the friar and their female parishioners, the *Ilustrado* portrayal of women revealed a strong strain of misogyny that condemned them as sexually weak willed and intellectually weak minded" (139). And, yet, there is more to Rizal's logic than the simple wish to usurp the place of the friars as the legitimate representative of moral authority.

When Rizal talks about helping Filipina women to return to their "pristine condition" ("To My Countrywomen" 27), he evokes the same image of the idealized pre-Conquest state that he traced in his annotations to Morga's *Sucesos*, a time when indigenous Malayan women and men alike were unpolluted by the corrupting influence of the friar curates and other colonialists. At the same time, he holds up Western women as a desirable, yet impossible, model for all Asian women to follow, claiming that Europe and America are powerful "porque allí la mujer es libre e instruida, lúcida de inteligencia y fuerte de voluntad" ("there the women are free and well educated and endowed with lucid intellect and a strong will) ("A las compatricias" 28; "To My Countrywomen" 27). European and American women, it would seem, represent the future, while the best that Filipinas can do is to return to their precolonial past, so as to recover their original, indigenous "pristine" state, which has been corrupted by colonization.[14] Rizal's depiction of his "compatricias" thus displays a tension between his approval of their desire for intellectual freedom, which he associates with the West; and his own nostalgia for Filipina sexual purity, which is, for him, an essential component of their lost Malayan indigenous identity.

Rizal's association of Western women with enlightenment and freedom does not reflect the conception of middle-class Western women that characterized the "coloniality of gender" in the Americas, according to Lugones:

> The European, bourgeois, colonial, modern man became a subject/agent, fit for rule, for public life, and for ruling, a being of civilization, a heterosexual, Christian, a being of mind and reason. The European bourgeois woman was not understood as his complement, but as someone who reproduced race and capital through her sexual purity, passivity, and being homebound in the service of the white, European, bourgeois man. (743)

Rizal prescribes the proper role of his "compatricias" in nearly identical terms to those Lugones uses to capture the place of the women as helpmeets to those colonial subjects who would become "men," that is, who would become "civilized" (743). Yet he associates precisely the sort of intellectual autonomy that the Maloleñas are demanding with the West, offering his "compatricias" a model that would have them emulate the passivity of their mythical indigenous foremothers—with the singular exception that they should resist the rule of the friars. By reinforcing the association between the West and social and intellectual superiority, Rizal again enacts a colonial gesture that undermines the larger anticolonial argument of the essay.

Further, in order to make his argument, Rizal reframes the racial identity of the elite signatories, who were *mestizas sangleyes*—descendants of both Chinese and indigenous people. In emphasizing their indigenous Malayan heritage, he elides their Chinese heritage.[15] Presaging Rizal's own repudiation of his Chinese heritage in the last hours of his life (Coates 312), Rizal thus identifies the Philippine with the Malayan, imagining the addressees of his letter in terms of the nexus of their femaleness and their indigenous heritage. When he writes to the Maloleñas in Tagalog, then, it is not only because he is following the suggestion of his friend Marcelo Del Pilar. More significantly, Rizal is writing to them *not* as equal companions in the modern anticolonialist struggle, but as his projections of an idealized indigenous pre-Conquest golden age, when women were sexually pure, unsullied by their own acquiescence to the colonizers. He writes to them as young Malayan indigenous Filipinas, as *doncellas* or girls. That is, as the letter's Tagalog title indicates, he positions them, not as the powerful, history-making women they are, but as *dalagas*. Through these rhetorical moves, he situates Philippine elite women firmly and safely in the past, reserving the creation of a new Philippine future as a project to be carried out exclusively by himself and his *Ilustrado* colleagues.

Twenty-one years after Rizal wrote his Tagalog-language letter to the Maloleñas (*Sa mga Kabakayang Dalaga sa Malolos*), when the Spanish empire in the Philippines had been replaced by the rule of the United States, the outlier *Ilustrado* Pedro Paterno published a short novella, which he included in his collection of Spanish-language didactic tales called *Aurora social* (*Social Dawn*) (1910). "La dalaga virtuosa y el puente del diablo: Leyenda Filipina" (The Virtuous "*dalaga*" and the Devil's Bridge: Philippine Legend), like Rizal's letter, is framed as an address to a group of young Philippine women— that is, to a group Paterno alternately calls "*dalagas*," "girls," and "hijas del pueblo" (daughters of the *pueblo*) (*Aurora* I–XVI).[16] Like Rizal, Paterno draws on the notion of a pre-Hispanic golden age, this time featuring not only a unified, peaceful, productive Malayan utopia, but a vast pan-Asian civilization. He begins his narrative with an origin myth based on the idea that the Philippine archipelago was originally part of the Asian mainland, until an earthquake split the ancient homeland off from the rest of Asia, forming the islands that would come to be known as the Philippines. On the basis of this myth of geological, cultural, and linguistic Asian unity, he builds his tale of inherent indigenous feminine virtue.

The authorial voice claims that the tale of the young maiden and the devil's bridge has survived "trastornos religiosos" (religious upsets) and "invasiones de nuevas razas" (invasions of new races) ("La dalaga" 10) and has been passed down from grandmothers to their granddaughters in order to inculcate the love of God and to teach them virtuous behavior ("La dalaga" 10). Although the story is presented as a pre-Christian morality tale, the indigenous supreme god Bathala who is invoked in the tale is indistinguishable from the Christian God. Paterno's identification of Bathala with the Christian God goes beyond syncretism; in fact, in his ethnographic writings, Paterno theorizes the existence of a pan-Asian universal religion. He considered this religion, which he calls alternately called "Tagalismo" and "Bathalismo," to be the precursor of modern Catholicism, existing in the

Philippines long before the Spaniards arrived (Paterno, *La antigua civilización* 148–66). According to Paterno, although Catholicism replaced Bathalismo during the Spanish colonization, the essential Tagalog belief in Bathala and in the virtues he exemplifies never really died out in the Philippines.

This explains why, in "La dalaga virtuosa," Paterno makes a point of mentioning the matriarchal oral transmission of the tale. While once grandmothers told the tale to teach their granddaughters to love Bathala, they now use the same tale as a lesson about the importance of loving God. For Paterno, it is not so much that God has replaced Bathala, but that the two literally are simply different versions of the same deity.[17] In this sense, Paterno manages to frame the tale as a thread that connects twentieth-century Philippine "girls" with their indigenous spiritual heritage. Yet the tale also strongly echoes Catholic morality tales about the dangers of sexuality and the rewards of chastity that were predominant during both Rizal's and Paterno's lifetimes.

In "La dalaga virtuosa," a beautiful maiden (called simply "la dalaga") is bathing in a pool one day when suddenly a gorgeous young man appears by her side. Startled, the maiden tries to cover herself, but the young "baguntau" instantly declares his love to her.[18] She demands that he prove his professed love by constructing a stone bridge for her so that she can cross the pool to go home after bathing. She goes to rest on the shore, congratulating herself for having thought of such an impossible task, but after only fifteen minutes she is terrified to see that the young man has already constructed the first arch of the bridge. Correctly interpreting this supernatural feat as proof that the beautiful young man is the devil, the maiden runs as fast as she can to take shelter in the temple of the priestesses of Bathala, where no men are allowed.

Intending to outsmart the temple priestesses and follow the beautiful "*dalaga*" into the temple, the devil discards his incarnation as a handsome young man and transforms himself into a woman. In contrast to the narrator's description of the chasteness of the "*dalaga*," who is as virginal as forest jasmine ("virgen cual sampaga de la selva") ("Dalaga" 11), the description of the she-devil is dramatically eroticized. Not only is the beauty of her shapely legs enhanced with rice powder, but she also knows how to "mover y manejar el escote de la camisa" (maneuver the neckline of her blouse) in such a way as to show off "la curva suave de los senos firmes y eréctiles" (the soft curve of her firm erect breasts) ("La dalaga" 26). When the she-devil tries to convince the priestesses that she is merely a woman seeking shelter, the priestesses recognize the erotic she-devil as Lucifer himself. They barricade the door of the temple and keep the devil out of their refuge. The devil flies into a fury and uses his magic to make the temple sink into the ocean, killing all of the priestesses. But the virtuous "*dalaga*" is saved, because Bathala hears her devout prayers and transports her safely home on a cloud. Survival is her reward for renouncing sexual desire, and all good "*dalagas*" should follow her example.

The incarnation of the Tagalog devil as an erotic woman seems to disrupt the colonial logic according to which "*colonized* females were understood in relation to Satan, sometimes as mounted by Satan" (Lugones 745; my emphasis). Female sexuality is diabolical in this narrative, even though it is situated in what Lugones calls the "non-modern" era (743). At the same time, the androgynous shape-shifting of the demon, which allows him to take the form first of a strapping young buffalo/man and then of an eroticized woman, reinforces the notion that the indigenous—even indigenous supernatural figures—were "bestial and thus non-gendered, promiscuous, grotesquely sexual, and sinful" (Lugones 743). In this sense, it is significant that, in the tale Paterno tells, all of the priestesses in this nonmodern world are killed, while the virtuous "*dalaga*" is transported safely to her home. Paterno thus neatly reëstablishes the domestic as the proper realm for the good Filipina, just as Rizal does in his letter to the Malolos women.

By explicitly dedicating his collection to the female students of several Manila schools, Paterno positions himself as a benevolent "paternal" source of moral guidance. Like Rizal, he appeals to the women's indigenous identity, and to the centrality of sexual virtue to that identity. Again, like Rizal, he does this by conjuring up an idealized indigenous past, which he posits as key to the essential identity of the modern Filipina. Yet Paterno's tale also presents a marked contrast with the address to the Malolos "*dalagas*" written by the Philippine martyr José Rizal. When Rizal addresses the Malolos "*dalagas*," he informs them of the terrible things that Spaniards say about their sexual looseness, and suggests that it is up to the Malolos women to change the dishonorable reputation of all Filipinas and return to their unsullied original—that is, indigenous—state. Paterno, on the other hand, uses his textbook to repeat the same moralistic lessons found in Catholic schools of his time about the dangers of feminine sexuality, under the guise of a traditional Tagalog legend that makes female sexuality literally diabolical. In narrating his indigenous legend, Paterno affirms that the Filipinas' sexual purity is not just a result of the success of their Catholic indoctrination. On the contrary, he suggests that their indigenous identity is at the root of their *essential* spiritual goodness and sexual purity.

By presenting his morality tale as a Tagalog legend that has survived the centuries of Spanish colonial domination, he suggests an unbroken tradition of Tagalog virtue, maintained through a female oral tradition that excludes men. Just as the priestesses of Bathala bar the doors of their temple to the sexual threats of the devil, Paterno suggests that, through the centuries, Tagalog women have managed to waylay the threat of male sexual invasion, thanks to a matrilineal narrative tradition. Implicitly, they have also managed to sustain an indigenous identity that posits female chastity as an essential Tagalog virtue. Thus, while Paterno echoes Rizal's suggestion that Filipina women were sexually chaste in the idyllic preconquest days, the former departs sharply from the latter's insinuation that Filipinas have lost that sexual purity. Paterno's discourse also differs from that of Rizal in that he makes no attempt to refer to the young women's future role as mothers of Philippine citizens. Instead, he emphasizes the sexual chastity of the Filipinas by infantilizing them, addressing himself, like Rizal, to the "*dalagas*," the "señoritas" or "girls" of the nation's capital. This trilingual shift, or code-switching, from "*dalagas*" to "señoritas" to "girls" reflects the shifting sands of the imperial presence in the Philippines in 1910.

It is in the nexus of language and ideology that the two texts show the most complicated contrast, and, through that contrast, the marked shifts in Philippine colonization that took place between 1888 and 1910. As we have established, when Rizal wrote his letter to the Maloleñas in Tagalog, he was not only appealing to their common heritage; he was also positioning the Maloleñas, and their Filipina identity, as indigenous. He was also implicitly claiming Tagalog as an appropriate language for formal written communication in Malolos, perhaps presciently signaling mid-twentieth-century Philippine language policy, which would establish Tagalog as an official national language. Yet Rizal's choice also worked to undercut the demand of the Maloleñas for a *Spanish*-language school to be made available to them. When he addressed the Maloleñas in Tagalog, Rizal was writing to them in a language he generally used only to communicate with close family members or with a few close friends. Since the open letter was in fact a carefully constructed essay, meant for public consumption, Rizal's choice to write in Tagalog transformed his essay into a hybrid discourse, at once a public manifesto and a more intimate epistle to his metaphorical little sisters.

Paterno, on the other hand, chooses to address his young female interlocutors precisely through the language that the Maloleñas had claimed as their linguistic right, and that of all Filipinos. Had he been writing, like Rizal, in 1889, the publication of a didactic text in Spanish would have been unremarkable. Yet by 1910, the United States government had already implemented its aggressive campaign to establish English-language schools all over the archipelago, shipping teachers from the United States to the Philippines and providing intensive English-language instruction to train local Philippine teachers. In multilingual societies, language choice itself always conveys meaning, whether it signals ideology, politics, or simply membership in a sociolinguistic community. In the first decade of the twentieth century, when the United States was actively establishing its hegemony, whether one spoke or wrote in English, in Spanish, or in one of the many vernacular languages of the Philippines carried particular weight.

By the time Paterno published his *Aurora social* in 1910, Spanish was neither the language of anticolonial protest favored by the *Ilustrados* nor the language that provided access to political power. The use of Spanish for the former function had been supplanted by Tagalog; and English was the new language of colonial and political power. Spanish was indeed the language Paterno knew best (Mojares 98), and in a mundane sense, it was his most obvious—perhaps only—real choice for any publication.[19] What is significant, then, is not that Paterno opted to write in Spanish, but that a didactic text addressed to young women and recreating a pre-Spanish paradise would be published in 1910, when Spanish was already the language of a dead empire.

Paterno's "La dalaga virtuosa" and the entire collection *Aurora social* are, in this sense, doubly nostalgic, in that they are situated both linguistically and thematically in the Philippines' past. The young women Paterno addresses are "hijas del Pueblo" and "señoritas," and they are now also "girls," given the aggressive language policies established by the new imperial power. But, Paterno implies, the women of the Philippines will always be primarily "*dalagas*," descendants of the idealized golden age of Malay civilization. Moreover, at least rhetorically, Paterno imagines the future of the Philippines embodied in the *female* members of the younger generation, in contrast to Rizal, whose vision of women's role in nation building was limited to that of helpmeet.

Both the Philippine national hero and the national antihero, one writing in the waning days of the Spanish empire and the other in the first years of a new empire, use didactic addresses to their countrywomen to construct a foundational fiction of indigenous female purity. For Rizal, the Spanish rule and subsequent *frailocracia* represented the destruction of an indigenous paradise, and the Malolos "*dalagas*" the promise of its recovery—provided they understood their proper role as chaste mothers and helpmeets. For Paterno, that paradise still existed, at least in his own exoticized fantasy of primeval woman; and its embodiment in the "girls" of the Manila Spanish-language private schools represented an enduring inspiration for the male founding leaders Rizal called "the brains of the nation" (Mojares n.p).[20] The Maloleñas Rizal addressed fought for free and public access to the language of the friars and the Crown; the "girls" of the Manila Spanish-language schools Paterno addressed maintained his dual dream of indigenous purity and of a lost linguistic empire. In their addresses to the "*dalagas*," both Rizal and Paterno invoked the notion of young indigenous women's sexual purity to rhetorically create an anticolonial national unity.

In their appeal to a notion of indigeneity tied to traditional Christian notions of sexual purity, both of these *Ilustrados* write against the backdrop of the long Philippine tradition of the *pasyon*, the vernacular-language performances of the Passion during Holy Week. As Reynaldo Ileto explains, while the *pasyon* was intended to inculcate passivity and obedience to Church rule in the colonized peoples of the Philippines, in fact this folk retelling of the Passion played a key role in fomenting revolution: "The second function, which probably was not intended by the missionaries, was to provide lowland Philippine society with a language for articulating its own values, ideals, and even hopes of liberation" (12). For Ileto, the consideration of folk practices such as the *pasyon* provides a methodology for writing a "history from below" (10). Rizal's and Paterno's use of Tagalog and their appeal to an idealized indigenous past that reflects contemporary Catholic models of womanhood take on new light when read in the context of the *pasyon*. Both authors employ a religious frame that melds contemporary Catholic precepts with an idealized version of indigenous spirituality, just as the *pasyon* does.

In both Rizal's and Ileto's texts, rather than encouraging the "*dalagas*" to articulate their own "values, ideals, and . . . hopes of liberation," Christianized indigeneity is invoked to encourage Filipinas to model precisely the sort of abnegation that would minimize women's contributions to the making of a new Philippine nation. However, when we consider the gendered dynamics of the *pasyon* itself, it becomes apparent that there is ultimately no essential contradiction between the *Ilustrados*' recolonization of gender and the backdrop of the *pasyon*. As Patajo-Legasto points out, in spite of the subversive uses of the *pasyon* to inspire male revolutionary heroism, it also reinforced the simplistic dichotomy between Eve and Mary, and in this way excluded women from the local revolutionary discourse (74).[21] Furthermore, given the privileged background of both of the authors and their intended audiences, their essays' resonance with the *pasyon* functions to falsely situate the "*dalagas*" they address as abject colonial subjects and to elide the degree of economic and intellectual agency from which they did benefit.

Ironically, both Rizal and Paterno looked to an idealized past to create a future for the nation. What both of them overlooked was that the young women of their respective times would not be content with the role of mere rhetorical figures. Each of the dozens of "girls" whom Paterno mentions in his dedication to *Aurora social* would face a future enriched by the tenacity and persistence of the flesh-and-blood women of Malolos. In 1905, several of the women of Malolos went on to found the Asociación Feminista de Filipinas, and to begin the struggle for women's suffrage. Three of Rizal's sisters were founding members of the Manila chapter. It may or may not be a coincidence that one of the founders of the Manila branch of the Asociación was a grown woman named Susana Paterno.[22]

Notes

1. Studies by Renato Constantino and by Nicholas Cushner are now classic; more recently, Paul Kramer, Reynaldo Ileto, Josep Fradera, and Vicente Rafael have all documented this intersection.

2. Act 74 established the Bureau of Education in the U.S.-occupied Philippines, and mandated that English be the language of instruction in public schools. See Gonzalez for a compact history of language policy in the Philippines.

3. As early as 1634, the Spanish government began issuing mandates, which reappeared periodically over the next two and half centuries, that education in Spanish be provided to the inhabitants of the Philippines. As late as February 1889, the liberal overseas minister, Manuel Becerra, issued a communication to Valeriano Weyler, the Governor General of the Philippines, reiterating the importance of implementing the 1863 decree that ordered that primary education be provided in all villages, including instruction on the Spanish language, and that it be free to those who were not able to pay. The 1863 decree also provided for the establishment of normal schools to train teachers, in Spanish. Sanctions were to be imposed upon villages that did not comply with the order.

4. See Vicente Rafael's extended analysis of this dynamic in *Contracting Colonialism*.

5. Resil Mojares, John Schumacher, and Megan Thomas, among others, have provided comprehensive studies of the thought, activism, and biographies of these two men.

6. Tiongson recounts one case of a lawsuit won by Loreto Lucero, a female Malolos schoolteacher, against the local friar curate, Santiago Pérez, in the 1890s.

Loreto alleged that the friar had dropped by her parents' house at a time when the parents were away, and that Pérez "used words that the lady found salacious (*malaswa*). There and then, Loreto pummeled the friar with blows and drove him out of her house. Not content with this, Loreto filed a complaint against the friar in court" (189).

7. At the time of the petition, the Malolos area was home to a cluster of anticolonialist leaders, including Marcelo H. Del Pilar, Graciano Reyes, and Teodoro Sandico. Sandico had opened a privately funded school in Malolos, a stopgap measure until free public primary education was instituted in the archipelago. In fact, allegedly it was Sandico himself who drafted the petition that the Malolos women delivered to the Governor General (Gatmayan 9–11; cited in Tiongson 171).

8. Del Pilar writes, "La actitud de las muchachas de Malolos revela que es allí constante la campaña de los nuestros. Esas muchachas son de la clase escogida del pueblo, respetadas por la honrosa reputación e hijas de *maginoos*. Si pudiese V. dirigirles una carta en tagalo, sería un auxilio más para nuestros campeones de allí y de Manila" (The attitude of the Malolos girls shows that our campaign there is not letting up. Those girls are members of the chosen class of that town, and are respected for their honorable reputation and as daughters of indigenous nobles. If you could possibly write them a letter in Tagalog, it would be one more way to support our champions there and in Manila) (Kalaw 120; my translation).

9. The Spanish translation is included in a special section of the *Revista Filipina*, composed by Epifanio de los Santos, under the title "Más sobre Rizal" (More about Rizal). De los Santos also includes, in footnotes, the entire texts of López Jaena's "Amor a España" (Love of Spain) first published in *La Solidaridad*; and an early study of Philippine language policy: "El castellano y los idiomas Filipinos" (Castilian and the Philippine Languages) by the Austrian ethnologist and reformist ally Ferdinand Blumentritt.

10. The 1962 English-language translation is the most accessible and the most widely cited. However, the first translation to English appeared in 1917, in *The Philippine Review/Revista Filipin*a, the same periodical that published the first translation from Tagalog to Spanish. The 1917 translation, credited to Epifanio de los Santos, who also did the Tagalog-Spanish translation, contains a footnote stating that the English translation is based on the Tagalog original. In this essay, I will refer to this earlier, and more reliable, translation.

11. Lugones's notion of reading "the hierarchical dichotomy" into Yoruba society is relevant here (749).

12. San Juan uses the Tagalog spelling of Sandico's name.

13. De los Santos provides a list of the extant works by Rizal written in Tagalog. Including the letter to the Malolos women, there are only four original works, and a half-dozen translations (27).

14. I am grateful to Joshua Goode for pointing out this contrast (Goode, personal communication, March 18, 2017).

15. Wickberg offers a comprehensive overview of the economic, legal, and cultural status of the Chinese mestizos in the Philippines during the Spanish colonial period, explaining their role as centers of cultural and economic power.

16. All translations of passages from "La dalaga virtuosa" are my own.

17. See Thomas for a thorough discussion of Paterno's theories of Bathalism as, literally, an early form of Catholicism (74–76).

18. The Tagalog term *baguntau* that Paterno uses to describe the young man is ambiguous: it could refer literally to a young water buffalo, or to an unmarried young man.

19. Note, however, that at least one of Paterno's works was translated to Tagalog. Lifshey discusses the debut of Paterno's radically anti-American opera, *La alianza soñada*, which Paterno wrote in Spanish. The work was translated to and performed in Tagalog, and translated to English in the same year under the title *The Dreamed Alliance: Philippine Opera in One Act Divided into Five Scenes*. William Howard Taft was present in the audience at the debut performance (16–43).

20. Mojares takes the title of his landmark study from a quotation he attributes to José Rizal (October 31, 1889): "If today the enlightened class constitutes the brains of the nation, within a few years it will constitute its entire nervous system and manifest its existence in all its acts." The quotation forms the frontispiece of Mojares's book.

21. Augusto Espíritu also draws on Patajo-Legasto's feminist reading of the *pasyon* in his analysis of the reception of two Philippine American intellectual figures of the twentieth century, Carlos Bolusan and Carlos P. Romulo. Like Rizal, Bolusan was admired for his liberatory stance, while Romulo, like Paterno, was reviled for his conservatism. Espíritu aims to question this "binary characterization" of the two figures (379).

22. See Tiongson for biographies of the twenty Women of Malolos, and for a list of all the founding members of the Asociación Feminista de Filipinas (248–406).

Works Cited

Blumentritt, Ferdinand. "El castellano y los idiomas filipinos." *La Solidaridad*, 15 julio 1890. Rpt. in De los Santos, pp. 31–33.

Coates, Austin. *Rizal: Philippine Nationalist and Martyr*. Oxford UP, 1968.

Constantino, Renato. *The Philippines: A Past Revisited*. 16th ed. Quezon City: Foundation for Nationalist Studies, 1998.

Cushner, Nicholas P., S. J. *Spain in the Philippines: From Conquest to Revolution*. Ateneo de Manila University, 1971.

De los Santos, Epifanio. "Más sobre Rizal." *Revista Filipina*, December 1916, pp. 24–35. *Hathi Trust*; hdl.handle.net/2027/mdp.39015011375527.

Espíritu, Augusto. "Beyond Eve and Mary: Filipino American Intellectual Heroes and the Transnational Performance of Gender and Reciprocity." *Diaspora*, vol. 12, no. 3, 2003, pp. 361–86.

Fradera, Josep. *Filipinas, la colonia más peculiar: La hacienda pública en la definición de la política colonial, 1672–1868*. Consejo Superior de Investigaciones Científicas, 1999.

Gatmaytan, Vicente. Letter to Marcelo H. Del Pilar. *Epistolario de Marcelo H. Del Pilar, Vol. 1*, Manila: Imprenta del Gobierno, 1955, pp. 9–11.

Gonzalez, Andrew. "The Language Planning Situation in the Philippines." *Journal of Multilingual and Multicultural Development*, vol. 19, no. 5, 1998, pp. 487–525. *Routledge* dx.doi.org/10.1080/01434639808666365/.

Guerrero, León María. *The First Filipino: A Biography of José Rizal*. Manila: Guerrero Publishing, 2010.

Hardacker, Erin. "The Impact of Spain's 1863 Educational Decree on the Spread of Philippine Public Schools and Language Acquisition." *European Education*, vol. 44, no. 4, 2012–13, pp. 8–30.

Ileto Clemeña, Reynaldo. *Pasyon and Revolution: Popular Movements in the Philippines, 1840–1910*. Ateneo de Manila UP, 1979.

Kalaw, Teodoro M., ed. *Epistolario Rizaliano, Tomo Segundo (1887–1890)*, Documentos de la Biblioteca Nacional de Filipinas, Manila, Bureau of Printing, 1931.

Kramer, Paul A. *The Blood of Government: Race, Empire, the United States, and the Philippines*. U of North Carolina P, 2006.

Lifshey, Adam. *Subversions of the American Century: Filipino Literature in Spanish and the Transpacific Transformation of the United States*. U of Michigan P, 2016.

López Jaena, Graciano. "Amor a España." *La Solidaridad, Vol. 1 (1889)*, translated by Guadalupe Forés-Ganzón, U of the Philippines P, 1967, pp. 12, 14, 16, 18.

———. "Love of Spain." *La Solidaridad. Vol. 1 (1889)*, translated by Guadalupe Forés-Ganzón, U of the Philippines P, 1967, pp. 13, 15, 17, 19.

Lugones, María. "Toward a Decolonial Feminism." *Hypatia*, vol. 25, no. 4, 2010, pp. 742–59.

Mas, Sinibaldo de. *Informe secreto*. Manila: Historical Conservation Society, 1963.

Mojares, Resil. *Brains of the Nation: Pedro Paterno, T. H. Pardo de Tavera, Isabelo de los Reyes and the Production of Modern Knowledge*. Ateneo de Manila UP, 2006.

Pardo de Tavera, T. H. "History." *Census of the Philippines, 1903, vol. 1*, U.S. Bureau of the Census, 1905, pp. 309–418.

Patajo-Legasto, Priscelina. "*The Pasyon Pilapil*: An-'other' Reading." *Women Reading: Feminist Perspectives on Philippine Literary Texts*, edited by Thelma B. Kintanar, Quezon City, U of Philippines P, 1992, pp. 71–89.

Paterno, Pedro Alejandro. *La alianza soñada*. Manila: Estab. Tipográfico de M. Paterno y Compañía, 1902.

———. *La antigua civilización tagalog (Apuntes)*. Manila: Manuel G. Hernández, 1887.

———. "La dalaga virtuosa y el puente del diablo: Leyenda filipina." *Aurora social*, Manila, La República, 1910, pp. 5–34.

———. *The Dreamed Alliance: Philippine Opera in One Act Divided into Five Scenes*. Translated by W. H. Loving, Manila, Imprenta de la Revista Mercantil de J. de Loyzaga y Ageo S. Jacinto, 1902.

Rafael, Vicente. *Contracting Colonialism: Translation and Christian Conversion in Tagalog Society under Early Spanish Rule*. Duke UP, 1993.

———. *Motherless Tongues: The Insurgency of Language amid Wars of Translation*. Duke UP, 2016.

Reyes, Portia L. "A 'Treasonous' History of Filipino Historiography: The Life and Times of Pedro Paterno, 1858–1911." *South East Asia Research*, vol. 14, no. 1, 2006, pp. 87–121.

Reyes, Raquel A. G. *Love, Passion, and Patriotism: Sexuality and the Philippine Propaganda Movement, 1882–1892*. U Washington P, 2008.

Rizal, José. "A las compatricias doncellas de Malolos." Translated by Epifanio de los Santos, *Revista Filipina*, diciembre 1916, pp. 27–31. *Hathi Trust*; hdl.handle.net/2027/mdp.39015011375527.

———. *Message to the Young Women of Malolos*. Translated by Encarnación Alzona, Manila: R. P. García 1961.

———. *Sa mga Kabakayang Dalaga sa Malolos*. Manila, *El Renacimiento*, 1902.

———. "To My Countrywomen, the Girls of Malolos." Translated by Epifanio de los Santos, *The Philippine Review*, January 1917, pp. 25–29.

———, ed. *Sucesos de las Islas Filipinas, por el Dr. Antonio de Morga. Obra publicada en Méjico el año de 1609, nuevamente sacada a luz y anotada por José Rizal y precedida de un prólogo del Prof. Fernando Blumentritt*. Paris, Garnier, 1890.

San Juan, E. Jr. *Beyond Postcolonial Theory*. St. Martin's P, 1999.

———. *Sisa's Vengeance: Rizal/Woman/Revolution*. Philippines Cultural Studies Center, 2010.

Schumacher, John N., S.J. *The Propaganda Movement 1800–1895*. Ateneo de Manila UP, 1997.

Thomas, Megan C. *Orientalists, Propagandists, and Ilustrados: Filipino Scholarship and the End of Spanish Colonialism*. U of Minnesota P, 2012.

Tiongson, Nicanor G. *The Women of Malolos*. Ateneo de Manila UP, 2004.

Whinnom, Keith. "Spanish in the Philippines." *Journal of Oriental Studies*, vol. 1, no. 1, 1954, pp. 129–94.

Wickberg, E. "The Chinese Mestizo in Philippine History." *Journal of Southeast Asian History*, vol. 3, no. 1, 1964, pp. 62–100; jstor.org/stable/20067476?origin=JSTOR-pdf&seq=1#page_scan_tab_contents.

9

The Spanish Carceral Archipelago

Concepción Arenal against Penitentiary Colonization

AURÉLIE VIALETTE

Introduction: Penal Colonies and Colonization

What place do criminals have in the society whose contract they have broken? One solution offered by eighteenth- and nineteenth-century European governments, such as England and France, was to send felons to remote islands with two purposes: first, to serve their sentences in penitentiary colonies, and second, once released, to populate the islands, to which they sent both male and female convicts. The practice yielded some results for both countries—between 1788 and 1868 in Australia (Botany Bay) and starting in the 1850s in French Guiana—and was, therefore, a central debate of prison reform in nineteenth-century Europe. Yet, during the 1877 Penitentiary International Congress in Stockholm, penal colonies were criticized by all participants except France.[1] Spain participated in these debates both nationally and internationally. The sociopolitical problems involved in the question of future penal colonies in the Philippines, the Marianas, and Fernando Poo were extensively discussed in the press and in intellectual and literary circles. The debates on sending criminals overseas emerged from the difficulties of dealing with them economically and politically, and of handling their physical presence in social life. The exchange of viewpoints shaped ideas about what it means to imprison offenders and to use their labor on remote islands.

Spain had prisons in its colonies (such as Cuba) that served the same purpose as those in the metropole; the country did not make use of wholesale penitentiary colonization. In the peninsula, social reformers and the government alike asked if this might be a good model to implement on archipelagoes such as Bioko (formerly Fernando Poo, in Equatorial Guinea), the Marianas, and the Philippines. This idea arose right at the time when the Spanish empire was in free fall, with the old colonies now gaining their independence. The maintenance of the Spanish empire was thus envisioned through the establishment of penal colonies: these lands would help grow a population of settlers in the islands that were of little interest to Spaniards themselves (Llorente Pinto 93).

The ensuing discussions, I argue, could be conceptualized as a biopolitical attempt to rationally organize the Iberian territories and their citizens—biopower being understood by Michel Foucault as the impact that the political power has on the biological lives of the individuals (*La naissance de la biopolitique* 323). The convicts in penal colonies were perceived and treated as a social group on which the state could assert its capacity to manage the lives of the criminal population as a whole. I propose to consider the project of penal colonies as a colonial biopolitical laboratory, where the islands are the channel through which a politics of incarceration and penal reform at the service of the empire were devised. The colonial biopolitical laboratory served to assert the capacity and power of a sovereign power to organize bodies, to model an ideal subject who will become a neocolonial figure to revive a crumbling empire. Its implicit social power was that it could be extrapolated to the rest of the criminal population, even those imprisoned in the metropole and not facing removal to archipelagos elsewhere.

I argue that the recourse to penal colonies as the ultimate option to save the empire implied establishing a space of exception in some Spanish islands, to which the state's perceived enemies, such as criminals, vagrants, prostitutes, and political prisoners, would be sent away and physically eliminated from the peninsula. Ironically, the existence of penal colonies also implied that even if these citizens were seen as incorrigible in terms of European political systems, they were nevertheless granted the status of becoming settlers on the islands after serving their sentences. My argument is that this plan implied a paradox: by sending the convicts to remote islands, it created the illusion of their rehabilitation and conversion into citizens; but, in fact, they were to become citizens in the colony only: they would never have the possibility to return to the peninsula. I contend that this conversion of the criminals is a mechanism of creation of colonial subjects as neocolonizers of islands that would remain in a legal regime different and isolated from the peninsula.

"The Spanish Carceral Archipelago" delves into the ethical, political, and social issues involved in this project of incarceration. In fact, these new politics meant using the island as a space of exception and conceiving the Spanish empire as a form of carceral archipelago, a term Foucault used to explain the way several elements and institutions in modern societies form a global network in which men and women live under a form of surveillance (*Discipline* 293–308). The technologies of discipline and regulation, the mechanisms of discipline attached to the carceral archipelago, would produce a population that would correspond to utilitarian principles and government rationality. Now Foucault's metaphor of the carceral archipelago becomes a literal geographical issue in this process of neocolonialism that intends to salvage the remnants of the Spanish Empire—and I want to underscore this geopolitical issue in the present project.

The idea of the island as a prison, as a camp, was already in place in the nineteenth century and foreshadowed contemporary politics that have created spaces of exception. Those spaces are, for Giorgio Agamben, zones of suspension of the law. The space of exception, a "no-man's-land between public law and political fact, and between juridical order and life" (1), is the space in which the state can both dispose of the bodies of its citizens, and have absolute power. But what are the biopolitical effects of the space of exception in the Spanish project of establishing penal colonies in the Philippines and the African coast? I assert that the handling of criminality helped reinforce the colonial endeavor and that the removal of criminals, who were considered socially unfit and unproductive for the industrialized nation-state, not only morally justified the colonial enterprise but also gave it an important economic and political structure. The eighth *Ley de Bases* of 1869 (a kind of legislation that falls on the responsibility of the government) stated that the ones to be sent away would be those convicts considered irredeemable. Those irredeemable in the metropole, were contradictorily cast as redeemable in the space of exception. What kind of colonization project intends to populate a territory with individuals considered beyond redemption and, if they are beyond redemption, how could they maintain the status of Spanish subjects and settlers? What is the role of redemption in the political discourse of colonization?

To start answering these questions and to explain the relevance of looking at this precise moment in history to think about broader political issues regarding citizenship, political economy and the bodies of prisoners,

I propose concentrating on Galician lawyer and anthropologist Concepción Arenal's public interventions in a field completely dominated by male intellectuals and professionals.[2] The other intellectuals who participated in the debates pertaining to the establishment of penal colonies included renowned lawyers and jurists such as Pere Armengol i Cornet, Francisco Lastres, or Fernando Cadalso.[3] Arenal's interdisciplinary research goes beyond these other individuals, as it involves looking at the ethical stakes of punishment from historical, social, economic, and legal perspectives. In addition, Arenal provided crucial insight into how a woman could participate in the legal debates connecting prison reform and neocolonial movements to keep the Spanish empire alive.

Indeed, penal colonies and colonization were interrelated in many ways. First, the Spanish government's desperate need to maintain a declining empire was fueled by the successes in Britain and France: they sent prisoners to serve their sentences in penal colonies and to stay afterward as inhabitants/settlers who consolidated the colonial structure. Second, the vision set out in Spanish legislation—in particular the "Ley de Bases" (October 21, 1869) and the Penal Code (1870)—allowed for the creation of agricultural and industrial penitentiary colonies. There, the convicts' labor would be used to build the material and social infrastructures of the colony. It is possible, then, to conclude that some Spanish legislation in the second half of the nineteenth century was intended to legalize the use of prisoners to renew colonial success.

The Promising Islands: State of Exception and Biopolitical Impact

The social tensions derived from the development of capitalism in nineteenth-century Spain have to be taken into account to understand the type of punitive society that was put in place. Who was the social enemy? And how was he or she perceived and fabricated (Foucault, *The Punitive* 198)? Reformers and the government alike were constantly searching for a definition of the criminal, of the "dangerous citizen." According to Foucault in "About the Concept of the 'Dangerous Individual' in 19th-Century Legal Psychiatry," the penal apparatus at that time started to implement its machinery with elements that would constitute material to be used by the law. These elements, the "confession, self-examination, explanation of oneself, revelation of what one is" ("About the Concept" 2), would contribute to understanding who the criminals were and help to construct their psychological portraits. This has been called the "psychiatrization of criminal danger" ("About the Concept" 3). Criminal anthropology became central to the debate around these questions. Indeed, anthropologists, such as Cesare Lombroso in *Criminal Man*, established the parameters by which an individual's social danger could be measured and eventually used in the definition of the criminal (Horn 126).[4]

In addition, the development of a police network implied a growing surveillance of urban space that both fabricated an image of the supposed enemy and led to the repression of social conflicts. The social enemy dutifully constructed by politicians, criminal anthropologists, psychiatric doctors, and other positivistic scientists was as much the criminal and the vagrant as the revolutionary, in a movement that conflated the criminal and the political offense. The close examination and control of urban space by the state apparatuses—including the police—is at the origin of a biopolitical project that was directed at people classified as unclean, whose actions "soiled" the urban space.

Workers were held liable for their lifestyles, and for the important urban socioeconomic changes that occurred with industrialization. Scientists published studies on what they called "mala vida," which was, in their view, the new forms of urban delinquency linked to the socioeconomic transformation caused by liberalism.[5] In fact, these studies reflected the elites' anxieties regarding the shifts occasioned by modernity. Campos explains that a moralizing discourse contributed to the idea of approaching social problems through a biological lens, which served to criminalize deviant behaviors. The disciplines of psychiatry, criminology, and hygiene all stigmatized the popular classes by presenting them as dangerous (2).[6] Felip Monlau for example, a Catalan doctor, an industrial hygienist and humanist, wrote in 1846 that society perceived the "clases desgraciadas" (27), especially the poor and vagrants, as being the "clases peligrosas" (25). Benito Pérez Galdós, in his novel *Misericordia*, elaborates on the politics of deportation of the beggars to the outskirts of Madrid and their relocation in rehabilitation centers.[7] The person him/herself, and his/her status in society, was a concern, as was civil society's responsibility toward him/her. All the questions asked pointed to the same matter: What were the means to these perceived dangerous individuals' rehabilitation, to their social and moral reform, and what could social institutions do to eradicate crime? Some solutions pointed to a control and rejection of their bodies.

Penal colonies were proposed as a means of fighting deviance but also more generally the dangerousness of industrialized society. They implied the development of a biopolitical project vying for the elimination of the so-called deviant citizens from the social body. Even by accepting the definition of criminality, Arenal submits to criticism the possibility of the island. In the islands, she pointed out, prisoners would never be reformed, would never receive the legal rights granted to citizens and would in a sense be treated as incarcerated colonial subjects. Furthermore, she excludes from the economy of morality the very agents of deportation: "porque desde que toda esta máquina jurídica da por resultado llevar a los hombres adonde se hagan peores, los que allí los conducen están fuera de la ley moral" (Because since all this legal machinery results in taking men where they become worse, those that lead them there are outside moral law) ("La pena"). She argued that no country had ever used penal colonies to reform criminals, but, on the contrary, had created them to eradicate their undesirable bodies: "La ley de transportación ha tenido principalmente por objeto alejar á los criminales" (The law of transportation has had as its principal objective to move criminals farther away) ("Las colonias" 96).[8]

Prisoners would effectively be expelled from the peninsula and stripped of their basic rights. The connections between prisoners and the colonized on the island become evident when reading Arenal's analysis of the juridical status prisoners would accrue in the colonial space: those rights would be different from the ones prisoners had in the metropole. This plan would transform the island into a space of exception for them. According to Agamben, the space of exception is a structure that includes living beings but "radically erases any legal status of the individual, thus producing a legally unnamable and unclassifiable being" (3)—hence its biopolitical relevance. The resulting situation from the establishment of penal colonies was that the state would not have to give any account of how the prisoners were treated. However, one of the narratives developed to support the project was that prisoners were sent to serve a higher purpose. Francisco Lastres championed this idea. For him, penitentiary colonization implied a mission of civilization. In *La colonización penitenciaria de las Marianas y Fernando Póo*, he identifies the geographic and strategic location of Fernando Poo off the African coast as excellent for commercial use, while describing its inhabitants as backward, superstitious, and lazy (35). It is a description that certainly echoes that of early modern colonizers. There is a clear intertextuality between the explorers' descriptions of what they encountered in the lands where they arrived and what Lastres wrote in 1878: he describes the island in all its splendor, fertility, packed with tobacco, coffee, wood and many other usable products—and commodities. His text is that of an explorer who wants to convince his audience of the value of the land he has encountered and of the need to "llevarles la vida de Europa" (To bring them European life) (59).

The life/*vida* he is talking about is that of the prisoners. A life that was rejected in Spain as irredeemable. Indeed, penal colonies would cleanse the social body of its most disturbing elements. But reformers needed a functioning rhetoric to sustain the project; according to the foundational myth of penal colonization, convicts would be sent to work, learn agricultural methods, enlighten the indigenous people of the islands, and return to the peninsula as newly reformed citizens. In the words of Lastres, "los nuevos delincuentes ganarían mucho con la colonización, sobre todo aquéllos que cumplida la pena volvieran al seno de la patria" (The new delinquents would gain a lot with the colonization process, especially those who would return to the homeland once their sentence is served) (68). In his view, then, the felons can indeed be redeemed and go back to Spain. Lastres devised a sort of pedagogical subject on the island, redeemed through the missionary impulse of the penal colony.

The idea of rebirth is a metaphor that explains the project of penal colony in the second half of the nineteenth century in Spain. It is an idea that some authors, such as Jacobo Villanova y Jordan, employed to talk about prison reform in general and about the benefits of the Panopticon in particular.[9] Villanova y Jordan translated Jeremy Bentham's work into Castilian and researched the state of the Madrilenian prisons. In his *Cárceles y presidios*, he addressed the advantages of the Panopticon for Spain and affirmed that it would change the lifestyles of the prisoners by reforming them: "despues de una tan rígida educacion, los presos acostumbrados al trabajo, é instruidos en la moral y en la religion, perderán sus hábitos viciosos por la imposibilidad de continuarlos, y volverán á nacer para la sociedad" (After such a rigid education, the prisoners, accustomed to work and educated in moral and religious matters, will lose their dissolute habits since they would be unable to continue to perform them, and they will be born again for society) (81). The metaphor that the author employs, "Volverán á nacer," is powerful because it implies a renewal of the social body and, as he concludes, that the nation would benefit from it by accepting a reformed citizen back into its public sphere (169).[10] In the project about penal colonies, the rebirth is coupled with the ideology attached to colonialism and, especially, to the conversion rhetoric of the colonial power. In this case, the subject that would benefit from a conversion is the convict. The conversion would be moral, social, and work-related in the eventual service of colonial power.

Arenal denounced this fallacious argument and postulated that prisoners would never be able to come back, explicitly undermining all arguments in favor of this system: the economic, the moral, and the colonial. Her line of argumentation is centered specifically on the humanitarian aspects of what it meant to send away felons to serve a purpose of colonization, highlighting the biopolitical impact that deportation would have on the bodies of the prisoners. First, she analyzes the British example of Botany Bay—one of the alleged models for Spain. She accuses the British government of having abandoned prisoners there and qualifies its attitude as criminal ("Las colonias" 38). For her, the penal colony is a synonym for the death sentence ("Las colonias" 98)—and indeed, in Roman law, the deportation of the criminal to the island constituted his social death.

In fact, one sees in her analysis how the Spanish island of Fernando Poo and the archipelago of the Philippines would escape the net of justice by being too far from the central judicial power of the peninsula, converting themselves into spaces of exception that would allow, in the words of Agamben, "the physical elimination not only of political adversaries but of entire categories of citizens who for some reason cannot be integrated into the political system" (2). Agamben's idea of "categories of citizen," whose integration into a normative society is seen as problematic, is in fact Arenal's main concern in all her writings. From *La cárcel llamada Modelo*, a text in which she underscores the humiliation that the prisoners suffer in the prisons, to *Estudios penitenciarios*, in which she philosophically reflects on the human being and the conditions that lead him or her to commit an offense, Arenal reasoned, well before Foucault, how deviance is fabricated and why the conditions put in place to fight crime reproduce the system: "el penado no brota de una manera espontánea sin tener antes del delito relaciones con la sociedad . . . el penado es un hombre más o menos culpable, más o menos ignorante, más o menos extraviado, pero un hombre, en fin" (The convict does not appear spontaneously without having established before his crime some relation with society . . . the convict is a man more or less guilty, more or less ignorant, more or less lost, but a man in the end) (*Etudios* 42). She presents a humane vision of the prisoners, insisting particularly on their dignity, and opposes the idea that their lives and their bodies do not matter, that they should be considered different from other citizens: "Hay en libertad hombres mucho más perversos que la mayoría de los que la ley condena. . . . Descendiendo en la escala de la criminalidad, a medida que ésta disminuye, aumenta la semejanza del penado con los hombres honrados, hasta no diferenciarse de ellos sino por circunstancias accidentales e insignificantes" (There are free men much more perverse that the majority of those that the law condemns . . . [I]f we descend the scale of criminality, as it gradually narrows, the similarity between convict and honorable man increases, until we cannot find any difference between them other than some accidental and insignificant circumstance) (*Etudios* 41).

What is to be underscored here is that, for Arenal, by no means did this project of deportation of criminals seem an adequate solution to fight against criminality. On the one hand, the work the state demanded of criminals to build the colonial infrastructure was a clear exploitation of their labor, what Arenal denounces as "tratar al penado como mero instrumento para realizar cálculos tenidos por ventajosos para la sociedad" (To treat the convict as a mere instrument to realize operations thought as profitable for society) ("Las colonias" 19). The objective of her argument is to defend a system of true and effective rehabilitation of the criminal, something missing in the project of penal colonies. She even goes so far as including torture in her discussion: "Es necesario procurar que el alma del penado sienta mucho, que sienta lo más posible, lo cual no se puede conseguir si se tortura su cuerpo" (It is necessary to try that the convict's soul feel a lot, that it feel as much as it can, which cannot be achieved if his body is tortured) ("Las colonias" 22). The tortured soul, as result of the tortured body, is what she concentrates on, reminding her readers of the interconnection between both in the process of rehabilitation of the prisoners and echoing *avant la lettre* Foucault's idea of the soul as the prison of the body (*Discipline* 29). It becomes clear then that she describes the island as a space in which all is allowed, from exploitation of labor to torture, which makes the establishment of penal colonies a project of creation of a space of exception in which power, forced labor, lawlessness, and bodily degradation are at the service of the Spanish empire.

Arenal against Penitentiary Colonization: The Defense of Human Rights

Arenal was concerned with many aspects of the treatment of the criminal in penal reform, and they all led to the goal of achieving justice and the equal treatment of the human subject. My argument in this respect is that Arenal's main concern was both to prove the uselessness of penal colonies and to demonstrate that they were an attack on human rights. For her, penal colonies could be considered a form of slavery. This is a fundamental point of Arenal's argumentation, which has to be interpreted as a frontal rejection of both slavery as an institution and the colony as a project. Knowing that slavery still existed in the Spanish colonies, Arenal nevertheless draws a parallel between early modern slavery and what she calls modern slavery, the latter of which is attached to industrial societies and, subsequently, in her argument, to penal colonies.[11] In this politics of penal colonies, the poor would become the new slaves because, she says, their lives matter less than the lives of the bourgeois or the rich, "como si rico fuera sinónimo de corregido y honrado" (as if being rich were a synonym of being reformed and honorable) ("Las colonias" 80).

Social changes during the Industrial Revolution made the lifestyle imbalance between the lower and upper classes more apparent in daily life. This imbalance became manifest in how social groups made use of public space. Vagabonds were called a threat to social order, and the term *vagrant* became a catchall for anyone who did not comply with the status quo—including the poor and the members of the working class. The Cadiz Constitution of 1812, in article 25.4, dictates that constitutional rights would be suspended "Por no tener empleo, oficio o modo de vivir conocido," (for not having employment, trade or known lifestyle), which was a way of defining the term *vago* without naming it. However, the *Reglamento* of the "Cuerpo General de Gendarmería" from March 19, 1812, the same day of the Cadiz Constitution, included the term *vago* and created a direct causal relationship between being a vagrant and disturbing social order: "celar sobre los vagos y ociosos, y perseguir sin excepción de ningún género a cuantos intentaren perturbar la tranquilidad pública y desobedecer al Gobierno" (To keep a watchful eye on vagrants and idlers, and to pursue without exception those who try to disrupt public peace and to disobey the Government) (in Martínez Dhier 60). The Penal Code of 1850 introduced the legal concept of "vagos" in article 258 and their punishment in articles 259, 260, and 261. Article 261 reads as follows:

> El vago a quien se aprehendiere disfrazado o en traje que no le fuera habitual, o pertrechado de ganzúas u otros instrumentos o armas que infundan conocida sospecha, será condenado a las penas de prisión correccional en su grado máximo, y tres años de sujeción a la vigilancia de la Autoridad. Iguales penas se impondrán al vago que intentare penetrar en casa, habitación o lugar cerrado, sin motivo que lo excuse.

(The vagrant who will be apprehended disguised or dressed in an unusual way, or equipped with picklocks or other instruments or arms that arouse certain suspicion, will be condemned to correctional imprisonment, sentenced to the highest degree, and to three years of surveillance by the authorities. The same sentences will be imposed on vagrants who will try to penetrate in a house, room or closed place without any justified reason.)

As we can see, from the 1812 *Reglamento* of the "Cuerpo General de Gendarmería," the term *vago* was connected with disobedience and disruption of public order. What was the state to do with "vagos," or the lazy poor, in the public space? Imitate what Britain had done: send them to penal colonies. However, in rebuttal, Arenal asserts that "pretender extinguirla [la miseria] alejando los pobres es como querer secar un pozo á donde afluye de contínuo agua corriente" (to pretend to put an end to it [misery] by moving the poor further away is like wanting to dry a well where water flows constantly) (48).

She presents the island as a dangerous space of exception. That is, on the island, the central element of the Spanish carceral archipelago, questions of citizenship and individual rights would be diminished and rejected. For instance, even if felons were condemned to a definite sentence, she shows that the deportation in many ways meant a sentence to life imprisonment (81) or even capital punishment (76). By pointing out this fact, she underlines how the structure of penal colonies would not implement anything reasonably in keeping with a common understanding of law. In her analysis, the island is not the place for the rebirth of the Spanish empire. On the contrary, it is where an infraction of national law would occur, should convicts be sent there with no assurance that they would be able to come back if they desired to do so after serving their sentence.

Among the many nineteenth-century theorists on the question—Lastres, Cadalso, for example—Arenal appears to be the only one to talk about justice and human rights. She most notably did so in her essay, "Las colonias penales de la Australia y la pena de deportación," which won the 1875 prize from the *Real Academia de Ciencias Morales y Políticas*. The theme of the contest was: "¿Convendría establecer en las islas del golfo de Guinea ó en las Marianas unas colonias penitenciarias como las inglesas de Botany-Bay?" (Would it be profitable to establish, on the islands of the Gulf of Guinea or in the Marianas, penal colonies such as those established by

England in Botany-Bay?). In her text, one of her main arguments is that penal colonies are equivalent to death: from the travel that criminals had to undergo, with the risk of suffering "grande mortandad durante la travesía" (great loss of life during the crossing) (38), that is, during which many of them would perish, to the difficult adaptation they would experience on the island.[12] In Botany Bay,

> en una poblacion de 1.000 personas hubo un dia en que pasaron de 200 los enfermos . . . despues de saltar a tierra; el número de enfermos llegó hasta 500. "La primera labor de la mañana, dice un testigo presencial, era abrir sepultura para los muertos de la noche" . . . No se comprende este inhumano descuido y ménos la desigualdad con que los deportados eran tratados durante la travesía.
>
> (Among a population of 1,000 persons, there was one day when more than 200 had fallen ill . . . after disembarking; the number of sick people rose to 500. "The first task in the morning," says an eyewitness, "was to bury the dead of the night before" . . . it is difficult to understand this inhumane neglect and even less the inequality with which the deported were treated while crossing.) ("Las colonias" 34–45)

The politics of penal colonization can be construed as a politics of colonialism, which implied a biopolitical project in which the bodies of the prisoners would be subjected to drastic consequences and to "abusos de la autoridad" (abuses of authority) (Arenal, "Las colonias" 46) that would let these prisoners perish only after exploiting them to death. For her, "island" was synonymous with remoteness and loss of life.

The project of establishing a penal colony in remote islands indicated that the Spanish government wanted to resolve tensions occurring in the social body in a drastic way. Jorge Núñez recently studied how for some reformers "la distancia geográfica, las largas condenas y la virtud 'regeneradora' del trabajo, ayudarán a su [el preso] conversión moral, transformándolo en un 'obrero laborioso'" (The geographical distance, the long sentences, and the "regenerating" virtue of work, will help his [the convict] moral conversion, transforming him into a "diligent worker") (154). Indeed, penal colonies were the last resort of a society that found it impossible to handle part of its population, and that refused to sort out the difficulties that arose with the industrial exploitation of a large sector of the population by a small minority. The solution was to send away those who would transgress established norms. In fact, the so-called *vagos* had already been sent to Ceuta (per the Royal Order of November 28, 1788) before being assigned to work for the Armada (Fernández Bermejo 54).

The fear of possible rioting by the lower classes is at the origin of many penal regulations and of the association between vagrancy, workers, and disturbances.[13] The "Ley de Procedimiento en las causas de vagancia" enacted during the reign of Queen Isabel II on May 9, 1845, had a political objective that led to the Ministerio de Gracia y Justicia's text on April 4, 1848, that defined the term *vago* as whoever tries to provoke a riot or rebellion. *Vagos* and workers had to be under surveillance because of how they were perceived to threaten the social order. This association reveals a politics that preemptively categorized the criminal as part of the social body, to be marginalized and sent away.[14] In fact, the interdependence between misery, vice, and crime, according to Ricardo Campos, was a historical constant. Starting in the nineteenth century, the socioeconomic transformations caused by industrialization and the instauration of liberalism made the relationship between the three more intense (Campos 2). For instance, another law, the *Ley de Orden Público* proclaimed on March 20, 1867, was directly devised to avoid commotion and rebellion in the public space.[15]

Within this panorama, the development of penal colonies in Spain's overseas islands was the promise of a new social order. Yet, Arenal's analysis of Botany Bay states a contrary opinion in a subsection titled "Islas infernales" (59). Island, for her, is not a synonym of promise but of lack of control and social unrest:

> Se ha llamado á la capital de las colonias penales inglesas en Australia la *Ciudad del crímen*, pero tal vez habria sido más exacto llamarla la ciudad del *vicio*. Cierto que se lamentaron crímenes y no pocos; que se vieron incendiados muchos edificios del Estado, robados los almacenes públicos y las propiedades privadas, y hubo tumultos, colisiones, y homicidios y asesinatos; pero el desbordamiento de los vicios fué aun mayor que el de los crímenes.
>
> (The capital of English penal colonies in Australia has been called the *City of crime*, but maybe it would have been more accurate to call it the city of *vice*. Surely, crimes were committed and not

a few; many State buildings were set on fire, public warehouses and private properties were robbed, and there were commotions, conflicts, and homicides and murders; but the outburst of vices was even greater that those of crime.) (63)

Arenal contends that deporting convicts to an island will not solve any existing or perceived violence. In fact, the data she brings into the discussion show that the isolation—or should we say *insulation*?—of the prisoners only worsens their violent tendencies. One by one, Arenal dismantles each of her opponents' arguments in favor of penal colonies—for instance, that felons become productive and are reformed after their stay on the island. In fact, she makes a solid argument that, even there, prisoners can still be "vagos":

> suspendíanse las construcciones y los trabajos agrícolas, porque los penados se negaban á trabajar y vagaban por los bosques [en Australia] . . . la dificultad de convertir en colonos á los emancipados y el gran número de ellos que burlando la ley ó aprovechándose de su imperfeccion vagaban en viciosa holganza debiendo su subsistencia á las estafas, á los robos de los almacenes del Estado.
>
> (Constructions and agricultural work were suspended, because convicts would refuse to work and they would wander in the forest [in Australia]. . . . the difficulty of converting the emancipated into colonizers and the great number of them who, evading the law or taking advantage of its imperfection, wandered in vicious idleness owing their subsistence to fraud, to robbery . . .) ("Las colonias" 37, 64–65)

Throughout her writings on the topic, she carefully uses the same language as her opponents and as the law ("vagaban," "convertir," "emancipados") to establish a direct dialogue and to take apart the arguments on the project. Using the same words and semantic fields with a different theoretical purpose amounts to reforming penal law from a discursive vantage point.

For Lastres, penal colonies could be used effectively only if Spain could develop a precise method of organized deportations. An island could not simply be chosen to function as a receptacle for any unwanted prisoner, but had to be a land from which the nation could benefit socially, economically, and politically, that is to say, a colony:

Mas á pesar de las prescripciones legislativas, no se ha organizado nunca de un modo serio la colonización penitenciaria, y sólo en momentos dados, y por medida gubernativa, se han enviado á Fernando Póo y á las Marianas á los conspiradores vencidos y algunas veces á los vagos y hombres de mala conducta; pero se ha procedido siempre sin método, sin preparación ninguna, y no es de extrañar por tanto, que los resultados hayan sido negativos.

(But despite the legislative prescriptions, penitentiary colonization was never organized in a serious way, and only in specific moments, and through governmental measure, defeated conspirators, and sometimes vagrants and men of ill conduct were sent to Fernando Póo and the Marianas; but it was always done without method, without any preparation, and it is no surprise that, as such, the results have been negative.) (Lastres 31)

Lastres's mentioning "vagos y hombres de mala conducta" that were sent to Fernando Poo and the Marianas is indeed revealing; "vago" was not only associated with the poor but was also applied to persons who violated societal norms in the public space.

Apart from the reformatory argument, champions of penal colonies underscored their economic advantages for a nation in which industrialization created conditions for a growing presence of the poor who were seen as unproductive for the economy in general. Arenal analyzes this aspect in her discussion of Botany Bay and concludes that the poor were sent there so that England would not have to deal with them in the Metropole: "Economista, M. Shaw, pretendió probar que si el Gobierno y la caridad combinados y haciendo un esfuerzo, enviaban á la colonia penal todos los pobres, podía extinguirse el pauperismo en Inglaterra con una economía de cerca de dos mil millones de reales. El cálculo era errado" (Economist M. Shaw hoped to prove that, with an effort, if Government and charity combined sent all the poor to the penal colony, poverty would die out in England and it would save more or less two billion *reales*. The calculation was erroneous) ("Las colonias" 48). Her analysis includes economic data to prove that the savings that a government ought to receive with the politics of incarceration in penal colonies was erroneous.

But more than any other argument, her texts on the topic stress the moral and ethical obligation to recognize that the human rights of any citizen, poor, rich, even criminal, should be respected. For Maria José

Lacalzada de Mateo, in a recent essay, Arenal's theoretical and practical defense of fundamental human rights such as the individual's right to life, to liberty, to happiness and their expansion to social, work, political, and religious life are connected to her defense of men's and women's dignity (176). In addition, the defense of equality and fraternity, and universalism in general, according to Lacalzada de Mateo, occurs in connection with her religious beliefs because, for her, the frontiers between sexes, races, nations, and even religions are artificial: "Esto significa además que los no creyentes o los que adoran a Dios 'de otro modo' no dejan por eso de ser también hermanos y de aquí deriva otro principio: el de tolerancia. Estas convicciones, hoy bien admitidas en la Iglesia Católica, colocaban sin embargo a Concepción Arenal en una posición controvertida en la España de su época" (In addition, this meant that those who do not believe in God or adore him "in a different way" do not stop being brothers, which implied another principle: tolerance. These convictions, today well accepted by the Catholic church, place Concepción Arenal in a controversial position in the Spain of her time) (176–77).

Arenal denounced not only the failure to consider criminals' dignity, but also the violence implied in the state's expulsion of their bodies from the national territory ("Colonias penales francesas"). The creation of overseas prisons, in Arenal's view, was a moral problem as much as a problem of justice. If the sentencing of the criminal was a reaction in defense of society and was not decided according to a system of just laws, then it constituted an abuse of power:

> Los que dan a la pena el carácter de *correccional,* evidente es que tienen que rechazarla cuando sea *desmoralizadora,* y que no pueden ver en ella una acción jurídica, sino un hecho de fuerza. No se da al Estado el terrible poder que sobre el penado tiene, sino a condición de que le corrija, de que le mejore, de que lo intente al menos. Si lejos de ponerle en condiciones de enmendarse, le coloca en situación de que se extravíe más y más; si emplea los medios de que dispone para sujetarle dentro de aquella atmósfera infecta, donde se respira vicio, crimen, y se envenena el alma.
>
> (Those who want the sentence to be *reformatory* must reject this solution when it is *demoralizing,* and because they cannot see in it a legal action but an act of force. You do not give the State the terrible power that it has over the convict except on one

condition: to reform him, to improve him, to try it at least. More than putting him in conditions to change, it puts him in a situation in which he loses his way more and more; if the State employs the means it has to subject him to this infected atmosphere, where you breath vice, crime, and your soul gets poisoned . . .) ("La pena depravadora")

The "hecho de fuerza" or "act of force" replaces the "juridical action," thus revealing the exceptional character of the island-colony where prisoners were not protected by a promise of correction, but rather by the removal of morality itself, or "de-moralization." The space of exception, Arenal reckons, foreshadowing Agamben, does not advance the bettering of the prisoners' lives, but rather—without right juridical action and moral compass—the permanence of the prisoners within an "infected atmosphere" where all they accrue is depravation. The Philippines and Fernando Poo were to become the perfect place for a settler colonial project.

Conclusion

Arenal's writings could not be more urgent, both during her times and today. The islands have historically and culturally either been attractive—from Plato's *Atlantis* and Thomas More's *Utopia*—or a space of rejection—for instance, the island as a land of exile—or a space of exception. Whether or not the island was a promising space in which to reform prisoners was a question that Spanish reformers and government debated in the nineteenth century. For many, penal colonies were a panacea, a way to cure the social body of its most dangerous elements. For Arenal, however, the penal colony was a machinery of injustice that was only rationalized by the Spanish empire's efforts of expansion. The contest she won on this topic (for the *Real Academia de Ciencias Morales y Políticas*) had an actual impact on the government; indeed, after she won, the law that anticipated the creation of penitentiary colonies in the Philippines and Fernando Poo was not implemented.

Arenal might appear to be a lone female voice in the field of penal reform in the nineteenth century. Women have been active participants in many debates on the most pressing issues of their times, despite having been excluded from official historical discourse. Penitentiary reform, however, is not without the participation of women intellectuals around the globe. In Spain, Arenal in the nineteenth century and, in the twentieth, the Radical

Socialist Republican Party member Victoria Kent, who became the director general of prisons under the Second Spanish Republic, are the most salient examples of the active contribution of women intellectuals to debates on penitentiary reform.[16] Isabel Ramos Vázquez mentions that women and men of the *Institución Libre de la Enseñanza* theorized about penal law, and that "hay que citar a otros hombres y mujeres que coadyuvaron también desde la práctica a la reforma penitenciaria desde diversas perspectivas o posiciones ideológicas" (We must also cite other men and women who also contributed in a practical way to penitentiary reform, from diverse perspectives and ideological positions) ("La reforma penitenciaria" 321). Yet she does not actually include the names of these women. Pere Armengol i Cornet's archive, preserved in the *Arxiu Nacional de Catalunya*, is representative of a nineteenth-century Spanish jurist's and researcher's archive. Dedicated to penal reform, this archive contains academic and legal documents, correspondence (for example, letters to the New York jurist E. G Wines), documents from Armegnol i Cornet's term as a magistrate in Barcelona's and Madrid's *Audiencias*, and other manuscripts (talks, theories on penal law, books, among others). Here, Arenal is, again, the only female name that appears as a peer.[17]

It is imperative to recognize that nineteenth-century women intellectuals had to overcome many barriers to participate in the debate on penitentiary reform. Undeniably, the prejudices against their gender and, more importantly, the complicated means for them to access knowledge and sources were two of the obstacles that they could encounter. Arenal is famous for having cross-dressed to study law at the Central University in Madrid. Her academic inclination is unquestionably what distinguishes her writings from those of other female writers of her time. In fact, Arenal did not cultivate any of the genres that women usually produced: she did not write poems, novels, or short stories. Rather, she chose to write formal studies and commentaries on the law, treatises on how to visit prisons and govern them, and newspaper articles on governmental decisions about the prison system.

Arenal wrote on an infinite number of issues pertaining to the prison system: from the *Cárcel modelo* in Madrid and Jeremy Bentham's Panopticon to theoretical analyses of Spanish criminal law, to philosophical and psychological approaches to the treatment of prisoners while incarcerated. All her ideas converged into one concern: how to reform men and women while protecting their human rights and enable their participation in civil life. According to Gómez Bravo, "los correccionalistas y [las] figuras como

Concepción Arenal retomaron un reformismo básico centrado en las condiciones de supervivencia y regeneración moral, a través de posturas muy críticas con la continuidad del orden moderado en política penitenciaria o, más bien, su inexistencia" (Reformers and figures such as Concepción Arenal reintroduced a basic reformism centered on conditions of survival and moral regeneration, through critical postures regarding the continuity of a moderate order in penitentiary politics or better yet, it inexistence) (295). Indeed, her efforts went much farther than the mere survival of felons in prisons; her writings aimed to raise consciousness in her readers and make them understand that prisoners were actually citizens.

Notes

I am very grateful to Akiko Tsuchiya and Michelle Murray for their criticism and advice while I was writing this text. I am also indebted to colleagues and friends who have heard or read previous versions of this chapter: Leslie Harkema, Lena Burgos-Lafuente, Adrián Pérez-Melgosa, Josep Pierce, Noël Valis, and Jesús R. Velasco.

1. On Botany Bay, see Gillen and Duncan. On the French Guiana, see Redfield.

2. Arenal, who was born in 1820, wrote and published during the pre- and postrevolutionary periods. The pre-*Gloriosa* Isabelline regime faced many difficulties, and 1866 marked a year of financial crisis in Spain. The First Republic, meanwhile, was a period of great advancement for prison reform. During the very first month of its existence, in February 1873, a commission to reform both the prison system and the Penal Code was created. The idea was to apply the new theories of *correccionalismo*, which aimed to reform and reintegrate the delinquent into society. Among the specialists chosen to lead this reform were Gumersindo de Azcárate, Luis Silvela, Fernando de Castro, Manuel Ruiz Quevedo, and one woman: Concepción Arenal (Gargallo Vaamonde 68). Some of the measures that were considered included the abolition of the death penalty, the separation of common and political prisoners, and the recognition of fundamental rights for the delinquents (Núñez 68).

3. Pere Armengol i Cornet (1809–1870) was a Catalan jurist, theorist, magistrate (*Audiencias* of Barcelona and Madrid), and researcher of the penitentiary system. His prestige on penitentiary questions was national and international. In 1878, he created the *Asociación General para la Reforma Penitenciaria* in Spain. He also participated in international congresses about penitentiary reform in Stockholm, Saint Petersburg, Rome, and Paris. He was the promoter of the *Escola Municipal de Reforma* (1884), the *Asil Toribi Durán* (1890), and the new cellular prison of Barcelona (*Cárcel Modelo*). Francisco Lastres i Juiz (1848–1918) was a Spanish social

reformer. He had a PhD in Law and was a criminal lawyer. He is most famous for his writings on prison reform. Fernando Cadalso (1859–1939) was a penal reformer. He directed several prisons (for instance, the *Cárcel Modelo* in Madrid), was *Inspector General de Prisiones* and participated in many international congresses on penitentiary reform.

4. Nineteenth-century knowledge in psychology and psychiatry not only served to represent the lower classes as dangerous, but was also used to classify those who were already seen as socially dangerous or insane. According to Fernando Alvarez-Uría in *Miserables y locos. Medicina mental y orden social en la España del siglo XIX*, finding remedy against mental illness was equivalent to neutralizing the capacity of rebellion of the proletariat (130–40).

5. On deviance in nineteenth-century Spain, see Tsuchiya (*Marginal Subjects*), Fuentes Peris (*Visions of Filth*), and Fuentes Peris and Cleminson "La mala vida."

6. According to Campos, scientific discourse, especially criminology and psychiatry, criticized and even oftentimes criminalized social class conflicts championed by working-class organizations (3).

7. On *Misericordia* see Gold.

8. I maintain the original orthography throughout the article.

9. The nineteenth century saw the construction of model prisons around the globe, from the *Prison de la Santé* in Paris (opened in 1867), to the *Lecumberri* in Mexico City (whose construction began in 1888 and opened in 1900), to the *cárcel Modelo* in Madrid (opened in 1884) and in Barcelona (whose construction began in 1888, but opened in 1904 due to budgetary issues). Jeremy Bentham's Panopticon was the architectural and reformist technique employed for these model prisons. Devised at the end of the eighteenth century, the Panopticon comprises a circular construction with a central tower that allows constant control of the prisoners' movements. The surveillance was absolute and discrete, and could be performed by one man if desired. See Trinidad Fernández's work on the Modelo prisons. On Bentham's influence in Spain, especially in the *Cortes* of Cádiz, see Ramos Vázquez ("La colonización" 186).

10. Villanova y Jordan, anticipating Foucault's theories on disciplinary societies, stated that the Panopticon would create a new instrument of the government by giving to one man the power to surveil many (86).

11. On slavery, see Surwillo, Schmidt-Nowara, and Tsuchiya (*Empire's End*, 1–14, 131–47, 191–203).

12. On health in Fernando Poo, see Sampedro-Vizcaya.

13. The new modes of production, which implied social impact that was still unknown, generated a fear that was directed toward the desire of the working class and the poor to access capital. The body of the worker, in particular, was a source of preoccupation: its physical presence and its closeness to the forms of capital were a central point of articulation of the fear that the rest of society experienced in the public sphere. In effect, Foucault explains that the industrial capitalist believed

that he controlled and even owned the body of the worker, which culminated in the feeling that the worker was deviant if he or she used his or her body for something other than working, such as going to the bar, entering into the circles of prostitution, or neglecting their personal hygiene. Workers were held in permanent suspicion. The question of the role of the body of the working class and, in general, of the poor in nineteenth-century Europe, was thus central to the politics of social order. These politics had the objective of creating a norm into which the body of the worker could fit; a body that, thanks to systems of control, would turn into a productive force.

14. According to Pedro Trinidad Fernández, the control of the population was achieved through repressive means and was especially directed toward the lower classes (233–35).

15. Article 1 reads as follows: "delito o falta contra el orden público . . . toda manifestación pública que ofenda a la Religión, a la moral, a la Monarquía, a la Constitución . . . y al respecto debido a las leyes, o que considerados el lugar y las circunstancias en que se realice, produzca escándalo, agitación, bullicio, tumulto, . . . motín, o que pueda ocasionar relajación de la disciplina del ejército" (crime or offense against public order . . . all public demonstration that offends Religion, morality, the Monarchy, the Constitution . . . and the respect due to the law, or that considering the place and circumstances in which it occurs, would produce a scandal, agitation, hustle and bustle, commotion, riot, or that could create an easing of discipline in the army) (López González 40).

16. Other European figures who have also impacted the reform of prisons in the nineteenth and early twentieth centuries, especially for women and children, include Josefina Butler, Isabel Fry, Mary Carpenter from England; the Swede Ellen Key; and Gina Lombroso from Italy.

17. Arenal's name is everywhere in the archive. Armengol i Cornet exchanges more letters with her than with anyone else. He refers to her work in his drafts, publications, notes, and in his correspondence with other people. They wrote to him to inquire about her, her writings, and learn more about her after her death.

Works Cited

Agamben, Giorgio. *State of Exception*. Translated by Kevin Attell. U of Chicago P, 2005.

Alvarez-Uría, Fernando. *Miserables y locos. Medicina mental y orden social en la España del siglo XIX*. Tusquets, 1983.

Arenal, Concepción. "La pena depravadora y el derecho de penar." Jan. 7, 1880. *Artículos sobre beneficencia y prisiones*. Vol. V. *Biblioteca Virtual Miguel de Cervantes*, 1999.

———. "Las colonias penales de la Australia y la pena de deportación." Madrid: E. Martínez, 1877.

———. "Colonias penales francesas." Artículos sobre beneficencia y prisiones. Jan. 31, 1879. Vol. V. *Biblioteca Virtual Miguel de Cervantes*, 1999.

———. "Informe al Congreso Internacional Penitenciario de Estocolmo." 1896. Artículos sobre beneficencia y prisiones. Vol. IV. *Biblioteca Virtual Miguel de Cervantes*, 1999.

———. *Estudios penitenciarios*. Madrid: Librería de Victoriano Suárez, 1895.

Campos, Ricardo. "Pobres, anormales y peligrosos en España (1900–1970): de la 'mala vida' a la ley de peligrosidad y rehabilitación social." *XIII Coloquio Internacional de Geocrítica. El control del espacio y los espacios de control*, Barcelona, May 5–10, 2014. ub.edu; http://www.ub.edu/geocrit/coloquio2014/Ricardo%20Campos.pdf; accessed June 4, 2017.

Duncan, Martha Grace. *Romantic Outlaws, Beloved Prisons. The Unconscious Meanings of Crime and Punishment*. New York UP, 1996.

Gargallo Vaamonde, Luis. *Desarrollo y destrucción del sistema liberal de prisiones en España: de la Restauración a la Guerra Civil*. Doctoral dissertation; http://www.revistadeprisiones.com/luis-gargallo-vaamonde-desarrollo-destruccion-del-sistema-liberal-prisiones-espana-la-restauracion-la-guerra-civil/; accessed June 12, 2017.

Gillen, Mollie. "The Botany Bay Decision, 1786: Convicts, Not Empire." *The English Historical Review*, vol. 97, no. 385, Oct. 1982, pp. 740–66.

Gold, Hazel. "Outsider Art: Homelessness in Misericordia." *Anales Galdosianos*, 2001, pp. 141–54.

Gómez Bravo, Gutmaro. "Cartografías penales para la España del siglo XIX." *Cuadernos de Historia Contemporánea*, vol. 25, 2003, pp. 289–304.

Fernández Bermejo, Daniel. *Individualización científica y tratamiento en prisión*. Ministerio del Interior. 2013. *institucionpenienciaria.es*; http://www.institucionpenitenciaria.es/web/export/sites/default/datos/descargables/publicaciones/Individualizacixn_Cientixica_y_Tratamiento_en_prisixn_Web_Premio_VK_2013_2_Accxsit_.pdf; accessed June 15, 2017.

Foucault, Michel. *The Punitive Society*. Translated by Graham Burchell. Palgrave Macmillan, 2015.

———. *Discipline and Punish: The Birth of the Prison*. Translated by Alan Sheridan. Vintage Books, 1979.

———. "About the Concept of the 'Dangerous Individual' in 19th-Century legal Psychiatry." Trans. Alain Baudot and Jane Couchman. *International Journal of Law and Psychiatry*, vol. 1, 1978, pp. 1–18.

———. *Naissance de la biopolitique*. Seuil, 2004.

Fuentes Peris, Teresa. *Visions of Filth: Deviancy and Social Control in the Novels of Galdós*. Liverpool UP, 2003.

———. "La mala vida." Fuente Peris, Teresa and Richard Clemnson, eds. *Journal of Spanish Cultural Studies*, vol. 10, no. 4, 2009.

Horn, David. *The Criminal Body. Lombroso and the Anatomy of Deviance*. Routledge, 2003.

Lacalzada de Mateo, Maria José. "Acerca de los derechos humanos en Concepción Arenal: fundamentación y objetivación dentro de la Revolución liberal." *Derechos y Libertades: revista del Instituto Bartolomé de las Casas*, 1995, pp. 175–202.

Lastres, Francisco. *La colonización penitenciaria de las Marianas y Fernando Póo.* Madrid: Eduardo Martínez, 1878.

Llorente Pinto, José Manuel. "Colonialismo y geografía en España en el último cuarto del siglo XIX. El proyecto colonial." *Eria*, 1987, pp. 93–107.

Lombroso, Cesare. *L'uomo delincuente, in rapporto all'antropologia, alla giurisprudenza e dalle discipline carcerarie.* Bocca, 1889.

López González, José Luis. *El derecho de reunión y manifestación en el ordenamiento constitucional español.* Ministerio de Justicia, 1995.

Monlau, Pere Felip. *Remedios del pauperismo: memoria para optar al premio ofrecido por la Sociedad Económica Matritense en su programa del 1º de mayo de 1845.* Valencia: M. de Cabrerizo, 1846.

Núñez, Jorge. *Fernando Cadalso y Manzano: Medio siglo de reforma penitenciaria en España (1859–1939).* Doctoral dissertation; http://uvadoc.uva.es/handle/10324/4222; accessed June 20, 2017.

Ramos Vázquez, Isabel. *La reforma penitenciaria en la historia contemporánea española.* Dykinson, 2014.

———. "La colonización exterior penitenciaria en España: proyectos y realidades." *GLOSSAE. European Journal of Legal History*, vol. 9, 2012, pp. 171–202.

Redfield, Peter. *Space in the Tropics. From Convicts to Rockets in French Guiana.* U of California P, 2000.

Sampedro Vizcaya, Benita. "La economía política de la sanidad colonial en Guinea equatorial." *Éndoxa: Series Filosóficas* 37, 2016, pp. 279–98.

Schmidt-Nowara, Christopher. "Spanish Prisoners: War and Captivity in Spain's Imperial Crisis." *Empire's End. Transnational Connections in the Hispanic World*, edited by Akiko Tsuchiya and William Acree, Vanderbilt UP, 2015, 131–47.

Surwillo, Lisa. *Monsters by Trade: Slave Traffickers in Modern Spanish Literature and Culture.* Stanford UP, 2014.

Trinidad Fernández, Pedro. *La defensa de la sociedad: cárcel y delincuencia en España (siglos XVIII–XX).* Alianza Editorial, 1991.

Tsuchiya, Akiko. Introduction. *Empire's End: Transnational Connections in the Hispanic World.*, edited by Akiko Tsuchiya and William Acree, Vanderbilt UP, 2016, pp. 1–13.

———. *Marginal Subjects: Gender and Deviance in Fin-de-siècle Spain.* U of Toronto P, 2011.

Villanova y Jordan, Jacobo. *Cárceles y presidios. Aplicación de la panóptica de Jemerías Bentham a las cárceles y casas de corrección de España . . .* Madrid: D. Tomás Jordan, 1834.

Contributors

Julia Chang is assistant professor of Spanish in the Department of Romance Studies and a member of the core faculty in the Feminist, Gender, and Sexuality Studies Program at Cornell University. She is currently completing a book project that investigates the gendered afterlife of the early modern ideology of blood purity (*limpieza de sangre*) in nineteenth-century Spanish fiction and medicine. She has two recent articles that deal with Spanish colonialism in the nineteenth century.

Nuria Godón holds an MA and PhD in Spanish from the University of Colorado at Boulder and is associate professor of Spanish at Florida Atlantic University. Her research interests revolve around theories of subjugation, colonialism, gender, and sexuality studies in modern Hispanic literature. Her book, *La pasión esclava: Alianzas masoquistas en La Regenta*, was published by Purdue UP (2017). Among her most recent publications are two volumes, both co-edited with Michael Horswell: *Transnational Discourses of Peripheral Sexualities in the Hispanic World. Journal of Language and Sexuality* (John Benjamins, 2016); and *Sexualidades Periféricas. Consolidaciones literarias y fílmicas en la España de fin de siglo XIX y fin de milenio* (Fundamentos, 2016).

Ana Mateos is assistant professor in the Department of Romance Studies at the Ludwig-Maximilians-Universität, Munich, and earned her PhD from the University of California, Berkeley. A guiding aim of her research has been to bring Spain's nineteenth-century slave-based imperialism to bear on issues of social formation such as gender and class deviancy, the transformation of race, the idiosyncratic modernity of liberal Spain, and the shifting boundaries between public and private spheres. Her work has appeared in the *Bulletin of Hispanic Studies*, *Hispanic Review*, *Revista de Estudios Hispánicos*, and

Revista Canadiense de Estudios Hispánicos. Her current project explores the question of bodily property rights in nineteenth-century Spanish fiction in dialogue with colonial slavery and abolitionism.

N. Michelle Murray is an assistant professor of Spanish at Vanderbilt University. She has published articles in *Crossings: Journal of Migration and Culture*, *Studies in Spanish and Latin American Cinemas*, *Letras Femeninas*, and *Research in African Literatures*. She has contributed to the volumes *Gender and Sexuality in Spanish Urban Spaces* (Palgrave, 2017), *Espectros: Ghostly Hauntings and the Talking Dead in Contemporary Latin American and Iberian Narratives* (Bucknell UP, 2016), and *Theorising the Ibero-American Atlantic* (Brill, 2013). Her book, *Home Away from Home: Migration and Domestic Economies in Contemporary Spanish Culture*, was published by the University of North Carolina Press in 2018.

Benita Sampedro Vizcaya is professor of Spanish colonial studies, and associate director of the Center for "Race," Culture and Social Justice, at Hofstra University. Her research interests focus on Spanish colonialism in Africa, Asia, and Latin America. She has written on the politics and processes of decolonization and postcolonial legacies, colonial carceral systems, colonial medicine, colonial archives, borders, and ruins. Her recent work includes a double special issue of the *Journal of Spanish Cultural Studies* entitled "Entering the Global Hispanophone" (2019), the collective volume *Re-Routing Galician Studies: Multidisciplinary Interventions* (2017), a critical and annotated edition of *Ceiba II (Poesía inédita)* by Raquel Ilombe del Pozo Epita (2015), and a special issue of *Revista Debats* on "Guinea Ecuatorial: Poéticas/políticas/discursividades" (2014). Her current book-length project is tentatively entitled "Deportee Narratives and Atlantic Translatability: From Cuba to Fernando Poo and Back."

Mar Soria is assistant professor of Spanish at the University of Missouri, Columbia. Her major research interests include nineteenth- and twentieth-century Peninsular Spanish literature and culture, nation-building narratives, and the representation of class, gender, and race. Her most recent academic essays have appeared at *Hispanic Research Journal*, *Routledge*, and *Revista de Estudios Hispánicos*. Her book *Geographies of Female Labor and Nationhood in Spanish Culture (1880–1975)*, forthcoming from the University of Nebraska Press, studies a relatively unexplored model of femininity in

Spanish culture—the working woman. Currently, she is working on another book-length project tentatively entitled *Imperial Desires and The Economics of Race: Embodying Blackness in Contemporary Spain.*

Lisa Surwillo is associate professor of Iberian and Latin American cultures at Stanford University, where she teaches courses on Iberian literature and transatlantic studies, with an emphasis on the nineteenth century. Her research addresses the questions of property, empire, race, and personhood as they are manifested by literary works, especially dramatic literature, dealing with colonial slavery, abolition, and Spanish citizenship. She is the author of *The Stages of Property: Copyrighting Theatre in Spain* (Toronto 2007), an analysis of the development of copyright and authorship in nineteenth-century Spain and the impact of intellectual property on theater, and *Monsters by Trade* (Stanford 2014), a study of slave traders in Spanish literature and the role of these colonial mediators in the development of modern Spain.

Joyce Tolliver is the director of the Center for Translation Studies and associate professor of Spanish, translation studies, and gender and women's studies at the University of Illinois-Urbana. She is a specialist in modern Spanish literature and culture, with a focus on discourse and gender at the turn of the twentieth century. Her books include *Cigar Smoke and Violet Water: Gendered Discourse in the Stories of Emilia Pardo Bazán* (Bucknell, 1998); *"El encaje roto" y otros cuentos/"Torn Lace" and Other Stories* (MLA); and *Disciplines on the Line: Feminist Research on Spanish, Latin American, and U.S. Spanish Women* (Juan de la Cuesta, 2004). Her more recent scholarly work focuses on Spain and the Philippines at the end of the Spanish empire.

Akiko Tsuchiya is professor of Spanish and affiliate in women, gender, and sexuality studies at Washington University in St Louis. She received her PhD in Hispanic literatures from Cornell University. Her areas of specialization include nineteenth- and twentieth-century Iberian literatures and cultures, with a focus on gender studies. She is the author of a book on Galdós and has published extensively on the nineteenth-century narrative and on women writers of contemporary Spain. Her most recent books include, *Marginal Subjects: Gender and Deviance in Fin-de-siècle Spain* (U of Toronto P, 2011) and a co-edited volume, *Empire's End: Transnational Connections in the Hispanic World* (Vanderbilt UP, 2016). With the support of an NEH Summer Stipend and a Faculty Fellowship from the Center for the Humanities, she is working on a new book project, tentatively entitled: *Spanish Women of Letters in the Nineteenth-century Antislavery Movement: Transnational Networks and Exchanges.*

Aurélie Vialette is an associate professor at Stony Brook University. She earned her PhD from the University of California, Berkeley in 2009. She specializes in Iberian studies, popular culture, working-class and social movements, gender studies, and transatlantic studies. She has published her research in Spanish, English, Catalan, and French in *Hispanic Review, Hispanófila, Revista de Estudios Hispánicos, Catalan Review, Siglo Diecinueve,* among others. Her first book is titled *Intellectual Philanthropy: The Seduction of the Masses* (Purdue UP 2018). She has a forthcoming edited volume on *Dissonances of Modernity: Music, Text, and Performance in Modern Spain* (North Carolina Studies in Romance Languages and Literatures). She is working on a new book manuscript, titled "Peninsular Crime, Colonial Punishment: the Carceral Archipelago and the Failed Rebirth of the Spanish Empire."

Index

able-bodiedness, 174, 182, 183, 184, 188–89, 191, 194
A'Bodjedi, Enénge, 19–20, 42, 44, 46, 50n23, 50n25, 50n27, 50n28
abolition and abolitionism, 107, 108, 110, 111, 119, 123, 124, 128, 131, 140–41, 142, 144, 161n7, 204–205, 213, 225, 226n3
Acree, William, 13n3, 14n9, 77, 89, 97n1, 227
aesthetic competence, 184, 191
Africa, Scramble for, 28
Afro-Hispanic women (*negra*), 109, 115, 116, 117, 118, 121, 122, 123, 128, 130
Agamben, Giorgio, 257, 260, 262, 271
Alas, Leopoldo (Clarín), 11, 97n3, 108, 177, 203–209, 212–14, 216–19, 221–23, 225 226n3, 227n10
  Regenta, La, 108, 206–11, 215, 220, 222–23, 225, 227n12, 228n16
Alexander, Jacqui, 6–7
Álvarez Castro, Luis, 83, 87, 98n12, 101n27, 101n31
Anderson, Tracy, 65–66
Arenal, Concepción, 11–12, 255, 258, 260–73, 273n2, 273n2, 275n17
  cárcel llamada Modelo, La, 262, 272
  Estudios penitenciarios, 262

Argentina, 2, 100n21, 101n31
Armengol i Cornet, Pere, 258, 272, 273n3, 275n17
Asociación Feminista de Filipinas, 249, 251n22
Asturias 66, 70, 74, 207, 209
Australia (Botany Bay), 255, 262, 266–67, 269, 273n1
autonomy
  colonial, 204–206, 213, 217, 232
  female, 208, 211–12, 214, 216, 217

Bahía de Gibara, 66–67
Balfour, Sebastian, 2, 13n4
Barbados, 123, 125
Barberán Reinares, Laura, 88, 94, 101n28
Barcia Zequeira, María del Carmen, 57, 67, 77n3
Bathala, 243–46
  Bathalismo, 243–44
Benga (ethnic group and language), 19, 20, 23, 31, 42, 44, 45, 46, 50n27
Bentham, Jeremy, 261, 272, 274n9
Bhabha, Homi, 2
Bhambra, Guminder, 2
Bioko. *See* Fernando Poo
biopolitics, 10, 173, 175, 181, 183, 186, 193–95, 196n12, 196n13, 256–60, 262. *See also* biopower

283

biopower, 182, 194, 196n11, 256. *See also* biopolitics
blackface, 10, 109–29, 132, 135–60, 160n1, 161n4, 161n5
blackness, 88, 109, 111, 115, 116, 118, 120–23, 125, 127–30, 137, 145, 151, 160. *See also* race
Blanco, Alda, 2–3, 13n6, 14n9, 81, 96–97n1, 185, 216
body, 108, 110, 111, 119–23, 127, 128, 178, 182–84, 186, 188–89, 190, 192, 218–19, 263, 274–75n13
   female body, 178, 186
   black body, 137
   black men's bodies, 154
   bodily purity, 127
   women's ownership of, 107, 110, 122
Boyd, Carolyn, 179–80, 189
bozal, 145, 146, 147, 152
Brazil, 109, 110, 112, 118, 122, 129n11–12
Burguera, Mónica, 107, 111, 123, 131n28

"Cádiz," 146, 163n22. See also *zarzuela*
Campos Marín, Ricardo, 181–82, 187, 197n20
Canel, Eva, 8, 55–77
   Lo que vi en Cuba, 55, 58–77
   mulata, La, 70–72
Cánovas de Castillo, Antonio, 58, 213, 215–16
   Discurso sobre la nación, 215
capitalism, 92, 156, 176, 227n11
Carabalí, 146–47
Catalonia, 72, 73–76, 77n8, 141, 143, 161n12, 162n19, 162n21, 204
   Catalan Block (separatism), 73, 74, 75, 76

independence (autonomy), 74, 163n25
nationalism (nationhood), 58, 141, 161n12, 162n13, 162n14
Catholic Church, The, 45, 58, 220, 231–32, 245, 248, 270
Catholicism, 243–44, 251n17
Céspedes, Benjamín de, 85, 86, 87, 90, 98n11, 99n17, 99n18
charity. *See* philanthropy
Charnon-Deutsch, Lou, 122, 196n8
Chaviano López, Lizbeth J., 131n25. *See also* Rodrigo y Alharilla, Martín
citizen-soldier, 179–80, 193
citizenship, 5, 11, 114, 130n16, 179, 257, 265
Cleminson, Richard, 174, 178, 182, 187, 195n3, 196n10, 198, 274n5
colonial matrix of power. *See* coloniality of power
coloniality of power, 137, 149, 176, 177, 206–207, 209, 227n11. *See also* Mignolo, Walter; Quijano, Aníbal, 137, 144, 176, 206–207, 227n11, 242
coloniality of gender, 149, 150, 176, 177, 178, 193, 242. *See also* Lugones, María
Columbus, Christopher (Cristóbal Colón), 1, 74
Consejo Superior de Investigaciones Científicas, 26
Constitution of Cádiz (Constitution of 1812), 5, 13n14, 114, 129n14, 130n16, 264
Cordero Torres, José María, 26
Corisco, 23, 28, 29, 40, 44, 45, 50n23, 50n28
costumbrismo, 129n12, 141
criollo/a (Creole), 86, 87, 89, 100n22, 100n23

Cuba, 86, 98n11, 108, 110, 111, 124, 125, 129, 131, 135–60, 161n5, 164n36, 175, 179–80, 197n18, 203–14, 216, 217, 222, 224, 225, 226
  anticolonial movement, 99n15, 141
  colonial (preindependence), 86, 139
  identity, Cuban, 70, 98n11
  independence, 55–56, 63, 162n16, 203–207, 209, 217, 220, 226n6
  Peace of Zanjón, 162n16
  US occupation of, 59

dalaga(s), 11, 239, 243, 245, 246, 247, 248, 249
decolonial theory, 149–50
decolonial feminism, 175–76, 207, 239. *See also* Lugones, María
decolonization, 12, 205
degeneration, 10, 85, 86–87, 96, 98n14, 101, 187, 209, 217, 221, 228n16
disability, 175–76, 184–89
"Disaster of 1898," 8, 13, 14n11, 25, 55–56, 63–64, 66, 69, 77n9, 98n14, 174, 175, 185, 187, 197n18, 198n18, 198n21, 227n8
discipline, 182–83, 189, 192, 194, 257, 275n15
domesticity, 5, 50n26, 71, 72, 108, 113, 206, 227n8
Domínguez, Daylet, 130n21, 131n23
Don Juan, 157–58, 159, 164n41, 209–11. *See also* Zorrilla, José
Dyer, Richard, 136–37, 152, 157

Edelman, Lee, 188, 197n21
Elizalde Pérez-Grueso, María Dolores, 149
Elobey Chico, 21, 28–34, 39, 42, 49n16
Elobey Grande, 28, 31

Elombuangani, 45, 50n27
emancipation, 107, 111, 126, 144, 147, 174, 205, 212, 216, 223–25, 226n3
  intellectual emancipation, 227–28n13
emigration. *See* migration
Equatorial Guinea, 3–4, 13n1, 21, 47n5, 256, 265
erotization, 94, 95, 191, 208, 220, 225
Espinosa de los Monteros, Gaspar, 150
Eurocentrism, 1, 10, 136–37, 144, 157, 176, 227n11

feminism and proto-feminism, 11, 41, 72, 110, 111, 133, 176, 220, 239
Fernández, Pura, 87, 98n8, 98n9, 99n17, 100n23
Fernández Cifuentes, Luis, 44, 196n4
Fernando Poo (Bioko), vii, 21, 23, 24, 25, 26, 31, 32, 34, 47n4, 47n9, 47n11, 49n16, 49n19, 50n21, 50n22, 255–56, 260, 262, 269, 271, 274n12. *See also* Equatorial Guinea
Feros, Antonio, 138, 214
Ferrer, Ada, 138, 139, 163n31
  Insurgent Cuba, 138, 139
Ferrer i Codina, Antoni, 140, 141–50, 162n15
  Carolinas, Las, 140–50
Ferrús Antón, Beatriz, 57, 59, 60–61
Fischer, Sybille, 122–23
Flores, Eugenio Antonio, 9, 83–84, 86–88, 92–94, 95
  Trata de blancas (novel), 83–84, 86–88, 92–94, 95
folletín, 89, 100n23, 109
Forrest, Alan, 178–79
Foucault, Michel, 90–91, 125, 175–76, 182–83, 189, 256–58, 262–63, 274n10, 274n13

Fradera, Josep María, 13n5, 97n1, 143, 249n1
frailocracia, 233, 235, 247
Fraternity, 204–205, 214–16, 227n7
Fuentes Peris, Teresa, 94, 197n20, 274n5

García Tudela, Ignacio, 24, 47n9
gaze, 9, 60, 87, 88, 127, 208, 225
　colonizing, 9, 87, 95, 96
　ethnographic, 9
　male, 9, 95, 96
　medical(ized), 9, 87, 95
　metropolitan, 9, 87
género chico, 10, 135–60
Global Hispanophone, 3, 13n2
Global South, 4–5, 14n10, 101n30
Gómez de Avellaneda, Gertrudis, 110, 111, 122–23, 211
　Sab, 110, 122–23
Goode, Joshua, 130n15, 138, 160n2, 175, 196n9, 197n17, 250n14
　Impurity of Blood, 138
Guantánamo, 68, 75
Gulf of Guinea, 21, 24, 44, 47n3, 47n5, 49n15, 265
Gutiérrez Garitano, Miguel, vii, 22, 27, 41, 43, 46n1, 46n2, 49n16
　Apuntes de la Guinea, 22, 27, 41, 43, 46n1, 49n16

Hartman, Saidiya V., 137, 154
　Scenes of Subjection, 137
Hartzenbusch, Juan Eugenio, 119
　Los amantes de Teruel, 119
Hernández Espinosa, María del Carmen, 125
Hispanism, 8, 55–60, 64, 68–70, 74, 76, 77n9
honor (honor code), 119, 157, 210–13
Hooper, Kirsty, 13n7, 196n8

Iarocci, Michael, 14n9, 173, 179, 196n8
Iberian studies, 2, 3, 8, 12–13n1, 13n8, 194
Iglesias Presbiterianas Ndowé, 20
Ilustrados, 11, 231, 233–36, 239, 241, 243, 247, 248
immigration. *See* migration
imperial economy, 9, 10, 91, 99n15, 101n30, 125, 162n12
imperial expansion, 1–2, 6, 9, 13n2, 13n5, 24, 28–29, 44–45, 48n11, 271
imperial loss, 2–5, 7–8, 12, 55, 64, 66, 81–82, 86, 96, 98n14, 140, 174, 185, 193, 197n18, 206, 210, 222
imperial nostalgia, 61, 81, 91–92, 101n27
imperialism, 6, 8, 11, 60, 76, 139, 149
　British, 2
　Catalan, 72
　European, 60, 138
　Spanish, 1, 5, 14n9, 44, 96–97n1, 185, 218, 220
　US, 11, 55, 56, 63–65, 67, 68
impersonation, 135, 136. *See also* blackface
indiano(s), 72, 82, 88, 97n3, 108, 124, 125, 207–209, 211–14
indigeneity, 11, 231–32, 234, 236, 248
Instituto de Estudios Africanos, 26
insurgent(s), 99n15, 139, 142, 161n6, 205–206, 208, 217, 226n7
inútiles, los, 10, 173, 175–76, 183, 191, 198n21
Iradier Bulfy, Manuel, vii, 21, 25–27, 32–33, 34, 35, 39, 40, 41, 43, 44, 45, 48n13, 49n15, 50n20, 50n21
　África: Viajes y trabajos de la asociación euskara la exploradora, 40

Isabel II (Queen Isabella), 128n2, 188–89, 267, 273n2

Jackson Veyán, José, 140, 149, 150
 perla cubana, La, 140–41, 150–59
Jagoe, Catherine, 178, 182, 196n14
Junta Directiva de Sanidad Militar (Sanitary Board Corps of Directors), 173, 182, 183, 195n1

Kenmonge, Jean, 57, 73
Kingsley, Mary Henrietta, 22–24, 42, 47n6, 47n7, 47n8, 49n17
 Travels in West Africa, 23, 47n6
Kirkpatrick, Susan, 14n13, 110, 111
Krauel, Javier, 13n5, 14n9, 14n11

Labanyi, Jo, 119, 208, 212
Lane, Jill, 129n10, 135, 145
Lastres, Francisco, 258, 260–61, 265, 268–69, 273n3
Ley de Moret (Moret Law), 205, 226n4
López Bago, Eduardo, 9, 83, 84, 85, 88–92, 94–96, 98n8, 98n11, 100–101n26, 101n28
 Carne importada, 83, 84, 88–92, 95
 separatista, El 100–101n26
López Jaena, Graciano, 234–35, 250n9
Loureiro, Ángel, 4
Lugones, María, 149, 150, 176, 177, 195n5, 207, 239, 240, 242, 245, 252n11. *See also* decolonial feminism

Mackey, Isabella Sweeney, 19, 44
Malayan civilization, 236, 241–42
Malolos, 11, 231–32, 234–39, 243, 245–47, 249
marriage, 10, 107, 108, 110–13, 119–23, 186, 207, 211–12, 227n9
 as a form of slavery, 10, 121
 as imperial conquest, 149, 158

Martin-Márquez, Susan, 2, 14n9, 35, 97n1, 113, 130n15, 177, 186–90, 195n6, 198n22
Martínez Carreras, José U., 140, 142, 161n10
masculinity, 10, 11, 86, 98n13, 141, 148, 149, 157, 158, 159, 173–74, 178, 182, 184, 185, 187, 191, 194, 195, 196n10, 231
 hegemonic masculinity, 86, 98n13
 military masculinity, 11, 178, 182, 185, 194
Mbembe, Achille, 4
McClintock, Anne, 4, 6, 9, 96, 102n32, 113, 131n28, 149
 Imperial Leather, 96
mestizaje, 205, 213–14. *See also* race
meteorology, 21, 28, 41, 50n20
Mignolo, Walter, 136, 137, 138, 149, 206
 Local Histories/Global Designs, 206
migration, 8, 99n19
 emigration, 57, 63, 76–77, 97n3
 immigration, 61, 84, 85, 88, 99n19
 migration to Argentina, 61
 migration to Cuba, 57, 63, 76–77, 98n9
 transatlantic, 76, 82
Miguel, Amando de, 97n2
Miles, Robert, 130n19
Mills, Charles, 5
minstrelsy, 151, 164n34
miscegenation, 86, 138, 158, 164n40
Miserables, Los, 108, 109–28, 129n11
modernity, 2, 67, 81, 136, 176, 196n8, 197n18, 206, 259
 and colonialism, 136, 206
Mohanty, Chandra, 6–7, 14n10, 14n14, 99n16
Mojares, Resil, 234, 247–48, 249n5, 251n20

Monlau, Felip, 131n28, 259
Monroe Doctrine, 58
monuments, 65–66
Moret Law. See *Ley de Moret*
Morocco, 4, 13n1, 49, 187, 188
motherland, 91, 204, 213
mulata, 70, 71, 72, 151, 154, 158, 159, 160. *See* Afro-Hispanic women
mulatto, 87, 93, 111. *See also* race
Muni Estuary, 21, 23, 28, 42, 45
Muñoz, Laura, 56, 59
myth, 210, 214, 243

Napoleonic Wars, 2, 13n3, 192, 195–96n7
Naranjo Orovio, Consuelo, 57, 77n9
Nassau, Isabel, 42, 44
nation (nationalism, nationality), 1–2, 3, 4–5, 6, 8, 12, 13n5, 58, 60, 61, 76–77, 81, 86, 92, 95, 98n12, 98n14, 130n15, 135, 138, 139, 141, 145, 147, 159–60, 161n12, 162n13, 162n14, 163n25, 175, 178–79, 186, 189, 191–93, 197n18, 204, 206, 212, 214, 220, 226n3, 247
   unity of (national unity), 179, 204, 214, 225, 248–49
naturalism, 83, 95. *See also* radical naturalism
Ndowé, 20, 42, 44
negrero. *See* slave trader
Nerín, Gustau, 25, 27
Newton, Melanie, 123, 125

O'Donnell, Leopoldo, 189–90, 192
orientalism, 3, 100n24, 130n22, 196n8. *See also* Said, Edward

Pardo Bazán, Emilia, 75, 82, 83, 88, 96, 97n3, 177, 228
Partzsch, Henriette, 107, 124, 128n4

pasyon, 248, 251n21
Paterno, Pedro, 11, 231, 234, 243
   "dalaga virtuosa, La" 11, 243–44, 247, 251n16
penal colonies, 11, 255–61, 263–69, 271
penal reform, 256, 263, 271, 272, 274n3
penitentiary colonization, 11, 256, 260, 263–71
Pérez Galdós, Benito, 10, 96, 108, 176–77, 179, 185, 188–89, 190, 192, 197n18, 197n19, 198n22, 206, 220, 227n9, 259
   Aita Tettauen, 176, 185, 197n18, 197n19, 198n22
   Episodios nacionales, 179
performance, 121–23, 152, 154. *See also* blackface
philanthropy, 111, 123–26, 181, 269
Philippines, 2–4, 11, 13n1, 24–25, 81, 97n1, 99n20, 231–34, 236–49, 249n2, 249n3, 250n9, 251n15, 255–57, 262, 271
   Philippine language policy, 231, 232, 246, 249n2, 250n9
   Philippine nationalism, 11, 234
   Philippine Revolution, 234, 248
Pilar, Marcelo del, 234–36, 238, 242, 250n7, 250n8
Platt Amendment, 55
popular theater. See *género chico*
postcolonial studies, 1, 2, 4, 7, 12
postcolonial feminist studies, 1, 6–8, 177
Pratt, Mary Louise, 57, 60, 198n22
property, 108, 109, 110, 113, 119, 120 121, 128, 130
   women's ownership of, 120
prostitution (and prostitute), 71, 83, 84, 85–89, 92–96, 97n4, 98n11, 98n12, 100n23, 100–101n26, 182, 217, 256

Publicidad, La (newspaper), 68, 69

Quijano, Aníbal, 137, 144, 176, 206–207, 227n11

race, 110, 113, 115, 118, 120, 121, 125, 126, 128–31, 160n2, 163n31, 175–79, 184–86, 188–89, 194, 197n19, 206–207, 227n9, 227n10, 227n11, 242–43, 270. *See also* blackness; skin color; whiteness

racial hierarchies, 1, 6, 10, 86, 112, 127, 136, 138–39, 157, 160, 160n2

racial identity, 110, 118–28, 136, 242. *See* race

racial impersonation. *See* blackface

racism, 68, 152, 196n12, 235

Radcliff, Pamela Beth, 161n9

radical naturalism 83, 87, 94, 98n9. *See also* naturalism

Rafael, Vicente, 232, 249n1, 249n4

Real Sociedad Geográfica de Madrid, 35

Revista Marítima, 48n13

Reyes, Raquel, 231, 239, 241

Rizal, José, 11, 231–49

"Message to the Young Women of Malolos," 231, 236

Rodrigo y Alharilla, Martín, 131n25, 136, 143, 163n25. *See also* Chaviano López, Lizbeth J.

Rodríguez Ocaña, Esteban, 174, 195n1

Rodulfo, Concepción, 68–69

Romanticism, 100n24, 109, 119

Royal Geographical Society of Madrid. *See* Real Sociedad Geográfica de Madrid

Sáez de Melgar, 9, 108, 124, 140

cadena rota, La, 111, 140

Said, Edward, 2–3, 60, 136

sainete, 141. *See also zarzuela*; *género chico*

Sampedro Vizcaya, Benita, 8, 13n2, 274n12

San Juan, E., 237–38, 250n12

Sánchez-Eppler, Karen, 107–108

Sanidad Militar (Military Corps). *See* La Junta Directiva de Sanidad Militar

Santamaría García, Antonio, 57, 77n9

Santos, Epifanio de los, 235, 250n9, 250n10, 250n13

Sartorious, David, 139, 161n6

Schmidt-Nowara, Christopher, 13n5, 14n13, 58, 139, 140, 161n8, 204, 226n3, 227n7, 274n11

Conquest of History, The, 58, 204

Sèbe, Berny, 23, 47n7

sentimental fiction, 122, 123

serial novel or serialized fiction, 83, 89, 100n23, 109, 128n5. *See also folletín*

Serrano de Wilson, Emilia (Wilson, Baronesa de), 60, 68

sex trafficking (or sexual commerce), 9, 82–83, 84–85, 96, 97n5, 97n6, 97–98n7, 98n12, 100n26, 101n30

sex work. *See* prostitution

sexual deviance, 85, 86, 90

Simón Palmer, María del Carmen, 57, 66, 75, 77n3

Sippial, Tiffany, 86, 97n6

skin color, 114–18, 125, 128n6, 129n14, 138, 151, 154, 156, 163n30, 163–64n31, 164n36. *See also* race

slavery (slave), 73, 107, 108, 109, 110–13, 121–25, 129–31, 139, 144, 147, 204–206, 214, 227n9, 263–64, 274n11

debates on, 107, 140, 142, 161n10

pro-slavery, definition of term 140, 161n7

slave trade (slave trafficking), 9, 76, 84, 143, 205, 212–13, 226n5

slavery (slave) *(continued)*
  slave trader (slave trafficker), 108, 124, 125, 156, 164n37, 213, 226n5
Sociedad Abolicionista Española (Spanish Abolitionist Society), 140, 205, 226n3
Sociedad Abolicionista de Señoras (Ladies' Division of the Abolitionist Society), 108, 140
soldado español, el (The Spanish Soldier), 10, 175, 178–79, 191
Solidaridad, La (periodical), 233, 236, 239, 250n9
space of exception, 256, 257, 260, 263, 265, 271
Spanish-American War (War of 1898), 64, 69, 176, 179, 185, 189, 197n19, 227, 234
Spanish-Moroccan War, 176, 179, 185, 189, 197n19
Spivak, Gayatri, 2, 73
Stoler, Ann Laura, 6–7, 85, 86, 89
subaltern subject, 8, 12, 73, 91, 94–96, 101n30, 197n19
Surwillo, Lisa, 4, 8, 14n9, 46, 81, 84, 97n1, 97n3, 131n26, 131n29, 143, 156, 164n37, 197n18, 205–206, 209, 212, 226n5, 227n9, 228n14, 274n11
  Monsters by Trade, 14n9, 84, 97n1, 131n26, 131n29, 205, 228n14
syphilis, 84, 87, 93–94, 101

Tagalog, 11, 232, 236, 238–39, 242–48, 250, 251n18, 251n19
  Tagalismo, 243
tango, 146, 163n22, 163n23
teatro bufo, 145. See also *género chico*
Tiongsen, Nicanor, 233, 237
Tofiño-Quesada, Ignacio, 13n7, 196n8
transatlanticism, 61

travel narratives (travel writing), 59–60
  colonial travel accounts, 45
Treaty of Paris, 55, 56
Tsuchiya, Akiko, 3, 9, 12–13n1, 13n3, 14n9, 14n12, 97n1, 111, 127, 128n4, 187, 218, 227n8, 274n5, 274n11

Ugarte, Michael, 13n6, 14n9, 195n7, 197n19, 97n1
Urquiola (de Iradier), Isabela, 19–46, 50n22
Urquiola, Manuela, 19–46
Urquiola sisters. See also Urquiola de Iradier, Isabela; Urquiola, Manuela

Vázquez García, Francisco, 174, 178, 182, 183, 187, 195n3, 196n10, 196n12, 196n13, 196n15, 198
Vidal Tibbits, Mercedes, 129n10, 161n11
Villanova y Jordan, Jacobo, 261, 274n10
violence, 44, 45, 89, 95, 130n21, 153, 154, 156, 192, 205, 224, 227n8, 268, 270
Violeta, La, 108, 124, 128n5
virility, 10, 174, 177–78, 184, 187, 194, 195n3, 195n4, 197n16. *See also* masculinity

War of 1898. *See* Spanish-American War
West Africa, 8, 22, 23, 28, 31, 35, 44, 46n2, 47n6
Weyler, Valeriano, 77n3, 175, 232, 235, 241, 249n3
whiteness, 72, 86, 92, 93, 109–11, 114–16, 118–29, 131, 138, 152, 177–78, 186, 195n6. *See also* race
white slavery. *See* sex-trafficking
Wilson, Baronesa de. *See* Serrano de Wilson, Emilia

Wirtz, Kristina, 145, 147
womanhood, models of, 10, 71, 72, 95, 111, 112, 124, 125, 248

Xifré, Josep, 143, 162n20

zarzuela, 140, 141, 146, 149, 150, 151, 155, 160n1, 163n26, 163n29. See also *sainete*; *género chico*
Zola, Émile, 83, 101n29
Zorrilla, José, 159, 164n41, 210

www.ingramcontent.com/pod-product-compliance
Lightning Source LLC
Chambersburg PA
CBHW032050230426
43672CB00009B/1550